POLICING as though People Matter

Dorothy Guyot

Temple University Press

Philadelphia

POLICING as though People Matter

Temple University Press, Philadelphia 19122
Copyright © 1991 by Temple University. All rights reserved
Published 1991
Printed in the United States of America

The paper used in this publication meets the minimum
requirements of American National Standard for Information
Sciences—Permanence of Paper for Printed Library Materials,
ANSI Z39.48-1984

Library of Congress Cataloging-in-Publication Data

Guyot, Dorothy.
    Policing as though people matter / Dorothy Guyot
      p.   cm.
    Includes bibliographical references.
    ISBN 0-87722-755-1 (alk. paper).—ISBN 0-87722-766-7 (pbk. :
alk. paper)
    1. Police administration—United States—Case studies. 2. Police
administration—New York (State)—Troy. I. Title.
HV8141.G89 1991
363.2'09747'41—dc20   90-34691
                                          CIP

Passages from "The Organization of Police Departments: Changing the Model from the Army to the Hospital,"
Criminal Justice Abstracts 9, no. 2 (June 1977), pp. 231–56, are reprinted in Chapters 1, 2, and 4 by permission.

Passages from "The Evidence Technician Program in Troy, NY," *FBI Law Enforcement Bulletin* 46, no. 9
(September 1977), pp. 2–7, are reprinted in Chapter 6.

Passages from Erika S. Fairchild and Vincent J. Webb, eds., "Political Interference versus Political Accountability
in Municipal Policing," in *The Politics of Crime and Criminal Justice*, 120–43, Perspectives in Criminal Justice 8,
copyright 1985 by Sage Publications Inc., are reprinted in Chapter 7 by permission of Sage Publications Inc.

Material in Chapter 10 draws on Dorothy H. Guyot and Kai Martensen, "The Governmental Setting," in *Local
Government Police Management*, edited by William A. Geller (Washington, D.C.: International City Management
Association, 1991), and Dorothy H. Guyot, "The Fine Line between Political Accountability and Political
Interference," *Public Management* 70, no. 6 (June 1988), pp. 13–15. Passages from Erika S. Fairchild and
Vincent J. Webb, eds., "Political Interference versus Political Accountability in Municipal Policing," in *The
Politics of Crime and Criminal Justice*, 120–43, Perspectives in Criminal Justice 8, copyright 1985 by Sage
Publications Inc., are reprinted in Chapter 10 by permission of Sage Publications Inc.

Passages from "Building Bridges between Police and Public," *FBI Law Enforcement Bulletin* 54, no. 11
(November 1985), pp. 1–8, are reprinted in Chapter 11.

To our children
Erik, Khin Khin, and Sanpet

Contents

List of Figures

List of Tables

Preface

The quality of police service in a city strongly affects the quality of life for the residents, the commuters, and the visitors. Nationally, the quality of police service has been rising and can be expected to continue to rise. This book provides a close-range view of efforts to improve police service over the long run and extracts from that experience a set of questions that can be used to scrutinize the quality of police service. The theme is that when police officers are treated as professionals by their department, they will act professionally toward citizens.

The first objective of this book is to present a full picture of one case of upgrading that was guided by a clear conception of goals. The second is to provide readers with an understanding of fundamental issues so that they can make reasoned inquiries into the performance of other police departments. The Appendix contains twelve sets of questions, one set for each chapter, that probe the quality of police service. The book is organized by issues to facilitate the casual reader's skipping among chapters of interest.

The focus is on the police department, the level at which management can have the most effect on the quality of service. More than a decade ago two outstanding works each presented an integrated view of policing. At the national level, Herman Goldstein's *Policing a Free Society* explores fundamental issues. At the individual level, William Muir's *Police: Streetcorner Politicians* inquires into what makes a good police officer. This work asks, what makes a good police department?

The seed for this study grew from my experiences with students at John Jay College of Criminal Justice in New York, where the police officers in my classrooms broke my stereotypes of cops. In 1975 I looked for a police department where I could test out methods for studying the diffusion of innovation. David Powell of the Law Enforcement Assistance Administration suggested the department headed by George W. O'Connor in Troy, New York. Initially, John Marks of the New York City Police Department joined me in making an inventory of the changes taking place in the Troy PD. Soon I discovered that a mere list of changes has little use but that understanding a pattern of change based on a coherent philosophy of policing can illuminate contemporary problems of policing. A single city small enough to fathom and large enough to have urban problems can illustrate the fundamentals of policing and the dynamics of the upgrading process. A city short on fiscal resources and long on resistance to change can show that substantial upgrading is possible without spending great sums of money. The crucial factors in my choice of Troy as a site for observing transformations were Commissioner O'Connor's comprehensive view of the police field, his candor, and his cordial welcome to research.

Since my purpose in writing about a single department is to give concrete examples of general conditions, I brush lightly over unique features of Troy in order to concentrate on common problems and their solutions. Occasionally, in referring to the upgrading of service elsewhere in the country, I choose examples known to me either through a site visit or through frank discussion with the people involved.

My thanks go first to the members of the Troy Police Department who generously shared with me their views of the police job. They have provided forthright, thoughtful answers to my many questions. George W. O'Connor opened his thoughts so that I might learn what questions are worth asking. Among the citizens of Troy, I owe special thanks to Mary and Robert Stierer, Terry O'Connor, and Nancy Jones.

While teaching at the Rutgers School of Criminal Justice, I was assisted by students on data collecting trips to Troy: Diane Steelman, James Kassack, Ray D'Alessio, James Powers, and Donald Rabovich. Chief John J. Givney, Jr., permitted research to continue during the year when O'Connor was not directing the department. I did not remain a mere observer of the Troy scene but in 1977–78 participated as the evaluator of the team policing project, a reform that was opposed by the police union. Max Chmura, who joined me in directing the collection of evaluation data, maintained his balance and sense of humor under trying circumstances. Christopher Taffe and Alan Geraci assisted research during the seven months of the evaluation. This effort produced two major citizen surveys that addressed problems requiring police attention and assessed the quality of police work.

After the cancellation of the Troy evaluation project, I gained new perspectives on police work in Newark, New Jersey, as field director for a study covering thirty years of governmental response to crime. Further experience as a participant observer came when I served as management analyst for the Yonkers Police Department while it underwent major upgrading. I learned much about choices in orchestrating change from Commissioner Daniel P. Guido and Staff Director Thomas J. Sweeney, who also joined Anthony Bouza, in an intense discussion of my approach. Over the years I have continued to converse on fundamental issues in policing with two officers from New York City, Edmund Stubbing and Peter Mancuso. The title of this book is a gift from Peter Mancuso.

Among the many colleagues who have given me bright ideas and sound criticism I wish particularly to thank Herman Goldstein of the University of Wisconsin, Elinor Ostrom and Roger Parks of Indiana University, Stephen Mastrofski of Pennsylvania State University, Paul Dunn of

Pike Place Market in Seattle, Darrel Stephens of the Police Executive Research Forum, Frank Leahy of the Commission on Accreditation for Law Enforcement Agencies, Erika Fairchild of the University of North Carolina at Raleigh, Susan Parato of Adelphi University, and Lottie Feinberg and Kenneth Moran of John Jay College of Criminal Justice. Staff members of the computer center of the City University of New York provided solid technical advice on data analysis. Ronald Taylor and other students of John Angell at the University of Alaska plus students of Kenneth Betsalel at Southwest Missouri State University are good sports for giving fresh advice long distance. Thanks to my mother, Frances Hess, our final efforts to eliminate errors in the manuscript have been an enjoyable venture.

In looking at one police department I have aimed to ask thoughtful questions about how police power can contribute to social well-being and justice. Now probing deeper to consider fundamental questions of the human condition, I am engaged in an enduring conversation with books, students, and fellow tutors at St. John's College.

Dorothy Guyot
Annapolis, Maryland

Service by Professional Police Officers

One fall night about six years ago when I was a young cop, my partner and I were parked in a lot, as usual, but this time I was at the wheel. A call came over the car radio that a yellow Mustang had just missed running down an officer on foot. Just then a yellow Mustang sped by. I took chase, but my partner reached over and turned off the ignition. I drove to the station and disobeyed his order to stay in the car. The desk sergeant listened to both of us and just ordered us back to work. Nobody spoke to me. The next evening when I reported to work, I was punished with a walking post up and down the long hill of Hoosick Street. Nobody ever told me why I was being punished. I was kept on that post during a bitter winter and through the spring.

Officer "Don Turner," 1969

1

Two Transformations in Police Upgrading

Punishment has historically been employed as a major method of controlling police officers. Uncontrolled police power is so threatening to a democracy that great effort has been invested to control the actions of officers on the street. The administrative tools of control have been supervision, regulation, and punishment. What is unusual about the 1969 incident related above, in which an energetic young officer was punished for defying his slothful partner, is that the young officer's action was then agreed to be right by police locker room views, right by police rules and regulations, right by law, and right by the broad values of American society. Yet this stark example shows an endangered officer on foot and an officer giving chase being treated as though they do not matter. These events were the product of an ill-designed and ill-managed police department with a long history of providing shoddy service to citizens.

Repressive ways became part of the repertoire of the young officer who was so severely punished for trying to catch the reckless Mustang driver. We will give the young officer the pseudonym Don Turner. Two years after all capricious departmental punishment had ended, Officer Turner was still acting hostile to citizens.

> I've got many complaints against me from women. I am nasty with them so that they don't get the upper hand. When there are just the two of us, I let the woman rant unless I am not up to stomaching it. If there is a crowd, I can't let her rant because that will stir up the others. I may act nasty when I don't feel like it. I've shouted, "Shut up, bitch." I've grabbed them by the arm and pushed them in the squad car.

When police officers matter, the people they serve matter. This book is about the transformation of police service from callous and shoddy to helpful and competent. We will look at the problems of transforming a department that demeans and punishes officers into one that treats them as professionals in the service of the public.

Since policing is a practical business, the issues are illustrated with events from the operations of a single department over a fifteen-year span. Only five individuals from Troy—two city managers, one commissioner, and two police chiefs—are named; the confidentiality of citizens and other officers is maintained through the use of pseudonyms. This study examines closely the application to police organizations of the human relations school of management. If this approach works, officers spend less time following the locker room advice "Cover your ass" and more time treating citizens in ways that show that people matter.

Police Work

A police department is a city's multipurpose agency for dealing with social disorders. No grand design lies behind the wide variety of problems that are police business today. The longer an organization has been in existence, the more different functions it is likely to perform, because to avoid shrinkage it picks up new functions whenever the demand for old ones slumps. Changes in technology, resources, and needs over the decades have permitted police departments to drop some problems, such as lodging for wayfarers, and have required the commitment of enormous resources to others, such as traffic safety. The tendency to diversify is accentuated when an organization is open twenty-four hours a day and its services are free. A contemporary view of the diversity of police work and why officers love it emerges from photographs and reflections of officers across the country collected in the book called *Tribute* (Lawrence et al., 1989).

The 16,000 departments in the world of American policing show tremendous variation. Departments differ in their mix of officers who treat people with concern and officers who are indifferent or cynical. When people call the police, they usually receive calming reassurance and direct assistance, but sometimes officers act callously. Some police officers work closely with the people of the neighborhood to reduce burglaries, but other officers know almost no one. Some officers calm unruly crowds, but others stir anger among peaceable people. Luck does not determine whether or not a city has many officers who are concerned about the people they serve and grow skillful in solving complex problems. Management does.

A useful step in sorting out the remarkable variations among police departments is to return to the groundbreaking work of James Q. Wilson, *Varieties of Police Behavior* (1968). When Wilson linked variation in police practices with the organizational structure of the department and with the character of the local political system, he identified three styles of policing: the "watchman style" of a sluggish department; the "legalistic style" of a department that emphasizes impartial enforcement of the law; and the "service style" of a department that provides a wide variety of services requested by citizens. Troy, New York, where the watchman style prevailed prior to 1973, provided the examples for this book. In developing the concept of the watchman style, James Q. Wilson had looked at three other New York cities that also lie in the Hudson River Valley: Albany, Amsterdam, and Newburgh. In a watchman-style department, citizens who are not powerful are treated rudely—Don Turner's domineering attitude toward women is an example—but such a department routinely gives preferential treatment to politically powerful people, ranging from ignoring their drunken driving to posting officers at their whim. To members of a watchman-style department, whether people matter depends upon who the people are.

The Transformation toward Professional Police Administration

The major twentieth-century advances in the quality of police service have been directed by professional police administrators, individuals

who transformed watchman-style departments into legalistic-style departments. O. W. Wilson, the foremost administrator of midcentury, set forth
in his classic text *Police Administration* (1950) the current version of the
reforms begun at the turn of the century by the Progressive movement.
Police administrators fought political machines, which had so dominated
policing that an officer's rank in the department depended upon his rank
in the local party organization. Although the scope of patronage was drastically narrowed in the early decades of this century, pressures on selection, promotion, and assignment are still common in many cities. Quite
obviously, officers cannot be expected to enforce the law impartially
against powerful people to whom they are indebted. Police administrators sought to shield officers from outside influence and to create strong
departmental controls to curb abuses against the powerless. They ham-
mered at incompetent police agencies in order to forge positive answers
to these questions:

Do police officers obey the law?

To what extent do police officers act impartially and courteously?

To what extent do performance statistics show high productivity?

The transformation from foot patrol to radio car patrol and the emphasis on efficiency and impartiality cut informal, friendly contacts between officers and the individuals they serve. In the extreme, some officers saw their work narrowed to crime fighting and saw themselves
dealing primarily with criminals and troublemakers, defined as people
who did not matter.

The tumultuous 1960s shattered complacency in the police field. The
racial character of many cities had shifted greatly without any corre-
sponding change in the racial composition or sensitivity of the police
department. Black militance, central to this change of political climate,
encouraged others to demonstrate for their particular causes. Students
demonstrated against the war in Vietnam and faced the police as their
domestic enemy. When President Lyndon Johnson's promises of a Great
Society led to higher expectations among the urban poor and government programs supported their mobilization, additional segments of society took to the streets. Meanwhile, the proportion of the population in
the crime-prone ages was growing rapidly. Young people were also turning to drugs in moods of curiosity, defiance, and disillusionment, and
some engaged in burglary and theft to support their addiction.

Public concern with law and order grew so intense that between 1965
and 1971 five presidential commissions had inquired into the problems
of the police. The first, the U.S. President's Commission on Law Enforcement and the Administration of Justice (1967a), can now be seen as outstanding in contracting for social science research and making far-reaching recommendations. Moreover, the experiences of the 1970s further
agitated the police field: the pell-mell federal funding of new programs

through the Law Enforcement Assistance Administration (LEAA), the influx of educational programs and educated officers, police union picketing and job actions, and the application of social science research to police problems. Consequently, the unevenness among police departments has increased: some have pulled far ahead, while others have remained mired in old ways.

The Transformation toward Professional Police Officers

The fresh approach to police work that emerged in the late 1960s now has practitioners scattered across the continent. The first seeds were sown long ago by August Vollmer, who in 1908, as head of the Berkeley, California, police department, sought to recruit college students as police officers. This approach takes for granted the professional competence of police executives and strives to develop the professional skill and independent judgment of officers on the street. The magnitude of this second transformation is as great as that of the first, which turned watchman departments into legalistic ones. The service-style department identified by James Q. Wilson in the mid-1960s was the precursor of departments now engaged in encouraging officers to create and implement tailor-made solutions to community problems.

The departmental impact of this transformation can be visualized by thinking of the standard organizational pyramid turned on its side. The leaders who once commanded now obtain allegiance to shared goals and now manage systems that facilitate cooperative efforts. Those officers who once were expected to obey but resourcefully devised evasions now develop judgment, responsibility, and self-discipline. The changes include a fundamental decentralization of authority and responsibility to the officers on the beat and a fundamental opening of departmental policies and operations to public inquiry and demands. Departmental leadership directs the focus of the members toward the people they serve and facilitates their work by efficient management of the support services: cars in good working condition, clear radio transmission, useful records, and appropriate coordination. The key questions underlying the new approach include the same three that are central to the first transformation, plus three new ones:

To what extent do officers use discretion to help citizens solve their problems?

To what extent is the department managed to support officers' use of discretion?

To what extend does the department inform the public?

The success of the two leading contemporary undertakings, community policing and problem-oriented policing, require the police department to increase the motivation and develop the judgment of officers on the street. If officers are lazy or narrow-minded, both these approaches fail. In this book the police leaders who promote officers' wide latitude in decisionmaking are called "police managers" rather than "police administrators" to emphasize that they manage resources in support of the individuals who decide the content of the direct services.

The hospital model is introduced to describe the new organization design, which promotes and supports sound judgment by the men and women who serve as police officers. This model draws analogies between police officers and physicians to highlight both the discretionary decisions that officers make and their broad service role. The old tradition of thinking about police departments as quasi-military organizations emphasized the authority to use deadly force and gave the illusion that police officers routinely work under the direction of superiors. In reality, however, police officers employ both persuasion and coercion; moreover, close supervision is impossible because police service is delivered by geographically dispersed officers working alone or in pairs. This study scrutinizes the changes that take place when the hospital model is the concept guiding changes in a traditional department.

The effort to develop the professionalism of individual officers and to support them with an open style of organization has been slow in coming to the police field, decades after the beginning of the human relations school of administration and decades after practitioners in other fields had become professionals. Still, the delay has had its advantages. Just as Japan in the late nineteenth century did not have to pass through the early stages of the industrial revolution but could immediately adapt current technologies, so police management is now in position to draw upon well-developed theories and practices from public adminstration and business management.

The Pace of the Two Transformations

The acceptance of administrative and scientific improvements from the first transformation has occurred far more quickly than incorporation of practices central to the second. Table 1-1 shows the uneven pace of advances in American policing by identifying both the date of initial adoption of an improvement and the decade of its widespread adoption. Dividing the advances into two separate lists, those in police administration and those in the development of professional police officers, makes vivid the differences. Police chiefs who hold the outlook of a professional administrator make improvements on the first half of the list; police chiefs who have the outlook of a police manager make improvements on both halves. Within each list the improvements are arranged in the order of first adoption by an American department, and only practices that have endured are included. Widespread adoption is considered to have oc-

Table 1-1 Two Transformations in American Policing

Improvement	First Use	Wide Adoption	Troy Adoption
Steps Toward Professional Administration and Scientific Techniques			
Fingerprint identification[a]	1904 St. Louis	1920s	
Patrol cars[b]	1913 Berkeley	1920s	1932
Crime laboratory[d]	1916 Berkeley	1950s?	not yet
Radio cars[c]	1921 Berkeley	1930s	1938?
Patrol workload formulas[e]	1926 Berkeley	late 1950s	1974
Uniform Crime Reports[f]	1930 IACP nationally	1930s	1930
Central numerical dispatching record[g]	after 1941	1950s?	1973
Internal affairs unit[h]	1950 Los Angeles?	1960s?	1973
Computers for operational information[i]	1969 Los Angeles?	1970s?	1985
911 emergency number[j]	Huntington, Ind., 1968	1970s	not yet
Portable radios for patrol[k]	President's Commission, 1967	1970s	1973
Investigative case screening system[l]	1969 Fremont, Calif.	1980s	1977
Agency accreditation[m]	1983 Mt. Dora, Baltimore County, and three others	not yet	not attempted
Steps Toward Professional Officers			
Mandatory training for new officers[n]	1870 St. Louis	1950s	1962
Officers earn B.A.s[o]	1918 Berkeley	1970s	1974
Applicant psychological screening[p]	1919? Berkeley	1970s?	1974
Substantial employment of nonsworn personnel[q]	1944 Los Angeles	1960s	1973
Women become patrol officers[r]	1968 Indianapolis?	1970s	1984
Law Enforcement Code of Ethics[s]	1937 FBI; 1956 California Peace Officers' Association	early 1960s	1974
B.A. required for entrance[t]	1965 Multnomah, Ore.	not yet	not yet
Team policing[u]	1970 Detroit	not yet	1978 attempt
Problem-oriented policing[v]	1981 Madison, Wis.	not yet	1980 attempt

Note: Date of earliest known use is given. Decade of widespread adoption is roughly when the improvement had been adopted by a majority of departments serving cities of 50,000 or more.
[a]Walker 1977, 73. Fosdick 1920, 348–51, notes resistance to fingerprinting.
[b]Parker 1972, 24.
[c]Parker 1972, 36.
[d]Deakin 1988, 53, 98.
[e]Parker 1972, 24–26 (the date was apparently between 1924 and 1926).

(*Continued*)

Table 1-1 (*Continued*).

[f]FBI and IACP 1930.
[g]After 1941: Wilson 1942 says that the FCC requires a radio log.
[h]Brewer 1988.
[i]Brewer 1988 reports that Los Angeles began to operate a computerized warrant system in 1969.
[j]A T and T 1983, 60.
[k]U.S. President's Commission 1967.
[l]Greenberg 1972–73.
[m]CALEA 1985, 2–6.
[n]Deakin 1988, 25; O'Connor 1962 shows that in 1956 less than 75 percent of the cities with population over 25,000 had preservice training.
[o]Deakin 1988, 95–96. A four-year college degree for police officers was proposed in Vollmer and Schneider 1917.
[p]Blum 1964, 99, places Vollmer's introduction of psychological testing in the 1910s.
[q]Brewer 1988 reports that the Los Angeles PD hired 678 nonsworn personnel in 1944 and 1,011—19 percent of the department—by 1947.
[r]Milton 1972, 10.
[s]Various codes were proposed for local law enforcement as early as 1937 (see Deakin 1988, 177, 214, 222). The code adopted came from California (O'Connor 1957, 33–34; personal communication from Gene Muehleisen, author of the code) and is reprinted annually in the Uniform Crime Reports.
[t]Clark and Chapman 1966, 21; Owen 1988.
[u]Block and Specht 1973, 13.
[v]Following a seminal article by Herman Goldstein (1979), the National Institute of Justice awarded a grant for a pilot implementation in Madison; see Goldstein 1990, 51–52.

curred when roughly half the departments serving populations of over 50,000 had implemented the improvement. Note that twelve years has been the median delay between the introduction and general acceptance of any administrative or scientific advance. By contrast, even basic steps to increase the professional competence of street officers, such as mandatory training, have taken up to sixty years from initiation to widespread acceptance.

What Makes a Good Police Department?

In brief, a good department can be distinguished by the excellence of the services to the public and by the quality of the worklife for its members. Employing sound administrative practices, using modern scientific techniques, and promoting professionalism among officers—that is, all the steps in Table 1-1—are means for improving the quality of services. Coherent departmental management can take such steps in an appropriate sequence to achieve a more effective organization, but the steps themselves are not measures of quality service.

Because all police departments provide multiple services, multiple criteria are appropriate for evaluating the quality of those services. The broad performance questions asked by police administrators and managers are the place to begin. Questions such as "To what extent do officers act impartially and courteously?" can generate other, more specific questions to pinpoint the quality of performance in solving various societal problems. The Appendix contains some of the many reasonable questions that could be asked about departmental performance. Most questions directly assess the quality of service to the public, but a few concern management practices that faciliate quality service.

Overview of the Book

To explain the processes of police upgrading in contemporary America, one department's changes are examined in depth. In 1973 George W. O'Connor came to Troy, New York, for the purpose of upgrading the quality of police service, and his efforts launched the department into the two transformations simultaneously. This focus on the work of a single police manager is not tantamount to a claim that his approach is unique; in fact, his approach is shared by a growing number of leaders in the police field. Rather, the claim is that these police managers work very differently from their predecessors and from the majority of today's police chiefs and police commissioners. Nor does this examination of a single department stake a claim of special success in upgrading. Rather, the ups and downs of change are instructive; hence, the examples both of outstanding police service and of police malpractice come from the Troy department during the years 1973–87. The Troy experience in catching up with the field is presented in the last column of Table 1-1. Note the spurt in administrative and scientific improvements in the mid-1970s. A summary of Troy's changes, probably a common pattern for lagging departments, shows swift catching up in administrative and scientific competence but slower development in the professional level of officers.

In exploring fundamental problems in the provision of police service and describing a coherent approach to their solution, we begin with the basic issues of direct service to individual citizens and build to complex discussions of policy. The book is about change: both deliberate organizational change stemming from a coherent view of policing, and unanticipated change. The specific changes in Troy made between 1973 and 1987 will be changed again. If future changes continue in the direction chosen since 1973, then these years will have marked a turningpoint for the department.

This study is organized around problems in the provision of quality police service. The first of four major parts inquires into the development of professional police officers and their service to citizens. Chapter 2 is richest in detail, describing many management steps that conveyed the message that both police officers and the people they serve matter. Chapter 3 discusses patrol by examining the great variety of problems that citizens brought to police officers, the officers' use of discretion, and the sources of citizen satisfaction with police service. Chapter 4 concludes Part I by drawing upon organization theory, which supports changing the organizational design of police departments to draw upon the hospital model.

Coping with crime is the topic of the three chapters in Part II. Arrest rates—reasonable measures of performance in handling one set of problems—are covered in Chapter 5, as are the treatment of arrestees and the results of subsequent court cases. Chapter 6 shows that a department organized in support of the professional police officer has a number of other modes for ameliorating crime problems: reducing the likelihood that people and property will be attacked, reducing the likelihood that some individuals will make attacks, and assisting victims. Chapter 7, on fear of crime, starts with an incident triggering public belief that the city was suffering from a crime wave. The discussion then turns to the positive concept, a sense of safety, and what police can do to enhance it.

Part III concerns police power. Chapter 8, which categorizes and explores remedies for police malpractice, returns to the fundamental principle shared by police administrators and the new breed of police managers, that police officers obey the law. Chapter 9 examines union power and the clash of interests in the adversarial relations between union and management. Chapter 10 develops and applies criteria to distinguish between political accountability and political interference.

Part IV returns to the central concern of service to the public. Chapter 11 explores the fundamental relations between individual police officers and the individuals they serve. When police officers provide a wide range of services to all members of the community, they build support and trust for their law enforcement responsibilities. Chapter 12 weighs issues of fairness, both in law enforcement and in provision of service.

The Appendix presents questions for each chapter, to aid inquiry into the degree to which specific American police departments provide excellent services to citizens. Readers can probably use them most effectively by reflecting on each set of questions in conjunction with the specific chapter that generated them. The questions perform the double function of summarizing the main argument of each chapter and succinctly addressing common problems in policing urban America. Citizens and police officers who wish to see improvements in their department's performance will gain insights into the nature of the problems by asking these questions. Citizens and officers who wish to document their own department's provision of quality service can use the questions to gain a systematic understanding in support of their impressions.

What I refused to do was come in with a standard in my head which said that everyone should be able to stand so tall and run so fast. I came in with the understanding that this is an old police department that had been here for 100 years and was going to be here at least that many more, and that it was eminently unfair to inflict a whole new set of standards upon people who had joined this police department under a different condition. I thought it better to give them the opportunity and, hopefully, the resources to grow. . . . I think in the long run that makes a more solid kind of organization.

George W. O'Connor, 1977

Overcoming Inertia

From his first day as public safety commissioner of Troy, New York, George W. O'Connor offered department members opportunities to grow in their sense of worth as police officers, in their personal standards for helpfulness to citizens, and in the satisfaction of meeting higher standards. Fears, ingrained habits, and attachment to current advantages generated resistance to change during his first few weeks on the job in 1973.

The first theme of this chapter is a portrayal of the poorly managed Troy Police Department before O'Connor's arrival. The second theme is that when a leader involves department members in the change process, they are not forced to choose between rejecting their past and rejecting the promised future; instead, they feel ownership in the continuity of improvements in their department's performance and do not single out the new practices as foreign imports. The third theme begins an exploration of ways to adapt an open style of management to policing. The fourth theme considers appropriate governmental controls on the police manager.

Resistance to Change

Isolation characterized the police department and the city of Troy, New York, during the twentieth century. This old industrial city of 51,000 is set in the Albany-Schenectady-Troy metropolitan region, which has a population of 800,000. The low, flat land stretching almost ten miles along the Hudson River contains factories, the central business district, aging three-story apartments, and small, detached homes. Hills rise sharply from the flat lands, cut by the streams that provided the power permitting Troy to become a leading industrial city in the early nineteenth century. Today, the presence of Rensselaer Polytechnic Institute, Russell Sage College, and Hudson Valley Community College make education the city's major industry. The Census Bureau has pegged the decline in the city's population at about 1% a year between 1960 and 1988.

Size is the most basic characteristic of a city. At 51,000 in 1990, Troy is at the national midpoint, since half the population of standard metropolitan areas lives in smaller towns. National trends are exhibited by Troy: sharply decreasing density; concentration of the poor and minorities in the center; increasing suburban employment of all types. As of 1980, 9 percent of the households were receiving public assistance, a proportion close to the national average of 8 percent. Fourteen percent were then living in public housing, mostly in two-story units well scattered throughout the city. In racial and ethnic composition Troy is not typical, having only 6 percent black residents and almost no Hispanic residents. In this regard, Troy is like one-fourth of the cities of over 100,000 population, which have black populations of 5 percent or less.

Troy's black residents are concentrated in a limited area of dilapidated housing just north of the central business district.

Like most cities under half a million, Troy is governed by a city manager who reports to a city council chaired by a mayor, who is one of the council members. Troy came late to the council-manager form of government, from a history of partisan conflict so intense that the city hall was not rebuilt for thirty years after it burned down in 1938. The triggering incident for the resignation of the first city manager in 1967 was his refusal to make a police promotion on the orders of the head of the party in power. During the first seven years of city manager government, five of the six managers were forced to resign. City politics in Troy creates exciting combat for the participants and a fascinating spectator sport for the voters.

The typology of municipal politics developed by Oliver Williams (1961) comprises four categories, each describing what the influential local people expect the role of the town's government to be: the provider of amenities, typical of suburbs; the booster, as in Phoenix, Arizona, where growth is the priority; the caretaker, as in Florida towns with low tax rates; and the arbitrator, where energies are consumed in conflict. In Troy, an arbitrator government, each policy question that arises immediately becomes a partisan issue: one party takes sides in an effort to derive some narrow advantage, and the other party swings to the opposition for the same reasons. Fundamental improvement in police service appears to be most difficult under arbitrator government, less difficult under caretaker government, and least difficult under booster and provider-of-amenities governments.

In Troy an appointed commissioner of public safety was in charge of both police and fire departments, each headed by a chief with civil service tenure. This double layer of leadership, found primarily in cities where police chiefs do have civil service tenure, is a mechanism that permits the city executive to appoint and remove the commissioner, the person in charge of the police.

In 1972 the Troy PD was composed of 122 sworn officers and four full-time nonsworn personnel. The absence of a lieutenant's rank accounts for a flatter organizational pyramid than in most departments. The small fraction of nonsworn personnel, three meter maids and one secretary, was characteristic of departments in an earlier era. Patrol staffing was low at sixty-eight officers of all ranks, administration had twelve, the detective bureau was large at nineteen, the juvenile bureau had six, and the traffic division was huge at fourteen officers plus fifty-five part-time crossing guards, another legacy from an earlier era. Three officers on the department's payroll did not work for the department but had been selected by the police court judge and the corporation counsel to work for them. The one sworn woman had a permanent assignment to the juvenile bureau, and the one black man had received his appointment in 1957, when political leaders sought him out to offer him a choice of employment in the police or the fire department.

A vicious circle kept the Troy department at a low level of performance. Bad working conditions and low salaries attracted few officers, many of whom exerted little effort, producing poor service, leading to low public respect, leading to fewer applicants. Failure had plagued a decade of halfhearted attempts to upgrade the department. In the mid-1960s the first city manager had failed to persuade the city council to contract for an assessment by the International Association of Chiefs of Police (IACP) as the first step in an overhaul. The council permitted only consultation from a retired state police colonel to revise the crime reporting forms. When police officers in 1968 sought to negotiate their first contract, they were unsuccessful for twenty-one months until the fire fighters forced the City with a brief strike. In 1969 a sergeant with more than twenty years of service attempted to force the repair of the police station by writing a long letter to the editor of the city's newspaper and by making a formal complaint to building and fire inspectors. The inspectors documented leaking pipes, broken toilets, loose wires, and combustible piles of trash, concluding, "Maintenance? There is or was none." The upshot of the investigation was that the police chief, on the orders of the public safety commissioner, forbade officers to communicate with the news media.

The city manager who came to town in 1970 initially gave little heed to police, but after the current public safety commissioner was indicted for extortion, the city manager began issuing orders to the department. When he failed to get the council's attention to the quick and damning management study he had commissioned from a retired New York City police administrator, he began cruising the streets during early morning hours to catch officers sleeping on duty and to bring them up on disciplinary charges. He next outraged the department by holding a lineup of police officers in an attempt to identify individuals who had beaten a college student, high on LSD, who was attacking an older officer. The dictates of this outsider unified the department behind the police union. The city council bargained with him to end his attentions to the police department in exchange for their agreement to contract with a nationally respected consulting firm. The contract, paid for completely from LEAA funds, was approved at the very meeting at which the council fired him for refusing to acquiesce in the stripping away of his appointment powers.

In July 1972, on the eve of the consultants' arrival, the city council's planning committee held a citizens' open house at the police station in order to publicize the building's deterioration, but only the press came. Administrative inertia was matched by public apathy. When the consultants arrived, the chief took a long vacation, but officers lined up after work to pour out their woes.

Bleak conditions at the departmental level do not automatically condemn all officers to giving shoddy service. An unusual episode from the late 1960s illustrates one officer's concerned and helpful service, despite the capricious mismanagement of his department.

☐ Carl Peterson recalled that one evening while patrolling his zone his suspicions were aroused that someone was inside a closed shoe store. Watching inconspicuously, he caught a seventeen-year-old boy stealing a single box of shoes. The boy seemed to Peterson like a good kid, but he sullenly rebuffed every effort to talk over what he had done. In making the arrest and collecting evidence of forcible entry, Officer Peterson had put together a solid case of burglary 3rd that carried an indeterminate sentence of up to seven years, but he felt very uncomfortable about the possible consequences for the boy.

When Peterson approached the boy's friends, whom he knew, they also refused to talk but finally admitted, "It's his old man. He beats him if he doesn't come home with liquor money." Peterson visited the boy's home, confirming the picture of two alcoholic parents who tyrannized their children, and a crisis that week when the boy's regular newspaper delivery and odd jobs had failed him. In the judge's chambers Peterson overcame his objections that the boy's brother was a repeat offender and obtained a conditional discharge. When the boy learned that he had been spared imprisonment, he emerged from his sullenness and eagerly took a job that Peterson found for him. Peterson also overcame the reluctance of the boy's older sister and her husband to let the boy live with them. The boy grew to manhood, and at his wedding and the christening of his first child, Carl Peterson was an honored guest.

This chain of events had begun with vigilance on patrol in spotting a burglary in progress, but the next steps were possible because police officers have the latitude to carry self-defined responsibilities to extraordinary lengths. In this case the officer worked in the manner of a family physician, probing to understand the history before making the diagnosis, prescribing a treatment that he personally supervised, and continuing his interest in the well-being of his client.

Critique from the Perspective of Professional Administrators

After examining the department the consultants bluntly concluded, "The Troy Bureau of Police is currently a poorly managed, poorly organized, inefficient police agency" (Cresap, McCormick, and Paget 1972, 1:III-1).

The police department had experienced no coherent policy direction since at least 1956, when the Democrats elevated a patrolman directly to chief. Although he had scored the lowest of seven who took the examination, he became eligible when men ahead of him on the promotion list were promoted to lesser ranks. Civil service tenure then froze him into the chief's position, but he never learned management. Officers knew him best for his capricious punishments. His most direct involvement in operations was to lead officers in mass arrests of partying college students. His version of fiscal responsibility was to accept an inadequate budget and then pinch pennies on maintenance and equipment so that a surplus could be returned to the City at the end of the year. The chief of detectives, until his death in 1968, had exercised the most power and had even written directives for the public safety commissioner to issue. The succession of Republicans who had held the part-time post of commissioner had brought no police expertise to the office, save the one appointed in 1968. The consultants summarized the chaotic state of the department in 1972: "The various Platoons, Bureaus and Sections of the TBP [Troy Bureau of Police] function as a loosely federated association of autonomous cells without adequate communication and coordination, and often appear to be pursuing divergent, competing or conflicting, rather than similar, ends" (Cresap, McCormick, and Paget 1972, 1:III-3).

Officers typically channel energy into protecting themselves when city leaders, commissioners, chiefs, and other commanders show little regard for their well-being. Troy officers strongly supported their union, the Police Benevolent Association. In 1955 the PBA had obtained a long overdue salary increase solely through members' efforts in launching and winning a municipal referendum. After New York State permitted collective bargaining, the PBA gained an exceptionally strong seniority clause to protect officers from arbitrary personnel shuffling and such punishment posts as the wintry slope where Don Turner had walked. The management consultants concluded that "members of the Bureau have organized and, by means of the PBA contract with the City, have acquired an excessive degree of control over Troy Bureau of Police operations. The efforts of these members appear to reflect primarily an attempt to provide a degree of control, direction, and stability to the Bureau which is otherwise lacking, and to protect their means of livelihood from unwarranted external interference. . . . They have, however, achieved this control to an extent which now threatens to undermine the potential for revitalization of the Bureau" (Cresap, McCormick, and Paget 1972, 1:III-2).

In September 1972, immediately after the key consultant appeared in a half-hour television interview, the chief retired. The way opened for the City to take the first step toward upgrading the department, to select a professional to head it. The choice of a new head for an organization, whether in business or in government, provides the best opportunity to change policy direction.

Fear of Change

Events in the appointment of the new commissioner of public safety illustrate a complete absence of reasoned public debate. Worse, the circumstances surrounding the appointment led to fearful gossip and ominous predictions within the police department.

The new city manager's operating style had created the vacuum into which rumors poured. John P. Buckley had turned to the consultants for advice, traveled to Washington to interview their sole nominee, and immediately offered the position to George W. O'Connor. Buckley was the only person in Troy who knew of O'Connor's existence.

Buckley had stepped from head of the water department, where he had built an excellent filtration plant, to acting city manager in March 1972 upon the firing of his combative predecessor. When the city council, composed entirely of Democrats, confirmed him in June 1972, his background as a native of Troy and his engineering competence outweighed the fact that he was a registered though inactive Republican. A bachelor, he was married to his work. His engineering background shaped his approach to city government in both his emphasis on building physical facilities and in his slowly diminishing discomfort in political matters. When Buckley took the job, his major projects for the city were a city hall, improved traffic flow, a new bridge across the Hudson, a north-south interstate highway, and urban renewal to build a downtown shopping center. Before ten years were out, he had succeeded with all but the highway.

With an engineer's eyes, Buckley saw problems as technical questions for the experts. He often withheld information from the city council, announcing his view only after he had taken action. Police matters were a particularly sore point with city councilmen, stemming in part from the fact that the mayor was the brother of the PBA's past president and in part from the council's resentment over the previous city manager's dictates to the department.

Buckley had kept secret even from the city council the fact that the consultants had completed their critical first volume and his decision to hire a commissioner. On 21 February 1973, Troy's newspaper, the *Times Record*, announced this triple shock: the consultants' blast, the *fait accompli* of an outsider as commissioner, and the city manager's refusal to fill the vacant police chief position. During the rest of the week the top local news stories quoted the consultants' condemnation of the department. O'Connor took office on 26 February 1973, amid pervasive rumors that he was a hatchet man. Vague fears that a commissioner with a mandate to overhaul might resort to dismissals had been heightened by efforts to learn more about this unknown outsider. When PBA leaders telephoned the Cleveland police association to learn how O'Connor had run the police department there, they learned of a layoff of two hundred officers. Other rumors circulated that the consulting firm had made the Troy police department look exceptionally bad in the eyes of the federal government so that Troy would be more eligible for federal funds.

The Commissioner

All this controversy and fear focused on a man who brought seventeen years of diverse experience in the police field to his new position. After graduating with a political science degree from Dartmouth, O'Connor had next enrolled in the criminology school at the University of California, Berkeley, where he served as a teaching assistant to O. W. Wilson. One of his final steps toward entry into police work was getting arrested. In 1955 Chief Wyman Vernon of the Oakland Police Department had come to the school of criminology to find a few volunteers to pose as winos. As O'Connor and a classmate lay in the gutter of downtown Oakland, the patrolmen who lifted them into the paddy wagon also lifted a wallet containing marked bills. O'Connor entered the Oakland department in 1956 and served primarily in patrol, but he also worked in the jail, dispatching, the juvenile bureau, and planning, where he developed crime prevention clauses for the municipal building code. In 1958 O'Connor departed for Cleveland, where he held a dual appointment as scientific investigator for the Cuyahoga County coroner's office and as clinical instructor in criminology at Case Western Reserve University.

O'Connor became director of training in the Chicago PD in 1960, the year that O. W. Wilson took charge of this department, which had drawn national ridicule when eight officers were discovered to be running a burglary ring. At that time one precinct had no functioning patrol cars. To make do, four officers had put police radios in their own cars and drove them on patrol. Such low performance had persisted because the public was not informed of the specific shortcomings and lacked standards for comparison.

In 1962 O'Connor joined the staff of the International Association of Chiefs of Police. His most influential work of the next seven years was to create the bi-weekly *Training Keys*. When the Law Enforcement Assistance Administration was established, O'Connor served in 1969–70 as the first chief of its police programs division.

Departmental responsibility came in 1970 when O'Connor accepted the appointment from Mayor Carl B. Stokes as Cleveland's director of public safety. In his first week on the job he abolished the computerized ticket fixing that had served hundreds of well-connected individuals. Because Cleveland felt the financial crunch of the 1970s earlier than other cities, O'Connor had to lay off more than two hundred young officers, one of the most painful acts of his career. A few months later Stokes announced that he would not seek a second term. O'Connor, judging that the election was unlikely to produce an administration supportive of change, joined the faculty of the University of Miami, where he developed a criminal justice program.

This career line is typical of a new breed of police managers, well-educated individuals who explicitly apply social science knowledge to management. Their ability to view the field from a national perspective is enhanced by working in more than one department. They see police services as contributing in many ways to the quality of life far beyond the reduction of street crime. They accept the fact that the complexities of police work require independent judgments by street officers and so manage their departments to enhance the quality of those judgments.

Among such police managers working in the 1970s and 1980s is R. Fred Ferguson of Covina, Riverside, and Salinas, California who is best known for teaching officers to experience life as members of a despised minority by having them spend a weekend as Skid Row bums. Cornelius Behan, after serving in New York City, has shaped an efficient and community-oriented department in Baltimore County, Maryland. Lee P. Brown of Multnomah County, Oregon, and then Atlanta, Houston, and New York City, strives to develop community-based policing. Under the leadership of Raymond C. Davis, the Santa Ana, California department developed the trust of the Mexican-American community, whose members had feared that officers would inquire into whether or not they were legal residents. David Couper of Madison, Wisconsin, sees the city as composed of citizens living in diverse and conflicting moral worlds (the porno consumers, the motorcyclists, the pot smokers, the solid citizens), and a crucial job for the police is to prevent these moral worlds from colliding. Darrel Stephens of Kansas City, Missouri, Lawrence, Kansas, and Largo, Florida has implemented problem-oriented policing in Newport News, Virginia and now serves as executive director of the Police Executive Research Forum (PERF), the professional organization of college-educated police leaders of large departments. The common vision shared by these and other police managers across the country is a fundamental upgrading of police service through an increase in cooperation between police officers and citizens.

The description in the following chapters of the work of George W. O'Connor focuses on the elements common to police managers and blurs the peculiarities of the Troy situation. The specific policies he developed are not prescriptions for other police managers; the head of every police agency needs the flexibility to translate general principles into specific policies appropriate to the history and characteristics of the agency and the city. The leaders who have developed consistent approaches to upgrading police service are strong personalities whose individuality is stamped upon their every action. Police managers do not work well if asked to follow a blueprint drafted by others. A police manager works best when the city's political leadership is willing to be educated by that manager in the fundamentals of policing.

Overcoming the Fear of Change

O'Connor's approach was to acknowledge openly the existence of problems and to involve the people concerned in working out solutions. On his first day as commissioner he announced that he did not feel bound by the consultants' recommendations for top-down change but would discuss all changes with department members. He met with the departmental commanders in the morning, with the PBA leaders in the early afternoon, and with the press in midafternoon. Between meetings he chatted informally with members at all ranks. Every time the "hatchet man" label cropped up, O'Connor explicitly stated that he took the job with the intention of working with the present department members and had no preconceived plan for dismissing anyone. Since department members had not seen the consultants' report, O'Connor placed seven copies at the central desk available for borrowing and a week later gave two copies to the public library. To minimize the damaging effects of misinformation, he posted "Rumor/Fact Notices" to rebut each rumor that surfaced. His answer to the first rumor indicates the tenor of his replies.

Rumor/Fact Notice #1

Rumor: There is a plan to rotate shifts.

Fact: There is no plan to rotate shifts. Any such plan would be developed only at the request of the majority of the members of each particular unit.

Serious consideration is being given to the rotation of assignments for newly hired and newly promoted members. The purpose of this type of rotation is to afford the member in a new position with an opportunity to experience the function, procedures and problems of most major units of the department in which he might work. If this form of rotation is adopted, it will be for a specific period of time and its purpose would be for training, indoctrination and for career development.

O'Connor immediately opened channels of communication within the department and between department members and citizens. He convened a meeting at a nearby labor hall where all members not on duty could air their pent-up complaints. He established working committees to plan changes in major aspects of departmental operations: physical plant, rules and regulations, training, and performance evaluation. These committees took their work seriously, especially the one revising the departmental rules and regulations. To enhance informal communication, the commissioner gave the PBA office space and the president an inside job on the day shift, Monday through Friday. In introducing officers to the city's social service agencies, he urged them to attend open houses on department time. His door was always open to every member of the department and every citizen. In reflecting on his first two years as commissioner, he estimated that he spent half his time listening and responding to complaints and suggestions.

Watchman-style departments tend to discourage initiative and openness. Bleak descriptions of how a police department has extinguished initiative are given in Van Maanen (1974) and Rubinstein (1973). Suspicion of virtually everyone and grousing over not being appreciated permeate the locker room culture that Mark Baker (1985) captures in the book of stories officers told him. Anthony Bouza (1990) characterizes the isolation and secrecy of the police world as viewed from his vantage point of leadership in the police departments of New York City, the New York City Transit Authority, and Minneapolis. Insightful analysis of the closed nature of police organizations appears in Manning (1977), and of mutual distrust within a police organization under the pressure of a scandal in Punch (1983). The literature should dispel any naive belief that a few years will suffice to accomplish lasting upgrading in the quality of service delivered by a police department that is not already open to continual change.

The Troy PD had long operated in the watchman style. My own acquaintance with the department, beginning in 1975, included conversations with a sample of officers at all ranks and in all units. Everyone but the current rookies vividly described his frustrations in his first years on the job, when older officers had criticized or belittled him for trying too hard. Over the years many young officers had come to resemble their seniors. One patrol commander spoke for many in summing up his rookie lessons from his patrol car partner: "When he drank, I drank. When he slept, I slept."

The most dramatic self-justification of low standards came from an officer in his late fifties, whom we shall call John O'Reilly. He had developed a routine and an outlook to protect his pride against all criticism of his actions and inactions, and his defensive method was well known throughout the department. The day I met him, two years after the beginning of the department transformation, he was steaming over the reprimand he had received from his captain for his handling of a call that very morning. This abbreviated retelling tones down the color of his language.

A local gas station called in a theft. I pulled into the station and honked at the men in the lube pit. When they came over, I asked them what they wanted.

"Some kids stole the keys to the washrooms."

"If you guys gave the keys to the kids in the first place, then they didn't steal them. What do you want me to do? Why don't you call their parents?"

"We have, but they aren't going to do anything."

"That's not my problem. You handle it."

"You cops are no damn good."

At that point I got out of the squad car and pulled this wad of hundreds from my pocket. I told them, "You are the ones who are no good. I don't need you, and I don't need this lousy job. See this $3,000 I have here. I don't need this stinking job."

This officer had not joined the department intent on avoiding work or bringing disparagement on himself and his fellow officers. On the contrary, he recounted that as a child he had always looked up to police officers, always wanted to be one, and considered them at the same level as judges, lawyers, and priests. His brother and his brother's sons were officers in the New York City Police Department. When he joined the Troy department, it was riven by Democratic and Republican factions, Irish and Italian cliques. As a Democrat of Irish descent, he experienced four years of choice assignments, which ended in 1960 when Republicans returned to power. After passing civil service examinations for both sergeant and detective ranks, he blamed his failure to receive promotion on the Republicans. When his own son wanted to follow in his footsteps, he responded, "I would rather support you the rest of my life than see you come on the Troy department." Such intense bitterness is self-perpetuating and cuts the expression of enthusiasm by others.

Opportunities and Resources for Growth

In a television interview at the end of his first week, O'Connor was asked his opinion of the police station and remarked that there ought to be a sign on the inside of the front door: "Please Wipe Your Feet Before Leaving. Keep Our City Clean." The reply from the department greeted him the next morning when he found the sign he had described hanging inside the front door. That very day O'Connor issued a memo outlining eight specific steps the department would take in housekeeping. A clean building quickly resulted, and construction began the next year on a total redesign of the police station that eventually produced a well-designed and pleasant working environment. In addition, a new system of automobile maintenance and replacement provided an adequate fleet within two years.

The overall aim of O'Connor's upgrading was to improve service to citizens through a redistribution of departmental rewards, status, and authority to the officers on the street. Although he did not introduce the phrase in his public discourse, he had the "hospital model" in mind, comparing the work situation of officers in patrol to the work situation of physicians. He articulated at every opportunity the importance of the work of officers on the street. During his first two years he gradually replaced traffic and investigative positions with patrol positions and induced voluntary switching from two-man cars to one-man cars to bring the number of patrol cars fielded per day from about sixteen to about twenty-seven. Patrol coverage on weekday evenings rose from 1.9 officers per 10,000 population to 2.5, the national average for departments of this size (Ostrom, Parks, and Whitaker 1978, 90).

A usual means of upgrading organizational performance is to improve the skills of employees through education and training. In his first months with the department, O'Connor created an intern program for college students, funded extensive in-service training, provided IACP membership for all executive personnel, persuaded the YMCA to give courtesy memberships to all officers so that they would have a place to exercise, encouraged officers to take college courses, and hired new officers with college backgrounds. On the two occasions when a Troy commander graduated from the eleven-week FBI management course, the commissioner flew down to Quantico to celebrate the achievement. Although in Chicago, O'Connor had created the nation's first field training program, he did not develop one in Troy because the union contract denied him authority to appoint individuals to any position, including new ones such as field training officers. The most significant training in Troy was an in-service school that all police officers and sergeants attend for a week each year. Begun in 1974 on a voluntary basis, because the PBA objected to mandatory training, the in-service school was not held again until 1979 but since then has run annually on a mandatory basis.

Police salaries had been extremely low in Troy in 1973, only 50 percent of the average for New York and New Jersey cities of over 50,000 population. O'Connor was surprised that officers were not streaming into his office to demand a raise. In the next contract he negotiated a 29 percent raise over two years to bring the base salary for the police officer rank up to the average local factory wage.

Above all, O'Connor set new standards for courteous, competent service to every citizen and treated shortcomings as correctable mistakes. In one of the first complaints to cross his desk, a fearful woman wrote that a dispatcher had failed to send an officer when she called about a prowler. O'Connor sent the complaint and supporting information to all three dispatchers and all three desk sergeants for them to read and initial. Since only one dispatcher worked each shift, O'Connor could easily have identified the officer accused of aggravating the woman's fears. Rather than attempt to weigh the circumstances of the specific complaint, O'Connor used the incident to educate department members:

I am not interested in determining the identity of the individual member who originally handled Miss D.'s call for assistance. . . . In my opinion, he exercised faulty judgment and hopefully will try to correct his techniques for dealing with such requests for service. There were two disservices which he did—first to the citizen who sought and was denied our help, and second to the members of the Bureau whose time and energy have been diverted in trying to recover from the initial error.

Civil Service and Union Impediments

Lack of departmental control over the three functions of hiring, promoting, and firing is typical of American police departments and seriously impedes the upgrading of service. Management in Troy suffered the further disadvantage of lacking control over transfers. Characteristic fragmentation of power over personnel decisions is illustrated by an episode in which the commissioner was forced to make an appointment and another in which he was prevented from doing so.

When O'Connor announced his first batch of promotions in June 1973, he left the chief's position vacant. Previously, O'Connor had explained that a chief was unnecessary because he was directing the department. The PBA immediately took the commissioner to court, arguing that his failure to appoint a chief not only violated the city charter and the PBA contract but also deprived officers at every level of an opportunity for promotion. In July the county judge ruled that filling the vacancy rested in the discretion of the commissioner of public safety. PBA leaders then addressed the city charter commission, which had been at work for over a year on an array of revisions. The changed language from "the Commissioner of Public Safety may appoint a police chief" to "shall appoint" forced O'Connor's hand. He appointed John J. Givney, Jr., from among the three department members who had scored highest on the civil service examination. Chief Givney had risen rapidly through the ranks by scoring well on civil service tests. He believed that higher education had no place in police work and tried to keep the public out of police business.

The commissioner was thwarted in filling a new position he had created, departmental planner. In June 1973 O'Connor appointed as planner and paid from the LEAA grant a young man who had served for two years as a police officer in California, had earned a master's degree, and had been teaching police science for two years at the community college in Troy. The Troy Civil Service Commission quickly classified the temporary, grant-funded position as permanent and declared the appointee ineligible on the basis of their own general job description for senior administrative assistants, drawn up three years earlier. O'Connor continued to employ his appointee on a temporary basis. The civil service commission set an examination to select the individual for the "permanent" position and finally permitted the young man to take the examination, scheduled for February 1974. But since the exam covered general administrative and office procedures irrelevant to police planning, the top three scorers had no knowledge of police work, and the planner barely passed. In August 1974 Commissioner O'Connor abruptly ended the tussle by abolishing the nonsworn position and creating instead a position open to sergeants.

Over the years the Troy Civil Service Commission also interfered with discipline by cutting punishments and by preventing the dismissal of an alcoholic who resisted rehabilitation.

The powers it exercised are typical: to create new positions, to define the eligibility of candidates, and to design and conduct the tests that determine who may be employed (Greisinger, Slovak, and Molkup 1979). Over 80 percent of departments with at least fifty officers were under some type of civil service system as of 1973 (Eisenberg, Kent, and Wall 1973). The extreme autonomy of independent civil service commissions continues today, despite the recommendation to abolish them of the National Civil Service League (1970), the body that helped draft the initial Civil Service Act of 1883.

Across the nation, union contracts also limit managerial powers. Few departments operate under the fetters of a union contract with a seniority clause as strong as Troy's. Only passing mention is given the myriad difficulties stemming from the seniority clause because the purpose of examining a single department in depth is to speak to fundamental common issues in American policing. In April 1972 the PBA had obtained from Buckley as acting city manager this ironclad protection: "In determining preference for the purpose of selection of vacations or assignment, seniority within rank shall control." When O'Connor arrived, application of this clause in patrol was resulting in a daily shuffling at roll call whenever an officer with seniority decided that he preferred to work in a different zone that day. O'Connor instituted a regular system by which all officers signed up semi-annually, in order of seniority, for the positions open to their rank, and in 1984 he gained union agreement for an annual choice of assignment.

Nevertheless, departmental operations were continually hampered by the absence of authority to assign specific individuals to specific responsibilities. Unhappy as most department members were with incompetence in key support positions, such as records room supervisor, they held to the seniority principle as their personal bulwark against possible distasteful assignments that might be imposed by a possible future department head. This fear was grounded in police traditions whereby administrators have used officers as interchangeable cogs, posting them without regard to their individual preferences.

Leaving the Cowpath for New Roads

A few months after O'Connor began work in Troy, he reflected on policing in a television interview:

> We have been following an old cowpath. Cows used to wander down
> the crooked path, and then somebody tied wagons to the back ends
> and put ruts in the path. Then guys came along with paving equipment,
> they paved it, and now we have got a crooked street. . . . I think we
> have followed some cowpaths in law enforcement for a long time.
> There are different approaches we can and should try.

O'Connor held out the hope of a better future, communicating his
confidence that the department could become the best in the region.
Officers generally saw each change as making sense; thus, in retrospect,
the individual changes did not stand out. When I became acquainted with
the department in June 1975, members were already taking for granted
many of the new ways of doing the job. As I talked with officers in com-
piling a list of the specific changes introduced, I repeatedly encountered
recollections that some technique or procedure had been in practice for
years, when in fact departmental records pinpointed its introduction in
1973 or 1974. When officers recognized recent improvements they generally believed they themselves had made them. Officers were experienc-
ing stability during the process of change. They could respond to that
process with realistic expectations of the changes ahead and were not
gripped with fear that unknown expectations, conditions, and standards
might be imposed upon them. O'Connor's personal style of not seeking
credit for improvements permitted members of the department to accept
the changes as a natural evolution. Officers took for granted the marked
change in organizational climate, from fear of unpredictable punishment
to a confidence that management would not harm them. When officers
reflected on the changed tone of the bosses, they quickly acknowledged
that O'Connor was fair but then credited the disappearance of vindictive
management to the strength of the union contract. There were isolated
complaints about some specific changes, but no one complained in 1975
that there had been too much change. This acceptance of change by officers on the street stands in contrast to the sabotage of management initiatives in the New York City PD, where street cops responded with confusion and resentment to imposed changes (Reuss-Ianni 1983).

Although this book is about change, its chapters are organized around
major themes in police work, rather than chronological development, in
order to clarify the issues in different aspects of upgrading police service.
The brief chronology in Table 2-1 and a few words here will serve as a
background to the ups and downs, periods when changes were easily
accepted and when they were stoutly resisted. The years from 1973 to

Table 2-1 Chronology of Major Developments in the Troy Police Department

Date	Development
Feb. 1973–Sept. 1975	commissioner opens department to continuous, planned change
Sept. 1975–Jan. 1977	chief directs department without a commissioner
1975–78	city council interferes in department operations
Jan. 1977	commissioner resumes direction of the department
Aug. 1977	city council fires city manager
1977–78	commissioner attempts to establish team policing
1977–79	police union is active politically and through the grievance process
1979–82	department recuperates from turmoil
Jan.–April 1981	a poorly handled high-speed chase and an off-duty shooting reflect badly on the department
July 1983	new chief takes office
1983–87	planned changes are smoothly implemented
1984	women become street officers
1985	computers are used for operational information
May 1987	new city manager forces commissioner's early retirement

1987 may be divided into four periods: the takeoff, political interference, recuperation, and sustained upgrading. During the takeoff, 1973 to September 1975, department members most welcomed change. At that time the new administrative and scientific techniques were implemented, and the professional level of officers rapidly increased. In September 1975 O'Connor accepted the assignment at the Police Foundation, the organization established in 1970 by the Ford Foundation to upgrade police service. There he helped to create a new professional organization, the Police Executive Research Forum. Everyone, including O'Connor, thought he had left the Troy department for good. The period of political interference began in mid-1975 and lasted to the end of 1978. Chief Givney's secretive administrative style clashed with the yen of new city council members to run the department. In early 1977 O'Connor accepted the city manager's offer to return to the commissionership, as his work in Washington had ended, and he was engaged in private consulting. Political turmoil increased when the city council fired City Manager Buckley in mid-1977. The climax came in 1978, when the PBA used the city council to battle team policing. Resistance to change tapered off through the period of recuperation, 1979–82, though the recovery was slowed by the occurrence of two unrelated incidents within a few months in 1981: a mishandled high-speed chase, and a shooting by an off-duty officer. These events divided the department and diminished all members in the eyes of the public. The period of sustained upgrading, 1983 to 1987, received impetus with the appointment of William P. Miller as chief in July 1983. The span covered by this book ended when a new city manager forced O'Connor's resignation in May 1987.

Authority over Police

The first of four issues of public control illustrated by events in Troy is that the city executive should either work through the head of the police department or remove him. However, the unsuccessful efforts of the Troy city managers to work around the chief from 1964 to 1972 are typical of many cities. Incumbent chiefs can ignore directives and even obscure the fact that they have done so.

Goldstein (1977), in a careful analysis of police upgrading, has identified the head of the police department as the central figure in initiating change. For an individual who knows how to use them, such a position provides an impressive set of powers. Beyond the crucial function of setting department goals, the person in charge guides planning and research, establishes the organizational lines of communication, controls much of the flow of information to the public, oversees auditing, authorizes inspections and investigations, directs the background checks to weed out the unfit during recruitment, designs in-service training, establishes the table of organization, and supervises the disciplinary system.

Unfortunately, the chief who heads an ineffective department may be so much a product of the prevailing system that he is incapable of carrying out necessary changes. Between 1964 and 1972 Troy's incumbent chief had successfully resisted all but peripheral changes, despite energetic efforts from two professional city managers. Similarly frustrated city executives are not rare—when police chiefs disregard their orders, they have difficulty learning that their directives have been ignored.

When a chief must be forced out, the exit should be as graceful as possible. In Troy the ammunition the consultants used to blast out the chief also blackened the whole department and created immediate departmental fear of change. A city executive pondering whether to force the chief's retirement can usually obtain a reliable assessment from an expert through a few days' consultation. Ethical and practical considerations then dictate that this expert not subsequently replace the ousted chief.

Second, consolidating managerial powers in a single police executive is consistent with holding that person responsible for the quality of service. However, authority over the police budget and over personnel matters is usually fragmented, leaving the police manager far less powerful than a manager in the private sector. In Troy, nine different bodies outside the department had some say in the decisions to appoint a chief and a planner: the state legislature, the state department of civil service, the city's civil service commission, the city manager, the city council, the police association through the contract, the county court, the city charter commission, and the voters. This multiplicity is typical. Further, periods of fiscal stringency intensify the pressure on a city government to bargain away managerial powers, in the long run a far more costly choice than raising salaries. Specifics of constrictive union contracts and fragmented managerial powers are covered in Chapters 9 and 10. The topic is introduced here because of the gravity of counterproductive constraints on the authority of the department head.

Third, the head of the police department should be held accountable through a fixed-term, renewable contract. This relationship is a moderate alternative to the present dichotomy between life tenure and service at the pleasure of the city executive. Any authority to dismiss at will is open to abuse. We may glance at Minneapolis, where from 1969 to 1979 the mayors played musical chairs with the office of police chief, rotating eight through the office as first one faction of the police department and then the other saw its candidate win the biennial mayoral election. A fixed-term, renewable contract provides some protection against secret political pressures and yet retains some flexibility for the city executive. The head of a police department dismissed before the expiration of his contract must be paid for the time remaining in the contract, a condition requiring city leadership to build a case for dismissal that the public can believe. The Police Executive Research Forum has identified sixteen elements that should be covered in such a contract (Guyot and Martensen 1991). Scrapping current terms of office is not easy; moreover, in many cities it would require amendments to the city charter.

Poor management practices multiply quietly during the administration of an inadequate police chief. Wherever civil service rules extend to this office, the police chief is removable only through enormous effort. Across the country, about one-fourth of the heads of municipal police departments of all sizes hold their positions through civil service tenure. In the Northeast about half have tenure. New Jersey and New York state laws require that the chief hold civil service tenure in every department where officers are covered by civil service regulations. Nationally, the average length of tenure for a chief is eight years (Witham 1984; Guyot and Martensen 1991). Employing both a commissioner and a chief is an unsatisfactory solution, because each position is superfluous from the perspective of the other.

Fourth, a new department head should be selected from a national pool of candidates. The advantages of appointing an insider to head the department are that he already knows the strengths and weaknesses of the department and has some knowledge of the city's political system. The insider can augment his own skills in managing change by bringing into the department one or two talented individuals to serve as staff aides. However, when a department is far behind the times or badly riven by faction, an insider carries a considerable handicap. Because illegal and unjust police actions are often tolerated in watchman-style departments, the insider perhaps has taken or condoned practices of dubious legality that as chief he now wants officers to abandon. Members of the department who can embarrass him with his past are a latent source of persistent pressure against change. In a divided department, few are able to remain aloof from factions on the way up the rank ladder. The most common problem is that those who never experienced supportive leadership directed toward planned change may not quickly learn the art.

An outsider brings the advantages of direct knowledge of practices elsewhere and a fresh view of all departmental practices. The more isolated the department has been, the greater the need for a police manager who can open it to the currents of change. Initially, an outsider is neither a partisan of existing departmental factions nor the bearer of previous obligations. The immediate disadvantages of fear and resentment diminish over time.

The British police system avoids the parochial perspective by requiring the head of a police force to have served in another police force. Many chief constables lead forces where they started their careers, but they have all had several years' experience in other jurisdictions. This career path, returning to head one's home department after service elsewhere, has been followed by a few American police leaders, such as Wyman Vernon, who upgraded the Oakland Police Department in the 1950s, and Patrick V. Murphy, who managed the New York City department in the early 1970s.

As should be clear by now, the moment when a city selects a new head for its police department is the time when the city has the most choice about future directions for the department. It is an opportunity for public debate revealing a whole range of citizen views on just what the department should be doing. Many advantages flow from channeling a wide range of citizen concerns to a police executive early in his work. He hears at the outset from some of the many constituencies that the police serve, witnesses the breadth of the city's consensus on goals for the department, and sees the spots where no consensus exists. Unfortunately, many city executives keep the entire selection process confidential, thus preventing citizen concerns from being heard.

Open, consultative selection methods have been developed and used successfully in some cities. National competitors can be winnowed through requiring an essay, and finalists can be interviewed by mixed boards of citizen and departmental representatives. The questions can probe the prospective leader's philosophy and plans for applying it to the city's problems. Drawing on experience in Seattle, Portland, St. Louis County, and some California cities, the Police Foundation and the International City Management Association have produced thoughtful guidelines for the selection of a city's police executive (Kelly 1975). Whatever the specifics of the method, the leadership of the city needs a sound system for choosing a police manager and holding the appointee accountable for the quality of police service.

I don't think the shine on a man's shoes is a measure of the
humanity, wisdom, strength, or intelligence he brings to bear
when confronting human problems.

George W. O'Connor, 1977

Patrol Officers: General Practitioners Who Make House Calls

The central question of quality police service is how good officers' decisions are. Can police departments attract young men and women who have humanity, wisdom, strength, and intelligence? Can management encourage and teach them to make decisions that are humane and wise? The steps to overcome the inertia of a neglected department, as described in Chapter 2, could have been taken by a chief with the outlook of a professional administrator seeking to replace a shambles with order. A police leader with the outlook of a manager, however, strives in addition to create an organization that educates and supports officers in the many decisions they make on the street.

The central argument of this chapter is that the diversity and complexity of tasks assigned to patrol officers require them to make hard decisions directly and prevent their automatically applying a rule or passing decisions to their supervisors. The first section uses data from twenty-four departments to describe statistically the variety of patrol incidents. The second section, the centerpiece of the chapter, explores five skills and traits that an officer needs in order to handle discretion wisely: curiosity, sound judgment of danger, a tragic perspective, moral calm in being decisive, and self-control. Descriptions of specific patrol incidents illustrate that the outcomes depend upon the skills of the officers involved. The next sections consider methods of evaluating the quality of patrol service and suggest surveys of consumers as the most appropriate. The final section leads into Chapter 4 by analyzing the barriers to the acknowledgment of discretion, which still persist in traditional departments. The Appendix provides a summary of the chapter by posing five questions that can be answered by department members on the skills officers bring to their exercise of discretion, two questions that citizens can answer in evaluating the service they receive, and a question, on patrol performance that can be answered with departmental statistics.

The Diverse Work of Patrol

Since the beginning of organized police service in London in 1829, when Sir Robert Peel established the New Police, officers have patrolled assigned territory to keep the peace. In those days a hue and cry let the officer know that something was amiss; now, officers hear citizens' phone calls indirectly, as summarized and relayed by a police radio dispatcher. In the phrase of Egon Bittner (1970), patrol officers handle "something-that-ought-not-to-be-happening-and-about-which-somebody-had-better-do-something-*now*."

The International Association of Chiefs of Police has formally recognized the diversity of police responsibilities. The IACP Board of Officers unanimously endorsed and continues endorsement of the standards for urban police developed by the American Bar Association in 1972. The recognition that the police have a broad range of responsibilities and that strong reasons support a continued broad mandate, is expressed in a list of eleven major current responsibilities belonging to the police by design or default:

1. to identify criminal offenders and criminal activity and, where appropriate, to apprehend offenders and participate in subsequent court proceedings;
2. to reduce the opportunities for the commission of some crimes through preventive patrol and other measures;
3. to aid individuals who are in danger of physical harm;
4. to protect constitutional guarantees;
5. to facilitate the movement of people and vehicles;
6. to assist those who cannot care for themselves;
7. to resolve conflict;
8. to identify problems that are potentially serious law enforcement or governmental problems;
9. to create and maintain a feeling of security in the community;
10. to promote and preserve civil order;
11. to provide other services on an emergency basis. [ABA 1973, 3–4]

Supporting commentary to the standards identifies five factors that account for the wide responsibilities given the police. First, the police usually have a broad legislative mandate. Second, the special authority of the police to use force lawfully results in reliance upon them in a wide range of potentially dangerous situations. Third, the investigative ability of the police is called upon not only for crimes but in myriad daily situations where something is awry. Fourth, the twenty-four-hour availability of the police gives citizens reason to turn to them when governmental and private social services agencies are closed. Fifth, pressure for more service from neighborhoods, commercial interests, and citizens' groups has the cumulative effect that police increase their services. To these, we can add a sixth factor. Police officers' rich local knowledge of neighborhoods can be applied to a broad range of social problems.

In endorsing the foregoing list, both the bar association and the police chiefs' association made clear that these responsibilities are not fixed for all time. The standards explicitly call for each local government to develop overall direction for its police department. The careful study of performance measures by the Indiana University Workshop in Political Theory and Policy Analysis came to the same conclusion: that local government is the appropriate body to select the broad responsibilities and then to set specific, measurable objectives (Whitaker et al. 1982). Thus, democratic accountability takes place as the local government decides upon objectives and priorities within the limits set by federal and state constitutions and statutes (see Chapters 10–12). The ABA list, however, is useful as an initial statement of current responsibilities common to American police departments.

Every responsibility on the list is shared by the patrol division. Management, which embraces these multiple services, sends out the patrol officer, an educated and thinking individual, with the encouragement, "We support your use of discretion in solving problems." The legal statutes are a resource in addition to the officer's own persuasiveness, physical ability, imagination, understanding of people, and knowledge of community resources.

The usual categories of patrol incidents—violent crime, traffic, nuisances—obviously cover an amazing variety of situations calling for different investments of time and skill. Similar situations are also handled differently by different officers. The Indiana University study of twenty-four departments in the St. Louis, Tampa–St. Petersburg, and Rochester metropolitan areas (Mastrofski 1983) provides observer data on officers' handling of calls and of the encounters they initiate, or "on-views." Table 3-1 lists crime categories first and then noncriminal incidents, each group arranged from the most to the least frequent type of incident. These data from the summer of 1977 are the most comprehensive statistical summaries of patrol work across American departments.

At least four conclusions underscoring the variety of patrol work may be drawn from this table. First, within every category there is a tremendous range in the time that officers spend on a call: from less than a minute to more than three hours for violent crimes, nonviolent crimes, and traffic problems. Officers have considerable control over how long they will spend in handling each incident. Even to matters usually requiring only two minutes, such as a request for information, officers have chosen on rare occasions to devote more than thirty minutes. Second, officers spend little time on most calls, resulting in median times of less than twenty-four minutes for each type of incident. Situations involving disputes, dependent persons, and medical emergencies are often complex yet are usually handled in about fifteen minutes, so quickly as to raise doubts concerning the adequacy of the police response. The last two columns of Table 3-1 show the percentage of each type of incident in which officers gave assistance and in which they used coercion. According to the researchers' definition, coercion includes drawing a weapon, handcuffing, gripping by the arm, other physical force, and threatening to arrest or search but excludes issuing a traffic ticket or making a peaceable arrest. Third, both giving assistance and using coercion occur within every category. Overall, however, officers give assistance far more often than they resort to coercion, four times as often in noncriminal incidents and three times as often in criminal incidents. Because a call for service initiated the vast majority of encounters over criminal incidents, officers

Table 3-1 Variation in Police Handling of Incidents

Type of Incident	% Total Incidents (n = 5,688)	Service Time (min.)[a] Range	Median	% Involving Assistance[b]	Coercion[c]
Crime Totals	29%			49%	15%
Nonviolent crime	15	0–224	18	53	9
Suspicion	10	0–157	9	37	17
Violent crime	3	2–305	23	23	26
Morals crime	1	1–133	14	37	47
Noncrime Totals	71			54	13
Traffic	24	0–221	9	40	9
Nuisances	11	0–161	10	57	23
Disputes	9	0–149	15	71	30
General assistance	9	1–161	10	60	4
Administrative	4	0–100	7	23	3
Information request	4	0–47	2	95	1
Dependent persons	3	1–142	15	69	14
Information offer	3	0–61	9	48	1
Medical	2	2–100	16	64	3
Gone on arrival	2	1–48	7	23	3

Sources: These data are from the 1977 study of twenty-four police departments (Mastrofski 1983) and his paper presented to the 1982 annual meeting of the American Society of Criminology. Interviewers recorded the actions, which were later coded into categories. The data were collected by trained observers riding in patrol cars. [a]Total number of minutes the officer spent arriving at the scene and handling the incident. The median is shown in the table, rather than the mean, to take full account of the many quick jobs. [b]Includes settling arguments, offering comfort, providing information, finding lost property, providing transportation, giving first aid, and making referrals. [c]Includes all uses of physical force, threats with a weapon, and verbal threats, but not peaceable arrests.

have many more opportunities to assist the victim than they have to arrest the suspect. Fourth, the mix of assistance and coercion in every category suggests the difficulty of culling from the police work load those incidents where law enforcement powers and coercion are not required. This mixture should give pause to those who seek to winnow out for officers the incidents likely to require use of force and to leave all other tasks to personnel with less training and lower salaries.

A summary table cannot convey the flesh-and-blood substance of what happens between officers and citizens. The abstract nature of this table becomes evident when two sharply contrasting incidents from Troy are considered in terms of its categories: the time when Officer O'Reilly ostentatiously pulled out his wad of hundreds, as his excuse for not taking seriously the theft of the gas station washroom key, would be recorded as "no coercion, no assistance"—and so would Carl Peterson's arrest of the boy for stealing shoes, because the arrest was peaceable and Peterson's exceptional help in finding the boy a new home and a job occurred afterward. The variety in the table is due in unknown proportions to both variation in the incidents and variation in officer handling. To date, no research has attempted to distinguish how much of that variety is due to whatever different circumstances require for excellence in service and how much is due to the quality of service delivered.

When anyone asks broad questions such as "How long should an officer spend handling a traffic problem?" or "Should an officer make an arrest in handling a domestic dispute?" the only reasonable answer is, "It depends upon the circumstances." The circumstances include the nature of the place, the time of day, the prior history leading up to an incident, the letter and intent of the law, and the culture, life-style, and desires of the participants. The very diversity of cultures in America brings police officers into contact with people who relish commotion as well as people who enjoy quiet, youths who fight with friends as well as foes and youths who never trade punches, people who speak hesitant English or only a foreign tongue or incoherently.

Officers cope with too vast an array of human problems for any departmental rules, guidelines, or training to specify exactly what they should do in each different instance. Rather, guidelines and training at their best can promote an officer's skills in assessing complex situations and making sound decisions. A single example stands for the multitude of unusual situations that officers encounter in the course of their work and points up the difficulty of setting down guidelines. To my request "Tell me about a decision you made that had good results," Tom White, an officer with seven years' experience, replied:

> I remember going to an emergency in central Troy. A baby had rolled down a ramp into passing traffic and had rolled under a Cadillac. The driver had come to an immediate stop, and when I arrived the baby was trapped underneath the car, near the hot muffler. An ambulance was already there, but the attendants were just standing around looking at each other. A crowd had gathered around the Cadillac, and nobody knew what to do. I immediately used my big voice: "Okay, everybody, lift!" Together everyone lifted the Cadillac. The ambulance attendants grabbed up the baby and rushed to the hospital. The child had only second degree burns and recovered well.

In view of traditional police administration, such a set of circumstances is a contingency so rare that it cannot be covered by department regulations and thus should be handled with common sense. Nevertheless, the argument runs, since regulations and procedures can cover the vast majority of situations, administrators should issue reasonable, appropriate regulations and hold officers to them. Departments in which officers are treated as professionals also use regulations and standard procedures, but management recognizes that the most important and common responsibilities are too complex to regulate.

Skill in the Use of Discretion

To discharge varied and demanding responsibilities requires an officer first to decide whether to look into the situation, and then to decide what to do. The term "exercising discretion" has long been understood in policing to apply to situations where an officer has legal authority to make an arrest or issue a ticket but decides not to do so. This definition is too narrow, because independent choice and action permeate every aspect of patrol work. Recently, the term "discretion" has acquired the broader meaning that includes all independent decisions made by line officers.

What abilities and attitudes do police officers need in order to use discretion wisely, so that their efforts contribute to the solution of human problems? The answers given here are tentative notions, but making a case for these specific skills and character traits may start the process of developing testable hypotheses about what attributes affect the quality of police officers' decisions.

Curiosity

First, officers need curiosity to prompt them to inquire into situations until they can determine whether or not the circumstances require intervention.

□ Carl Peterson was patroling about 3:00 A.M. on a warm Saturday night in September 1975, and I accompanied him. Suddenly he caught sight of some shadowy figures in the headlights of a truck far down a cross street. I had noticed nothing. Carl circled the block and spotted someone darting into the bushes. He quietly asked whoever it was to come out. "How come you aren't hitting the books?" he ask the youth, who appeared to be a college student. The student explained that he and his friend were bored while waiting for a third friend to pick them up for a trip to New York City. They had begun to play chicken by lying down in the street and jumping up only as a vehicle approached. "You're too intelligent to do such a foolish thing again," Carl quietly admonished. The student hung his head in agreement and promised to prevent his friend from resuming. As Carl was about to leave, he added, "By the way, I could have arrested you for criminal mischief." Shocked, the student gave quick thanks.

Alert curiosity is developed by many officers who quickly detect the unusual because they understand the ordinary flow of events. Younger officers begin learning this street sense from experienced officers and sharpen it through practice. A keen sense of curiosity is a valuable asset for police officers. With curiosity they have more success in investigations, put more of themselves into the job, and gain more satisfaction. The officer with curiosity will take the time to probe a situation until he or she is satisfied that there is no problem or sees a way toward a resolution.

On the same night that the student played chicken, Officer Peterson followed his curiosity in three other situations. He responded to a call at 1:30 A.M. from a mother who wanted a noisy boy on a motorbike chased away so that the racket would not keep her baby awake. Carl conversed casually with the mother, curious to learn whether he knew the noisemaker. He did, and promised he would speak to the lad. About 2:00 A.M. the dispatcher sent him to a pocket park where neighboring residents had complained of shouts and laughter. All was still when he pulled up the patrol car. In such a situation a less energetic and curious officer radios the dispatcher that this job is a GOA (gone on arrival) and immediately is gone himself. It is an occupational hazard of patrol officers to become glued to the seat, conducting only the business that can be done from inside the car. Instead, Carl got out, curious to see where the revelers had gone. Shortly, he spotted four teenagers running out the far side of the park. He radioed the other zone car that he was going around the block, saw the kids reenter the park, and then both officers pulled up near the kids. Carl said softly over his car speaker, "Would you come over here a minute, please." The kids did, he told them of the neighbors' complaint and let them go back to their partying with the promise that they would keep it quiet and his promise that he would come back if they didn't. About 2:30 A.M. Carl saw a car come out from behind a dime store. He jotted down the license number and followed the car only a short way, since the driver showed no guilty reaction at being tailed. A few minutes later Carl swung behind the dime store to check for any evidence of a break-in or vandalism. His curiosity over what had been going on back there was satisfied with the discovery of leftovers from eating and drinking on the curb.

Boredom on the midnight shift is a hazard for all officers. Although complaints of being overworked and short-staffed are as common among police as in other occupations, on midnights an officer can drive the empty sheets for hours without a call. Those lacking curiosity have difficulty staying awake. The tremendous variation in the number of calls from hour to hour, from Saturday to Sunday, from hot nights to rainy nights forces patrol officers sometimes to dash from one call to another and sometimes to endure long lulls. Observational studies of patrol officers have found that on average, 60 percent of officers' time is noncommitted: that is, not spent on work assigned by a dispatcher or a sergeant. In Troy, after staffing the patrol division well and making generous estimates of the time spent handling calls for service, Commissioner O'Connor concluded that in 1986 about 67% of patrol time was noncommitted on the day tour, 67 percent on evenings, and 80 percent on midnights.

The curious officer discovers what others miss. An officer will choose to investigate or ignore, depending upon the press of other responsibilities, personal priorities, and current mood. An officer's failure to be curious or failure to follow the prompting of curiosity are not known to anyone else. Over the years officers grow more divergent in their curiosity levels and in their willingness to exert themselves during their noncommitted time. The same department typically houses both the dullard who no longer recognizes an open window in the winter and the sharp-eyed observer who detects the carrying of an illegal handgun by spotting a change in body language. The use of discretion to investigate or to ignore is so variable among officers that assigning additional officers to patrol a neighborhood may make no difference if their curiosity is low or misdirected.

Judgment of Danger

The most difficult aspects of discretion lie in an officer's decisions about how to handle a situation once he has intervened. William K. Muir, Jr. (1977) has made important contributions to understanding the nature of police discretion in his study of the moral and intellectual development of twenty-eight young officers. The discussion here uses Muir's ideas and terms from *Police: Street Corner Politicians*, with somewhat different emphasis. Briefly, he concluded that officers who are skillful in applying discretion to street situations draw upon these abilities: correct judgment of the dangerousness of a situation, an understanding of the tragic quality of life, and equanimity in using coercion. Because he chose to study police officers in order to examine the predicaments of power, he focuses on coercion. Because this study focuses on quality police services, I regard coercion as central to some police actions, as in subduing a maniac, and tangential to others, as in rescuing a traffic accident victim.

Exposure to danger is always part of the police job. When the "something-that-ought-not-to-be-happening" is an armed robbery or a hostage situation, there is obvious personal danger. Frequently, however, the hazards of a situation are not immediately apparent. An officer must be alert for possible danger even in circumstances that seem ordinary and uneventful and must correctly assess who, among the many people present in a dangerous situation, is immediately dangerous. An officer should approach a situation warily, looking for clues to danger in the circumstances and in the citizens' behavior. In well-chosen words the skillful officer gives "dangerous" citizens the opportunity to choose to become less dangerous.

Some officers have developed extraordinary skills in understanding dangerous situations and in reducing the danger. A few years before the Troy department had trained an emergency response team, Sam Griffith, an officer with five years on the job, described his actions upon receiving a radio call that a man with a rifle had barricaded himself in his apartment.

> My partner and I went to the back of the building. A couple of young officers went right to the front where they were in full view from the apartment. They could have gotten shot. They were shouting at a man coming down the street that he had to stop and turn back. The man could sense that the officers were nervous and unsure of themselves. The louder they shouted, the closer he came. As I came up, they were threatening to arrest him. When I first get to a scene I always try to figure what's bothering the different people there. I figured he was a friend of the man with the gun and was concerned about his safety. I went right up to him and assured him that we would not hurt his friend. I asked him where he lived, told him to go back home and stay by the phone, and if we needed him we would call him. That made him feel important. He left immediately. We cleared the building of all the other tenants, and then two of us went to the front door and two to the back. As we entered, a screaming woman rushed up, showing us she had the rifle. The man was in the bedroom, unarmed.

Fast-moving events such as this one place multiple demands upon officers: prudence in maintaining their own safety, sensitivity to the concerns of the citizens present, reassurance to citizens regarding the safety of their friends, decisiveness in telling citizens to go home, command presence to organize other officers to empty a building, clear explanations so that citizens quickly leave their homes for safety, foresight in planning an approach to the barricaded apartment, readiness for whatever happens once they are inside.

Even a superb judge of human character is likely to make a few mistakes when making snap judgments. The risks an officer takes in being mistaken are uneven. If an officer mistakenly judges a man to be cooperative when in fact he is dangerous, there is risk of injury to both until the officer brings the citizen under control. The consequences of the opposite mistake are not so obvious or so serious: if an officer judges a cooperative person to be dangerous, most likely that citizen will continue at least grudging cooperation even while resenting the officer's harshness. Still, the cumulative effect on citizens may be an undermining of their respect for all officers, based on their experience with harsh ones. Muir describes the action of an officer who continually misjudged peaceable people as dangerous and thus provoked some into becoming dangerous, in effect, fulfilling his expectations.

A Tragic Perspective

The most important element in an officer's use of discretion appears to be a compassionate understanding of people, what Muir calls the development of a "tragic perspective." Frequently, officers intervene when people are no longer pretending that everything is all right. Day after day, they see people suffering the misfortunes of life: the unemployed young addict caught breaking into a drugstore, children scarred by parental abuse, a married couple breaking up their possessions in a fight, a young man who has committed suicide over lost love. To sustain compassion when encountering the worst in people, police officers need great personal courage. When officers take a tragic view of life, they place the immediate situation in a larger context of human struggles, pain, and suffering. They look upon other people as basically like themselves, exposed to the hardships of life and weathering them as best they can. Although officers learn many dirty secrets about people's private lives, those with a tragic perspective have no interest in gossiping. The term "tragic" sums up an understanding that one can offer assistance to people even when their misfortunes cannot be reversed.

When officers with a tragic perspective respond to a call for help, the caller receives reassurance. A woman in her early forties recounted an experience when Officers Chuck Holt and Al DeCarlo came to her door.

Well, my son, he's seventeen, had supper with us and said he was going to the store—which would have been six o'clock. It's very unusual for Donny not to come right back. We thought maybe he visited a friend, but at ten he still never came home. We were concerned, so we called the police. I've never had contact with the police before. Two officers arrived in about ten minutes, but I was very upset. They calmed me down and said it wasn't unusual and that seventeen-year-old boys do that, and the majority of boys come home. They took all his friends' names down. They asked what Don looked like and if he had been in trouble before. They were great. They were understanding. They made it seem like they were going to look for him. I was carrying on, but they understood and tried to calm me down. They made me feel better by telling me this happens to other people.

If the officers had lacked a tragic perspective or if departmental policy had been based on a narrow view of efficiency, this woman's problem would not have been ameliorated. Many departments have recently dropped long-standing policies that postponed investigation of a missing person until twenty-four hours had elapsed. Since the missing person almost always turns up within a day, the old view argued, police need not waste their time trying to solve a problem that almost always will soon solve itself. The broader view, a tragic perspective, tries to alleviate the overwhelming fear and helplessness that parents may suffer when their child is missing.

In developing this tragic perspective, officers build upon whatever understanding of people they have shaped from experiences prior to joining the department. To the extent that officers are curious and satisfy their curiosity through talking and listening, they learn the complexities of people and their problems. Officers working with people of diverse ethnic groups may develop insights into different cultural patterns in the relationships between mothers, fathers, and children. In observing the diversity, they recognize similarity. Officers come to understand people's feelings, their hopes and fears, their triumphs and despairs. They use this understanding to encourage people to take steps to solve their own problems. To the extent that officers reflect on and talk over the incidents they have handled, they gain a rounded view of the diverse people who inhabit the city. These officers understand that their efforts will not eliminate crime or injustice. They continue to offer their help to people overwhelmed by problems in the belief that their assistance may make a difference, may help people transform their present problems into more manageable ones.

Sam Griffith, the officer who had instantly recognized what was going on in the incident of the man with the rifle, explains poverty this way:

My mother was poor and kept about five jobs cleaning house in order to raise us eight kids. We kids were so fortunate. Of all the people in my patrol zone, the ones who are most unfortunate and make me most discouraged are the third generation on welfare. The mothers are sixteen, and their daughters have children at fourteen, and maybe their daughters will have a child at twelve. They have no control over their lives. If they do get the determination to leave welfare, they will encounter the stresses of life, and those stresses will be too much for them. People who are used to being responsible for their lives may not even pay attention to these stresses, but for these people the stress is too much, and it pushes them back to dependence. I see a very thin line between the people who are doing all right and the ones without hope. Officers should recognize that someone in their own family, perhaps their parents or their grandparents, made the extra effort and got their family to where it is today. Without them, the officers could be in the position of the very people they look down on. They shouldn't look down on these people.

Officers with a tragic perspective can keep their balance even through a quick succession of problems as they enter and leave people's lives. The tragic perspective probably cushions to some extent an officer's personal suffering as a witness to the misfortunes of others. The tragedy that most officers find hardest to bear is the death of a child. When the driver of a semitrailer backs up, unwittingly crushing the little boy who was tailgating on his bicycle, police officers must keep their presence of mind. They must assist the stunned driver and the grief-stricken mother, pick up the child's remains, and restore the street to normal. Some officers who do not accept their own emotions at such times have nightmares afterward; others become faint when their own child has a slight injury. An officer who recognizes his common bond with the parents of the dead child calls home: "How are the kids?" Returning home from work, he may stand gazing at his sleeping son or wake him up with a loving hug. A departmental climate where officers feel comfortable in talking about suffering probably assists them to regain strength to face the next tragedy.

Decisiveness

An entirely different dimension of discretion is described by Muir as moral calm in using coercion. Americans dislike obeying orders and yet authorize police officers to give orders that must be obeyed and to detain people by force. An officer who has developed a moral calm in compelling others to obey his decisions recognizes both that his decisions hold for a limited duration and that in crisis a quick decision is essential, even if hindsight proves it to have been faulty. A decisive officer applies force or threats when necessary, recognizing that some situations cannot be resolved without using coercion.

Commissioner O'Connor made clear his acceptance of the use of force, including deadly force, by explaining that the department uses hollow-point bullets, which inflict additional injury on the attacker, for the purpose of increasing the likelihood of stopping the attack. In the rare situation that presents a choice between the life of a victim or an officer and the life of the attacker, the officer takes a life. The most common event requiring physical force is resistance to arrest. Officers with an integrated view of coercion choose an appropriate level of force, a come-along hold or a well-placed blow with a nightstick. In tense confrontations where no crime has been committed, decisive officers can convincingly threaten arrest and thus control the situation short of actually making arrests.

This story of decisiveness in pursuing their course of action and readiness to use force is told by officers with the pseudonyms of Mike Mullin and Jack Rice, who both had college education and five years of street experience.

One hot Saturday night in August, Sarah Brown was ready to fight her neighbors across the street. Sarah is a black woman who is a tower of strength, with grown sons who are strong and tough like her. One of them is a homosexual. Sarah and her sons live on Oak Street, which is so narrow that people conversing on one stoop can hear the people on the stoop across the street. On a summer night it seems like there are a hundred people out in the street. Each apartment is crowded, and everybody has friends. The white couple across the street made no bones about their dislike of black people and homosexuals. Sarah accused the white woman of slapping her son, and insults had been going back and forth for two weeks or more.

This Saturday we answered a call and found about five big guys hanging around on Sarah's stoop, waiting to see if there would be a fight. Sarah had told friends from Schenectady to come over. We went right up to them. "We know why you are here. If there is a fight you will be the first to go." These guys knew we were serious and would arrest them on every charge we could legitimately bring against them. We kept telling Sarah that she should see the judge and bring charges against the woman. We stood around and made jokes with the people on Sarah's stoop. Even while we were there the white woman rekindled the animosity with some remarks. Eventually we left, but we kept coming back all evening. The fight was averted, and Sunday night there was no showdown. The feud cooled down.

An officer who fears to be decisive lets street situations get out of hand. Officer Chuck Holt discussed Philip Denning's troubles of the previous night.

At the bank plaza up Hoosick Street, teenagers have been hanging out and vandalizing the place, making a mess. It's a good neighborhood up there where the kids will all go to college. Phil took the call. I wasn't there, but I heard what happened. The kids were standing in a ring around him making jokes at his expense. While he was reasoning with one kid, another behind him dashed up, gave him a pound, and dashed back to the circle. In lots of cities there is talk about police brutality to citizens. What about citizen brutality to police?

At this time Officer Denning had been working in patrol for seven years. He had exhibited indecisiveness six years earlier when I accompanied him in his work as an evidence technician: in a house where jewelry had been stolen from the master bedroom, he spent ten minutes aimlessly poking around in the attic, musing on whether or not a burglar might have been up there. Denning's work as an evidence technician suffered little from his lack of decisiveness, but in the hurly-burly of patrol he was severely handicapped.

Decisiveness and acceptance of the consequences of one's decisions may be a broader view of the skill Muir describes as moral calm in using coercion. Because Muir's reason for studying police officers was to explore the effect of coercive power on those who employ it, he focused on the dichotomy between officers who are comfortable in exercising coercion and those who flee from the exercise. If using coercion is part of a broader pattern of decisiveness, then officers who have an equanimity in employing coercion will also be comfortable with their quick decisions in situations where there is no need for coercion. For instance, an officer provides emergency medical care for an injured passenger without immediate remorse that he is simultaneously unable to give care to the injured driver. If first at a fire, a drowning, a building collapse, he makes an instant decision to embrace danger or to assist from a distance. Afterward, he lives with his decision. Empirical research among police officers could show what relationships actually exist among the two attitudes and two types of behavior: acceptance of the necessity of coercion, psychological comfort with decisions made in noncoercive situations, employing coercion, and taking decisive action in noncoercive situations.

The reason to place the use of coercion in a larger context of decisiveness is the need to abandon a narrow focus on enforcing laws. In the 1960s and 1970s research and comment on police work stemmed largely from interest in crime control, often defining the job in terms of the officer's authority to use force. Because police work is now seen as an array of community-oriented services, the skills for the job should also be viewed more broadly.

Self-Control

The ability to control one's emotions is the last essential police skill discussed here. Fear and anger intermingled appear to be the emotions that most often hamper good police work. When Sam Griffith arrived outside the apartment of the man with a rifle, the two younger officers had already lost their emotional control and increased their shouts as the man's friend advanced. The officers had reason to be fearful, since the barricaded man could at any moment have started shooting out the window, and the failure of a citizen to obey immediately can cause an officer's anger to flare. Any officer who has not learned to act coolly while fearful and angry has limited professional skills. The most effective officers may have developed such a thorough understanding of people that they are not surprised and angered when someone tries to provoke them. When Officers Mullin and Rice talked Sarah and her neighbors out of a street brawl, they had grounds to fear for their physical safety. If a fight had started, they would certainly have received many kicks and punches in quelling it. When the white neighbor made nasty remarks, they saw her as directly and deliberately undermining their peacekeeping efforts. Yet they controlled their anger and kept coaxing Sarah out of starting the fight.

The emotions of grief and horror that paralyze some people are handled by experienced officers in ways that do not interfere with presence of mind. Tom White, who used the crowd to save the baby trapped under the Cadillac, had infants at home, but he described the event in such a matter-of-fact manner that I did not think at the time of asking whether he had felt a surge of anxiety for his own children. If we compose a list of the situations that police officers handle, we find many that can raise fear, anger, or disgust—emotions that officers need to control in order to act effectively.

Individual Approaches

Different officers develop markedly different approaches to handling the complexities of the street, reflecting the degree to which they have developed their curiosity, judgment of danger, tragic perspective, decisiveness, and emotional control. Muir has suggested a means of comprehending the diversity among police officers through looking at only two characteristics: whether or not an officer develops a tragic perspective; and whether or not an officer accepts the necessity to use coercion, the attitude viewed here as decisiveness.

Muir's typology, shown in Table 3-2, is an excellent place to start observing patterns behind the diversity of police officers' working styles. With Muir, I recognize that such a typology oversimplifies complex questions of human character, but I believe he is correct that police officers encounter so many difficult human problems that they cannot evade developing a consistent outlook. Further, I suspect that encounters with members of the public have an amplifying effect, that young men and women who begin by feeling sorry for people in trouble develop the compassion of a tragic perspective as they come to terms with their encounters with grief.

Muir uses the term "professional" for the officer with both a tragic perspective and decisiveness in the use of coercion. Carl Peterson and Tom White had reasoned through the complexities of the human condition and reached an understanding of their roles as officers even under the adverse conditions of the old department. Sam Griffith, Mike Mullin, and Jack Rice became professionals when department leadership nurtured such growth. All these officers are well rounded in their development. They can talk tough one minute and trade jokes the next, as the situation changes. They recognize that citizens can be their resource, as when Officer White commanded the crowd to lift the Cadillac. To call them "professional" highlights the similarity between these officers and members of the established professions that aim to change the behavior of the client, such as teaching and medicine.

As Table 3-2 indicates, some officers do not succeed in mastering both the skills essential to professional accomplishment. If an officer develops

Table 3-2 Diversity of Individual Approaches to Police Work

	Tragic Perspective	Cynical Perspective
	Professional	**Enforcer**
Decisive, able to use coercion	Carl Peterson Tom White Sam Griffith Mike Mullin Jack Rice	Don Turner
	Reciprocator	**Avoider**
Indecisive unable to use coercion	Phillip Denning	John O'Reilly

Source: Based on categories developed in Muir 1977. The names are the fictitious ones given to Troy police officers whose work is described in the text.

a tragic perspective but fails to come to terms with the necessity to use force, he or she is a "reciprocator." A reciprocator such as Philip Denning uses reason, but if that fails to stop the taunting teenagers, he has no recourse. Officers who are reciprocators are uncomfortable with the conflicts of the street and go to great lengths to avoid making arrests.

Officers who lack a tragic perspective tend to become cynical. They come to regard most people as essentially different from themselves. These officers protect themselves by narrowing their worlds to "we," the "decent people" versus "they," people who do not matter. Cynical officers see the world as a war in which the police are almost alone in protecting civilization from its enemies. Cynics protect themselves from disappointment by holding low expectations of others, by defining them from the outset as "no good." Their communication goes only one way, for they fail to listen to people, yet people must listen to them because of their power.

An officer who combines a cynical perspective with a willingness to use force is an "enforcer." Don Turner was schooling himself to be nasty to women. An enforcer acts tough and learns from citizens' hostile reactions to treat people even more roughly next time. In the world of the enforcers, might makes right, and they have the might of two fists and a gun. Far from solving problems, enforcers usually intensify them.

An officer who combines a cynical perspective with an unwillingness to make decisions is an "avoider." Over the years John O'Reilly, with his wad of hundreds, had become an avoider. Such officers are not interested in people's problems. They neither handle situations where the skillful use of force is necessary nor show compassion for people who come burdened with problems. Instead, they develop many ways to tell citizens, "I can't help you."

Police Service as Evaluated by Recipients

The diversity of patrol incidents and the diversity of approaches that officers use leads to the conclusion that merely counting events is inadequate for evaluation. This section and the next two propose that consumer satisfaction surveys are the most appropriate technique, that response time has limited value as a performance measure, and that the trend in calls for service can be a measure of consumer demand that expresses consumer satisfaction. Performance measures for police need to take account of the diversity of the problems and the outcomes. Since incidents are not recorded on videotape, such specific knowledge must come from those on the scene: the officers themselves, the citizens involved, and, if present, supervisors or alert bystanders.

Citizens who have requested police service can report the degree to which the officer listened to their problems and helped them toward solutions. Consider, for example, two residential burglaries investigated by Troy officers in the spring of 1978. Departmental records show they were bascially alike and similar to the majority of burglary investigations that occur across the nation. In each case the householder discovered the break-in on returning home; patrol officers responded promptly and completed incident reports; no sergeant came, and no detective followed up; no property was recovered, and no one was caught. Despite the superficial similarity, however, comparison of what the householders told a survey interviewer reveals vast discrepancies in the quality of work performed.

A twenty-five-year-old woman used bitter words to describe the investigation of her ransacked apartment:

> The officer walked in and looked around. He was very nonchalant. He asked me what was missing, filled out the report, and asked me if I lived alone. He came to the conclusion that it was my ex-husband who did it and told me to contact him. He said he would give the report to the detective. His whole attitude was as if he was just there from nine to five, as if he thought, "Why did I have to come for this?" He got annoyed when I asked why he suspected my ex-husband. I thought he would be a little more concerned. He could have taken fingerprints or something, because a metal box was broken into. He told me the way the doors were secured that I might as well leave them open. I felt very degraded. I felt like I was the criminal.

In contrast to the woman's anger over the avoider's callousness, an old man expressed gratitude to the officers who came after his vacation money was stolen from his home while he was visiting his wife in the hospital.

The officers made an investigation to find the point of entry, which I couldn't find. They made another call to headquarters for . . . someone to come down who took pictures and picked up fingerprints from various items. They waited till he came and just talked. They went out of their way to help me by giving me good pointers on things I could do. For example, I have eight switches that go on at night. They told me to set them for different times and that they would check my house when I'm on vacation. The patrol car in the neighborhood would make sure nothing was unusual when they went by. They told me I could leave my guns at the police station when I went on vacation. They were very courteous and knew their job.

These divergent assessments underscore the importance of citizens' perspectives in answering a major performance question stated in the Appendix: "To what extent do police officers use discretion to help people solve their problems?" For Commissioner O'Connor the most important work that a patrol officer can do is to respond to citizens' calls in an effective and caring manner. Starting in 1966 with the President's Crime Commission, survey research has developed a substantial body of knowledge on citizens' views of the problems police address and of the services that officers provide. Comparing citizen recollection with notations from trained observers, Roger Parks (1982) has concluded that citizens have quite accurate recall. He makes a persuasive case for using surveys to assess departmental performance. Through survey research, citizens' views on the handling of their problems may be communicated to the department, so that patterns of excellence may be encouraged and patterns of shoddy service may be identified and corrected.

In Troy both a service survey of 349 citizens who had called the police and a cross-section survey of 950 residents were conducted during the spring of 1978, with financial support from the Law Enforcement Assistance Administration (LEAA). With guidance from Commissioner O'Connor and a national advisory committee, I designed them to elicit people's recent experience with officers and their sense of personal safety. The service survey dwelt on the citizens' perceptions of how an officer responded to their calls for service; the residential survey examined citizens' reactions to being stopped by the police, witnessing praiseworthy and blameworthy police actions, and directly cooperating with police in crime prevention, as well as their views of crime problems, recent experience with burglary, sense of personal safety, and priorities for the police department. All quotations from citizens in this book come from these two surveys.

The most general question asked in the service survey was this: "On the whole, how would you rate the service the police officer(s) gave you?" Overall, 62 percent rated the Troy service as very good, 25 percent as good, 6 percent as fair, 3 percent as poor, and 3 percent as very poor; 1 percent declined to say. Satisfaction with police handling of suspicious incidents was highest, close to 100 percent, for these are occasions when an officer's mere appearance scares off troublemakers. People were least satisfied, only 76 percent, with the handling of conflicts among acquaintances, incidents with long histories and little likelihood of conclusion.

Answers should be compared across departments only when similar methods are used to solicit citizen replies. In Troy, both surveys were conducted by telephone by independent polling firms that made repeated callbacks to reach the appropriate person. Strenuous efforts to reach citizens usually bring out more negative and indifferent opinions than do phone interviews without callbacks. By contrast, when a police department directly conducts mail or telephone surveys, frank criticism is less likely.

The service survey asked people what they particularly liked about the responding officers' actions. Courtesy was the most frequent answer, mentioned by 68 percent and listed first by 38 percent. We may speculate that courtesy is particularly important because citizens who call the police are doubly vulnerable: they are beset by the current crisis, yet faced with a powerful individual who could belittle them with impunity. The next most frequent response was that the officer was concerned. Typical answers here included "Reassuring"; "Sympathetic"; "Calmed me down"; "Seemed to know how I felt"; "You couldn't ask for anyone kinder"; "Said it was a shame it happened"; "Realized the situation embarrassed me"; "Suggested we could have lost a lot more." Overall, 65 percent of the citizens questioned gave their first praise to supportive actions such as courtesy, concern, and friendliness. Only 21 percent first praised task accomplishment. Another 8 percent expressed praises in a manner too vague to classify, and 6 percent liked nothing.

People selectively praise various aspects of police work depending upon the type of problem they suffer. Table 3-3 groups the problems into three general classes comprising eleven specific categories. Shown across the top of the table, they are roughly arranged from the most serious threats on the left to the least serious inconveniences on the right. The various elements of service that people liked are grouped into two major categories: emotional support and task accomplishment. For each type of incident, the percentage of respondents praising each police response is recorded only where it is substantial.

The majority of citizens praised officers' courtesy in almost all types of incidents. Officers' concern was particularly appreciated by people who suffered personal harm or theft. Where citizens feared a repetition, they appreciated officers' suggestions for preventive action. Citizens who were

Table 3-3 Officers' Actions Especially Appreciated in Different Types of Incidents

	Personal Harm and Annoyance					Crimes against Property			Motor Vehicle Problems			
Actions Praised	Violent Attack	Harm to Person	Harassment	Dispute	Suspicious Situation	Burglary	Theft	Vandalism	Traffic	Car Blocking the Way	Parking in Front of House	Average %
Emotional Support												
Courtesy	67%	73%	63%		57%	85%	67%	68%	52%	73%	100%	68%
Concern	100	67			56	54	56					51
Friendliness		27							33			18
Took time to talk			22									6
Will return if needed			11							9	11	5
Advised protective steps						15	12					4
Promised to patrol								12				4
calmness	13				11							5
Task Accomplishment												
Got results										64	85	27
Competent		27			33							16
Efficient									25			14
Came quickly	33											8
Explained					22							5
Took a report						7			7			2
n =	15	9	15	48	27	41	39	59	27	22	47	349

Note: Because citizens could give three replies to the question "What did you like about the way [the officer] acted?" the averages total 233 percent. Percentages are included for each type of incident when more than 50 percent of respondents praised an action or when an action was praised at 50 percent above the average rate for its type.

agitated admired the officers' calm. We see that for task accomplishment, getting results was praised most often in the simple situation of a parking problem. Citizens emphasized efficiency only for handling traffic problems. Quick arrival was particularly valued only for violent attacks. The incidents that generated the least praise were disputes, often ill-resolved episodes in protracted struggles. In sum, courtesy and concern were far more often praised than were all aspects of task accomplishment, a major finding of the survey.

The service survey also specifically addressed people's emotional well-being by asking early in the interview whether they were upset or calm when the officers arrived and later asking how they felt when the officers left. Initially, 60 percent of the citizens queried felt calm, 26 percent somewhat upset, and 14 percent very upset. Officers succeeded in leaving 80 percent of the citizens in a calm frame of mind, 15 percent somewhat upset, and only 5 percent very upset.

The finding that citizens place less importance on the accomplishment of tasks than on emotional support has far-reaching consequences. Generally, police task accomplishment is low because there are no easy solutions to many of the problems that prompt people to call the police: a purse snatcher's shove breaks an old woman's hip; a neighbor's child continually and deliberately smashes windows; neighbors disagree over the proper volume for music. Officers are often weighed down with intimate knowledge of how much goes wrong in people's lives. Setting out on a burglary call, they know they are probably headed for failure to make an arrest and failure to recover the stolen property. Leaving a burglary scene, they often feel frustrated and discouraged that they "can't do anything." The survey found that in the seventy-five cases of burglary and theft, officers recovered the property of only three people, yet 90 percent of the victims considered their service good or very good. Helping people to feel better and motivating them to take precautions to prevent a recurrence have traditionally received little recognition as goals for patrol officers. Indeed, officers tend to discount supportive actions by labeling anything that helps a person to feel better as "a P.R. job." However, this survey shows that by listening sympathetically, officers have already done something important. In the 349 responses to the survey, no one ever said or implied that officers were insincere or manipulative.

Human nature is at work here. If we look beyond the technology of 911 emergency numbers, computer-aided dispatching, and speedy radio patrol cars, we see that someone who is seeking help is visited by a person whose job is to give help. That the seeker appreciates courtesy and concern from the giver is only natural.

As should be clear by now, the most appropriate performance measures are based on an assessment of what a situation requires and judgment of how well officers address the requirements of the specific situation. Police officers, patrol sergeants, and other experts can assess an officer's skill in both task accomplishment and psychological support. Citizens responding to surveys can make nontechnical judgments of how helpful and supportive an officer is. Yet despite the power of survey research to obtain citizen perspectives, police management has barely begun to use this tool for obtaining feedback on performance. The crying need for judgmental evaluation techniques was hidden until a few years ago by the denial that officers exercise discretion and by the reliance upon objective statistics on response time.

Response Time as a Misused Performance Measure

Americans in the twentieth century have a craving for hard numbers to "prove" that products and services are efficient and effective. The police field is not exempt from this need, yet the complexity of the problems that police handle and the complexity of police skills defy easy measurement. From the 1950s through the 1970s a fast overall response time was the dominant measure of patrol performance. The Indiana University study mentioned earlier found success on this measure: in 1,100 emergencies handled by twenty-four departments, officers arrived within three minutes for 50 percent, within five minutes for 75 percent, and within eleven minutes for 95 percent (Antunes and Scott 1981). The suburban departments were quickest for every type of emergency, and central city departments were next; sheriffs' departments were understandably minutes slower.

However, research has shown that citizens are satisfied with a slower response to nonemergency calls (Farmer 1981; McEwen, Connors, and Cohen 1984). Even for crimes in progress, rapid response is usually ineffective. A careful study by the Kansas City, Missouri, Police Department (1977), followed by a four-city study by William Spelman and Dale Brown (1984) of the Police Executive Research Forum, found that in only 3 percent of the total incidents of robbery, rape, aggravated assault, burglary, larceny, and motor vehicle theft reported by the public did an arrest result from fast response. Further, there is little opportunity for improvement, because about 75 percent of these crimes are discovered after the fact, and even for fresh crimes citizens typically delay ten to fifteen minutes before calling the police.

A department can shave minutes off the overall response time by upgrading dispatching and patrol allocation. The dispatching volume has been cut through new techniques of systematic triage: quick patrol car response, delayed patrol car response, and alternatives to patrol car response. Once these improvements are in place, achieving even faster response time requires that more patrol cars be made available to take calls, either by fielding more cars or by instructing officers to spend less time on each call. Since increasing the patrol force is expensive, administrators have urged officers to handle their calls quickly. The traditionally unnoticed cost of fast response time is to pull officers away from work so that they can resume looking for and waiting for work.

One reason why this practice did not appear wasteful to efficiency-oriented administrators lies in the power of language. Since the invention of the radio car in 1921, the term "in service" has had the standard meaning of driving on patrol without specific assignment; "out of service" has meant that the officer is busy, whether eating lunch or questioning a robbery witness. Police chiefs have demanded, and officers have accepted as a principle of good police work, that calls for service be handled swiftly so that officers can quickly get back "in service." This demand also fits the personal desires of cynical officers to cut their involvement with the "no-good types."

Over the years, police departments have stressed the importance of procedures: the pull on the call box, the recording of all actions in the activity log, the report written on every call, the radio activity cards recording the speed of response. All these recordkeeping systems have been carried to counterproductive extremes. Herman Goldstein (1979) has analyzed this predicament and aptly termed it the "means over ends syndrome." The continuing attractiveness of precise performance measures is that they seen to offer certainty in a field so full of complexities, ambiguities, and intractable problems. Slowly, the field gives up its attachment to specific means, and now overall response time has been scrapped by many departments and fast response time acknowledged to be a process measure appropriate only for emergencies.

Consumer Demand as a Rough Measure of Consumer Satisfaction

The desire for some quantified measure of patrol performance can be met by using the volume of dispatches in response to citizens' calls for service. A rapid rise in the volume of dispatches measures the increased frequency of patrol officers' assistance to people who have problems. The ability of a department to dispatch patrol officers is the product of its competence in receiving phone calls, making dispatching decisions, and staffing patrol. Any or all of four conditions can bring about an increase in dispatches: an increase in the number of crimes and disorders; an increase in citizen willingness to rely on the police; an increase in the proportion of calls to which the department decides to respond; and an addition of new types of incidents for which officers take responsibility. Whatever the mix of causes, officers on patrol are performing more work.

Troy's dispatches, 300 per 1,000 city residents in 1971–72, jumped to some 400 in 1974 and 500 in 1975. The rapidity of this rise suggests that initially citizens had many unmet needs for police service. Citizen willingness to call the police may have risen because prompt, helpful service in serious situations motivates people to call also about less serious problems. For example, citizens reported 180 thefts of auto accessories in 1972 but 402 in 1974. Yet there is no reason to believe that this form of thievery had doubled during the two years, because reported auto thefts stayed steady: 224 in 1972 and 211 in 1974.

Departmental upgrading does not trigger an endless escalation in the number of minor incidents brought to police attention. Future comparative research into patrol services will probably bear out that the larger the proportion of poor people, the larger the percentage unemployed; and the larger the proportion of teenagers, the greater will be the per capita rate of calls for service and dispatches. Troy's dispatches leveled off in the late 1970s between 425 and 500 per 1,000 residents. Since the early 1970s a fairly steady 70 percent of the department's dispatches have been for incidents that are not crimes.

The Long, Hard Road to Open Exercise of Discretion

However much discretion police officers actually exercise, the police field has ignored, denied, and discouraged discretion. Instead, it has made control the paramount issue throughout the history of American policing. Certainly departmental rules and regulations are essential for such fundamental matters as restricting the use of deadly force and forbidding the acceptance of gratuities. They establish procedures for routine actions, set the limits on discretion, and lend formal recognition to priorities, but they serve poorly as the major means for controlling most actions.

In 1967 the President's Commission on Law Enforcement and the Administration of Justice opened the debate on the proper role of discretion. Once the exercise of discretion is admitted, many uncomfortable questions arise. How can the enforcement of laws and the provision of services be fair if they are not centrally controlled? Traditionally, departmental regulations were supposed to delineate proper actions, and sergeants were supposed to see that their subordinates adhered to the regulations. To complete the picture of how unrealistic it is to expect to control discretion by means of the chain of command and how counterproductive such efforts can be, we shall look at examples of police-initiated incidents from three very different departments.

An example from New York City shows the consequences of a regulation that prohibited officers from patronizing local eating and drinking establishments—an effort to reduce the opportunities for graft.

□ At the end of their evening tour a pair of radio car partners went to eat and have a drink at a local grill, knowingly violating a written departmental regulation designed to reduce the opportunity for officers to receive graft. As the two officers drove away from the grill, they spotted smoke pouring from a tenement. They rushed inside and dragged an unconscious man from his burning bedroom. Once they had seen him safely off to the hospital, they spent much more time to invent a plausible story for the bosses to explain why they were still in the precinct after hours.

A few years later the department dropped this regulation, not because it was counterproductive but because it contravened individual freedom for officers off duty.

Patrol officer compliance with directives mandating positive action is also difficult to obtain. The police chief of a working-class New Jersey town in the inner suburban ring around New York occasionally receives letters of praise and appreciation for the courtesy his officers have extended. The letters concern everyday situations where an officer has had the legal authority to issue a summons but instead has chosen to obtain compliance by politely advising the person that his action was against the law: a resident drinking beer on his front steps; a used car dealer forgetting to put plates on a car he was demonstrating; a grocer displaying his merchandise beyond his property line on the sidewalk. In each case that has come to his attention, the police chief has reprimanded the officer for failing to "enforce the law."

Here is a final example of police officer discretion, seen at three different levels. In 1976 an officer in Berkeley, California, whom I will call John Ross, had developed his own technique for avoiding hassles and receiving thanks when issuing a ticket. Through research of the municipal and state codes, he found that the municipal ordinances were sufficiently broad to cover most improper driving practices. When Officer Ross issued tickets for violations of the municipal rather than the state code, his explanation to the driver, that the fine was lighter and carried no points against the license, consistently produced thanks and a promise to drive more safely. An added benefit, although not of importance to Ross, was that the fines went to the city, not the state.

The Berkeley department has an unusually strong tradition of encouraging officer discretion and thus attracts many well-educated men and women. Yet to my surprise, when I praised the approach of Officer Ross to a patrol sergeant, he wanted to know the identity of the officer in order to correct his behavior. This sergeant reasoned that citations must be given only under the state code so that accurate tallies can be maintained of points against drivers, who then can be barred from driving. The sergeant's own working style was always to give a ticket and never a warning. The chain of command had not worked to identify for the sergeant actions contrary to the way he believed laws should be enforced.

Nor had the chain of command worked to impress upon the sergeant the way that Chief Wesley Pomeroy wanted the job done. When told of Ross's way of getting thanks, Pomeroy highly approved, because he is convinced that the beat officer has to be encouraged to use discretion. Further, Pomeroy believes that the purpose of traffic enforcement is to educate, not to punish or collect fines. An officer's own sense of fairness in each circumstance should guide the decision whether or not a ticket is an appropriate educational technique. The driver, too, should feel that the ticket was fairly given.

All three members of the department did agree that good police work requires stopping dangerous drivers, and they had no regard for the common practice of ignoring driving violations. But we have no research that compares the effectiveness of a friendly manner with that of points against the license. This absence of statistical proof of effectiveness is typical of police work. Clearly, when certain techniques have been demonstrated to be more effective than others, the training of officers should include the teaching of those techniques and the research behind them.

The examples could be multiplied and the analysis extended. External controls on police officers are most effective in obtaining compliance in outward appearance, the shine of the shoes. They have not proved effective in controlling the way police officers treat citizens, in whether or not officers assist citizens toward the solution of their problems. Efforts to replace officers' judgment with central direction are generally misguided. Central direction is appropriate only where simple, routine work is the norm or where a supervisor is continually present.

When the exercise of discretion is recognized as legitimate for police officers, a whole new agenda for change appears. At the county level, the prosecutor needs to understand and support long-standing police discretion in exercising the power of arrest. At the state level, a statute would be useful to recognize and define police discretion in making arrests (Andrews 1985, 9). New state laws could structure and guide reasonable actions that officers can take now only without legal justification (Force 1972). At the beginning of the 1990s officers lack legal authority to end a fight by ordering the combatants to leave, to order unruly crowds to disperse, to take iron bars away from a gang of youths, to remove guns from a home where serious domestic violence has occurred, to take a mentally ill person home. Legislation on public intoxication, however, does now authorize police in two-thirds of the states to transport inebriated individuals home or to shelters without arresting them. This prototype can guide thinking toward other problems that might be addressed through specific new powers for police. Such far-reaching legislation will take years to develop, but fundamental transformations at the department level are already underway.

The characteristic which will distinguish the new from the old police system will be its central focus of attention and energy upon the needs of its clients.

George W. O'Connor, 1976

The Hospital Model

George O'Connor developed the analogy of the hospital in order to encourage creative thinking about how police departments should be redesigned to serve their clients. A fundamental explanation of the slow pace of progress in policing is that the field has been working with an inappropriate model—one taken from the military. Supplanting it with the hospital model is a starting point for rethinking fundamental questions, for almost never should police officers act like soldiers, but often they should act like physicians. Force and killing lie at the core of the military model; persuasion, healing, and compassion lie at the core of the hospital model. To think of police work as human service akin to that of medicine permits a bubbling up of new images, notions, possibilities, considerations, and approaches that do not arise within the confines of the police quasi-military tradition.

The organizational arrangements of hospitals are appropriate as a model for police departments primarily because police officers, like physicians, exercise broad discretion as they work face to face with clients. When Officers Mike Mullin and Jack Rice found Sarah Brown ready to brawl with her disparaging neighbor, their diagnosis took into account their broad knowledge of race relations and their particular insights into relations on Oak Street. Their therapeutic aim was to keep the neighborhood peace, and their treatment was a deft combination of serious threats of arrest and humorous cajoling. When Officer Carl Peterson helped the boy he caught stealing shoes to live his own life away from the tyranny of his parents, he worked in the manner of the old-fashioned family physician. He considered the whole person in making his diagnosis, prescribed a treatment that he himself supervised, and continued a personal interest in the well-being of his client. The fact that Peterson rendered these services at a time when the department was giving no support whatever to this mode of work shows what a determined officer can do despite the prevailing police system.

To be clear about what the hospital model means, consider the situation of a patrol officer responding to a mother's complaint that on coming home from work she learned from the baby-sitter that three fifth-grade boys had beaten up her eight-year-old daughter. The officer, in the role of attending physician, would assess the nature of the problem and decide what he ought to do; what specialists, if any, he ought to bring into the case; and what referrals, if any, he should make. It is easy to imagine the patrol officer calling in a youth services officer to learn about the circumstances of the attack directly from the girl, and almost as easy to imagine the patrol officer conferring with the zone officer who works days and with relief officers to learn whether any of these boys have been accused of other attacks. It is only a little harder to imagine the patrol officer and youth officer talking to the various parents. A stretch of the imagination pictures a departmental secretary setting up appointments with the parents if the officers cannot make immediate contact and the responding officer and the youth officer conferring afterward on whether or not to bring school or recreation department personnel into the solution.

This chapter is about changing the system. First we examine concepts from organization theory that characterize the activities of organizations and the settings in which they work. The argument advanced is that hospitals and police departments both deal with complex human problems that can be ameliorated as people change their behavior, yet their present organizational structures are fundamentally different. The hypothesis guiding the changes in Troy was that a redesign of the department's structure along the lines of hospital organization would improve the quality of service. The core of the chapter examines five areas of organizational change: selection of officers, individual accountability, departmental accountability, skill enhancement, and organizational goals. For each area we look at specific steps taken in Troy to reshape the department from a halfhearted imitation of the military model into an organization capable of growth toward the hospital model.

Insights from Organization Theory

Instead of seeking the Holy Grail of a single structure that is right for every organization, contingency theory proposes that different organizational structures are appropriate for different modes of work environments. James D. Thompson (1967) classified organizations by identifying three fundamentally different systems of work, which he called technologies. An organization's technology includes the goals, the objects worked on, the personnel, the equipment, and the accumulated lore and knowledge of the field. In *long-linked* technology, a routine series of processes takes place, as on an assembly line; in *mediating* technology, clients such as bank depositors and borrowers are linked; and in *intensive* technology, a variety of techniques are applied to change an object, depending on feedback from the object. People are often the object of intensive technology, but it is also applied in scientific research, where each research question requires custom applications; and in building construction, where design, terrain, and weather shape the process. A bundle of services specifically configured to meet the individual needs of the client is characteristic of intensive technology.

That the work of police officers utilizes an intensive technology can be seen by considering a common occurrence, a household burglary. Different members of the household may be in need of reassurance or psychological support to assist their recovery from the shock of the intrusion or from the loss of possessions of great sentimental or monetary value. The householder may need technical advice on reducing the likelihood of a recurrence, may have lost uniquely identifiable property that diligence can recover, may need help in filing an insurance claim, may have neighbors who caught sight of a stranger moving suspiciously, or may even need to be dissuaded from taking vengeance on the presumed thief. There may be physical evidence that can help identify the burglar. How the patrol officer obtains the necessary information and conveys appropriate advice is shaped throughout the conversation by the way the client responds.

Tailoring services to individual burglary victims is an example of the specifics that underlie the more abstract statement of responsibilities in *Standards Relating to the Urban Police Function* (ABA 1973), quoted in Chapter 3. Depending on circumstances and personal interest, an officer may advance the general objective of identifying and apprehending criminal offenders, may reduce the opportunity for a future burglary of the premises, may restore a feeling of security, and on rare occasions may preserve order by preventing a vendetta. In contrast, some police departments as a matter of policy provide only limited service for burglary victims by employing clerks to take reports over the telephone or by ordering patrol officers to be quick in getting the facts needed for an incident report. When nonsworn personnel or officers act as clerks, the organizational goal is an accurate record of the burglary, which facilitates the victim's insurance claim and is included in official crime statistics. Where only minimal service is rendered, the department is employing a mediating technology, a routine linking of records. Such routine provision of a simple, standard service is quite different from an officer's weighing the situation and deciding that an accurate report is the only service appropriate.

The second major concept that Thompson uses to distinguish the demands on organizations is the character of their task environment, those aspects of the setting that are relevant to the organization's goals. Environmental factors may be considered in four groups: clients, suppliers, competitors, and regulatory groups. Two fundamental questions for an organization are whether the task environment is homogeneous or heterogeneous, and whether its rate of change is slow or fast. Lawrence and Lorsch (1967) of the Harvard Business School found that the most successful firms in the diverse and changing environment of the plastics industry placed more authority in middle-level managers and relied less on hierarchical controls than did their less successful competitors. In the stable and homogeneous environment of the container industry, by contrast, the most successful firms were more tightly hierarchically controlled than their competitors.

The diversity of incidents that patrol officers handle suggests how heterogeneous are the clients. Heterogeneity is particularly vexing when police officers must maintain order, as in quieting a noisy party, because one citizen's idea of fun is another citizen's annoyance. Officers with a "crime fighting" or military mentality disparage such incidents as not "real police work." The military model simplifies the perception of the environment by neglecting the victim and focusing on the burglar. In fact, the citizens who actually come in contact with officers are only part of the clientele. A municipal department discharging its responsibilities to facilitate the flow of traffic and to enhance people's sense of personal safety is serving everyone who lives in or enters the town.

Continual changes take place in the mix of incidents from day to night, from season to season, from one neighborhood to the next. When officers speak of a rash of burglaries in the central business district, they correctly imply that the present high frequency will decline. In this quick look at the task environment of a police department we have considered only the clients because dealing with them is the aspect addressed directly by officers on the street.

The heterogeneity and instability of the environment have consequences for the organization. Thompson argues that in complex and fluid settings, organizations are more likely to achieve their goals if each unit operates on a decentralized basis. Each unit then sets up procedures that it modifies as it monitors and plans responses to the fluctuations in its sector of the task environment. Organizational units situated in a stable task environment, on the other hand, do better to follow set procedures. The old police organization was modeled on the nineteenth-century British army, which directed the efforts of the men through standard routines, rules, and orders passed down from the commanders. The rules and routines in the police version of the military model stipulate how to write an incident report and how to document an arrest but not how to handle incidents and when to make arrests. Yet Thompson notes that even in the military, modern combat teams with a multiplicity of specialized skills take cognizance of the changing task environment by moving toward an intensive technology.

An Overview of the Hospital Model

Experts agree that hospitals employ intensive technology in a heterogeneous and changing task environment (Thompson 1967). The modern hospital, shaped by a profession as a place to work, is run by two separate systems of management: administrative and medical (Starr, 1982). Administrators are responsible for the comfort of the hotel services, the efficiency of the records system, the maintenance of the buildings and equipment, the quality of nursing, the accuracy of lab work. The fact that hospitals bring into cooperation far more occupations than do police departments does not diminish the usefulness of the model. The fact that hospitals create a controlled environment that willing clients enter is a limitation of the model. However, the central point is that the hospital's chief executive officer is responsible for overall policy and every decision that is not a medical judgment on an individual patient, whereas physicians are responsible to their clients, to themselves, and to their peers for the quality of their medical decisions. The controls on physicians come not from a hierarchy of supervisors but primarily from their own internalized standards, originating in their arduous recruitment and training. The peer review organization, pathology review, and fear of malpractice suits are secondary controls.

O'Connor was under no illusion that physicians and hospitals always hold to account those responsible for errors. Learning hospitals from the inside during his two years in the Cleveland coroner's office, he had been deeply affected to find that fatal errors by medical practitioners were excused under the euphemistic label of "therapeutic misadventures." Still, O'Connor considers more malleable the problems of limiting abuses of discretion by physicians through inculcated values and peer pressure than the problems of controlling police abuses of discretion through a department's chain of command.

The hospital model defines the direction in which the police occupation ought to evolve—toward a profession. It does not describe current reality. The diverse body of literature on professions agrees on what the core professions are but finds the boundaries fluid and indistinct. Talcott Parsons (1968) defines the professions in terms of three criteria: formal technical training that gives prominence to an intellectual component; the development of skills in the application of the technical knowledge; and institutions to assure that the competence will be put to socially responsible uses. Far back in Western civilization, the priesthood was the only profession. The hallmark of the twentieth century is the increase in occupations that have become professions and in those staking disputed claims to professional status. Occupational upgrading to professional status has been analyzed by Wilensky (1964) and Habenstein (1970) to include the establishment of a training school; the formation of a national professional association; a redefinition of core tasks such that the "dirty work" devolves on subordinates; conflict between the old guard and the profession-oriented newcomers; hard competition with neighboring occupations; political activity to gain legal protection for the occupational prerogatives; and ideals embodied in a formal code of ethics.

The description of patrol work in Chapter 3 should have made clear that one cannot reduce the discrepancy between the breadth of the job and the narrowness of the officer by restricting the job. The acceptance of the hospital model is a commitment to broaden the job of a police officer into a profession. A testable proposition is that if young men and women are required to master a body of social science knowledge and acquire skill in interpersonal relations before they become police officers, they will more adroitly handle the job and, in consequence, improve the quality of police service.

When a police officer is viewed as capable of becoming a professional akin to a physician, a new agenda for upgrading emerges. The most basic change replaces the traditional system of command and control with a support system that supplies and coordinates while leaving professional judgments to the individual officers. The American legal system supports expansion of the professional responsibility of the street officer because it vests law enforcement authority directly in each individual officer. Legally, in every state, police officers as individuals hold the power to arrest by virtue of their authority as agents of the state. By contrast, sheriff's deputies are the agents of the sheriff, holding their authority only by virtue of his authority. Since more than 80 percent of officers in local law enforcement hold individual authority, we may speak generally in noting that no supervisor has authority to order a police officer to make an arrest.

A fundamental item on the agenda for change is to shift the domain of police work from a narrow focus on arrest and repression of crime to a positive and broader view of collaborating with citizens to increase their well-being. Among the many actions O'Connor took to convey this shift was a spur-of-the-moment decision one evening during his first months in Troy to respond to a call for service. He caught a call on his car radio that a woman was attempting suicide and drove over to the house so that he could provide officers an example of assistance to a distressed person. When he entered, however, a number of officers stood around outside saying, "Well, here's the Commish. Let him handle it." As a result, O'Connor gently calmed the woman behind a closed door while officers waited outside. Since she was embarrassed by the attention that the police cars attracted, he asked the officers and the ambulance to leave and then took her to the hospital in his own car. In retrospect, he considered that this lesson had failed because those who were supposed to learn from it did not witness it.

The People Attracted to Police Work

Finding Talented and Committed Individuals

High on the agenda for redesigning police departments is the employment of a diverse mix of intelligent and well-motivated individuals who are open to cultivating a tragic perspective. When the composition of a department is close to the social, ethnic, and linguistic composition of the community, the members may be better prepared to understand community conditions. When the personnel have diverse intellectual skills, they can bring special abilities to bear on complex problems. O'Connor has remarked that if the United States can remain at peace long enough, police departments will no longer be flooded with men who came out of the military "loving it" and looking for similar work in policing. Although the popular view of police work, as shaped by television dramas in the military tradition, lauds superior police firepower, the human side of policing has finally been shown on *Hill Street Blues* and *Barney Miller*. In Troy, publicity to attract police applicants portrayed the police officer as a person who can make the difference between a fearful citizen and a secure one, between a neighborhood soiled and broken by vandals and one where citizens can live peacefully (Troy Department of Public Safety, 1984).

Across the broad range of efforts to augment the talent pool, Commissioner O'Connor was least successful in making changes that required the consent of the Troy Civil Service Commission. By law and local practice, police jobs were traditionally open only to men who were local residents and awarded preferentially to veterans. O'Connor was unable to make college preparation mandatory for entrance, to eliminate absolute preference for city residents, or to hire any black officers. Only in 1984 did Troy hire any women as patrol officers. However, the commissioner quickly instituted selection criteria in areas not regulated by the civil service commission, a system of thorough background checks and psychological testing.

Scattered among well-motivated, emotionally stable applicants there are usually a few domineering individuals who will amplify their cynical and vindictive inclinations if permitted to become officers. Even well-balanced individuals who function capably in jobs with ordinary levels of stress may be incapable of professional response to the tragedies and the dangers of the street. To the extent that police departments set high standards for entry and use diligence in screening applicants, they are applying concepts from the hospital model to prevent malpractice. As police departments increase their use of psychological and psychiatric diagnosis, more experts in mental health will apply their knowledge to the specifics of policing.

A formal interview was set by O'Connor as the final selection device. Bill Alsip, a successful applicant with a graduate degree, went for his interview with confidence, having skillfully handled previous job interviews, but he was amazed.

It turned out to be more like a graduate school orals exam. The commissioner was sitting on one side of the table, the chief on another, and I on the third. They asked me a series of probing questions about the fields of social science. Then they asked a question they had posed to many of the candidates, "What would you do if you were a provisional officer and you drove to a bar and your senior partner went into the bar saying, 'Stay here,' and when he came out two hours later he was so drunk he couldn't stand?" I thought that I had solved that one when I said I would take him to the station and tell the sergeant. They came back at me, "Suppose the sergeant says, 'He does this all the time. Take him on out'." I was very disturbed by that and had to reflect. I told them, "Because there is a sense of brotherhood among officers and they must support each other, it would be hard to just turn the man in." Finally, I said I would go to each succeeding level of supervision until someone handled the problem or I reached the chief.

Police salaries have historically been too low to attract college graduates except during the Depression and the present era. O'Connor holds that the major factor keeping police salaries down in the long run is that officers are paid for just existing rather than for the work they accomplish. If police departments fired the poor performers, their salaries could be shared among those remaining, and no decline in service would occur. In 1972, 90 percent of the Troy officers interviewed by the consultants had second jobs (Cresap, McCormick, and Paget 1972, 1:III-18), typically occasion employment, but a few had steady full-time jobs in violation of the state law limiting secondary employment to twenty hours per week. Although most continued their outside employment despite the hefty increase in police salaries, new officers generally did not take secondary employment.

The national contrast is sharp between modest pay for officers and high income for physicians. The two occupations have also been distinguished by the fact that physician's income typically derives from client fees, although in this regard physicians are becoming more like other professionals, as 31 percent are now salaried (Marder et al. 1988; AMA 1987). Another contrast is the level of mobility. Police officers are usually tied by their pensions to their original department almost as tightly as serfs were tied to their lord's land. Discontented officers who do not leave within the first few years linger until they become eligible for their pensions after twenty or twenty-five years.

In educational requirements and collegial exchanges, as well, the police system falls far short of the hospital model. Having mastered a minimum of eleven years of education and training beyond high school, physicians keep up with the field through reading, conferring, and taking required continuing education courses. By contrast, less than 15 percent of American police departments require more than a high school diploma (Carter, Sapp, and Stephens 1989, 54). Police academy training is set at a minimum of ten weeks in New York state and less in most states (Flanagan and Jamieson 1988, 43). Union membership is usually an officer's only organized contact with the police world beyond the department.

In, Troy, educational preparation of new officers rose sharply as more candidates taking the state civil service examination applied to Troy and the educated applicants outscored the others. In 1968 there had been only ten applicants for Troy; in 1970, only sixteen. At the next exam, 1974, the number jumped to ninety-six. Only 15 percent of the officers joining the department between 1965 and 1972 had any college education, but the proportion rose to 87 percent of the recruits admitted by the 1974 exam. Nationally, during the same period, the proportion of recruits possessing some college education started higher, 22 percent in 1965–69, but rose more slowly, to 34 percent in 1970–74 (Sherman and National Advisory Commission 1978). In 1986 the Supreme Court upheld the Dallas PDs entrance requirement of forty-five semester hours of college. Minnesota state law now requires all officer applicants to have completed two years of college. Both recruitment and enrollment of officers have pushed up educational levels for departments serving jurisdictions larger than 50,000: 65 percent of such officers now have some college, 43 percent have two years, and 23 percent have four or more years (Carter, Sapp, and Stephens 1989). In view of the complexity of the police job, O'Connor believes that a bachelor's degree should be required of all new officers.

To promote professionalism, O'Connor, with union agreement, wrote a clause into the 1975 contract forbidding the City to hire any provisional officers except in a formally declared emergency. This elemental barring from practice of those who have not passed screening and training is not observed by many New England and mid-Atlantic departments, which frequently hire extra personnel in the summer. O'Connor persuaded the civil service commission to extend the probationary period from six to twelve months and used the time to rotate recruits systematically through all major units of the department. They worked three weeks on each patrol shift and a week or more in criminal investigations, youth services, the radio room, planning, and traffic. The commissioner wanted all new officers to gain many organizational perspectives so that they would see how their jobs meshed with all the other jobs of the department. When senior officers who had never worked outside of patrol expressed envy, the commissioner arranged their rotation as well.

Civil Service Barriers to Nonresidents and Women

A few departments deliberately seek candidates nationally, but many restrict their search to the state, and some require local residence. Pre-employment residency is an appropriate criterion only if jobs are viewed as benefits. Although civil service systems were created a century ago to prevent political machines from awarding jobs as benefits, some civil service commissions have been dominated by local party leaders much as some governmental regulatory agencies have been dominated by the industries they regulate. The Troy civil service requirement that a candidate live in the city for four months prior to taking the examination imposed a substantial sacrifice on outsiders, because the average wait between the examination and appointment is over a year. Limiting the talent pool to Troy residents severely cut the department's ability to find highly qualified candidates. To be specific, Troy's population is just over 1/5,000 of the U.S. population. If we assume that the same fraction of Troy residents as of U.S. residents are interested in and qualified for police work, then restricting recruitment within city boundaries cuts the talent pool to about 1/5,000 of its potential size. If we further assume that none of the eligible are willing to move out of state, then the talent pool is cut to about 1/350 of its potential size. Among minority groups in Troy hardly any men or women took the civil service examination during the years 1973–86, and not one scored high enough to be eligible for appointment.

Civil service regulations also discriminated against women. In June 1973 when Commissioner O'Connor learned that 5 feet, 8 inches was the minimum height requirement for officers, he wrote the chairman of the Troy Civil Service Commission: "I note that . . . [the New York State regulations] apply the male height standards to female candidates. I do not think this is appropriate except as a technique for barring female applicants." He recommended basing height standards on national norms for men and women and then allowing "the employment of shorter persons whose psychological and physical assessments indicate that they do not have emotional problems relating to their stature *and* they are capable of defending themselves and others in life-threatening situations." This succinctly states the two types of handicaps that short stature might impose on an officer and proposes means to determine whether or not an individual is free of those handicaps. The lack of sound social science research on the effects of height on performance has led courts to reject all height standards as discriminatory against women and certain ethnic groups.

So favorably inclined toward tall officers was the Troy Civil Service Commission that it exceeded its authority by setting the city's limit at 6 feet, 6 inches, despite the state limit of 6 feet, 4 inches. One civil service commissioner's argument against women of average height, in O'Connor's recollection, was that they would be too short to shoot over the roof of a patrol car while taking shelter behind it. O'Connor's participation in state-level hearings assisted the state adoption of separate height requirements for men and women in early 1974. That same year Troy's civil service refused O'Connor's request to waive the height requirement for a young man, half an inch shy of 5 feet, 8 inches, who was finishing college and serving as a police intern.

The civil service next prevented three shorter women from taking the 1974 examination. O'Connor suggested they take their case to the Troy

Human Rights Commission. After hearings, a court order barred the City from making any appointments from the list based on the 1974 examination. In March 1976 a county judge waived the hiring ban on the grounds that public safety required the department to expand by ten officers in response to fear of a crime wave (see Chapter 7). By early 1977 the Troy Civil Service Commission was still maintaining the 5 foot, 8 inch standard, even though the state had dropped all height requirements. O'Connor wrote the state attorney general, asking his office to advise the local civil service commission that it was no more likely than the state to succeed in defending a height requirement. When the Troy commission dropped height requirements for the October 1977 examination, several women passed, one with the top score, but were eliminated by the agility test. The city commission then failed to arrange for Troy's participation in the 1979 state exam, despite O'Connor's standing request for annual exams, and the state agency would not permit Troy candidates to travel to neighboring cities to take it.

The Troy commission extended the life of the 1977 list, with appointments now coming from far down on the list. A man who had scored 44th on the 1977 examination had been eliminated from consideration because he was not a resident at the time he took the test. He became an investigator in the district attorney's office, moved into Troy, took the 1980 exam, and tied for first. Even after state civil service released the 1980 list, the Troy commission again extended the 1977 list. The candidate brought a civil suit challenging the validity of maintaining the old list in the face of a new one. During the court proceedings the city was again barred from all hiring, and the young man eventually received appointment.

By 1983 two of the top women candidates were married to officers in the department, and one was the daughter of an officer. In the agility test, not only did the two women fail, but all the scores were terrible in the judgment of the examiner. O'Connor, who was present, concurred that performance was universally poor because of the slickness of the gym floor. He and the examiner jointly decided to rerun the test for all candidates in another gym and saw them all pass with higher scores than on their first try. In January 1984 the first woman joined the department as a full-fledged police officer.

Increasing Individual Accountability

The agenda for change breaks with the traditional view of police discretion as a dangerous power that must be contained, limited, and controlled by the chain of command. There are two sides to accountability: individual officers hold themselves accountable for the quality of their work; and the department holds them accountable. Both types of accountability are needed in every work organization, but the more intensive the technology and the more heterogeneous the clients, the more essential is individual accountability.

O'Connor's method was to structure the work so that individual officers would expand their own sense of personal accountability for the well-being of the people they served. His first alteration in the work situation of patrol officers was to adopt practices that are routine in well-managed departments: consistency in working conditions, and individual responsibility in single-officer cars.

Consistency in Working Conditions

Five types of consistency give stability to a street officer's work, which is highly unpredictable from hour to hour: consistency in shift, geographic zone, partner, squad, and sergeant. Consistencies across time and space reduce the diversity of street problems. In Thompson's terms, they reduce the heterogeneity of the task environment. The officer who handles the vandalism by adolescents going home from school does not also have to deal with patrons at bar closing time. In a single neighborhood, officers learn who the troublemakers are and who the peacemakers. When officers have their own piece of turf, they can direct their possessive feelings toward protecting and serving the people who live, work, and play there. Reciprocally, some residents come to know them personally. In the broadest sense, when officers know generally what to expect, they are best prepared to deal with the unexpected.

Consistency has other benefits. A system of steady shifts may end the toll on the body produced by rotating from one shift to the next, especially for officers who can maintain the same regular schedule of sleep on their days off as on workdays. Numerous studies have thoroughly documented the adverse short-term physiological effects and identified highly probable adverse long-term effects of shift rotation (Mitler et al. 1988; Monk 1988, 1989a, 1989b; Naitoh 1982; and Ottmann et al. 1989). However, a comprehensive survey in 1987 by the Bureau of Justice Statistics found that 45 percent of the departments with at least 135 officers still forced them to rotate around the clock, 12 percent requiring a weekly change (Reaves 1990; Bureau of Justice Statistics 1989).

Consistency in working groups enhances coordination. The most complex forms of coordination take place most easily between people who are members of the same organizational unit. The ever present potential for danger is a strong motivator for officers to know well what to expect of fellow officers. In May 1973 Troy's new patrol system created steady zones, partners, and squads to augment the long-standing consistency of steady shifts. In February 1974 O'Connor assigned sergeants to specific squads with the same schedule as the eight or so squad members, making possible consistency in supervision. As he developed the work chart

over the years, he designated a few positions on each shift as "extra."
Individuals who like variety select the "extra" positions; whenever ab-
sences occur, they will fill in, whether in the radio room or a different
patrol zone.

Single-Officer Patrol Cars

O'Connor strongly favors one-officer cars to promote individual responsibility and to increase contacts with citizens. Danger to officers is the
major argument against single-officer cars, but the results of a year-long
experiment in San Diego still hold: that officers working alone have
fewer instances of arrestees resisting arrest, equal experience with assaults in high-hazard zones, and less in low-hazard zones (Boydstun,
Sherry, and Moelter 1977).

In Troy the PBA had fought the previous city manager's stripping of the
patrol division by specifying in the 1972 union contract the minimum
number of two-officer cars on each shift. Platoon captains had fielded no
one-officer cars on evening and midnight shifts unless pairing left an odd
officer. The department's evolution toward predominantly single-officer
cars began in 1973 when O'Connor shifted more officers into patrol and
designated all patrol positions beyond the contractually set minimum as
one-officer cars. The percentage of officers working alone rose in one
year from 8 percent to 26 percent. By January 1975 the positions available
in one-officer cars had become so popular that no one with less than
nine years' seniority could obtain one. Then O'Connor obtained a small
clause in the 1975 contract that permitted partners to choose on a daily
basis whether or not to work separately, regardless of the total number
of two-officer cars on the road. After six weeks of the new contract, Carl
Peterson and his partner, whose working styles diverge, opted for separate cars. Since the stock argument against the single-officer car is that it
diminishes officer safety, one may ask why men on the midnight shift led
the way. An answer is that these officers, who enjoyed relative independence from the daytime command staff, prided themselves on being the
most capable shift. More partners chose to split up and try out this new
mode of work, pushing up the percentages on evenings to 60 percent. By
April 1976 every officer had tasted working alone. In 1978 the union
agreed to drop from the contract the final blockage to single-officer cars,
the minimum manning clause. Thereafter, officers themselves decided
when to work alone and when to work in pairs. Between 45 percent and
60 percent consistently choose solo patrol (Guyot 1977a, 245; Guyot
1985, 5).

In a department where the union vigilantly guards the rights of officers, there has never been a complaint that management has acted arbitrarily about one-officer cars. This acceptance contrasts dramatically with
the Troy PBA's opposition to other management initiatives and with

union opposition elsewhere that has put single-officer cars at the center of the most heated controversy in deployment for more than a decade. The reasons that officers choose to work alone are varied, but the most common one is that they like to make their own decisions.

A realistic sense of personal safety is a prerequisite to officers' willingness to work alone. O'Connor's double aims were to increase safety on the job and to increase officers' sense of safety. He gave high priority to early installation of a new radio system and doubled the staffing in the radio room. Departmental policy gave officers in one-man cars priority on portable radios during the years when they were in short supply. While widely regarded as lenient, O'Connor made known his intolerance of any failure of officers to back each other up. In 1974, when one officer apparently disregarded another's call for assistance, O'Connor opened an investigation with this charge:

> This, on its face, is the most serious violation which the Professional Standards Unit has had in the time that I have been here. I want the fullest and most complete inquiry made to determine what occurred.

Over the years, departmental policies have consistently promoted a realistic sense of officer safety. When New York state set up a program to finance purchase of lightweight body armor, the commissioner ordered vests for all officers but emphasized that there should be no publicity; he hoped to avoid reminding potential attackers to aim elsewhere on the body. In developing the department's plan for coordinated response to bank robbery, the physical safety of citizens and officers had top priority. Some officers cover likely escape routes, and others converge on the bank but wait until the robbers exit before confronting them. In describing the first robbery after the adoption of the plan, a high-ranking field commander praised the officers for giving the robbers no incentive to take hostages or to engage in a shootout. The fact that the robbers escaped from the scene and were not apprehended until later did not dim this commander's view of success, so paramount had safety become. At the in-service school there has been opportunity for officers to deal openly with their fears. Since 1980 a police expert has led sessions in stress reduction. In a wide variety of ways, then, the department conveys the message that an officer needs prudence, not a partner, for protection.

The shift to single-officer cars appears to have enhanced the quality of work performed by patrol officers in at least three ways: increasing initiative, increasing interaction with citizens in nonstressful situations, and increasing positive handling of stressful situations. In the absence of rigorous before-and-after observational study of Troy's patrol officers at work, we must rely on comparative studies from other departments.

A substantial body of research on work organizations finds that new employees tend to be more highly motivated to produce than oldtimers, who often establish informal norms to keep output at a "reasonable" level. Direct evidence on the less energetic performance of older officers comes from an analysis by Robert Friedrich (1977) of the seminal patrol study conducted for the President's Commission in Chicago, Washington, and Boston. At the end of each of the 1,300 shifts on which observers rode, they gave an overall rating to the work efforts of officers during their noncommitted time. The more years officers had served, the less they worked. An organizational change to single-officer cars permits junior officers to escape the stifling of their initiative, epitomized in the phrase, "When he slept, I slept."

A second positive result may be more frequent interaction with citizens in nonstressful situations. Officers in single cars, the argument runs, are more likely to hold casual conversations with citizens because they lack the conviviality of a partner. The greater the number and variety of an officer's friendly contacts with citizens, the better his understanding of people and the more confidently he can handle stressful encounters. In turn, citizens who have been treated considerately by one officer are more likely to be supportive when the next officer needs them.

Third, an officer who must handle stressful incidents alone is more likely to treat citizens in a positive, friendly manner than when accompanied by another officer. This reason was especially important to O'Connor because as a patrol officer in Oakland, he had observed that a particular officer with a nasty reputation would get rough only when there were other officers present. The tough officer working alone is constrained by the likelihood that he may get hurt, but when such an officer has a partner, that partner becomes his most important audience. If an officer who is not ordinarily domineering has any doubts about how to handle a situation, he is likely to fall back on the stereotype of the tough cop in order to avoid appearing weak before his partner. Evidence from Friedrich's analysis of the three-city study supports this argument. In over 15,000 encounters he found that officers with partners were friendly 14 percent of the time and that single officers were friendly 22 percent of the time with offenders and 24 percent with others.

Tom White, the Troy officer who rescued the baby trapped under the Cadillac, had been working alone for a year as an evidence technician when he recounted this experience of befriending a boy.

> One evening a couple of weeks ago I was just finishing backing up a gun call in another zone when I heard a nearby call, boy trespassing. I found the zone officer standing on the lawn over a miserable boy of sixteen. He had been trying to kill himself by slashing his wrists with a piece of broken glass. Since Jerry was stymied, I settled down to talk with the boy. The kid poured out a string of woes, family problems, no friends, just been fired. I listened to him and attempted to reason with

him. I felt sorry for him that he had life in front of him yet he believed he was worthless. At last, just when I thought I was getting somewhere, he said, "Give me your gun. I want to shoot myself."

I called an ambulance to take the boy to the hospital psych center, but I was concerned that the attendants might just drop him, so I followed them to be sure that the boy was all right. As I thought, the attendants dumped him. I stayed quite a while trying to get the receptionist to bring immediate help for the boy, who was all alone in a waiting room. She kept insisting that the boy would be all right, so I left. Within minutes, the hospital called the department to say that the boy had run away. I rushed back to the hospital to find that he had just attempted to jump down a thirty-foot drop from the hospital parking lot. This time I stayed at the hospital until a doctor began helping the boy. Later that evening I saw the boy again, wandering alone down the street. I knew that I would have to find a better place to bring a person in crisis.

When Tom told me of this episode, I asked him why he felt so free to go so far out of his way, so far from his assigned end of town, and so far in checking up on how others were doing their jobs. He replied, "I believe that this is the most important kind of work I can do as an officer. I know that this is the kind of police work that the commissioner believes in. Years ago, I was outside the room once when he helped a woman who had tried to commit suicide."

Weak Departmental Accountability

The police field took a giant step forward in promoting departmental accountability in 1979 when four professional associations created a voluntary, nongovernmental accreditation process. The Commission on Accreditation for Law Enforcement Agencies resulted from the joint efforts of the International Association of Chiefs of Police, the National Sheriffs' Association, the National Organization of Black Law Enforcement Executives, and the Police Executive Research Forum. The commission has developed and adopted over nine hundred standards requiring written policies, programs, and procedures on all aspects of administration and operations. By March 1990, 143 departments had achieved accreditation through demonstrating compliance with commission standards. Meeting the accreditation standards is of value both for departments emphasizing orderly professional administration and for departments aiming to develop professional police officers. Their fundamental merit for a department that supports officer discretion is that they establish a firm basis of standard procedures for the routine work, which enhances coordination and frees energies for solving complex problems in the community.

Prior to his retirement Commissioner O'Connor had taken the preliminary steps to involve the Troy department in the process of self-scrutiny and administrative upgrading required to achieve accreditation, but the department's involvement in the national program ceased at his departure.

Just as individual accountability has a model in the accountability that physicians maintain in their profession, accountability for smoothly running support services has a model in the chief executive officer's direction of a hospital's hotel services. Assessment of such direction asks, is the operating room properly cleaned? is the bed occupancy rate high? A single question will stand for the many similar questions that should be asked of a police department: are the patrol cars maintained in good operating condition? Reliable car maintenance is least difficult to achieve when the mechanics are police department employees and work on the premises, arrangements O'Connor made in 1975. In both hospitals and police organizations, systems of routine maintenance and feedback keep facilities and equipment in good order.

Accountability through Sergeants

In police departments, as in hospitals, the most important accountability issues concern the treatment of clients. However, police departments have neither used the chain of command effectively nor followed the medical school mode of intensive guidance that teaches young doctors good workmanship. In analyzing commands and standards of workmanship as two systems of control, Egon Bittner (1983) deplores the usual police department practice of focusing on officers' attention to rules and prior orders but neglecting to assess the quality of their workmanship, which cannot be prescribed in advance but can be judged afterward.

The responsibilities common to first-line supervisors, whether in a police department or in a shoe factory, include coordinating, monitoring, training, and motivating. Consistency in the police working group provides the sergeant with a small number of officers whose strengths and weaknesses he or she should know. However, patrol supervisors have particular difficulty in performing every supervisory function because the work consists of services, which cannot be inspected as goods can, and because those services are typically performed out of sight of the supervisor. A mechanical solution employed from the late 1800s until the 1950s, the call box system, required foot patrolmen to make hourly pulls to show that they were alive and awake. By remaining in the precinct station where the call box bell rang, a sergeant used this device to monitor his men. Today, the radio is employed similarly in time checks. More important, the radio has stripped the sergeant of job allocation and monitoring powers. If an officer appears to be taking excessive time to handle a call, the dispatcher will make that judgment. Further, computer-aided dispatching systems have as an optional feature a locator system that continuously gives the position of each radio car. The modern electronic systems, like the old mechanical bell pull, can monitor where officers are, but they cannot control what officers do. Although the portable radio has the potential for greatly increasing the contact between sergeants and patrol officers, it has rarely been utilized for supervision. The most usual form of supervision is after the fact, a review of written reports.

Excellence in monitoring, training, and motivation does not require gadgetry. R. Dean Smith (1975), who served many years as a key member of the IACP staff, once reflected on the best patrol sergeant he had known, his supervisor when he was a young officer in Oakland, California. Often, when Smith finished handling a call, his supervisor would be waiting. They would then sit together in one car or the other to discuss the incident. Sometimes before their conversation the sergeant would tell Smith to sit tight, go inside himself to learn what the citizens thought of their service, and return armed with the citizens' views. The sergeant would then help Smith to reflect on alternative ways he could have handled the incident to bring about better outcomes. A sergeant who has a tragic perspective can guide his or her officers in learning how to work with the complexities of human nature. Goldstein (1990, 157–59) deftly sketches ways in which sergeants can support officers' creativity in solving community problems.

In most departments, however, patrol sergeants customarily see little of their officers outside of the roll call room. The only quantified observational study of patrol sergeants was conducted in Minneapolis in 1981. Mary Ann Wycoff (1982) found that even with observers as a stimulus to more active supervision, sergeants spent only 11 percent of their time in face-to-face contact with the officers they supervised. From intensive observation of a traditional department, John Van Maanen (1983) characterized sergeants as emphasizing procedural regularity, being uninterested in service to the public, and conniving with officers to deflect demands coming down the chain of command. In Troy, during the first ten years of upgrading, most sergeants most of the time took little interest in the work of their officers. Never having experienced constructive guidance as patrolmen, they did not know how to give it.

Consistent, constructive supervision became less rare in the Troy PD by the mid-1980s, when officers who had internalized professional values gained promotion. Sam Griffith provides an example:

> In my squad there is a young officer from a good family who uses bad language to citizens, even calls people niggers. Probably he was somewhat sheltered as a youth, and when he became an officer, he picked up locker room talk without realizing that officers don't use that language on the street. I had heard about him from a couple of citizens and from some officers.

Then came a complaint from a black woman where he had gone on a call for service. I asked him what had happened, and he described the events without mentioning any bad language. After telling him what her complaint was, I said that probably his recall was not quite accurate and her recall was not quite accurate. I was not going to judge what happened, and I was not going to take her side. I explained that I had other complaints about his language. I told him that he was young and that I didn't want him to form bad habits. I said that at age twenty-two he thinks he has experience, but in five years when he looks back, he will see his situation entirely differently. The officer felt uncomfortable and accused, so I repeated that I was not blaming him.

At the end of this long conversation I asked him to remember how it began. "You asked me what happened." "Yes, and after every incident, I want you to ask yourself what happened." That conversation was a couple of months ago, and I have heard from his buddies that he is cleaning up his language.

Civil Service and Union Impediments

Job protection for incompetent and even dangerous officers is the most serious of many impediments to strong departmental accountability. When John O'Reilly pulled his wad of hundreds to show he didn't need the job, he knew he would not be fired, because the Troy Civil Service Commission would protect him.

In work organizations, promotion is the standard reward for excellent performance, but in police departments under civil service systems, job performance is irrelevant to promotion. Skill with a pencil one Saturday morning is what counts. The automatic nature of civil service systems permits almost no choice among candidates who pass entrance or pro-motion examinations. Candidates' test scores, plus points for seniority and veteran status in New York and several other states, establish their exact ranking on the civil service list from which appointments are made. For promotional examinations some states also award points for years of service. Following the standard rule of three, the police manager may select one from among the top three candidates. A moment's reflection will show that the more candidates the manager needs to appoint from the same list, the less valuable is the power to skip two of them.

A second set of impediments to departmental accountability often stems from the union contract and the actions of the police union. Troy's contract has the exceptionally restrictive clause that management has no right to make job assignments; instead, officers choose their positions in order of seniority. The clause achieves its authors' aim in preventing any sergeant or command officer from inflicting punishment posts, but it greatly reduces management's ability to hold officers accountable, since management cannot assign personnel in accordance with their talents or reassign individuals who consistently perform below standards in a particular position.

In many cities the union plays such an active role in opposing management that the conflict deserves a full explanation (see Chapter 9). The Troy PBA leadership from 1974 through 1985 actively discouraged individual initiative, maintaining direct pressure on officers to stop work promptly at shift change, for example, rather than work a few minutes longer without overtime pay. A serious blow against officer initiative and departmental accountability took place in 1975 when the union objected to an officer's receiving a temporary investigative assignment.

Officer Richard Ogden, a respected, powerfully built man of eight years' experience, smashed his patrol car when he fell asleep at the wheel at the end of a midnight shift. An ill wife and young children had prevented his getting more than a few hours' daily sleep for the previous ten weeks. After the accident he asked the PBA executive committee to allow a hardship transfer to days. The union participated in this managerial decision because Ogden's assignment to days gave him a benefit not available to officers senior to him and thus went against the contractual stipulation of assignment by seniority.

After the PBA board and O'Connor agreed to the transfer, Ogden developed a lead on heroin coming into Troy. He sought permission to relinquish his patrol duties in order to investigate. To forestall a grievance that the investigative assignment resulted from favoritism, O'Connor directed Ogden to make a written request showing his initiative. The PBA did bring a grievance, technically against the chief and the commissioner for making the assignment, but when Ogden faced the PBA executive board and their lawyer in the commissioner's office, he felt as though he were being brought up on charges. Ogden did follow his lead to Harlem and locate an apartment that federal authorities confirmed was under surveillance, but fellow officers never knew of his success. Ten months later the PBA dropped their grievance and did not fine Ogden for breaking PBA bylaws, but he felt so undermined that he vowed that he would never again leave himself open to such an attack.

In assessing changes in the Troy department, in 1977 I used the scale of the University of Michigan Institute for Social Research to measure organizational climate (Taylor and Bowers 1972). The 87 members who participated in the survey agreed that the department did not provide incentives to work hard. Table 4-1 reflects their judgment that only a low percentage of coworkers had any extrinsic reason to apply themselves to their work. Typically, promotion and pay raises in policing, do not depend upon how hard a person works. Also typical is the absence of two key sanctions against laziness: fear of losing one's job, and the sting of

Table 4-1 Lack of Reasons for Working Hard as Seen by Troy PD Members, 1977

Why Do People Work Hard in This Organization?	Positive Response	Conditions in Troy PD and Common Elsewhere
Extrinsic Reasons		
To seek promotion	6%	civil service tests control promotion
To avoid being chewed out	7	supervisors rarely expect more than a minimal job
To make money	8	salaries are fixed by rank with increments for longevity; opportunities for overtime work are limited
Because people they work with expect it	11	"mind your own business" is the motto of many officers
To keep their job	14	civil service protection makes firing incredibly difficult
Intrinsic Reasons		
Because the public needs the services of this organization	33	
For the satisfaction of a job well done	57	

Sources: The seven reasons are from Taylor Bowers, 1972. In April 1977, 59 percent of the 135 sworn officers and 12 nonsworn employees, responded to these items in a 34-item questionnaire.

peer disapproval. In Troy, supervisors so rarely reproved officers that a reprimand was not seen as a reason to avoid laziness. Only the intrinsic reasons, personal satisfaction in good performance and service to the public, were considered important by at least one-third of the department.

At the extreme, about one-fourth of the officers saw no reason to report to work if they felt like staying home. Officers had enjoyed unlimited sick leave until the first union contract set a limit of twelve months' continuous sick leave. O'Connor was unable to obtain the city manager's support to replace the incumbent police surgeon with a system to monitor and control sick leave. Among the immediate supervisors, who should handle sick leave abuse, so many had been compromised over the years by their actions and inaction that they were unable to say, "Never mind what I used to do; we'll do it right from now on."

Table 4-2, compiled from sick leave figures kept by O'Connor, measures one consequence of weak departmental accountability. The Troy average never fell below fourteen days per officer per year, far above the six- to eight-day averages found in over one hundred departments by a manpower consultant (Hobson 1989). About one-fourth of the Troy de-

Table 4-2 Sick Leave Use by Sworn Personnel

Year	Average Days of Absence[a]	Losing No Days	Losing 20+ Days
1976	19	28%	23%
1977	20	24	25
1978	23	22	30
1980	15	30	19
1981	14	22	21
1983	20	28	27
1984	26[b]		
1985	21	22	25

Sources: Reports from the commissioner's office: 1976–78, "Police Sick Leave Usage, 1976–1977–1978"; 1979–81, "Analysis of Sick Leave Use, 5 Year Period, 1976–1980"; 1984, "Sick Leave Used by Troy Police Officers, 1 Jan through 14 Oct 1984"; 1985, printout from city hall.
[a]All sick and injury days are included.
[b]Extrapolated from 9.5 months.

partment members used more than a month of sick leave each year. By contrast, another fourth were never out sick during a year. As might be imagined, the same officers fell into these two groupings year after year.

Increasing the Skills and Status of Police Officers

All O'Connor's efforts to improve the quality of police service also aimed to propel individual officers toward professional responsibility. Earlier in this century, policemen were often portrayed in drama and on film as stumbling, stupid, and drunk. O'Connor's intention to bury that past is reflected in his memo refusing a request for officers to play the fool:

It is my understanding that the Troy Retail Merchants plan a special sale on April 1st and that they would like "Keystone Kops" available. I will *not* authorize working officers to become clowns. However, an . . . intern might be suitable.

O'Connor had created eight intern positions from two clerical positions in 1973. This new, lower rung on the organizational ladder raised the status of street officers by relieving them of errand running. Gradually, O'Connor filled some key support positions with nonsworn personnel. When senior patrolmen or sergeants hold support position they tend to act as though they are doing a favor when a young officer asks them to check the records; but when a young newcomer holds a nonsworn support position, he or she does what the officer asks as a matter of course. Across the nation, an important yet little-noticed consequence of civilianization in police work has been to raise the status of the police officer rank by creating positions below that rank.

Before 1973 the status gap between detectives and patrolmen in Troy had been so great that patrolmen did not dare to go upstairs to the detectives' office. The department ended the assignment of detectives to the midnight shift in 1973 and opened detective positions to the police officer rank in 1979. O'Connor resisted repeated pressures to return detectives to midnights, including a public attack in 1981 by the district attorney. O'Connor's announced reason, to prevent inefficiency, was based on the infrequency of midnight cases requiring immediate intensive investigation. His fundamental reason was that assigning detectives to midnights would downgrade the responsibilities of patrol officers on that shift, who were disproportionately young, well educated, and well motivated. While working an unattractive shift, they at least had the intrinsic satisfaction of increased investigative responsibility.

Expansion of training, as already mentioned in Chapter 2, is an effective technique of police upgrading. Whenever officers requested specific training, whether for underwater rescue or stress reduction, O'Connor arranged it, even when his priorities lay elsewhere. He chose an evidence technician program as a concentrated early effort to increase the professional skills of patrol officers. In larger departments, evidence technicians are often nonsworn personnel attached to support services or the detective bureau. Troy's program began in 1975 with nineteen officers volunteering for the six positions, which provided increased expertise, responsibility, authority, and continued patrol responsibilities but no increase in pay. The orders establishing the program gave evidence technicians absolute authority over the physical evidence at crime scenes. Such authority, based on expertise rather than rank, is unusual (Fields, Lipskin, and Reich 1975). Its effectiveness was tested in the program's fifth week by a homicide in the woods. Previously, in Troy as elsewhere, homicide scenes had attracted a number of officers who unthinkingly contaminated physical evidence. This time, the evidence technician and the identification sergeant roped off the sites and made clear plaster casts of the murderer's footprints. Their work, together with leads from field questioning, led to an arrest within twenty-four hours.

The evidence technician program is an example of the unevenness of progress in building a professional department. Between 1975 and 1987 sixty officers had chosen to work for at least six months as evidence technicians. By 1987 forty-four of these men were still serving as police officers, and nine had become sergeants; only seven had left the department. The officers carry their technical skills in crime scene analysis to their work throughout the department. The weakness that initially cut the effectiveness of the program was the inability to bring evidence to bear on arrests. During the first four years of operation, when the department was averaging 105 adult burglary arrests annually, only about nine adults a year were convicted of burglary on the basis of evidence obtained before arrest, about twelve a year on evidence obtained after arrest, and the majority without physical evidence. Unused evidence lay in the files, a common problem in policing. In Troy, the utilization of fingerprint evidence improved a decade later when the state developed the computer capability to match single prints.

Similarities between Policing and Public Health Medicine

Hospitals as model organizations share two limitations with traditional police departments: a tendency to create passive, unquestioning clients, and a tendency to focus on acute episodes while underplaying preventive measures. Because clients actively engaged in preventive measures are found in public health medicine and in health maintenance organizations, it is worthwhile to examine these institutions that go beyond the hospital model.

The development of a broad base of public involvement is a prominent new goal for policing. O'Connor (1976) observed that "the walls of suspicion and distrust which have been built in city after city between the police and their publics are reason enough to justify an effort at reconstruction. If nothing else is accomplished, those walls need to be leveled." The complexity of developing collaboration between police and citizens is discussed in Part IV; here we will merely note that involvement of citizens is crucial.

The typical neglect by hospitals of preventive health care results from their specialization in acute illness. When patients recover, their health is no longer the hospital's responsibility. Hospitals exacerbate the discontinuity by running outpatient clinics as enterprises completely apart from the inpatient floors. Similarly, the police field gives central attention to the incident. Officers tend to see every call for service and every on-view incident as a self-contained event, beginning when specific problems come to their attention and ending when they leave the scene. My discussion of policing has, up to this point, explained police work as the handling of a series of incidents, but later chapters deal with societal problems underlying patterns of incidents. Unfortunately, many police agencies operate only at the level of incidents. The head of such a department typically describes his job as "putting out fires."

More effective service results when police enlarge the focus from the single incident to patterns of incidents. Once identified, the pattern is the problem that requires departmental attention. Herman Goldstein (1979; 1990) has created the powerful concept of "problem-oriented policing," by which a department investigates and analyzes the common factors underlying a set of incidents and then creatively works out tailor-made solutions. In problem-oriented policing, members of the department ask, where do these incidents occur? at what times? to what kinds of people?

stemming from what causes? and with what consequences? Officers employing the problem-oriented approach are aware of how a particular incident fits into larger problems.

Better-managed police departments have long applied a forerunner of problem-oriented policing, crime analysis. However, problem-oriented policing broadens the crime analysis approach along three dimensions. First, it is applied to whatever societal problems become police business—drunken driving, loud stereos, stolen bicycles, debilitated alcoholics. Second, it looks systematically beyond the immediate solution of the current pattern of incidents, such as reducing drunken driving by making arrests, and seeks the adoption of preventive policies to reduce the likelihood that intoxicated men and women will attempt to drive. Third, it develops tailor-made responses to specific problems in collaboration with appropriate public and private organizations plus concerned citizens.

An immediate precursor of problem-oriented policing, known as zone profiling, began in San Diego in 1973. Officers who worked steadily in a given neighborhood assessed local problems, created an inventory of local resources, and outlined proposed solutions. As problem-oriented policing is now evolving, problems are tackled across the geographic areas where they occur, and resources are drawn from all manner of social and public agencies. Early efforts in Madison, Wisconsin, tackled specific problems with analytic assistance from outside the department (Goldstein 1990, 51–52). Baltimore County, Maryland, used a special new unit to apply the problem orientation first to fear of crime and then to a wide range of specific issues (Goldstein 1990, 52–53; Taft 1986). Newport News, Virginia, has pioneered in achieving the problem-solving orientation throughout the entire department (Eck et al. 1987; Goldstein 1990, 55–57). When police departments operate in this mode, they have gone beyond the hospital model, with its focus on acute care, to a public health focus on prevention.

Whenever a department employs problem-oriented policing, it is making policy, often at the initiative of officers on the street. Usually, effective new policies do not eliminate a problem but merely move and reshape it into a more tolerable form (Goldstein 1990, 35–36). By analogy to medicine, few solutions to social ills are like the small-pox vaccine that eliminates a pestilence. More are like blood pressure monitoring and a low salt diet, where persistence prevents backsliding. Commissioner O'Connor directed Troy's departmental efforts toward effective solutions to dogs eating garbage, vandalism of cars in the north end of town, debilitated alcoholics in the streets, and fear of crime in the central business district.

A societal problem that has been a police responsibility for a century, personal injury in motor vehicle accidents, is one that O'Connor tackled early and returned to intermittently at times when the accident rate was rising. He worked with the traffic engineer to identify and correct hazardous intersections. He introduced standard safety education programs for children into schools and the community. He calculated the department's enforcement index, the number of tickets issued for moving violations divided by the number of personal injury accidents, at 4 in 1972, far below the time-honored standard of 20 (Leonard and More 1975, 613–14). By 1974 the commissioner had prodded officers to issue tickets at a rate that equaled 10 for every personal injury accident. The rate of injury accidents fell from 771 per 100,000 population to 610 in 1977 but rose later as the patrol division slacked off in issuing tickets, a common occurrence in the performance of a single, self-initiated task by individuals with diverse, competing responsibilities. Some officers ignore hazardous driving because they want to avoid being "the bad guy" to drivers. They easily use their interest in other police responsibilities to excuse their sloth in traffic enforcement. Whenever departmental leadership directs attention to a single responsibility, enough individuals increase their efforts so that departmental output rises. Then, as new policies and new problems divert attention from a perennial problem, total efforts slacken. The commissioner redirected departmental attention to the city's accident problem several times during his tenure.

Just before the 1980 Christmas season, O'Connor took a different approach to educating department members on the seriousness of traffic injuries. He issued a memo to the whole department comparing the city's injuries and deaths from traffic accidents to the total injuries and deaths from robberies, rapes, assaults, and murders. In Troy, as nationwide, traffic accidents pose twice the danger of crimes in inflicting both injury and death (Rice, MacKenzie, et al. 1989). Between 1971 and 1986 the annual number of homicides in Troy averaged two and never exceeded four, but the number of motor vehicle fatalities had averaged four and even reached nine. Police officers often have a gut feeling that homicides reflect badly upon their city and even on the department. O'Connor tapped this sentiment and channeled it to a problem where police intervention can be effective.

To sum up, just as preventive medicine and health education direct attention to preventive measures, so police departments are more effective as they take a broad view. When citizens call the police, they are identifying pieces of a larger problem. When police and citizens see these pieces in context, they can work toward broad preventive measures. In 1988 the Police Executive Research Forum began publishing a newsletter, *Problem Solving Quarterly*, that circulates brief descriptions of new approaches to specific, commonly occurring problems. As a whole, the police field is ripe for widespread experimentation in ways to identify and solve community problems.

Coping with Crime

While crime fighting, in the sense of effective investigative work resulting in the arrest and conviction of individual offenders, must not be de-emphasized, the current fad of describing local police work as being part of a so-called "war on crime" needs immediate abandonment. Most importantly, it needs to be clearly rejected by the police officers themselves. The analogy between war and crime is inappropriate and dangerous, since it tends to sanction military or wartime tactics in civil, peacetime matters.

George W. O'Connor, 1972

Arrests

The hospital analogy points up the futility of seeking a few simple tactics to eliminate "crime," just as physicians do not seek a few simple medicines that will cure "disease." Wars end, but crime and disease continue. Because crimes include all human acts that have been considered sufficiently harmful or annoying to have been declared illegal, governmental and citizen responses should vary with the specifics of the problem. Yet the search for simple solutions continues, nurtured and promoted by thinking about "crime" as though it were a single specific category of social ills.

How well does a department employ civil, peacetime tactics appropriate to the specific type of crime to achieve high performance in arrest and conviction? The first of these three chapters on coping with crime deals with arrests; the second considers other techniques for solving crime problems; and the last ponders management steps in reducing fear of crime. This chapter starts with the basics of legal arrest procedures and the safety of prisoners, then highlights broad public involvement as that aspect of the hospital model most crucial to excellence in arrest performance. Rather than generalizing about all street crimes, we concentrate on residential burglary, because it is a common crime that leaves some victims feeling vulnerable. In asking questions about departmental performance, we explore the usefulness of arrest rates per 100,000 population and the unreliability of clearance rates. The chapter closes with an examination of the changing patterns of arrests for drunken driving and public intoxication as examples of increased attention to dangerous behavior and decreased attention to annoyances.

Legal Arrests

We begin with a very difficult question: do officers make only legal arrests? An essential characteristic of a free society is that the power of arrest must be exercised within boundaries set by law for probable cause as the grounds for arrest. Vigorous investigations can both identify the guilty and exonerate the innocent. The fearful experiences of people in dictatorships, where the innocent may be seized on the street, should be kept in mind. In Philadelphia in 1980–81 two officers in a decoy unit made a string of illegal arrests, seizing pedestrians, beating them, and charging them with attempted robbery. The court convicted a number of innocent men who were poor and black before the *Philadelphia Inquirer* exposed the scheme, by which the officers had connived to gain prestige and overtime pay. Exposure of such knavery is very rare, both because these illegal arrest schemes are themselves rare and because they are hard to identify.

The usual method for questioning the legality of a department's arrests is to examine all cases the prosecutor decides to drop in order to identify lack of probable cause, illegal entry, illegal searches, and failure to safe-guard prisoners' rights. Unfortunately, the written record is usually silent as to why prosecutors drop cases. Systematic studies of prosecutorial decisions using the Prosecutor's Management Information System (PROMIS) found very few cases dropped because of illegal arrest. The Institute for Law and Social Research (INSLAW) study of 1977 data from six sites found that failure to observe due process in all felony cases taken together accounted for 4 percent of the dismissals in New Orleans down to 0.2 percent in Washington, D.C.; drug cases account for most of the due process rejections (Brosi 1979; U.S. Department of Justice, National Institute of Justice 1982).

In Troy, my examination of records on all 127 adult robbery arrests between 1971 and 1978 and a systematic sample of 113 burglary arrests for the years 1971–72 and 1974–78 found one documented case of false arrest. In the fall of 1978 a new officer responded to a robbery call from a commercial establishment, where witnesses gave him the license number of the getaway car. The officer checked vehicle registration, found the owner's address, went to his house, and immediately arrested the car owner, despite his protests that he had lent his car to a friend. The officer lacked probable cause to place the owner at the scene of the crime, a serious mistake. This false arrest was quickly nullified without coming to the attention of the prosecutor or the media. The actual number of false arrests in a city is very difficult to determine and cannot be measured by the number of lawsuits for false arrest.

A complementary problem appears when one looks at the basis for decisions not to arrest when evidence is present to justify an arrest. Although the myth of full enforcement is not taken seriously within the police field, members are not eager to expose it. Data on 1,500 incidents from the patrol observation study performed in Boston, Chicago, and Washington in 1966 has been analyzed by Friedrich (1980) to show that the likelihood of arrest was increased by the seriousness of the offense, the ungovernability of the offender, the racial prejudice of the officer, the visibility of the incident to the partner, and the visibility of the incident to the department. Five man-years of participant observation of patrol encounters in a midwestern city and two suburbs in 1972 identified some 520 incidents where an alleged offender was present; officers made arrests for 41 of 42 probable felonies, in only 41 of 282 instances of probable misdemeanors, and in none of 146 encounters where information available to the officers indicated that no violation had occurred (Sykes, Fox, and Clark 1976). The Indiana University data on 5,688 police-citizen encounters in 1977 found that arrests occurred in 17 percent (Parks 1982). The likelihood of arrest was predicted by the antagonism of the suspect, the desire of the victim to press charges, and the seriousness of the crime, and to a lesser extent by the presence of bystanders, the suspect's being a stranger to the victim, and the suspect's being black. All the statistically significant variables taken together contributed only slightly to explaining the decisions. Those are the facts of the exercise of discretion, in which officers make their own judgments. The challenge for departmental leadership is to reduce the vindictive decisions and to increase the wise ones.

Proper Treatment of Prisoners

The police are responsible for the physical safety of prisoners until their release or their transfer to a city or county jail. The two paramount threats to the safety of prisoners in police custody are beatings by officers and suicides. However tranquil the circumstances, an arrest is an act of conflict in which the activities of a citizen are interrupted. Officers with a tragic perspective know how to maintain the self-esteem and dignity of the arrestee as well as their own. Some prisoners heap verbal abuse upon the arresting officers, some attempt to flee, and some struggle. Cynical officers frequently see themselves in a personal contest with prisoners and may be tempted to drive home their victory with abuse. A fundamental problem of any police lockup is the lack of importance attached to good care for prisoners. Since the whole orientation of policing is toward the street, work connected with the lockup is seen as peripheral and dull at best. In departments the size of Troy's, the desk officer has responsibility for prisoners in addition to patrol housekeeping and all the walk-in business. In larger departments the special unit running the lockup is often staffed by officers who previously had used excessive force on the street, because commanders view lockup duty as a convenient place to bury those unfit for patrol responsibilities. Department leaders typically do not hire individuals to work specifically in the position of lockup guard, because the police tradition as a corps organization designates officers as generalists who can be freely transferred to any assignment (see Guyot 1979).

In 1973, when Commissioner O'Connor began the redesign of the Troy department's physical plant, he inquired into whether the Rensselaer County Jail would accept prisoners immediately after booking. Upon receiving a refusal, he upgraded the lockup and designed a station entrance for police and prisoners only. The desk officer has specific and detailed responsibility for the safety of prisoners. Abuses that older officers recounted as having occurred in the 1960s apparently did not recur after 1972: prisoners' hands deliberately crushed by the iron cell doors; prisoners stripped in winter and dowsed with hoses. However, in the 1970s a few instances did come to light of officers who beat prisoners before they were placed in cells (see Chapter 8).

The most serious failures of the Troy department to safeguard prisoners were two suicides between 1973 and 1987. Young men arrested for the first time in their lives are particularly at risk. Some, overwhelmed by the disgrace they have brought upon themselves and their families, find ways to hang themselves. New York state figures for 1984 showed 14 suicides and 103 attempts in police lockups outside New York City. The lack of attention to suicides is accented by the contrast with the attention to police shootings, responsible in upstate New York for an average of nine deaths per year between 1981 and 1985 (New York State Commission on Criminal Justice and the Use of Force 1987, 160). Beginning in 1987, however, the state has provided training in suicide prevention, in which the Troy department participates.

A Broad Base of Public Involvement

The likelihood that offenders will be arrested depends upon the quality and timeliness of information that police officers can bring to bear upon specific criminal incidents. To the extent that police management can facilitate the flow of information from citizens to department members and within the department, management can enhance arrest performance. O'Connor (1976, 45) itemized seven executive tasks to upgrade the management of criminal investigation. This list shows systematically how essential citizens' information is to police handling of criminal incidents.

1. Increase the ability of police to become aware of planned criminal events prior to their commission.
2. Enhance the likelihood that police will discover an act in progress or as rapidly as possible after its completion.
3. Increase the likelihood that citizens will report the event to the police.
4. Improve the quality and quantity of information obtained from the victim.
5. Increase the likelihood that witnesses will cooperate by providing information as soon as possible.
6. Assure that physical evidence is discovered, protected, collected, and analyzed.
7. Improve the quality, quantity and likelihood of pertinent information from existing data sources [being] extracted and linked to the particular case.

Such a list drawn up in 1990 would also emphasize grouping similar crime incidents into coherent problems, assessing current approaches to those problems, and developing new approaches.

In 1978 a Troy neighborhood merchant recounted how he provided timely information that the department failed to use.

When we were tipped off that a burglary was going to take place at our business, I called the police and told them what was about to happen. They told me to watch the merchandise and call them when the actual theft occurred, which I did. The police came, took information down quickly, and chased after the thieves. We waited four hours at my business to see if they caught the thieves. They have never so much as contacted us since that incident, which occurred one week ago. I'm completely disgusted with the police on this matter.

A common failing of police departments is to undervalue citizen tips because many are false. Apparently, when the police operator told the merchant to make his own stakeout, he made an instant decision rather than passing the information to the patrol commander for evaluation, notification of officers, and consideration of a police stakeout. Moreover, given the merchant's efforts, the zone officers and any investigators had special responsibility to inform him of the results of their efforts.

When a department is redesigned in accordance with the hospital model, the openness encourages citizen involvement. Lucky timing makes arrests easy.

□ A graduate student out walking on a November morning saw an elderly woman running across a parking lot chasing a teenager wearing a bright blue jacket. Figuring that the teenager had snatched the woman's purse, the student followed him two or three blocks, lost sight of him around a corner, and then caught up with him as he stood in a doorway. The student asked the neighbors who he was, but they did not answer. When the teenager stepped out of the doorway, the student snapped his picture with the camera he happened to be carrying. Meanwhile, the old woman had called the police. As the student left the neighborhood, he saw a police van, told the officers what he knew, and then went on to the station to give his film and a sworn statement. As soon as the officers arrived on the block where the young man was last seen, he quickly came out and surrendered.

This unusual confluence of citizen reporting, good victim information, and witness cooperation should serve to emphasize the importance of each. Not only was this old woman eager to report the purse snatch; she tried chasing the thief. Her information clearly established the facts of the crime. The active cooperation of the graduate student as witness compelled the immediate surrender of the thief.

To solve crimes through follow-up investigation, citizen participation is essential.

□ Just after midnight in deep winter, two young men armed with a shotgun held up the attendant at a Mobil station. A security guard driving home from work caught sight of the fleeing robbers and chased them into the nearby park. Patrol officers immediately stopped all suspicious vehicles and searched the park, finding a shotgun thrown under a log. Sergeant Don Turner of the criminal investigation division became the case investigator, the same man who had been punished fifteen years earlier with a walking post. He had dropped his nastiness to women, long before this, probably because he had scored high enough on the civil service examination to be promoted to sergeant and had then chosen assignments outside of patrol. Sergeant Turner had the shotgun traced by the Bureau of Alcohol, Tobacco and Firearms, which reported within two weeks the 1976 original sale. He persistently tracked the possession of the shotgun, documenting each step with a sworn statement. The purchaser, Mr. Allen, had given it as a gift to his friend, Bob Burnham, for his older son, Charles. For many years Charles had kept the shotgun, but one fall his nineteen-year-old brother, Dave, took it for skeet shooting and left it at the house of his sixteen-year-old friend, Ernie. Because Dave had no money to pay Ernie for some wheels and tires, Dave left the gun as tacit collateral. When Ernie's friend, Frank, proposed a holdup, Ernie provided this weapon. After Sergeant Turner traced the gun to Ernie, his older brother, older sister, and mother, who all had known of the robbery for more than two weeks, obtained a lawyer. Ernie confessed, implicating his nineteen-year-old cousin and Frank. The cousin also confessed, but Frank fled.

Nowhere is voluntary citizen cooperation more evident than in Sergeant Turner's step-by-step tracing of the path of the shotgun. If Mr. Allen or any of the others in the chain had claimed not to know who had the gun, the robbery could not have been solved. Alternatively, the robbery could have been solved much sooner if Ernie's older brother on discovery of the facts had made him confess instead of thrashing him. The incident also illustrates the importance of citizen initiative. If a passerby had not seen and chased the robbers, they would not have stashed their gun. Criminal investigation of this degree of excellence is possible only when citizens have confidence in the department. An as yet untested hypothesis is that the frequency of solving crimes through witness information increases in direct proportion to management's reshaping of a department in accordance with the hospital model.

The great majority of burglaries and robberies are never solved, but the proportion could be reduced by officers' tapping information in the community. Analysis of the National Crime Surveys shows that for 40 percent of assaults, rapes, robberies, and personal thefts combined, the attacker was known to the victim; over 80 percent could estimate the age of the attacker; and over 90 percent recalled the race. Few officers systematically query bystanders for useful information, even though victims recall that a witness was present at 38 percent of the robberies and 63 percent of the assaults (Skogan 1985). In sum, criminal incidents generally fall into one of two categories: those where police officers can quickly learn from citizens the identity of the attacker, and those where sophisticated use of multiple sources of information might identify the attacker. Computers make possible revolutionary advances in criminal identification and crime analysis, as William Spelman's booklet *Beyond Bean Counting* (1987) shows in discussing the advantages of the new national crime reporting system.

Arrest Performance

The requirement of a report for every crime investigated and every arrest but not for other social ills places immense emphasis on crime. Naturally, reports are necessary as part of the information flow that can lead to the solution of crimes, but they give importance to the trivial, such as the taking of a bag of lollipops from a parking lot kiosk. By contrast, police officers do not write reports on assistance, even if it resolves a five-year neighborhood feud. Reliance on a few measures directs effort away from the unmeasured aspects of police work. Multiple performance measures that rely on citizen feedback, such as consumer surveys, are necessary to counterbalance the specific, narrow focus on arrest statistics.

The public consensus that crime is an important police responsibility gives reason to develop performance measures for arrest that can replace crude and false measures previously in use. Arrest statistics can serve as an appropriate basis for measuring performance, if they are used with due caution. At minimum, such a measure should allow valid comparison of a department's current achievements with its past record. The statistics used should (1) concern serious crimes for which police departments have primary investigative responsibility, (2) be easily available, (3) be reasonably accurate, and (4) be sufficiently precise as to type of crime. Such a performance measure implies that the least dangerous adult should be arrested for committing any offense within the crime category. Through a democratic process the citizens of a locality should determine which crimes they regard as sufficiently serious to be the basis for performance measures. Here I draw on a national opinion survey based on Marvin Wolfgang's concepts of severity (Bureau of Justice Statistics 1985c) to select homicide, rape, robbery, and burglary.

National and departmental arrest data and crime incidence data have been available since 1930, when the International Association of Chiefs of Police and 400 departments began to compile the Uniform Crime Reports (UCR), published annually by the FBI as *Crime in the United States*. Doubt about the accuracy of arrest statistics has been cast by a 1982 study from the Congressional Office of Technology Assessment, by a 1983 state audit in Missouri, and a 1984 Police Foundation study of four diverse departments (Bureau of Justice Statistics, 1985b). The Police Foundation study concluded that inaccuracies and ease of falsification rendered arrest statistics inappropriate for evaluating departmental performance; my reanalysis of the data, however, shows that the errors cancel each other out for homicide, rape, robbery, and burglary but are cumulative for aggravated assault. Departments *can* assure accuracy, as does the St. Louis PD, which routinely employs an auditing firm to check its crime and arrest statistics. An appropriate level of precision requires making distinctions among types of crimes at least as fine as the traditional UCR categories. If arrests for all felonies are added together, assaults are jumbled with homicides to create needless imprecision.

All varieties of arrest statistics should be used as internal management feedback to help direct departmental priorities (such as a crackdown on drunken drivers), to spot trends in neighborhood problems (such as vandalism), and to distinguish active patrol squads. Feedback to management is quite different from a performance measure held up for public scrutiny, because management can unobtrusively examine patterns in complex and sophisticated ways, whereas articulated performance measures will tend to redirect effort toward activities that are measured at the expense of effort toward unmeasured goals.

Performance in Burglary Arrests

The development and application of a performance measure for burglary arrests illustrates what is required for a performance measure suitable for police work. First, the UCR definition is clear: a burglary arrest is one in which the most serious charge is a completed or attempted entry into a building with the intent of committing a crime. Arrest statistics count only one arrest per prisoner, no matter how many criminal charges are brought simultaneously. When a police department increases its burglary arrests from around 60 a year in the early 1970s to 150 a year in 1977, as the Troy department did, it is obviously doing better. We begin simply with Figure 5-1, the trend in total burglary arrests, based on Troy's data sent to the Uniform Crime Reports. Many departments fail to use this simple comparison of performance over time, because they lump together all felony arrests.

Second, every performance measure established must include safeguards on the legality and appropriateness of arrests. A departmental measure should never be transmitted to individual officers as a quota. Some of the conniving in illegal arrests and the distortion of police work encouraged by individual arrest performance measures have been detailed by Rubinstein (1973) for Philadelphia. Less serious abuses in overcharging, such as third-degree burglary instead of criminal trespass, are

Number of
arrests

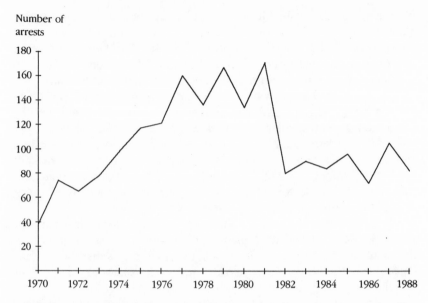

Source: Annual departmental reports to the Uniform Crime Reports, giving the total number of adult and juvenile arrests.

Figure 5-1 Trends in Burglary Arrests in Troy, 1970–88

committed routinely by some officers in some departments. A crucial step in maintaining arrest performance measures is to receive feedback from prosecutors, public defenders, trial lawyers, and judges on their knowledge of any illegal arrests or of any overcharging.

Third, beyond the basic contrast of present and past performance is comparison outside the department, most appropriately with national averages. The raw number of arrests is converted into a rate per 100,000 population, then the published UCR data facilitate comparison with the national average, which in 1988 was 176 burglary arrests per 100,000 population, and also with averages for cities of various sizes, 207 for cities of 50,000–100,000 population.

A drawback in making arrest comparisons, for which there is no easy remedy, is that burglary arrests should be compared to the number of active burglars. A city might have far more burglars than the national average and thus need no particular competence to reach an arrest rate of 176 per 100,000. Alternatively, a city might have few burglars and thus really be twice as productive as the typical department in reaching the average rate of arrest. Knowledge of a city's demographics, both the distribution of poverty and the size of the crime-prone cohort, helps one estimate whether or not a city's burglary experience is atypical.

Two Methods of Estimating Crime Rates

It is appropriate here to take stock of the current methods for estimating the prevalence of crimes in order to lay the foundation for discussion in this and the next two chapters of false performance measures. The most reliable estimate of how many burglaries occur in the United States is that for every 1,000 homes about 46 successful burglaries and some 14 attempts take place each year; in 1987 national crime victimization surveys estimated that a total of 5,623,000 household burglaries occurred. Similar estimates for stores, public buildings, churches, and other nonresidential buildings were last made in 1976, when approximately 160 successful burglaries and 50 attempts were occurring annually for every 1,000 buildings, to yield a total of 1,575,000 nonresidential burglaries. *Criminal Victimization in the United States* (see Bureau of Justice Statistics 1990), contains annual estimates from the National Crime Survey. Conducted by the Census Bureau, the survey asks all residents aged twelve and up in about 60,000 households about their experiences with crimes of violence and theft during the previous six months, and each household is surveyed again at six-month intervals for three years. Criminologists knowledgeable in survey research believe that the national surveys *underestimate* by varying amounts the occurrence of crimes.

Striking differences emerge when the victimization estimate of the annual occurrence of residential burglary is compared with the Uniform Crime Reports estimate (see Skogan 1975). Far below the 1987 victimization estimate of 5,623,000, the UCR figure for residential burglary was only 2,190,000. This is the total number of residential burglaries officially known to over 12,000 participating police agencies, plus an estimate for the 4 percent of the population not covered. Figure 5-2 shows that the victimization surveys in the 1970s and 1980s consistently estimated three times as many residential burglaries as were reported to the UCR.

Inexplicably, newspapers and political leaders still discuss data from the UCR as though it accurately measures how much crime has occurred. References in this book to crime rates based on the Uniform Crime Reports use the term "reported crime rates" to emphasize the dependence of this measure on citizen initiative in reporting to the police. The gaps between victimization estimates and UCR data exist primarily because citizens do not bother to report many incidents to the local police and secondarily because police departments fail to record accurately all citizen reports. If a police department succeeds in encouraging citizens to report burglaries, the UCR makes the city appear crime-ridden. The most reasonable explanation of the victimization survey drop in burglary rates between 1981 and 1984 is that there was a substantial drop in the size of the cohort in the burglary-prone ages, fifteen to eighteen. The fact that

Number of burglaries
in millions

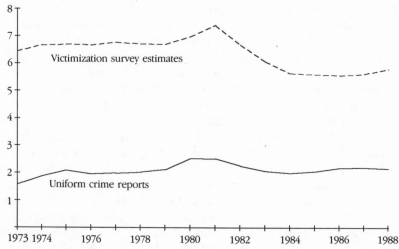

Sources: *Criminal Victimization in the United States*, issued by the Bureau of Justice Statistics; Uniform Crime Reports, *Crime in the United States*, issued by the FBI.

Figure 5-2 Victimization Surveys and Uniform Crime Reports Showing National Trends in Residential Burglary

the UCR figures remained steadier through 1988 was probably due to increased police encouragement of citizen reporting and to greater accuracy of police records through the use of computers.

The UCR's gross undercount of the occurrence of burglary is repeated for most crimes covered by the victimization surveys. Table 5-1 places burglary in context by also showing vehicle theft as an example of a well-reported type of crime and larceny as an example of a poorly reported type. Note that the victimization survey estimate in the first row and the UCR count in the second are fairly close for motor vehicle theft, further apart for burglary, and highly discrepant for larceny. Comparison between the second and third rows reveals how close the two sources are after the percentage of crimes reported is taken into account. A victim's hope of recovering the car or at least receiving insurance compensation is a practical reason why 71 percent of motor vehicle thefts are reported. For larceny, the minor value of most items stolen may explain the low 27 percent. This table demonstrates that the number of crimes recorded in the UCR depends upon citizen reporting rates.

A victimization survey of a neighborhood, city, or metropolitan area is a valuable tool for estimating the incidence of crime but is rarely conducted because of the expense involved. The few such surveys available disclose local variations in reporting burglary to the police ranging from

Table 5-1   Effect of Percentage of Victims Who Report Crimes on Number of Crimes Known to Police (U.S. 1985, incidents in 1,000s)

	Noncommercial Motor Vehicle Theft	Residential Burglary	Personal and Household Larceny
Number of incidents estimated by National Crime Survey[a]	1,270	5,594	21,653
Number of incidents officially reported to UCR[b]	970	2,050	5,887
Estimated number of incidents reported to the police calculated from the National Crime Survey[c]	897	2,780	5,842
Percentage of victims saying they reported the crime, National Crime Survey[a]	71%	50%	27%

Note: The UCR and the National Crime Survey use slightly different crime categories. Because the survey has no current data on crimes against commercial targets, I have made the following estimates to exclude them. For vehicle theft, the UCR reports that 24 percent of the targets are trucks, pickup trucks, and buses, one-half of which are assumed to be commercial vehicles and have thus been excluded. For burglary, no upward adjustment has been made in the UCR figure by estimating burglary of detached household garages, which the UCR considers nonresidential and the survey considers residential. For larceny, the 15 percent that are shoplifting and theft from coin operated machines have been excluded; no downward adjustment has been made for theft from commercial buildings or vehicles.
[a]Bureau of Justice Statistics 1987c.
[b]FBI 1986.
[c]Computed by multiplying number of incidents in first row by percentage in last row.

below 42 percent to over 70 percent, as shown in Table 5-2. Consistently, suburbs have higher reporting rates than central cities. The 70 percent rate for Troy should be taken as a rough estimate of an actual rate quite likely to be at least 62 percent. Given the disarray of the department in the early 1970s, Troy's reporting rate then was probably below the national average, and the rise to 1978 was probably as large as in Portland, where positive citizen assessment of police service and two years of citizen participation in crime prevention efforts increased the rate of reporting burglaries from 50 percent to 70 percent. The authors of the Toronto study attribute that city's high reporting rate of 62 percent to a general civic consciousness and the fine reputation of the police department. Caution should be exercised in making these comparisons, because the various surveys use modest samples and employ somewhat divergent survey methods. The diversity among locations is averaged into the remarkably steady national rates of reporting burglary.

Clearance Rates as False Measures of Departmental Effectiveness

One conclusion to draw from the great variability in citizens' crime-reporting rates is that the Uniform Crime Reports are an unreliable basis for estimating the prevalence of crimes. Unfortunately, police rely on UCR statistics as the base for their standard performance measure, the

Table 5-2   Rates of Reporting Residential Burglary to Police

Location	Reporting Rate	Year of Survey	Number of Burglaries in Sample	Researchers
Troy	70%	1977–78	101	Guyot
U.S.A	47	1973	5,600	NCS
U.S.A	49	1975	5,500	NCS
U.S.A	49	1977	5,300	NCS
U.S.A	48	1979	5,000	NCS
U.S.A	51	1981	5,300	NCS
U.S.A	49	1983	4,200	NCS
U.S.A	50	1985	3,800	NCS
U.S.A	52	1987	3,000	NCS
Minneapolis–St. Paul	42	1971	95	Reynolds
Minneapolis suburb	56	1971	16	
London: Brixton	48	1973	11	Sparks, Genn, and Dodd
London: Hackney	55	1973	20	Sparks, Genn, and Dodd
London: Kensington	60	1973	29	Sparks, Genn, and Doss
Metro Toronto	62	1973	116	Waller and Okihiro
Portland, Ore.	50	1972	1,525	NCS
Portland, Ore.	70	1974	500	NCS and Schneider (after $10,000,000 crime campaign)
Washington, D.C.	64	1982–83	68	NCS
D.C. suburbs	74	1982–83	105	NCS

Sources: Waller and Okihiro (1978, 20) provided their own data on Toronto and summarized the findings of Reyonds from Minneapolis and of Sparks, Genn, and Dodd from London. The NCS (National Crime Survey) data are from Bureau of Justice Statistics, *Criminal Victimization in the United States* (published annually); Bureau of Justice Statistics 1985a; and Schneider 1976.

clearance rate. To compute a department's annual clearance rate for burglary or any crime category, one divides the number of cases solved that year (regardless of when the crime occurred) by the number of cases reported to the police that year. Clearance rates by crime category have utility when applied to investigative units, provided they include only cases *cleared by arrest* and are computed as a proportion of cases assigned to the unit.

At the department level, however, clearance rates are totally inappropriate. A glance at Figure 5-3 shows Troy's 150 percent increase in the number of burglary arrests per 100,000 population between 1972 and 1977 while the clearance rate, as shown by the dashed line, inched up from 11 percent to 22 percent in 1979 but dropped back to around 10 percent for most of the 1980s. The reason the clearance rate did not soar during 1973–77 with the increase in arrests is that the department energetically solicited burglary reports from citizens and made departmental records accurate, thus augmenting the base against which clearances are measured. Troy's performance may be compared with the national average for cities of similar size: the city's arrest rate for burglary rose from less than half the national average to roughly even by 1977, remained there for five years, and then in 1982 dropped to about three-fourths of the national level. The misleading nature of the clearance rate is shown in the 1980s, when arrests were consistently higher than before departmental upgrading but clearance rates were about the same.

Organizational Changes to Facilitate Burglary Arrests

To explain the 1973–78 increases in Troy's burglary arrests, we first sort the cases by the circumstances of the arrest: by patrol initiative, by patrol in response to a citizen's call, by detectives after a short follow-up investigation, and on a warrant after longer follow-up investigation. Figure 5-4 shows arrests of adults, defined by New York state law as individuals aged

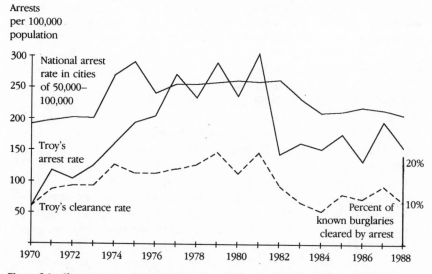

Figure 5-3 Changes in Troy's Burglary Arrests and Clearance Rates Compared with National Averages

sixteen and above. Youths are excluded, despite their prominence, because of inaccuracies in the department records, a common problem stemming from the legal requirement that juvenile records be kept separate from adult records. The figure shows that from a 1971–72 baseline, growth first took place through patrol initiative, then from 1975 through patrol-citizen cooperation, and after 1976 through warrants and detective work. The 1972 increases in officers discovering burglaries in progress can be attributed to the early upgrading of patrol operations: consistency in assignments, the new radio system, crime analysis to pinpoint geographic patterns, and patrol officers' occasional use of unmarked cars. For example, a steady zone assignment enabled Officer Sam Griffith to use his knowledge that a house was vacant for remodeling to suspect that two men he glimpsed in the back yard were either relieving themselves or about to break in.

Next came improvements from citizens calling the police, shown in Figure 5-4 to account for at least half the arrests from 1975 through 1978. Widespread citizen confidence in the police was well documented by the 1978 residential survey. First, among citizens who considered that a serious crime had recently occurred in their neighborhood, 84 percent recalled that the police had come, and 83 percent believed that the police did all they could. On the negative side, 7 percent believed that the officers did not do all they could, 2 percent said the police never came, and 7 percent did not know whether or not the police had come. Second, when citizens were posed a hypothetical situation, "Suppose you reported a crime to the police," over 80 percent said that the police would believe their account and would try to solve the crime. Third, among citizens who had actually seen a crime occurring or observed a suspicious incident, two-thirds of them notified the police. Fourth, about 13 percent of the citizens recalled that in the previous year an officer had asked them for information about some trouble that had just happened. Of these 84 percent said they gave information, 13 percent had none to give, and only 3 percent admitted to giving partial information. None said they refused information.

Police departments are generally not pushing against the limits on citizens' willingness to provide information for follow-up investigations; rather, they fail to solicit and use it. In 1977 the Troy department adopted systematic techniques of managing criminal investigation, including formal case screening using solvability factors, rather than assigning all unsolved cases to investigators. This managerial change stimulated a marked increase over all previous years in quick follow-up investigations and longer ones that required an arrest warrant. However, follow-up in 1977 accounted for only 30 percent of the burglary arrests and only 40 percent of the robbery arrests. These investigative results can be compared with 1980 data for DeKalb County, Georgia, where the follow-up

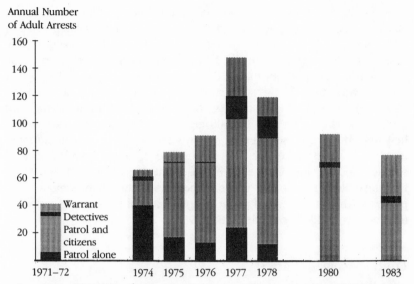

Annual Number
of Adult Arrests

Sources: Arrest and incident reports in files of Troy Police Department. Warrants resulted from cooperation by detectives and patrol. The totals are accurate, and the estimate of arrests from each source is based on sampling. For 1971–72 and 1977–78 the samples are full counts. For 1974–76 one-third of the cases were sampled. Estimates for 1980 and 1983 are based on full counts for April through September. In 1983 no distinction is made between arrests by patrol alone and with citizen assistance.

Figure 5-4   Sources of Adult Burglary Arrests

accounted for 61 percent of the burglary and 74 percent of the robbery arrests; to St. Petersburg, Florida where follow-up achieved 47 percent and 56 percent; and to Wichita, Kansas, where follow-up with team policing accounted for 40 percent and 41 percent (Eck 1983, 205, 208).

Because O'Connor considered residential burglary the city's most serious crime problem, he established a burglary squad in January 1985, which had responsibility for follow-up investigation. A letter over the commissioner's signature gave each victim the name of the investigator assigned to the case and asked for an evaluation of the quality of service the citizen had already received from the patrol officer and the evidence technician. In the previous year, investigators had made arrests in only 27 cases; in 1985 the two squad investigators made arrests in 41 cases. Nevertheless, when the discouraging nature of burglary investigation became onerous because the investigators had no easy crimes to solve, (such as aggravated assaults), the commissioner agreed to their request to return to the generalist method, in which each investigator carries a mix of cases. The number of burglaries solved in 1986 through follow-up investigation dropped back to 29.

O'Connor holds the view that any crime is solvable—if enough effort is expended. He gives the example of a kidnapping and murder on Long Island in the 1950s, where a major clue was the handwritten ransom note. Since the FBI had reason to believe that the murderer lived in New York state, they went manually through the files of applications for drivers' licenses until they matched the handwriting. The corollary is that it is not worth the effort to solve most crimes. The 1987 national victimization survey estimates that there were more than eight million thefts of under $50, as compared to 140,000 rapes and 700,000 robberies. As the first step in formal case screening, Troy's incident report form, adopted in 1985, provides places for the patrol officer to judge both the ease of solution and the importance of the case. The 1983 report of the Police Executive Research Forum recommends systematic management techniques for investigation and the adoption of a problem-solving approach that focuses on likely offenders (Eck 1983).

Court Outcomes of Arrest

Good police work can bring up the conviction rate by providing firm evidence to establish that a crime occurred and to link the accused to the crime. Groundbreaking studies produced by the Institute for Law and Social Research (INSLAW) show that the quality of arrests influences the conviction rate (Forst, Lucianovic, and Cox 1977; Brosi 1979). A RAND study of Los Angeles county found that departments using arrest statistics to evaluate officers' performance had lower conviction rates, presumably because the reward for the number of arrests motivated some officers to neglect quality (Petersilia, Abrahamse, and Wilson 1987). In studying the performance of a police department, one can look at the court outcomes to see whether conviction rates rise, with the caveat that a prosecutor's decisions are influenced by his or her case load and the seriousness of the crimes: was the entry by force? was the burglar armed? was this the suspect's first offense? Because prosecutors, also called district attorneys, generally regard a high conviction rate as the prime measure of *their* performance, they tend to offer plea bargains on well-prepared cases to obtain a sure conviction in misdemeanor court rather than chance a conviction on heavier charges in felony court. The adequacy of prosecutorial staffing for additional investigation and the availability of judges influence the proportion of cases a prosecutor brings to felony court, where time demands are great.

In order to achieve convictions, street officers must conduct their work with an eye to building strong court cases. Sergeant Sam Griffith explained how he teaches probable cause to the officers in his squad.

It is like building a bridge to Green Island. Sure you want to get to Green Island, but you don't want to plunge into the river and get back all wet and dirty with your prisoner. You want to take your time and step by step build a bridge called probable cause that will take you over there and that will carry the weight of your prisoner when you bring him back. Suppose you know that a burglary has just been reported nearby and you see a man who is moving suspiciously. When you get close, you recognize he has been arrested before for burglary. You ask him to stop for questioning. You have the authority to pat him down, and suppose you find a bulge in his pocket. Because it might be a weapon, you have authority to go into his pocket. Then you find women's jewelry. You hold him so that the burglary victim can identify the pieces. Step by step, you have constructed a bridge called probable cause, and you can reconstruct it for the DA.

The Troy department's investigative quality can be compared with two of the INSLAW findings, that the presence of physical evidence and the availability of witnesses result in higher conviction rates. The Troy records from 1975–78 show that the majority of convictions followed on-scene arrests where no physical evidence was gathered. What the evidence technician program accomplished was to investigate almost all burglaries where there was no immediate suspect, to find conclusive evidence in a few cases, and thus to bring about a few arrests in cases that otherwise would have remained unsolved.

The pattern of witnesses, which can be pieced together for about half the sample of burglary cases, shows a marked rise. In 1971–72, burglary convictions in the felony and misdemeanor courts combined took place with an average of only 0.4 witnesses for every conviction; in 1974–78 average per conviction was about 0.9. Robbery arrests showed a larger increase. For every conviction there were 0.8 witnesses in 1971–72, 1 in 1974–75, and 2.1 in 1977–78. In sum, during the first five years of upgrading, the records show modest improvements in the quality of criminal investigation.

The court outcomes are shown in Figure 5-5, the first bar for each year representing the cases decided by misdemeanor court and the second bar representing cases decided in felony court. The portion of a bar above the baseline represents the number of prosecutorial successes, and the portion below represents the dismissals and acquittals. After the initiation of police department upgrading, more cases went to both courts. The proportion of arrests carried to felony court rose from about 15 percent in 1971–72 to about 30 percent in 1974–76. However, when 1977 brought a large increase in arrests, the prosecutor chose to handle his expanded case load in misdemeanor court, where convictions are more quickly and easily obtained. In the two courts combined, the proportion of arrests ending in conviction hovered steadily between 87 percent and 97 percent.

Number
of Cases Won

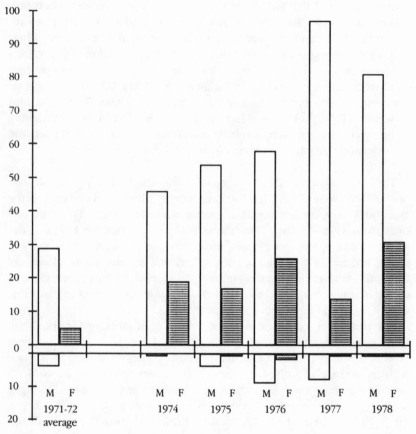

Note: For each year, the first bar represents cases decided in misdemeanor court (M), and the second bar represents cases in felony court (F). The portion of a bar above the base line represents cases the prosecutor won: conviction, conditional discharge, and adjournment in contemplation of dismissal. The portion below the line represents the prosecutor's losses: dismissal and acquittal. The sampling is the same as for Figure 5-4.

Figure 5-5 Adult Burglary Arrests That the Prosecutor Won and Lost in Misdemeanor and Felony Courts

Reasonable performance measures for police-prosecutor collaboration are the proportion of arrests for burglary, robbery, and selected other serious crimes that end in conviction. Present performance many be judged against past performance. The systematic study by INSLAW of six jurisdictions shows a range of 53 to 100 percent of burglary cases sent to felony court, and shows felony convictions as a percentage of arrests ranging from 33 to 78 percent (Brosi 1979, 139,142). Because the study does not cover outcomes at the misdemeanor courts, it does not provide a basis for comparison with jurisdictions like Troy, where the prosecutor handles most burglaries as misdemeanors. In comparison across jurisdictions, the working style of the prosecutor and the size of his staff may have as much influence on conviction rates as the excellence of case preparation by the police.

A closer look at the convicted burglars in Troy provides some explanation of why only one-fourth of the burglary cases went to felony court and why over 40 percent of those convicted received probation, both before and during upgrading: 60 percent of the adults arrested for burglary were between the ages of sixteen and nineteen and hence received lenient treatment. The second Troy consistency is that the prosecutor dropped less than 5 percent of the cases, quite different from the patterns in six other jurisdictions, where between 10 and 28 percent were dropped (Brosi 1979, 142).

Using the Hospital Model to Produce New Patterns of Arrest

When a police manager rebuilds a department, he guides and supports police officers to use arrest as one of several means of addressing problems more effectively. The rates of arrest for criminal attacks on persons and property may rise while other arrest rates fall. Two examples will illustrate why overall arrest rates and even overall felony arrest rates are inappropriate as performance measures.

First, the use of illegal drugs has been a major national social, criminal, and medical problem for three decades, but the vast majority of municipal police departments are not well equipped to detect and arrest the importers, manufacturers, wholesale dealers, and large-scale distributors. In 1982 Commissioner O'Connor drafted an internal memo on the twelve months' work of the department's Special Operations Section, finding that it had made about 27 of the department's 66 narcotics arrests.

- The quantities of controlled substances confiscated during the period were approximately five pounds and 30 ounces of marijuana, plus 18 cases with "small quantity" reported. . . . Small quantities of hash, pills, and other unspecified drugs were also recovered.
- The sentences upon court disposition in the [27] cases reported produced $875 in fines, 330 man/days of county jail time, and 300 man/hours of community service time. . . .
- I estimate that the cost of operations of the unit for the period was in excess of $150,000, and that approximately 9,100 man hours of duty time were expended. . . . It appears that:

- Each arrest took 260 man hours or 6.5 weeks.
- Each arrest cost $4,285.
- The marijuana cost $18,750 per pound.

The conclusion which I come to is that the unit's influence upon the drug traffic is nil. It seems apparent that in terms of our interrupting, interfering with, or inconveniencing drug dealers, our operation represents no significant threat. . . . Unless or until we develop some sophisticated undercover operation staffed by members not known within the city, we are simply wasting our time.

It is imperative that some pressure be maintained on the drug business within the city. It seems to me that we must call more upon the outside agencies, such as the state police. Perhaps our role might better be defined as developing a single officer to gather data and to serve as liaison with outside agencies which have the resources and anonymity to carry out the extended and complex investigations required in this field.

If a municipal department worked effectively against narcotics traffickers, it would arrest those most deeply involved, but they would be barely visible in that city's annual count of all drug arrests. The easiest way for a department to produce a higher volume of drug arrests is to go after the marijuana users. The UCR consistently reports that three-quarters of all drug arrests by local police are for possession and that possession of marijuana continues to be the largest arrest category, 35 percent of all drug arrests in 1988. In O'Connor's view, law enforcement sanctions should be applied to the drug dealers, but users are more effectively reached through a combination of law enforcements cutting the supply and other agencies' using social, educational, and medical techniques to diminish the demand. Hence, Troy's rate of arrest for drug offenses was consistently about one-third the national rate for cities of its size. Nationally, by the close of the 1980s the failure of traditional law enforcement methods to cope with drug problems had resulted in federal funding to five large police departments to experiment with problem-oriented approaches (PERF 1989).

The second example is the use of arrest in tackling a pair of problems produced by the consumption of alcohol: driving while intoxicated (DWI) and disorderly behavior in public places. The changes in Troy's arrest rate were like changes across the country, but they occurred at a faster pace. Officer Don Turner told of former practices in dealing with drunken drivers.

Back in the late 1960s the department did not look seriously at DWI. Once I had the wheel and stopped a DWI, but the senior man who was my partner let him go with a warning. The driver pulled away before we did, and as we were leaving we heard from the radio about a traffic accident ahead. The DWI had smashed three cars. Another time my partner let the DWI go, and in a couple of blocks he had smashed into a telephone pole. The third time I was alone, and the DWI pleaded, "Let me just go the two blocks to get home." I did, and he wrecked up. I sized up my actions—the same mistake three times—and never repeated it.

The solid, jagged line rising sharply after 1972 in Figure 5-6 shows the departmental increase in DWI arrests, which reach a plateau in the late 1970s. The steadier national increase is shown by a dashed line. The descending lines for both Troy and the nation are arrests for disorderly behavior of all types, mostly involving intoxicated people. The trends are consistent with the new view that drunkenness is a mortal danger in a driver but a mere annoyance in a pedestrian. This orientation is captured by a performance question: "Does the department make more arrests for drunken driving than for disorderly behavior?"

Up to this point the discussion has dealt with arrests intended to bring an individual before a court to determine guilt or innocence and to impose an appropriate punishment on the guilty. However, a large propor-

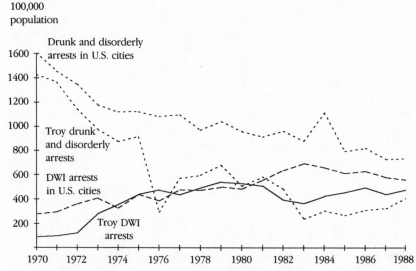

Sources: Uniform Crime Reports and New York State Division of Criminal Justice Services. Drunk and disorderly arrests include public intoxication, disorderly conduct, vagrancy, loitering, and curfew violations. Driving while intoxicated (DWI) also includes driving under the influence of drugs. U.S. cities shown here have populations between 50,000 and 100,000.

Figure 5-6 All Arrests for Disorderly Behavior Compared with Arrests for Driving while Intoxicated (DWI)

tion of arrests are not apprehensions of individuals to be brought to trial; rather, they are interruptions of rowdy or disturbing situations or even the provision of overnight safety in a lockup. These arrests—for public intoxication, disorderly conduct, loitering, vagrancy, and (among youths) curfew violations—may be considered together because the behaviors cited are largely overlapping, and the charge "disorderly conduct" is very broad. Officers with a tragic perspective often devise better solutions to street disorders than a night in the police lockup. Officers with a cynical perspective do not lock up all rowdy people they encounter but concentrate on those who "fail the attitude test": that is, citizens who fail to show them deference. Goldstein (1990, 134–38) argues persuasively that patterns of arrest not leading to prosecution indicate a need for police to find alternatives.

In 1970, arrests for these five types of disturbing behavior totaled 36 percent of the arrests in all cities, 34 percent of the arrests in all American cities of 50,000 to 100,000, and 43 percent of the arrests in Troy. A long-term national decline has been due in part to decisions by state legislatures and the Supreme Court. State after state has removed public intoxication from the penal code in the recognition that jail terms do not solve these social, psychological, and medical problems. In 1970 public intoxication was the charge placed for 25 percent of all criminal arrests by municipal police departments. Nationally, the proportion plunged to 15 percent in 1975 and continued downward to 11 percent in 1980 and 6 percent in 1988. Impelled by a series of Supreme Court decisions, arrests for vagrancy, curfew, violation, and loitering dropped to 3 percent of the total in 1970 and to less than 1 percent in 1988.

A fascinating aspect of the downward trends is that police departments actually changed their street practices. Police officers, squad sergeants, precinct captains, patrol commanders, and police executives all could have compensated for the repeal of any statute by using the broad and vague laws forbidding disorderly conduct. Instead, officers made millions of decisions not to arrest, and so the decline continued. Figure 5-6 shows that in cities of 50,000 to 100,000 all arrests for disturbances fell from 1,750 per 100,000 in 1970 to 735 in 1988, to merely 14 percent of the total.

The rate of Troy's arrests for disorderly behavior also fell precipitously between 1970 and 1976, from 1,427 per 100,000 population to only 293. New York state's removal of public intoxication from the penal code, effective in 1976, accounts for the first low point in the Troy curve. The rate rose to around 600 for the next five years and then returned to 300 (a rise and fall further explained in Chapter 8). In the 1980s the Emergency Medical Service that Commissioner O'Connor established within Troy's fire department picked up about 250 alcoholics a year. By 1986, disorderly situations accounted for only 9 percent of Troy's arrests, less than one-fifth of the proportion in 1970. This drop was in line with O'Connor's preference that officers use their discretion in resolving disorderly situations, employing a wide variety of techniques of which arrest is only one.

In sum, arrest is one of the tools that police officers use in dealing with a wide range of problems, from serious predatory crime to minor disorders. As criminologists develop better understanding of the influences of social and economic factors on the occurrence of different types of serious crime, arrest performance measures can be compared against estimates of actual crime rates quite apart from the rates known to the police. Cautious use of arrest statistics as performance measures should not degenerate into the numbers game once played in the precincts of large cities: "Who made the most felony arrests?" Many factors must be considered in answering the question, "Is the department making arrests for each type of serious crime at rates as high as should be expected?"

It is not rational to expect reported crime to decrease in Troy. . . . As we build ever stronger ties to the citizens we serve, their confidence will grow. With that growth come additional requests for help—requests which three or four years ago would not have been made. We understand that we do not generate crime but can respond to it. We do not consider ourselves solely responsible for the incidence of crime just as physicians do not take the "blame" for disease. We, like the physicians, will work to detect and arrest that condition which diminishes the citizens' well-being.

George W. O'Connor, 1975

Solving Crime Problems

Concerted efforts of police and citizens may not reduce crimes to levels considered acceptable. When citizens perceive that crime is not being kept within reasonable bounds, many blame the police or the courts rather than looking further to underlying social changes, such as the dwindling demand for unskilled labor, which has shaped a class of the perpetually unemployed. Neither citizens nor political leaders have reasoned standards of how much of what sort of crime is acceptable. Even if a city achieves a remarkable reduction in the prevalence of muggings, how can city officials hold a ribbon-cutting ceremony? Each police department when issuing the city's crime statistics can be held to a false standard, a measure of how many crimes the police have failed to prevent.

The chapter begins by explaining why reported crime rates are counterproductive as measures of police performance. The heart of the chapter concerns police and citizen efforts to reduce the incidence of crimes and minimize the harm inflicted by them. These endeavors may be grouped into four major categories:

1. dealing specifically with the individual offender;
2. dealing generally with the factors that dispose some people to commit some types of crimes;
3. dealing generally with the factors that make victims and their property easy targets;
4. dealing specifically with the individual victim.

The preceding chapter demonstrated the essential role of citizens in arresting individual offenders. Here we examine other efforts in Troy to increase the security and safety of citizens.

The Crime Index as a False Performance Measure

Despite sustained efforts by police and episodic efforts by citizens, predatory attacks recur. Old ladies are knocked over for their purses; homes are ransacked. Police frustration over high crime rates is the more keenly felt because the news media often judge police departments by a false standard, the Crime Index. This UCR summary figure, which is often uncritically considered to represent the actual number of serious crimes that occurred during a year, in fact is dominated by trivial crimes. The index adds the number of murders, rapes, robberies, aggravated assaults, burglaries, larcenies, and motor vehicle thefts, known as Part I crimes (the Part II category includes all other crimes). In 1988 the national Crime Index stood at 13,923,000. The index is so dominated by larcenies, with 7,705,900 reported, that if citizens could be persuaded to increase their rate of reporting larceny from the current level of about 27 percent of the time to about 70 percent, the Crime Index would double. Yet if a murder wave were to sweep the nation which raised the number of murders by a factor of ten, from the 1988 level of 20,675 to 206,750, the index would creep up by only 1 percent.

Since the Crime Index does include extremely serious street crimes, J. Edgar Hoover, during his long tenure as FBI director, succeeded in making it a symbol of national degeneration. To avoid the appearance of failure, some police leaders have resorted to underreporting their local statistics. In Newark, New Jersey, ever since street crime became a political issue in 1958, the Crime Index has paused six times in its upward rise. Each of these pauses occurred during the year immediately preceding municipal elections (Guyot 1983). A very different phenomenon results when a professional police manager takes charge of a department that has fallen behind the times. In 1960 the country's foremost police administrator, O. W. Wilson, took charge of the corrupt and inept Chicago PD, and Clarence Kelley retired from the FBI to clean up the Kansas City department. Between 1959 and 1961 Chicago's UCR rate of burglaries per 100,000 rose from 461 to 1,111, Kansas City's from 361 to 1264.

Table 6-1 shows the number of Part I crimes that Troy reported from 1970 through 1988. Note the rise in the Crime Index from 1972 to 1974. This particular surge in reported crimes had damaging consequences in contributing to a climate of fear, which is examined in the next chapter. If anyone living in Troy in 1975 doubted that crime was increasing dangerously, the doubling of the index appeared to provide proof. Given an increase of such magnitude, people look to lay blame—and find the police.

The assumption that the more the Crime Index goes up, the less crime the police have prevented rests on three false premises. First, holding police solely responsible for fluctuations in actual crime rates disregards societal influences, such as the size of the crime-prone age group and the unemployment rate, over which they have no control. Second, it is assumed that citizens report a constant percentage of crimes. Third, it is assumed that police departments record all crimes known to them: specifically, that all patrol officers write crime reports at every opportunity and that records room personnel resist all easy tricks to hide the occurrence of crimes.

The first step in understanding changes in a city's Crime Index is to look at changes in composition. Between 1972 and 1974 we see that the rise is concentrated in burglary and larceny. Commissioner O'Connor assessed the increases in a February 1975 special report to the city manager intended for public dissemination.

Were such measures to be accepted as being the full and complete measure of the extent to which Trojans pilfered from one another, it would signal a deterioration of the moral fiber of the community un-

Table 6-1 Reported Part I Crimes in Troy

	1970	1971	1972	1973	1974	1975	1976	1977	1978	1979	1980	1981	1982	1983	1984	1985	1986	1987	1988
Murder and nonnegligent manslaughter	3	0	0	3	2	4	3	0	1	3	2	3	1	2	1	3	4	6	0
Rape	8	7	17	17	18	11	14	16	14	16	19	20	14	13	26	24	21	19	17
Robbery	45	55	64	58	63	98	68	65	44	69	65	77	67	76	117	76	101	83	66
Aggravated assault	76	95	111	170	161	124	127	174	405	218	228	207	233	156	149	106	87	82	40
Burglary	567	549	603	718	1,184	1,167	1,070	1,430	1,285	1,305	1,351	1,271	961	1,190	1,226	810	858	873	784
Larceny	404	296	263	928	1,464	1,560	1,258	1,687	1,474	1,590	1,736	1,543	1,498	1,630	1,715	1,808	2,005	1,678	1,363
Motor vehicle theft	275	248	224	133	211	184	157	131	213	167	179	149	120	130	179	173	153	215	149
Arson										60	14	1	32	26	21	15	42	7	18
Crime Index	1,378	1,250	1,282	2,027	3,103	3,148	2,697	3,503	3,436	3,368	3,580	3,270	2,894	3,197	3,413	3,000	3,229	2,956	2,419
Department leadership	incumbent chief				O'Connor		Givney					O'Connor						Miller	

Sources: Annual Uniform Crime Reports.

Note: The crimes in this table are the Part I crimes. The Crime Index is a sum of all Part I crimes. Arson became a Part I crime in 1979. Larceny of goods valued at less than $50 was excluded from the index in 1958 and returned in 1973.

equalled in recorded history. If we can assume that the basic nature of Trojans did not change drastically in 1974, what accounts for the fact that there were almost 1,000 more reports of theft crimes as compared to 1973? [O'Connor 1975]

The three-part answer begins by observing changes in societal trends that were probably stimulating increases in property crimes. First, the rate of unemployment in Rensselaer County rose sharply from 4.4 percent in 1973 to 7.9 percent in 1975. In Troy the number of youths in the crime-prone ages of fourteen to twenty continued to climb until the late 1970s. New York's stiff drug laws came into effect in September 1973, raising the street prices of drugs and hence the volume of property crimes necessary to support a habit.

Second, citizen crime reporting probably rose. O'Connor had made clear to citizens that the department wanted to know about every crime they suffered. He never judged the importance of a crime by the monetary loss, for something precious to the owner might have little market value. The finding of the 1978 Troy victimization survey, that about 70 percent of burglaries were reported, supports the argument that reporting rose, since it is highly unlikely that the old department could have achieved reporting twenty percentage points higher than the national average. Two examples of commercial burglaries that occurred in 1975 provide some anecdotal support for the argument that citizens quickly enlarged their notions of what crimes were worth reporting. In one, a liquor store burglary, what was taken was not whiskey, but a can of deodorant from the windowsill. In the other, thieves broke into the parking lot kiosk of a bank to steal fifty cents and a bag of lollipops. Why did businessmen report such minor thefts? Perhaps because the commissioner had made clear that he was assigning personnel in accordance with need, and that only increased need would persuade him to allocate more patrol coverage to the central business district.

Third, I have documented most of the rise in Troy's index between 1972 and 1974 as the consequence of changes in police recording practices. The first source of underreporting is police administrators' laxity over whether officers write reports on minor crimes, since officers in patrol generally dislike paperwork. A trick by either patrol officers or records room staff is misclassification a Part I crime as a Part II crime. A national decision returned larceny of goods valued under $50 to the Crime Index in 1973. In Troy, if petit larceny had already been included in the 1972 Index, the 1973 increase in total larcenies would have been a modest step from 884 to 928, not the recorded leap from 263 to 928. The simplest explanation of why the leap was so large is that probably the department had consistently downgraded grand larcenies to petit larcenies in its reports. Other common misclassifications of Part I to Part II crimes convert burglary into criminal trespass, aggravated assault into simple assault, larceny into miscellaneous crime.

Yet another trick is miscounting. The easiest way to spot a likely miscount is to look at the detailed breakdown between attempted and completed Part I crimes. Omitting attempts from the count can be rationalized by a conscientious officer who sees the UCR as a performance measure and knows that attempts are not real crimes. The old Troy PD had substantially undercounted even completed burglaries in its monthly reports to the FBI. I went through the case files for the first half of 1972, counting all completed burglaries that had been classified by the street officer and filed by the department. I found 175 cases of commercial burglary and 277 cases of residential burglary, but the department had reported only 141 and 104. By contrast, my count in the files for 1975 matched the department's report to the UCR.

In sum, the stunning growth in Troy's Crime Index from 1,282 to 3,103 in two years can be accounted for by improvements in citizen reporting and departmental recordkeeping. The actual occurrences of Part I crimes may have been nudged upward by societal trends, or they may have remained steady, or they may have fallen slightly. The paper growth that occurred in Troy has taken place in cities across the country, though usually on a more modest scale. These examples from Troy suggest precautions for anyone examining reported crime rates in a given city: one, examine Part I and Part II crime figures over several years; two, compare the local figures with national figures; and three, ask police management for explanations rather than assuming that street crimes have increased. A reasonable conclusion is that the Crime Index should never be used as a police performance measure.

Preventing Crimes by Working with Youth

A few kids who get their kicks breaking into homes can wreak more havoc than the Hell's Angels. National statistics on youth arrests are unreliable because states differ in setting the upper boundary of "youth," and local departments define youth arrests differently. The 1986 national figures on what happens to youths taken to the police station are typical of the 1980s. About 30 percent of the delinquents, those charged with the least serious offenses, were simply released and 2 percent were turned over to a social agency. About 60 percent subsequently appeared before a family court. The 7 percent who were the most serious offenders appeared in criminal court or were turned over to another police agency. The smaller the city, the larger the proportion of arrested youths sent to criminal court.

These recorded contacts with youths are merely the tip of the iceberg, however. Police officers admonish, chase away, and counsel youths on the street much more frequently than they take them into custody. Almost always an officer's decision not to arrest is unknown beyond the circle of participants. There is no firm evidence to show under what circumstances each course of police action is effective in deterring disruptive behavior among either the youths caught or their friends who run away. The assumption underlying police contact with youths is that, if a police officer intervenes in some fashion with youths who are committing a nuisance or crime, they and their friends are less likely to commit subsequent offenses than if the officer ignores the situation.

Departments structured in accordance with the hospital model encourage officers to become well acquainted with the youths who hang out on the streets of their patrol zones, to provide informal guidance, and to bring them to the station for misbehavior that should come to the attention of their parents. Before 1977 the rate of arrest and referral for youths in Troy was low, and the number of unrecorded interventions on the street was probably likewise low. Youth arrests remained below two hundred a year from the late 1960s through 1976. Then, from 1976 to 1977 the number of youths brought to the station doubled and in 1978 rose further. Since Commissioner O'Connor never issued directives or expressed any desire for this higher volume, it is likely that when youth arrests took an upward leap, other interventions also rose.

The commissioner's step in April 1977 that brought about this increase was to abolish the separate youth service division and to place the youth services positions within the criminal investigation division. His action came as a shock, because the police field had developed these specialist units in the 1950s to cope with increases in youthful crime and had come to regard them as standard for all but the smallest departments.

The Police Benevolent Association tried to prevent the change, but there was no clause in the union contract on which to hang a grievance. The union's attempt to obtain a court injunction was thwarted because the commissioner had already obtained an opinion from the corporation counsel that the abolition was legal. The PBA did find eager listeners in the public safety committee of the city council. At a special meeting of the committee the union's president and attorney and juvenile detectives backed their objections with statements of protest some school administrators, the county youth agency, and other providers of youth services. When all had had their say, the commissioner explained that the same officers who had investigative responsibility yesterday would have it tomorrow and that the policewoman who handled matters from the office would continue to do so. Since the city manager supported the commissioner, the public safety committee took no action.

The logic behind O'Connor's move is that whenever a specialist unit is responsible for a function that is also among the responsibilities of the patrol division, patrol officers tend to neglect situations in which they might otherwise take action: "This is *their* problem." Thus, even in the heyday of community relations units, when O'Connor was commissioner in Cleveland, he had refused to create one lest patrol officers regard community relations as the concern only of the specialists. Because youths were the cause of numerous problems, O'Connor sought to increase all patrol officers' attention to those problems by eliminating the label on a specialist unit to which the buck could be passed. The stir also roused youth officers to bring more troublemaking youths to the station. During 1971–72 they averaged 59 youth arrests per year for burglary and criminal trespass combined. Their average rose to 66 per year in 1973–76, then jumped to 98 in 1977 and remained there through 1980.

Degeneration from a boy's delinquent acts to an adult's predatory crimes occurs so often that many police officers go beyond simply arresting youths in their efforts to nip a criminal career in the bud. Two incidents handled by experienced Troy officers portray the divergent ways in which officers exercise discretion in dealing with youths. Recall the unusual episode when Officer Peterson helped the boy he had arrested for stealing shoes to start a new life: he persuaded the judge to give a suspended sentence, got the boy out of his tyrannical parents' home, and found him a job. Peterson's professional manner contrasts sharply with the behavior of an officer who fits the category of an enforcer, one who is both cynical and decisive.

□ Rocky Davis was watchfully driving on patrol one Sunday when he noticed something going on in a closed commercial garage. He caught two twelve-year-old boys who were wreaking havoc. After taking the money from the vending machines, they had started the cars with the keys left in the ignition and were smashing them into the wall when Davis came in. Davis, certain that the family court judge would do nothing, gave each a beating. Then he took the boys to the station, had their parents come for them, and accompanied the boys home to make them show their parents the tools they had confessed taking previously.

Each of these officers persisted in his approach to youth at a time when the departmental leadership disapproved of his methods. Officer Peterson sought leniency from the judge in the days of the former chief, and Officer Davis gave the boys a beating when Commissioner O'Connor was in charge. The impediments to police executives' knowing how officers treat youths also makes research difficult. Research has not yet demonstrated what types of police intervention have what effects on what kinds of youths. In the absence of specific research findings, officers who share O'Connor's approach assume that an officer's ability to enlist the assistance of relatives, friends, and voluntary organizations will redirect the interest and energies of young persons, thus reducing their inclination and time available for predatory and destructive activities.

The Troy department supported a wide range of programs of governmental and voluntary agencies. The commissioner worked quietly with the heads of the probation department and two residences for delinquents, but he kept his connection unobtrusive lest some youths transfer their antipathy for police to these agencies. Among other efforts, O'Connor chaired the district Boy Scout nominating committee in order to attract capable men to lead local scouting. When the city undertook a major project of neighborhood planning, he worked with the planners to prepare a neighborhood analysis for the whole city of the frequency of youth problems, park acreage, and the long-term need for recreation programs. Police officers have contributed both as individuals and through the PBA to sports and other youth programs.

Reducing the Access of Potential Offenders

Routine patrol in marked police cars has been the primary police effort to prevent crime ever since police departments could afford to provide cars for the patrol division. The greatest policing furor in recent memory greeted the findings of a careful, year-long experiment in Kansas City, where the Police Foundation found no significant difference in crime levels when patrol presence was cut to less than 40 percent of normal or boosted to over 200 percent (Kelling et al. 1974). The initiative in selecting this particular million-dollar research experiment was made by a task force of patrol officers in the south command of the Kansas City Police Department, who questioned their own driving around on patrol because they sought blocks of noncommitted time to apply to the suppression of specific crime patterns (Kelling et al. 1974, 25).

The Troy patrol division was slow to adopt systematic crime suppression techniques, despite Commissioner O'Connor's introduction of a number of routine practices. For instance, in 1975 and again in the early 1980s he introduced field interview cards, a technique of proven effectiveness in which officers report basic information about suspicious individuals whom they stop for questioning (Boydstun, Sherry, and Moelter, 1977). However, Troy officers did not bother to note the names of their contacts, and supervisors did not require them to do so. In this instance of weak departmental accountability, O'Connor chose not to hold the chain of command responsible. He reasoned that stopping a citizen on the street is so serious a matter that officers should never interfere with passersby unless their suspicions are aroused. Moreover, the inconvenience of field interviews is not evenly shared among citizens, because the likelihood of committing a predatory crime is not randomly distributed. Officers stop young black men far more frequently than old white women. O'Connor did not want officers stopping citizens in order to look good on paper to their supervisors.

Residential burglary in the Hillside section of Troy came to public attention as a pressing problem in the summer of 1983 when the *Times Record* ran an article about the work of the "Hillside Burglar," and the next summer another reporter returned to the theme. Consequently, whenever a burglary occurred uphill from 8th Street, people said, "That's the work of the Hillside Burglar." In fact, it is very unlikely that a single burglar was responsible for all the break-ins, because there was no striking common characteristic in the methods used. The similarities among the burglaries were merely their occurrence between 2:00 A.M. and dawn, the use of some backyard object as a stepping stool under a rear window, and the slitting of the screen.

The department was particularly concerned because the average age of the victims was over sixty, an age at which people are more fearful and less able to replace their property losses. Investigators put extra effort into follow-up in the area, and the patrol division fielded some special duty patrol in an unmarked car on an overtime basis. Any displacement effect of this extra attention to the area and of the reporter's feature story after riding along on the special duty patrol is unknown. Some said there had been displacement when the state police made burglary arrests in East Brunswick, out beyond the Hillside area.

One hypothesis, investigated but never confirmed, was that some of the burglaries might be the work of a person normally out before dawn, such as a newspaper delivery boy. No evidence from investigations led to any suspect. Troy officers made some burglary arrests, but just how many break-ins the arrestees were responsible for is unknown. Were the arrestees deterred from future burglaries while awaiting the court outcome? Did knowledge of their arrests deter others from committing burglaries? How many burglaries were prevented during the months that the convicted burglars served jail terms? No one knows. The facts are that nighttime residential burglaries known to the police in the Hillside area tapered off during 1984 and did not become pronounced in the summer of 1985. The unanswered questions in this episode illustrate how difficult it is to know to what extent police actions have affected the local occurrence of crimes, through displacement of crimes to other areas, or general deterrence of those inclined to commit crimes, or the incapacitation of those jailed.

Crime Prevention through Work with Potential Victims

In 1976 the Troy department under the direction of Chief John Givney launched a federally funded crime prevention program using the slogan "Fight Crime with Us." On O'Connor's return the next year he coined the slogan "Safety and Security—for the People, by the People." The distance between these slogans is the distance between the military model and the hospital model. From their military traditions police draw the negative conception of fighting an enemy. The hospital model contains the positive conception of safety and security as a broad notion of well-being not limited to the prevention of crimes. A concern with the physical safety of citizens and their sense of security embraces many separate responsibilities of the police, from stopping a reckless driver to carrying a child from a burning building. The involvement of citizens in the responsibility for their own safety is deliberately promoted by police. As potential victims, citizens have two sets of methods available for protecting themselves and their property from criminal attack: "target hardening," or making physical changes to prevent access to victims and their property; and "protective neighboring," which is mutual watchfulness.

Target Hardening

From a national perspective the Troy department's formal programs in target hardening were nothing new, but for this city they were a fresh approach. The department's main effort to prevent burglary was the evidence technician program. An officer who is reconstructing a crime scene has an excellent opportunity to explain to the householder precisely how the burglar broke in and to give specific advice for preventing a recurrence. The period immediately after a burglary is a salient time for advice, particularly because buildings that have been successfully burglarized are more likely to be hit again. Departmental data from 1984 show that evidence technicians visited almost every burglary victim that year.

A bicycle registration program begun in April 1974 combined tips to youngsters about traffic safety with voluntary registration of the ownership, description, and identification number of each bike. The department reached children through the schools and new owners through bicycle dealers with the message to lock their bikes and report any that were stolen. A police-sponsored property registration program diminishes some of the most common reasons citizens give for not reporting: lack of proof, belief that police would not want to be bothered, inability to recover property because of lack of identification (Bureau of Justice Statistics 1989, 88). With the new program, records on bicycle theft were moved out of the youth services division into central records. The number of stolen bicycles reported to the police increased from 69 in the previous year to 294 during the first year of the program. It is reasonable to suppose that thievery stayed about the same while reporting and recording increased. In the absence of victimization surveys, it is difficult to tell whether such a police program prevents any crimes.

Protective Neighboring

A second set of methods for crime prevention has been called protective neighboring. As the concept has been developed by Anne Schneider (1987), the term refers to the ways in which people become one another's guardians. Whatever the formal or informal arrangements among neighbors, the police department is the silent partner, because the neighbor who spots trouble calls the police.

□ "Mr. Alert," in his early thirties told an interviewer:
"Somebody just hit a ball through the window in the school. It was an accident. They were kids playing baseball who were not from this area. I drove up, and the kids scattered. I called the police, and the dispatcher asked if the hole in the window was big enough for someone to crawl through. He was concerned. I was very dissatisfied and upset with waiting what seemed like an hour because I was standing out in the cold. When an officer finally arrived, he explained why he couldn't be here right away, that he was diverted by a fight at the north end. I understood. He took a complete report, asked me questions, and I signed a statement. He was very professional and was nicely dressed. He treated me very well as a person. It was an inspiring thing. It made me think the police are thorough. He made me feel I was a good citizen for watching the school."

This citizen first saw his problem as waiting a few minutes to make sure no kids crawled through the hole they had made. After he had waited impatiently in the cold, his new problem was whether he had wasted his time. If the officer had only brusquely explained his belated arrival and taken the report quickly, Mr. Alert would probably have felt like a fool. Instead, he described the officer's actions as "inspiring." The officer had confirmed to Mr. Alert that he was "a good citizen for watching the school." Yet like so many incidents that police officers handle, this one came and went without the citizen's ever finding out whether anyone addressed the underlying problem of kids running away from responsibility for the damage they did. Because Mr. Alert did not recognize any of the boys, it is almost certain that his reporting of the incident never transmitted any message to the parents about the behavior of their sons.

Some insight into increasing citizen cooperation over time can be obtained from the data that departments routinely collect in their records of calls for service. If the Troy experience is typical, then three changes in citizen cooperation occur together. First, a swift rise in the total number of calls for service takes place at the outset of departmental upgrading. As discussed in Chapter 3, this increase may reflect both growing citizen confidence and the increased capability of the department.

Second, increased citizen efforts at crime prevention is reflected in the number of times citizens mobilize the police when trouble is brewing. Although one cannot know the number of times they flag officers on patrol, one can count the number of times they telephone to help avert a crime that is about to occur or to stop a crime in progress. As defined here, "crime prevention calls" include all suspicion calls and reports of ongoing violations that are likely to result in serious harm. Suspicions—"prowler," "woman screaming," or "man with a gun"—may be mistaken, but citizens who bring out an officer are reassured. In-progress situations—"men fighting," "boys throwing rocks at people," "reckless driving"—may end tranquilly without intervention, but if an officer arrives quickly, less harm is likely to occur. Crime prevention calls should be seen as part of the total pattern of citizen calls for service. The significant rise in the number of crime prevention calls in Troy, from only about 6 per 1,000 residents in 1972 to about 15 in 1975, is shown by the dotted line in Figure 6-1. Crime prevention calls continued to increase after total calls for service had quickly reached a plateau in 1975. By 1983 the rate of crime prevention calls had doubled again from the 1975 level to about 34 per 1,000 residents.

Third, an indicator of trust in the police and in the neighbors is the increasing willingness of citizens who call the police to give their names. The distance between the top line and the middle line shows the number of callers in Troy whose names were recorded by police operators— actually an underestimate, given some operator laziness in recording. Troy department policy is to encourage but not to demand that callers give their names. Note that the proportion of citizens who identified

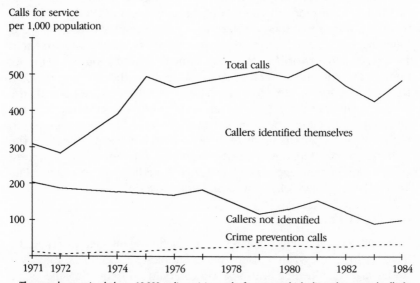

The sample contained about 10,000 radio activity cards, forms on which dispatchers noted calls for service and administrative matters. All days of the week and all hours of the day are equally represented in the samples. February, May, August, and November are the sample months. In 1972 and 1976 the samples contained 28 days; in 1975 and 1977, they contained 14 days, in 1979, 1981, and 1983, 7 days.

Figure 6-1   Rise in Crime Prevention Calls and in Callers Identifying Themselves

themselves grew most rapidly at the beginning of upgrading but also continued to grow during the plateau in total calls for service. Unless callers trusted the department enough to give their names, a responding officer could not seek them out to give personal reassurance.

Generally, people are willing to supply their names in criminal incidents, because they expect to give a patrol officer additional information for an official report. They are less willing for other conflicts, because they want to avoid getting in trouble with their neighbors. Citizens who withhold their names or operators who do not record them can frustrate the responding officer, who cannot talk over the situation with the person who was distressed enough to call. An extreme example occurred in Philadelphia when responding officers did not know who had called regarding noise from a bar. Eventual inquiry by a sergeant discovered that an elderly woman had called 500 times in six months because a blaring juke box stood again the wall of her apartment (Goldstein 1990,).

The general argument advanced here is that citizens see many incidents appropriate for police involvement but often do not bother to summon help or, if they do, sometimes fail to identify themselves. To the extent that officers convincingly convey the message that they want to be of assistance, people in doubt will increase their cooperation with police officers and with their neighbors.

A standard police program to augment protective neighboring is a vacant-home inspection program. Persuading residents to tell the department in advance that they will be out of town requires overcoming any lingering doubt that perhaps not everyone at the police department is 100 percent trustworthy: "Suppose someone tells a burglar I'm not home?" In Troy, the program began modestly in the summer of 1974, reached less than 1 percent of the homes, and then petered out. By the following summer the patrol captains had not taken responsibility for the program, and neither the commissioner nor the chief took the time to rejuvenate it. Neighbors usually rely upon each other, not the police. The 1978 survey found that of those who went away for a few days, 75 percent asked neighbors to keep watch. Residents of public housing asked neighbors only 50 percent of the time, and none asked the police.

Helping Victims

Police officers can significantly reduce the suffering inflicted by crimes by direct help to the victims. Here is the simplest of examples, told by a young man of nineteen who was concentrating on counting the office money for deposit when he heard a car door slam but paid no attention because he thought it was a fellow employee.

When I went to get my coat, it was gone. An officer came promptly and asked for a description of my coat. He asked me to go to the garage next door with him to see if they heard or saw anything. He seemed concerned almost as if it had been his coat that was stolen.

Police officers are in position to respond immediately on a human level to people in trouble. In many cases the help is merely a considerate attitude in taking a preliminary report when both victim and officer believe that the stolen property is unlikely to be found. Usually, once officers leave the scene, their assistance ends. However, because the new programs to assist victims are rarely known to victims, police officers are in a crucial position to make referrals. The programs outlined in a report from the National Institute of Justice (1987) can be divided into three types: financial assistance, recognition of victims' rights, and protection for especially vulnerable victims. Financial assistance, begun in California in 1966 with the establishment of a victim compensation program, had expanded by 1989 to forty-seven states, where modest programs assist a few thousand individuals. In addition, states have slowly increased restitution programs whereby a court presides over the offender's direct compensation to his or her victim. The rights of victims in some states now include notification of court proceedings, participation in sentencing, and representation by legal counsel. Changes in court rules about what is admissible as evidence permit police to spare the victim unnecessary hardship by using photos of recovered purses, bicycles, rifles, and so on, instead of holding the items themselves until the cases are adjudicated. Special programs for particularly vulnerable victims first began for rape victims, and now shelters for battered women are widespread. Child abuse too has become the focus of formal cooperation between police officers, health professionals, and educators who can refer victims to appropriate programs.

For a century before the first formal victim assistance program had a penny of funding, police officers provided informal assistance. To Commissioner O'Connor, this is a central opportunity and responsibility for officers. Research supports what individual officers have experienced, that a person is most in need of reassurance and most receptive to help and suggestions immediately after becoming a victim. The relationship that can develop between an individual victim and the individual responding officer is a personal tie between one who is suffering and one who understands suffering. The officer's calm helps the victim to recover some measure of calm; the officer's concern gives emotional and psychological support. The mere fact that the victim's initiative caused a police officer to arrive transforms him or her from an unwilling, passive person into an active citizen who has done something to begin to right the wrong. Among citizens who call the police (as shown previously in Table 3-3), the more serious the crime, the more they appreciate the concern that officers show.

If a woman tells me she is afraid because her purse was snatched, I reassure her by telling her that in all my years with the department I never met a woman whose purse was snatched twice. If she is afraid because her house was burglarized, I tell her that we will give her place extra attention. I tell the officers to swing by her house a couple of times a shift and shine their light into her yard. I remind the officers at roll call all week that I want them to drop by for the next *six* weeks. When someone is fearful, it takes a while for the scar to heal.

Sergeant "Sam Griffith," 1987

From Fear of Crime
to Sense of Safety

Unpredictable criminal attacks provoke fear, and when fear keeps people indoors, the streets are left to the muggers. Sergeant Sam Griffith, who viewed the wrongs of the world from a tragic perspective, believed that he and the officers of his squad could alleviate exaggerated fears.

This chapter looks at a typical wave of fear that produced an outcry for more police protection and critiques two popular demands, more manpower and neighborhood police storefronts. After briefly identifying differences between crime problems and fear problems, it examines explanations of why people feel safe. Because an individual's sense of safety may be diminished by a perception of a prevalence of attackers, we review an unusual episode from Troy in which the department attempted to reduce the amount of crime news carried by the local newspaper. Because the sense of safety may be heightened by a perception of a prevalence of protection, we examine new programs in other cities by which police work to enhance people's sense of safety.

Wave of Fear

Commissioner O'Connor stood for three hours on the evening of 28 May 1975, receiving angry, fearful accusations from an overflow crowd in Germania Hall in the Lansingburgh section of Troy: "'Since you became Police Commissioner, I don't know what you have done. What the hell are you doing?' A thunderous round of applause broke out" (*Times Record*, 29 May 1975). In a city where three murders a year are a lot, a wave of fear had been set in motion by a third murder within five months in Lansingburgh, the northern end of town.

Once an independent city opposite the mouth of the Mohawk River, Lansingburgh was incorporated into Troy in 1900 but maintains its separateness to the extent of running its own school district. For several years before this event there had been some complaints that the police could not deal with juvenile delinquency and vandalism in the Burgh. After a few muggings near the high school, elderly men and women had spoken out against permissive parents and lenient courts. Against this general background of unease about crime, a high school boy took his friend to the wooded hill below the cemetery in the middle of a May night and shot him. Although the police had solved the crime and arrested the boy three days before the Lansingburgh meeting, fears were not allayed.

A prospective candidate for city council, one who never received party endorsement, seized upon the youth's murder as proof of a crime wave. He demanded "decisive action . . . not just answers, to end the rash of burglaries, violence and murders." A convenient locus for venting fears and frustrations was a public meeting in Germania Hall, which the commissioner had previously scheduled with two neighborhood associations of Lansingburgh.

A raucous, rude crowd of about 450 men and women came to demand action. Every candidate and hopeful for city council turned out to the meeting and echoed the refrain, "The police must do something." Some people presented a petition that the county sheriff patrol the streets of Lansingburgh. One person suggested that the police teach dogs to attack criminals fleeing from the scene and to hold them until an officer arrived. The commissioner began to explain that attack dogs were not desirable, but was interrupted by a shout, "Why can't we have a 9:00 P.M. curfew?" The citizens poured out proposed solutions—more police, a precinct station, auxiliary police, unmarked cars, more police.

The commissioner's measured speaking pace and outward calm contrasted strongly with the agitation of the crowd. Men and women shook their fists to drive home to him that they lived in fear of a crime wave. O'Connor explained that there was no crime wave, that Lansingburgh already received adequate police protection, and that murder between acquaintances is not preventable by police officers. He used reason, facts, statistics. His figures showed that adding ten more officers to the present 125 would cost the city at least $145,000 annually. In questioning whether additional manpower would have a noticeable effect on crime, he asked, "What else could the money buy to prevent crime?"

To answer his own question, O'Connor explained that the misbehavior of youth was the primary cause for concern. The $145,000 might be better spent on recreation programs, youth centers, youth leaders, or employment training. Gradually, the crowd became attentive, but their attention was still riveted on physical signs of increasing law enforcement such as more police officers and a precinct station. The recently elected head of the Police Benevolent Association joined the demand for more officers. The desire for a precinct station was fed by memories of the distant past when Lansingburgh had had its own precinct station and by the vague knowledge that Arbor Hill, in neighboring Albany, had established a storefront base for its team policing program. The community members clung to the belief that they were endangered by a crime wave. It was after 11:00 P.M. when O'Connor closed the meeting and headed home, profoundly discouraged that he had failed to reach these citizens. And apparently they had failed to reach him.

The commissioner soon realized that he had approached this problem the wrong way and offered this reassessment in a report to the city manager.

Expressions of fear related to three unconnected murders during 1975, coupled with what have become chronic complaints regarding teenage misbehavior, have created pressures for programs aimed at reducing fear through increased or more obvious police presence. The task of reducing fear must involve making more visible those symbols of security which people believe can help to create a sense of well-being. Logic, statistics, and other intellectual but intangible response—regardless of their validity—have little impact on the ways people feel. Because people react and behave according to how they feel, only actions which create a greater feeling of security will be considered acceptable. In other words, it is necessary to build a heightened sense of security and safety through programs which people can see, rather than to seek to convince them that the problem is more imaginary than real. [O'Connor 1975b]

The dynamics of a wave of fear have been analyzed. A particularly frightening series of crimes reported in the mass media, such as rapes or child molestations, draws public attention to crime in general. Fishman's (1980) case study in New York City documented how two newspapers and a TV station manufactured a "wave of crimes against the elderly" through their selective attention to the elderly as victims. In quieter communities, waves of fear are often triggered by a quick succession of atrocious crimes, as Taft (1986) has reported for the suburbs of Baltimore. After a surge, people's fears slowly ebb as other issues divert their attention.

Waves of fear are local peaks on national levels of fear, which have changed markedly over the decades. Nationally, fear reached its highest measured levels in 1974, when 40 percent of young adults and 56 percent of the elderly were afraid to walk at night within their own neighborhoods. The number of citizens considering crime to be the top national problem has risen as the number of fearful people has risen, but these two groups do not coincide (Furstenberg 1971). Many of the very fearful people are so beset with other difficulties that they choose other concerns as the nation's top problem—poverty, unemployment, housing, or discrimination. Political concern about crime is strongest among members of the middle class. The bundle of related issues that includes crime, rioting, drugs, and other problems of social control had very low priority as a national issue from the mid-1930s through the 1950s, took a large upsurge in the mid-1960s, remained high to the mid-1970s, and declined in the late 1970s and early 1980s. Figure 7-1 demonstrates the ups and downs in national concern about crime issues.

A police department can best cope with fear of crime by recognizing it as a set of problems separate from the crime problems themselves and then applying creative problem-solving. However, when citizens fear that they are engulfed in a crime wave, political leaders tend to become involved and less willing to give the police department latitude in deciding how to respond.

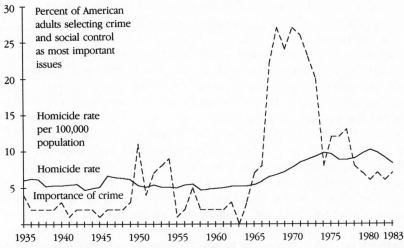

Sources: Margaret Zahn; the FBI, *Uniform Crime Reports*; and Smith (1985).
Note: The Gallup Poll question was most often worded, "What do you think is the most important problem facing the country today?" Crime and social control issues include violence, riots, crime, juvenile delinquency, drugs, moral decay, and the lack of religion.

Figure 7-1   National Change in Importance Attached to Crime and Social Control Compared to the Homicide Rate

Throwing Manpower at Crime

In Troy, a city with a history of turbulent political competition, 1975 was an election year in which four of the seven city council seats were contested. Following the Germania Hall citizens' meeting, a prospective candidate urged the city council to hold a special meeting for Lansingburgh residents. From the amorphous fears a solution began to emerge—ten more officers. The commissioner resisted: "I am not convinced they would do anything significant to prevent crime" (*Times Record*, 2 June 1975, p. 2). During the next week a consensus built among the Democrats on the city council, led by a well-loved councilman from South Troy. The only lawyer on the council promised to introduce the legislation. To substantiate the need, he cited statistics to show that in the last year violent crime had risen by 20 percent and property crime by 30 percent. The councilman's figures came from the commissioner's special report, written on his own initiative three months earlier. The twenty-three-page document provided full Part I crime statistics from 1970 to 1974 and a detailed explanation of why *reported* crime had risen dramatically, as O'Connor had predicted when he came to Troy. The report had stimulated a confused discussion when issued but had been quickly forgotten. Among the city leaders, only City Manager John Buckley demonstrated a full understanding that the volume of reported crimes can increase while actual occurrence remains steady or even drops.

At the regular council meeting of 5 June the mayor introduced the legislation. In a straight party vote, five Democrats to two Republicans, the city council ordered the hiring of ten more officers without suggesting where to find funds. Commissioner O'Connor dragged his feet on the appointments because he considered the solution completely inappropriate to the problem. During June, he put his energies into short-term steps and a long-term plan to increase people's sense of safety. The fortuitous timing of the next police academy graduation on 20 June permitted immediate assignment of the new officers to the street. Transfer of an intern to youth services in the evening enabled a juvenile services officer to spend more time on the street. Coordination with the parks department placed unarmed park rangers at work primarily in the evenings. For more attention to the burglary problem, O'Connor added an unmarked anti-burglary unit to patrol. For the long term he designed a citizens' council for channeling the energies generated by the fear of crime into constructive programs (O'Connor 1975a). However, a council composed of individuals outside the criminal justice system and staffed by a full-time executive was too threatening to New York state criminal justice professionals in 1975, and the funding request was rejected by the state Division of Criminal Justice. Two years later, however, when Washington promoted citizen involvement, New York adopted O'Connor's concepts and language in its new community-based crime prevention programs.

At the regular July 1975 meeting of the city council the Democratic majority was angered to learn that the new hiring was not yet under way. The mayor, whose brother had served in the police department since 1959, pointedly criticized City Manager Buckley:

> He's telling us he's keeping the force up to 125. I expect him to do that all the time. We want 10 additional policemen. . . . The administration chose to ignore the wishes of the Council and people. Most people have said they want more patrol. [*Times Union*, 4 July 1975, p. 3]

The mayor was quite right. Citizens often ask for more police as the solution to any problem, whether they are expressing themselves to elected representatives or to a survey interviewer. The city council pressed the issue by scheduling a special council meeting for 15 July. Only five citizens spoke, three opposing the hiring, and then Buckley argued cogently against adding ten additional officers:

1. The hiring was proposed without consulting the city manager, the commissioner, or senior members of the department.
2. The City cannot afford the additional expenditure.
3. The City has no funds to transfer from other departments.

4. The police department is flexible and able to solve the problem by shifting priorities.

Buckley concluded by making the issue a direct confrontation between himself and the council.

I know it is very easy for a few to say that the City Manager isn't thinking of the safety of the people. This is pure political rhetoric. As a lifelong resident and taxpayer of Troy, I have always placed the welfare of our citizens above any personal consideration. The City Council and the Mayor, in particular, know very well that it is only necessary to introduce a resolution stipulating that John Buckley is not doing his job for the benefit of the City and to the best of his ability, in order to get a rubber stamp that will always do the Mayor's bidding.

Disclaiming any notion of firing the manager, the council took a straight party vote that again required the expansion of the police department from 125 to 135 officers. An editorial in the *Times Record* criticized the council for disregarding the advice of the city manager and the commissioner; nevertheless the city council had made its commitment to stop an imaginary crime wave.

O'Connor's opposition to additional officers stemmed from a broad view of police work as one of many city services. He predicted that Troy would continue to experience financial difficulties as the population slowly declined. Without expansion of either the total city budget or the police share, paying for new positions would consume funds that could otherwise be used for increasing salary levels. In every city, officers should realize that if there are more of them eating the pie, the shares of the pie will be smaller. O'Connor knew that his opposition to police expansion would annoy many in the police field who consider themselves both indispensable and overworked and would disturb police managers who see many creative ways to use additional personnel. In his view, however, if a city must cut the budget, police service is not the last place to cut. Within the functioning of the city as a whole, he saw garbage collection as the most essential; next came fire fighting, where usually no more than small cuts can be made. Moreover, reduced recreation or other social service budgets could make police responsibilities more difficult.

The willingness of mayors in financially strapped cities to maintain huge police departments is shown in a Northwestern University study of ten major cities covering the period 1948–78 (Jacob et al. 1982). Over the thirty-one-year span the five poorest cities—Newark, Philadelphia, Boston, Oakland, and Atlanta—each had higher per capita spending on police than the five richest cities: Houston, Indianapolis, Minneapolis, Phoenix, and San Jose. The three cities in the Northeast maintained exceptionally large departments on low salaries.

Throwing manpower at crime is a reflex action. In the Troy situation the city council started with the vague notion that "crime has increased" and provided the vague solution of hiring more officers to do whatever it is officers are supposed to do. Let us be clear. More manpower can be a deliberate and appropriate means to address a specific crime problem. For instance, a patrol captain may assign an officer to foot patrol in the central business district during the Christmas shopping season with the knowledge that purse snatching can be expected to rise at this season and with the aim of using visible police presence to reassure shoppers and deter would-be thieves. A sergeant may work with his squad to increase surveillance of a school parking lot where a rash of vandalism is occurring. However, when crime problems are only vaguely sensed, the solutions cannot be definite. When the leadership of a city decides to expand the police force, the positions are not temporary but permanent. The hidden implication is that short-term efforts on the part of additional officers will not reduce the problem to its pre-crisis level so that the department can be reduced to its pre-crisis size. In Troy, long-term financial constraints did force the cutting of authorized positions, from 135 to 130 in 1980 and to 123 in 1983. That is, the department lost the very positions the city council had forced upon it. Good budget management prevented any layoffs during the departmental shrinkage, but officers still viewed the cuts as serious blows to morale.

The immediate difficulty with adding officers as the solution to a current crime problem is that at least six months will elapse before the new officers are out on patrol. On 5 June 1975, when Troy's city council mandated the hiring, a civil service list of eligible candidates still existed from the 1974 exam. Without that list, the city would have had to wait four months until the state held its annual entrance examination and then three months more for the results. Given a current list, a city can begin screening candidates with a medical examination, physical agility tests, a psychological assessment, a character investigation, and an interview. But even so, successful candidates usually have to wait a few months for the next recruit training class, which will run three or four months. In Troy the ten additional officers did not begin patrol until a year after the decision to hire them.

A coda on this council venture into department staffing is that every councilman up for reelection was defeated. When crime issues arise, they usually work to the disadvantage of the incumbents.

A Building to Radiate Crime Prevention

A second specific demand born at the Germania Hall meeting was to open a neighborhood police storefront. Commissioner O'Connor deflected the demand in 1975, but when Chief Givney directed the department without a commissioner in 1976, he did obtain federal funds to use a trailer as a crime prevention unit in Lansingburgh. O'Connor appeased a more vociferous outcry during the 1977 city council campaign by creating three neighborhood units located in fire stations and staffing them with nonsworn personnel. The 1977 political fight over neighborhood stations triggered the firing of the city manager, which is covered in Chapter 10. Here we look generally at the case for neighborhood police stations.

In every city, people welcome the opening of a precinct station or police-manned storefront in their neighborhood as a visible symbol of police presence. It is as though citizens believe that, when a victim calls for help, officers will come pouring out of the station in the same way that fire fighters pour out at the sound of an alarm. The Houston Police Department in cooperation with the Police Foundation conducted a carefully controlled experiment to pin down changes in residents' perceptions of safety after the opening of a neighborhood station (Wycoff and Skogan 1985). Among residents who were interviewed twice, the researchers found small but significant decreases in fear of becoming a crime victim and in estimates of the prevalence of personal crimes. Comparing all residents surveyed before the opening of the storefront with all residents surveyed afterward, and with a comparison neighborhood as well, the researchers also found decreases in the perception of the prevalence of property crimes and disorder. Yet the 65 percent of the residents who were aware of the existence of the neighborhood police station felt as safe as but no safer than the others.

The most serious obstacle to firm conclusions is that the effects of the building cannot be separated from the effects of other components in a multifaceted program of community services that are provided in other cities without a neighborhood station. In Houston, the four officers and the four nonsworn employees who worked out of the station engaged in a wide range of outreach efforts. They visited schools and neighborhood businesses, invited civic clubs and churches to select a member for a ride-along program, and launched a children's program of fingerprinting and a seniors' program of taking blood pressure. Police actions on the street reclaimed the local park for community enjoyment through appropriate patrol and police-citizen ballgames. All these interventions together, and perhaps unnoticed events as well, had the effects measured. An example of the irrelevance of the building is that when residents gathered for the first monthly community meeting and overflowed the neighborhood station, a local minister offered his church for this and subsequent meetings. A typical shortcoming of funding for police research is to require measurement of effects too soon, in the Houston case after only eight months of the program. No studies have continued long enough to find out whether an enhanced feeling of safety is temporary, remains stable, or increases over the years.

The reality is that a building requires personnel to keep it open, personnel who might otherwise be on the street. Most community stations, open between forty and sixty-five hours per week, require at least two positions. The Houston neighborhood station received about one visitor every three hours in the first three months and built up to an average of one per hour by the fifth month. Phone calls from citizens had a similarly slow upward trend. In reply to the common request for an officer to come to the scene for emergencies the storefront personnel had to ask citizens to phone again to central dispatching. This level of work put the storefront staff in contact with very few members of the public. Mary Ann Wycoff (1987), who has both a deep understanding of the Houston department and a broad view of police upgrading, considers that the community storefront was a symbol to people of the neighborhood that they had not been forgotten and a symbol to officers in cementing their commitment to the neighborhood people. More broadly, researchers evaluating the fear reduction efforts in Houston, Newark (Pate et al. 1986), and Baltimore County (Taft 1986; Cordner 1986) have concluded that the key resources are officers' time to talk with citizens and officers' initiative to respond directly to their needs. Time to talk and authority to act are found in well-managed patrol divisions, regardless of the geographic location of the physical plant.

Crime Problems and Fear Problems

All studies of fear of crime among Americans show that women are much more fearful than men, and older people somewhat more fearful than middle-aged ones. Fears well grounded in reality, such as fear of slipping and falling on icy pavement, are realistic assessments of the risk of such an occurrence and the potential seriousness of the results. The degree of damage that an elderly woman can reasonably fear from a purse snatch includes broken bones from being knocked down. For women over fifty the average risk of being injured in any way by robbery or assault is 7 percent per lifetime (Koppel 1987).

The divergence between the low risk of occurrence and the high presence of fear is made clear by looking separately at men and women. Table 7-1 shows the mismatch between the likelihood of becoming a crime victim and fear of walking alone at night. The table for men shows that the fear of walking alone at night rises after age 50, despite a decline in the estimated risk of victimization from each of five different types of street crimes. The same pattern holds at a more intense level of fear for women. For every age group, women's levels of fear are higher than men's, even though their rates of victimization hover at half the men's rates. One reason for men's higher rates of victimization is that they tend to associate with tougher people and are attacked more often by their acquaintances. One hypothesis is that fear of crime may be influenced by a fear of strangers, a fear perhaps more common among women. Another

Table 7-1 National Comparison of Fear of Walking Alone at Night with Rate of Attack (per 1,000)

	12-19	20-24	25-34	35-49	50-64	65+
			Men			
Fearful of Walking Alone at Night $n = 1407$	9%	7%	8%	5%	10%	14%
Victimization Rates						
Robbery with injury	4	4	4	2	2	1
Robbery w/o injury	12	12	7	4	3	3
Aggravated assault	23	31	19	7	3	2
Simple assault	38	38	27	13	5	3
Personal larceny with contact	4	4	2	2	3	2
			Women			
Fearful of Walking Alone at Night $n = 1042$	19%	29%	25%	28%	31%	40%
Victimization Rates						
Rape	3	3	2	1	0	0
Robbery with injury	2	3	2	1	1	1
Robbery w/o injury	5	6	5	3	2	1
Aggravated assault	10	10	8	3	2	1
Simple assault	27	30	18	10	4	2
Personal larceny with contact	2	4	5	2	4	4

Sources: ABC, 1982. Bureau of Justice Statistics, 1984, table 5.

hypothesis is that women may take a more serious view of being attacked than men do. Both explanations point up the difference between problems of crime and problems of fear of crime.

Recent research in risk assessment and risk perception offer systematic techniques that can be applied to understanding the fear of crime. Risk assessment estimates probabilities of the occurrence of events, a totally separate process from making cultural judgments of how serious the results are. Experts in applying risk assessment use standard objective measures such as the annual probability of death (Wilson and Crouch 1987), which shows that people are more than twice as likely to die as victims of motor vehicle crashes than as victims of crimes. People's perceptions of risk, however, are colored by their cultural judgments, such as the voluntary nature of the risk, its controllability, and its familiarity (Slovic 1987). When people worry, a possible injury in a car accident feels more familiar and more controllable than a similar injury from a mugger's attack. Unfortunate events that are the result of evil intentions, and where the risks are not well understood, can be seen as signals of larger problems and can affect people who do not even know the immediate victims. In the Lansingburgh section of Troy many of the hundreds gathered for the Germania Hall meeting may have believed that the local murder was a signal of rampant and growing lawlessness.

Another factor identified by O'Connor as possibly contributing to the outburst of public concern over crime was a fear that poor black people would move into Lansingburgh. During the early 1970s, demolition and excavation for the planned redevelopment of the north end of the central business district had forced the relocation of that area's residents, many of whom were black. It was generally understood that they had moved northward to an adjacent neighborhood, and some Lansingburgh residents feared that they would push farther north into the Burgh. Meanwhile, the area where the apartments had been razed remained a gaping hole for years, a constant sign of social decay.

Explaining the Sense of Safety from Criminal Attack

Initially, most discussions of these problems focused on fear and how to reduce it rather than on how to build a realistic sense of safety. Fortunately, the standard question in national surveys utilized to estimate fear actually asks people how safe they feel from crime. Since the President's Commission of 1967, fear of crime has usually been explained through examination of individual characteristics. Following the groundbreaking study by Biderman et al. (1967), other researchers including Hindelang, Gottfredson, and Garofalo (1978), Skogan and Maxfield (1981), Baumer (1985), and Ortega and Myles (1987) have documented that women are more fearful than men; members of minority groups more than white people; older people more than younger ones. Inconsistent results as to whether and how experience as a victim contributes to fear of crime have puzzled a number of researchers, among them Garofalo and Laub (1978) and Skogan and Maxfield (1981). In Troy, too, no consistent relationship appeared between ever having been a victim of a serious crime and feelings of safety at night.

An alternative to individual explanations has been put forward by researchers at Northwestern University. Lewis et al. (1979) suggest that fear of crime stems from people's perceptions of the area where they live. A study of ten neighborhoods in Chicago, Philadelphia, and San Francisco found striking differences in the percentage of people who were afraid, ranging from 24 percent to 55 percent. These researchers explain fear as the result of the balance between people's perceptions of social disorganization (as measured by abandoned buildings, trash, awareness of crime, and assessment of the risk of being a victim) and the availability of social resources (as measured by neighborhood levels of income, education, home ownership, social integration, and community involvement). The argument that community scars from vandalism may be more detri-

Table 7-2   Men's and Women's Sense of Safety in Troy

	Women			Men		
	Teens	20–49	50+	Teens	20–49	50+
Almost always feel safe	14%	28%	15%	56%	62%	45%
Often feel safe	14	17	4	17	15	12
Sometimes feel safe	26	18	9	17	15	10
Seldom feel safe	20	14	5	4	4	6
Almost never feel safe	6	9	13	5	3	9
Fear keeps in	13	9	28	0	0	9
Stay in for other reasons	8	6	26	2	1	11
n = 946						

mental to a sense of safety than robberies that leave no trace was developed by Wilson and Kelling (1982) in an essay called "Broken Windows." Why would a broken window create more fear than a robbery that sent the victim to the hospital? Because the robbery would be over in a minute, but the gaping hole would affront passersby for days, weeks, months, or years. This argument was the basis for the Houston neighborhood police station experiment and other fear reduction efforts.

In bringing the Troy data to bear on the issue of what promotes a sense of safety, we must look at both individual and neighborhood characteristics. The positive phrasing of the Troy survey question "How safe do you feel from crime *in your own neighborhood?*" is in keeping with O'Connor's view that when the fear problem is recast in terms of safety and security, a broader array of solutions involving cooperative action will become relevant. Table 7-2 compares the sense of safety of men and women across the age span. For both sexes the sense of safety at night which had risen during the teens, holds a plateau for young adults, and drops sharply after age fifty. In Troy, as nationally, at no age did women feel as safe as men.

The survey asked why each individual felt particularly safe or unsafe. The 69 percent of men and 30 percent of women who almost always or often felt safe had strong belief in the prevalence of protection. They expressed confidence in themselves and their neighbors as sources of protection. Fearful women and men believed in the prevalence of attackers. The area of Troy where residents felt least safe in 1978 was not the poorest, the inner city, but Lansingburgh, where distress may have lingered following the imaginary crime wave of 1975.

Because feeling safe is a greater problem for women, let us look at their survey results. Figure 7-2 groups the women into six categories based on how safe they felt when out alone at night. For each of these groups we looked at how the women knew about recent crimes. Over 70

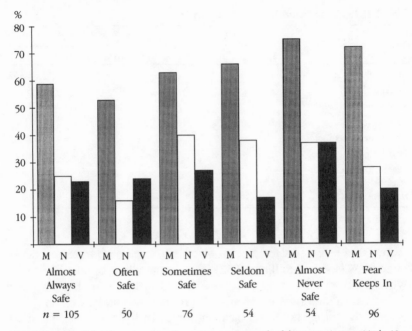

Note: The graph shows the percentage of women answering each of these questions positively. Mass media (M): When you listen to to TV and radio news or read the paper, are you hearing more about crime these days? or less? or about the same? Neighborhood crime (N): Has a serious crime happened in your neighborhood recently? Was victim (V): Has a *serious* crime ever been committed against you or your property?

Figure 7-2 Sources of Women's Belief That Attackers Are Prevalent

percent of the two most fearful groups, and slightly fewer of the other groups, had heard from the mass media that crime was rising. Among women who felt safe most of the time, few knew of a recent, serious neighborhood crime. Fewer of the fearful women who stay indoors at night knew of a neighborhood crime or had experienced a crime themselves than of the very fearful who did venture out. One curious finding was that women who *often* felt safe had somewhat less reason to believe in the prevalence of attackers than women who *always* felt safe. As found in research elsewhere, having been the victim of a crime had only modest bearing on the level of fear. From a policy perspective an important finding is that women too afraid to go out at night and those who almost never feel safe are the ones most frequently fed crime news by the mass media.

The belief that the community has sources of protection is a major counterbalance to the feeling of being surrounded by potential attackers. Figure 7-3 shows that the safer a woman felt in going out at night, the more likely she was to believe that neighbors would assist her if she

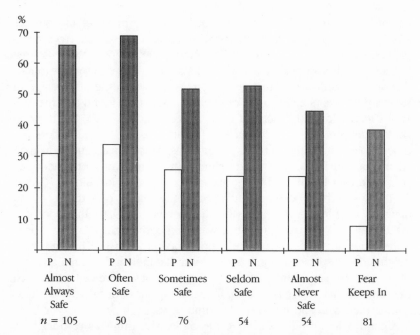

Note: The graph shows the percentage answering each of these questions positively. Helpful neighbors (N): Suppose you were walking alone at night in your neighborhood and you thought someone was going to attack you. What do you think would happen if you shouted for help? Know police officers (P): Do you know any police officers who patrol your neighborhood well enough to speak to them?

Figure 7-3 Women's Belief That Protection Is Available

shouted for help. Knowing an officer who patrols the neighborhood was true of one-third of the women who felt safe but the proportion dropped to about 10 percent among women who stayed home out of fear. From a policy perspective these findings suggest but do not prove that protective neighboring and neighborhood policing may help alleviate fear of crime.

A Conflict over Crime News

Police programs to increase citizens' sense of safety are recent offshoots of community-based policing. They have concentrated on extending the sense of protection that comes from knowing police officers personally and from cooperating with neighbors. Before looking at some of the leading programs in the nation, let us examine an effort in Troy to reduce the perception that predators abound. One woman, aged sixty-three, who lived alone in an apartment just south of the central business district spoke for many: "It's awfully tough to feel you're not in danger when you hear about muggings and burglaries all the time."

Knowledge of how crime is portrayed in the mass media has been concisely summarized by James Garofalo (1981) from over fifty studies. Americans get most of their information about local crimes from newspapers, followed by local television. Among newspapers there is great variation in the proportion of space devoted to crime news, a variation that is unrelated to the number of crimes known to the police. For instance, thirty years ago a study of twelve newspapers found that the *New York Times* allocated 7 percent of its space to crime news, but the *New York Daily News* gave it 28 percent (Deutschmann 1959). Murders and other violent individual crimes receive disproportionate attention from all media. Stories of individual crimes have a high rate of readership, surpassed only by election news, according to a study in Chicago (Graber 1980). Research is beginning to identify the effects of a diet of crime news on people's fears; studies by Gerbner et al. (1980) and Doob and MacDonald (1979) have found that watching crime dramas on TV is associated with higher fear of crime among people who live in high-crime neighborhoods. The survey in Troy found that men and women alike felt somewhat less safe going out alone at night if they perceived an increase in crime news in the mass media. In addition, fear of burglary was higher among men who had heard more crime news.

A conflict in spring 1985 pitted the police department's responsibility to withhold certain crime information against freedom of the press. The family-owned *Times Record* had been sold years before to a chain based in Ohio, and retirement had gradually claimed the older staff members, who had worked with great pride in the city. This sale of the *Times Record* is part of a long-term trend, fostered by tax laws, from 97 percent local ownership of daily newspapers in 1910 to about 30 percent in 1982 (Dertouzos and Thorpe 1982). Editors and managers operating a particular daily on behalf of a national chain can be expected to give less weight to local pride and to local definitions of the good of the community and more weight to profits.

Early in his work as commissioner, O'Connor had covered press relations in the departmental rules and had assisted the *Times Record* editor in writing guidelines for accuracy and good taste; these specified the withholding of the names of victims and arrested juveniles. Departmental rules authorized the officer in charge of a crime scene to grant access and supply information to the press. Any officer who felt that access or information would be contrary to sound police practice was required to refer the press to his or her immediate supervisor for further decision. No police department can or should release all information to the press.

Nor should newspapers print everything reporters know. In 1975, when Lansingburgh experienced the wave of fear, the *Times Record* showed restraint by not revealing sensational details of the murder that triggered the public outcry. In the 1980s the *Times Record* crime stories became more sensational and more numerous, in the judgment of Commissioner O'Connor and Chief Miller. They faulted the newspaper for stories that needlessly harmed the subjects, sensational detail in major stories, and numerous stories of trivial crimes "to keep the ads from rattling." A suicide by a woman student was covered in detail. When minors were accused of serious crimes, the newspaper printed their names, even though state law forbids police departments to release them. Publication of the many specifics of a murder under investigation complicated police efforts to check the truth of a confession of intimate details that could otherwise be known only to the murderer. Neighborhood burglaries became the topic of a series of stories when the *Times Record* linked all of one neighborhood's break-ins by calling them the work of "the Hillside Burglar." Chief Miller raised the possibility that the glamour of the name and the description of the mode of entry may have prompted a few young imitators.

The *Times Record's* wealth of crime stories—in comparison with crime coverage in the family-owned daily of neighboring Schenectady and in the Hearst-owned daily of Albany—made Troy appear crime-ridden. This image detracted from the long-term efforts of the police department to build a realistic sense of citizen safety, and it undercut a new city campaign to highlight Troy's attractiveness as a residential town. Meanwhile, the Guardian Angels, the tough youths who patrol New York City's subway, had opened a chapter in Albany over the protest of the mayor, and the rumor spread that they would come to Troy.

Crime news is the easiest kind of news to obtain because the potential stories are already written as police reports and can be easily rewritten with little or no additional detail. Some newspapers play up sensational crimes to boost circulation. Editorial decisions to publish more crime stories generate more column inches by reporters with beginning salaries. And because the police desk is often the first assignment for fledgling reporters, those covering the police beat change every year or two. The department had to educate each one in judgment and taste. An additional strain was put on police-press relations in 1985 when the current reporter obtained unauthorized copies of internal management documents.

In January 1985 the department adopted a revised incident report form that included a box where the officer could exercise judgment to indicate "no publicity"; a new reviewing procedure also restricted the availability of reports. As O'Connor saw it, two monopolies, the press and the police department, both had responsibility to operate in the public interest in their dissemination of information. Under the new procedure the chief or assistant chief reviewed the case reports each morning, held back felonies and other cases under active investigation, and then released reports on arrests, misdemeanors, ordinance violations, and traffic accidents. An eighteen-day tally made in April by the department showed that 88 percent of the reports were released. The police blotter, on which all crimes were recorded for the information of desk personnel, continued to be open to reporters. In a similar conflict ten years earlier, in July 1975, the department had held back all incident reports and instead provided an incident summary in order to prevent the *Times Record* from printing the names of victims in a daily column called "Police Log" (*Times Record*, 18 July 1975). When the newspaper quickly agreed to abide by the guidelines, the department had again made copies of all crime reports available.

In 1985 the *Times Record* attacked the department, starting on 24 March with an editorial incorrectly asserting that the policy was to release no reports until cases were solved. The executive editor complained about the "news blackout" in person and by letter to the city manager, who backed the department. A bitter editorial of 30 March stated that the department's restrictions would have made Hitler's minister of propaganda smile. The *Times Record* sought and received an advisory opinion on 4 April from the state Freedom of Information Office, based solely upon the paper's accusation, that if the department was acting as charged, it was acting illegally. As a countermove, the chief sent documentation of the department's procedures to the state office, but the decision confirming the department's practices as completely legal was not issued until 17 May.

Meanwhile, the *Times Record* intensified the attack; at least ten articles and editorials published in April criticized the suppression of crime information and asked the public to report crimes directly to the newspaper. In a new line of attack a six-column headline on 17 April proclaimed that the *Times Record* had interviewed fifty officers and found department morale at an all-time low. As might be expected, none of the officers' complaints concerned the department's policy on releasing crime information. The newspaper gained the support of the sole Republican councilman, who frequently criticized the city manager. The councilman attempted to introduce legislation to require the release of all crime reports, but the chair of the council's public safety committee refused on the grounds that the matter would soon be resolved (*Times Union*, 26 April 1985). On 6 May the editor dropped the initial line of attack by firing the police reporter on the pretext that he had fixed three parking tickets for the paper's delivery vehicles. In fact, he had carried tickets for standard voiding because the department voids all tickets placed on vehicles while the driver is making deliveries.

On 2 May the FBI's national arrests of members of the motorcycle gang called Hell's Angels for drug trafficking provided the newspaper with a new weapon. The six-column headline of 8 May proclaimed, "FBI Links Angels, Two Troy Cops." The origin of the charge was an affidavit filed in Baltimore that an unnamed informant had told an undercover FBI agent that an unnamed Troy police officer had offered to tell James "Gorilla" Harwood, one of the gang leaders, where police roadblocks would be sited. The FBI agent in charge at Albany immediately said there was no corroboration that any Troy officers were involved with the Hell's Angels (*Times Union*, 9 May 1985), and the shoddy nature of the "evidence" quickly became clear: the supposed link, a Sergeant Doug Wallzenberg, had never been a member of the Troy department. However, the *Times Record* persisted in running follow-up stories on 9, 10, 11, 12, and 15 May, culminating in an editorial on 18 May attacking the commissioner for denying that any link existed. This tarring of the department incensed the PBA, which retaliated by running a message in lights on a downtown electric signboard: "THE TROY POLICE BENEVOLENT ASSOCIATION DOES NOT SUPPORT THE TIMES RECORD."

After the state's Freedom of Information Office issued its opinion in support of current departmental policy, the department relaxed its restrictions to release reports of felonies under investigation but with sensitive sections excised. In a private meeting the city manager demanded correction from the publisher, who refused to issue a correction, retraction, or apology. In prepared remarks at the annual PBA dinner on 1 June, O'Connor called the repetition of lies a tactic of the McCarthy era. He characterized the Troy newspaper as acting like an absentee landlord, caring more for immediate profits than for the long-term future of the neighborhood. He maintained that the police had matured into a responsible community agency, the equal of the newspaper in education, intelligence, experience, and sensitivity to local citizens. O'Connor concluded that the police department had a legal right and a moral obligation to exercise judgment in assuring citizen safety and privacy.

The aftermath continued. On 11 May the national journalism weekly *Editor and Publisher* carried an earlier story from the *Times Record* about the department's withholding of crime information. In early October the *Times Record*'s stories on the police–Hell's Angels link received the top award for in-depth reporting from the New York State Associated Press Association (*Times Record*, 3 October 1985). Finally, the newspaper received in the Associated Press Managing Editors Association Freedom of Information Award for "its successful fight against the Troy police department and the city administration." City Manager Buckley asked in vain for a reconsideration of the award (*Times Record*, 24 December 1985).

In retrospect, the attempt of the police department to reduce crime news shows that this form of external restraint is considerably less effective than newspaper self-restraint. The newspaper's retaliation damaged the department's reputation because during the spring of 1985 the public read only accusations and never a retraction. The public could conclude that their police had illegally shut off crime news and had links to a drug-trafficking motorcycle gang. The department continues its policy of releasing the bulk of incident reports and of excising key information from reports of crimes under investigation. The newspaper has not again highlighted details of suicides or reported sensational details of murders, but stories of trivial crimes are still major space fillers.

Police Programs to Promote a Sense of Protection

The American Bar Association's *Standards Relating to the Urban Police Function* (ABA 1973, 68) described this goal:

> While rarely articulated, it seems obvious that police have assumed the responsibility for creating a sense of security in the community—for helping to create an atmosphere that makes it possible for people, exercising reasonable care and precaution, to carry on their ordinary, daily activities with the expectation that they will not be endangered, interfered with, or subjected to criminal attack.

Depending on the way police operations are managed, citizens will gain impressions of either safety or danger. A two-officer patrol car suggests to citizens that the city must be very unsafe if a police officer is needed to protect a police officer. That O'Connor made this observation is unusual, for police leaders seldom look at the symbolic aspects of the work.

Recently, a few police departments have initiated a variety of programs to build citizens' realistic sense of safety. The Santa Ana, California, department has maintained ambitious efforts to involve citizens directly in their own safety by creating block associations. The Baltimore County, Maryland, Police department has addressed fear of crime by creating a special unit, Citizen Oriented Police Enforcement (COPE), which has the flexibility to tackle the community problems that breed fear of crime (Taft 1986). In addition to the neighborhood police station in Houston, the Police Foundation evaluated four other programs in that city plus three in Newark (Pate et al. 1986). Houston's other programs include contact patrol, community organizing, victim recontact, and a newsletter. Each program was established in one of six similar, racially mixed neighborhoods; the sixth was maintained without a program to serve as the control. Residents and business people were surveyed before and after some months of operation. In the three neighborhoods where officers took the initiative to meet citizens personally, some reduction of fear took place. Although it is not possible to isolate any one cause of fear reduction, the only common finding in all three successful neighborhoods was that people who recalled seeing an officer recently were less fearful than others.

In the Houston contact patrol program, five regular officers and five relief officers had the responsibility of making special efforts to initiate contact with citizens, typically by going to homes to ask whether they knew of any neighborhood problems that police should address. In this neighborhood, fear of crime went down, and the proportion of citizens who personally knew an officer working in the neighborhood went up from 15 percent to 22 percent. What individual officers actually did in the contact patrol program supports a theme introduced in Chapter 3: that the sum of individual officers' skills and inclinations largely determine what policing is. A single officer made 45 percent of the 427 contacts during the eight months of the study; the four other regular officers each made 10–15 percent of the contacts, averaging less than two per week; and five relief officers made only 2 percent of the contacts. The active officer had persuaded the department to try contact patrol and to assign the program to his patrol zone for the study. Thus, because the department recognized and supported the good work of an individual officer and ordered nine others to do as he did, all nine together slightly surpassed his lone efforts. In the neighborhood without programs, the proportion of people knowing officers personally remained low, 5 percent and then 8 percent. We may wonder to what extent the work of this one officer contributed to the fact that even before the program began, citizens in his neighborhood knew officers at three times the rate in the comparison neighborhood.

Reflection upon the Houston programs and on police programs generally offers a reasonable initial working hypothesis, that a new program is likely to redirect very little police effort. An officer who makes one ten-minute contact per tour is spending slightly more than 2 percent of an eight-hour workday. A two-hour monthly meeting adds up to less than 2 percent of an officer's time. Day in, day out police activities loom large compared to new programs. In looking at the likely impact on citizens of any new program, one must place it in the context of the ongoing and usual links that people have with the police, such as service calls, follow-up investigations, being stopped for a moving violation, or reading newspaper stories about police activities. No matter how energetic the contact patrol, if police officers otherwise neglect or mistreat citizens, the program will not achieve the objectives.

We may make the argument clearer by putting the matter in the extreme, contrasting high quality with shabby service while ignoring the middle ground that makes up so much of police work. In emergencies, officers may arrive instantly or only after repeated calls. On driving patrol they may stop frequently to chat with citizens, or they may ignore an urgent hail. Juvenile officers may gain the cooperation of even hostile parents in the guidance of their children or may show contempt for the children and their parents. Detectives may give wise reassurance to crime victims or may belittle them. Police leaders and union leaders may take every opportunity to build citizens' realistic sense of personal safety, or they may play upon fears to emphasize the importance of police. Different officers have told burglary victims, "Here's how you can protect your home," or "That's what you get for living in this rat trap." If one pictures a department where the regular work is skillfully conducted with concern for the well-being of citizens, it becomes clear that opening a neighborhood station or establishing a dozen of the other programs in vogue may have little impact because many officers are already directing their efforts toward the program's objectives. If one pictures an incompetent and hostile department, one sees that new programs are hopeless because no foundation exists to support them.

Special programs do have a place. In some instances they reorganize the regular work so that achieving particular objectives becomes easier. In all instances programs signal to department members and to citizens what is important. Since so much of police work takes place without supervision and without record, it is essential to understand what police officers are doing with the time not spent on programs—the vast majority of their time. To the extent that a program motivates and facilitates officers to modify their habits in the course of their daily work, the program is likely to produce measurable results.

Friendly Relations to Promote a Sense of Protection

Several aspects of community policing appear to enhance citizens' sense of safety. To the extent that findings from the 1978 Troy survey are supported by other research, they may be cautiously generalized beyond the place and date of their origin. First, women more than men increase their sense of security if they know of positive police behavior. Second, knowledge of positive police behavior helps teenagers and persons over fifty feel safer but makes no discernible difference to men and women in the self-assured ages of twenty to forty-nine. Third, people who live alone feel as much reassured through personal acquaintance with officers as do those living in families.

Women of all ages who have had any of a variety of positive connections to the police department feel safer out alone at night than those who have not. These connections may include satisfaction with police service to the immediate neighborhood; confidence that if they report a crime, officers will believe them and try to solve the crime; and, for adult women, knowing someone to contact in order to change the way police officers work in the neighborhood. Ironically, women over fifty are the demographic group least likely to know officers personally (only 13 percent do), yet most likely to feel safer for the acquaintance. Among the few older women who knew two or more officers, about 40 percent felt safe, compared to about 25 percent of those who knew a single officer and about 15 percent of women who knew none.

Just how people form and re-form their feelings of safety and the ways that police can be involved in promoting a sense of safety are not well understood. Sound research requires an open police department, skillful researchers, and generous funding. The new willingness of police managers to conduct careful, controlled experiments makes such sites more abundant than researchers and funding. Years will probably elapse before research pins down the effectiveness of particular programs in promoting feelings of security among particular groups of people.

Meanwhile, police departments can run programs to increase community cohesion and improve police-community relations, programs that are fully justified on other grounds. If they also augment people's sense of safety, that would be an unknown benefit. Whether or not a department has formal outreach programs, individual officers can conduct their daily work so as to build a realistic sense of security among the people they contact.

One elderly man from Lansingburgh summed up what he liked best about police officers in the neighborhood:

It's always nice to see them cruising around in the car. Quite often they're around for accidents and fires. In October we had a sign in front of the church, and one evening I found it all pulled apart. The police came, found out that it was teenagers, and the next day the kids came and apologized.

Police Power

Survey question: When parents tell their children about police officers, what should they tell them?
A reply: Whether you are right or wrong, you are wrong.

Police Malpractice

Most acts of malpractice that individual police officers commit are based on their judgment that they are right and the citizen is wrong. On occasion an officer has killed an unarmed teenager fleeing from a burglary, and the officer's actions have been judged right by himself, by his department, and by the court. Officers have sometimes beaten a handcuffed prisoner "to teach him a lesson" and felt justified, and their story that the prisoner received the bruises while resisting arrest was never challenged. The trend of the last century has been a marked reduction in abuses of police power, but the fact that such incidents can still occur gives grounds for concern.

The orthodox solution to police abuse of power has been to rely on an internal disciplinary process, which has fundamental defects: most people who feel aggrieved never complain; many investigations fail to reach clear conclusions; and the process focuses on an individual's shortcomings, not departmental deficiencies. The Troy disciplinary system during the years of upgrading suffered these defects. Had an effective disciplinary system been essential to restrain police abuses, then malpractice would have been rampant and citizens fearful. Yet the citizen survey found a low incidence of police abuses and a 95 percent majority of city residents without fear of the police. This puzzling combination, an inadequate disciplinary system yet malpractice rare and citizens unafraid, suggests looking beyond the disciplinary system for reasons why citizens need have no fear of police. A reasonable explanation is that most officers have their own high standards of conduct.

The first section of this chapter describes a set of incidents in Troy where police officers were accused of committing some wrong; the second examines the department's disciplinary system at work in handling each of these incidents and the limited role of external review. The third section sketches means of assessing the prevalence of serious malpractice within a given department and the fourth section summarizes positive, systematic means of encouraging sound practice and discouraging malpractice. Hard questions that can be asked about any department are given in the Appendix.

A word of warning is appropriate here. Some details describing acts of malpractice in Troy came from conversations with department members. Anyone wishing to learn from officers about a department's patterns of malpractice should think through in advance how he or she will use information on current and recent wrongdoings. Officers are likely to be frank only if promises of confidentiality are made and kept. Officers who work the street know details of excessive force and harassment. To understand patterns, an inquirer needs no specifics on who did what to whom. When attempting to understand the nature of the problems, an inquirer will encounter exceptional difficulty if he or she attempts also to promote justice in specific instances. Unless the inquirer has witnessed the act of malpractice and is willing to testify, it is very unlikely that the inquirer's efforts will bring about an appropriate disciplinary outcome.

Instances of Police Malpractice

Unlike legislators, judges, and administrators, who have time to deliberate, police officers have broad authority to intervene instantly. Thus, there are no mechanisms to detect and curb abuses of police authority while they are occurring; external controls must be after the fact. Nor do police officers produce a full written record comparable to that of a court hearing to facilitate a review of their decisions. The most effective control on police authority will be the self-control of the officers at the very moment that they are exercising their authority.

The job of a police officer provides an especially rich variety of opportunities for wrongdoing, which may be divided into four categories based on the nature of the act:

- crimes,
- abuse of discretion,
- shirking and negligence,
- proscribed off-duty behavior.

We begin with the actions most damaging to the police function and conclude with the least damaging, although each broad category includes acts ranging from serious to trivial.

Crimes

Wife beating, driving while intoxicated, and other crimes occasionally surface among police officers, as among many otherwise law-abiding citizens. In addition, officers have frequent opportunity to commit street crimes, such as lifting a bottle of scotch while investigating a liquor store burglary, or slipping the money from the wallet of a drunk. Because they deal with all manner of offenders, police officers have opportunity to offer to overlook crime committed, in exchange for an offender's commission of a fresh crime at the officers' command—such as the theft of a car belonging to a hostile reporter. That crimes are more serious when committed by police officers than by others is a view firmly held by both professional police administrators and the newer school of police managers. Obedience to the law is the foundation for other commendable behavior. The democratic system of holding the government accountable to the people is undermined if the very individuals who enforce the law fail to obey the law.

Police work keeps raising the fundamental question, in what circumstances do good ends justify evil means? How far should officers go in using repugnant or dangerous means when morally good means will not achieve the good end? Gary Marx (1988), who began research for his book on undercover work with the assumption that deception is not es-sential to the control of morals crimes, has concluded that undercover work is a necessary evil. Carl Klockars (1980) wrestled with the justifica-tion of evil means and came to approve of torture as an extreme attempt to save a life. Delattre (1989) reveals the confusion in Klockars's reason-ing and recommends that the decision to use illegal means after exhaust-ing all alternatives should be made only by an officer of great integrity, who will then bear the consequences.

In my view, the line dividing illegal from legal actions is fundamental. Citizens may be acting morally when they choose civil disobedience, but the concept does not easily fit the police officer's role. As suggested in the conclusion of Chapter 3, some laws need to be changed to give offi-cers authority to take peacekeeping actions that are now illegal, such as immediately removing guns from a home where family members are threatening to kill each other. In the absence of appropriate legislation, circuitous legal alternatives can sometimes be created, such as finding grounds to arrest the most aggressive disputant and quickly obtaining a court order to remove the guns. An officer of great integrity who failed to find a legal way to separate the disputants from the guns should not make an illegal confiscation. I believe that an officer who has made stren-uous efforts within the limits of what the law allows is not at fault if afterward one family member shoots the other.

A strong statement supporting complete adherence to the law is given by Wesley Pomeroy (1985), a police manager of more than thirty years' experience and the holder of a law degree: "Police simply cannot be allowed to use *any* means under *any* circumstances that are outside the law. Men and women who are police officers have absolutely no identity or power as police officers outside the law. . . . If they operate outside the law, they become criminals, just as everyone else, and should be punished."

The most serious crime that can be committed by an officer is to kill a person without justification. Such events happen rarely, and when they do, they elicit strong public criticism. For off-duty officers, as for other citizens, bars and fast food restaurants are spots where fights are partic-ularly frequent. In 1982 a young Troy officer, whom we shall call John Logan, killed a man with whom he had picked a fight at a bar. The inci-dent, as presented by the prosecutor to the jury that convicted him, be-gan as name calling between Logan and his friends and a black homosex-ual and his friends who were walking past the bar. The pedestrians walked away from the encounter, but Logan and his friends jumped into a car, caught up with them, piled out of the car, and resumed name calling. The black man, backed up against a wall, seized a bottle and broke it to make a weapon. Logan shot him, and the man died in the hospital.

The types of crimes that most undermine the foundations of police as a law-abiding agency are crimes of office, those acts committed when individuals abuse their official police powers. Crimes of office are as diverse as police responsibilities. The power to enforce the law also carries the potential for self-serving nonenforcement and over-enforcement, providing every officer opportunities to engage in corruption and favoritism. All crimes of office involve the misuse of authority by police officers in a manner designed to produce personal gain for themselves or for others. The term "corruption" may be broadly defined to cover all crimes of office or narrowly restricted to financial gains. Naturally, law enforcement in the areas of drugs, gambling, prostitution, and other morals offenses provides particular opportunity for corruption, since individuals engaging in those businesses are ready to buy favorable treatment. Some notion of the diverse opportunities for corruption is given by this summary from a longer list made by Herman Goldstein (1977) of actions for which officers get payment, free goods, discounts, or the appreciation of friends:

1. failing to make an arrest, issue a ticket, or inspect a licensed premise;
2. revealing police records, reducing the charges, dropping the investigation, altering police records, destroying evidence, or altering testimony in court;
3. providing services beyond those normally.rendered, such as frequenting places of business or guarding parked cars;
4. making referrals to bail bondsmen, defense attorneys, ambulance services, physicians, tow truck operators, or others whose services are needed in a crisis;
5. making false arrests that result in overtime pay for court appearance.

Crimes of office can also occur without the connivance of other individuals and without payment. Cases have come to light in which officers tampered with evidence in order to obtain the conviction of a suspect they "knew" was guilty, or to keep a friend out of trouble. Consider this incident involving Troy police officers which occurred in January 1981. The terse statement of the facts given below includes only those that were undisputed in 350 pages of testimony and 50 pages of documents (N.Y.S.C. Appellate Division 1984).

□ A high-speed chase originated across the Hudson from Troy, shortly before 1:00 A.M. on January 17. The Troy dispatcher broadcast that a red Pontiac had already struck two police cars and was likely to strike any car in its way. Then the fleeing Firebird entered Troy, pursued by police cars from the neighboring jurisdictions of Colonie and Watervliet. Most units from Troy joined the pursuit, including a pair of partners who drove into the suburbs where they believed they might intercept the speeding car. As the Firebird left Troy, a two-man unit from the Rensselaer County sheriff's department joined near the head of the chase. At an intersection some two miles outside the city limits, the Firebird swung down the road where the Troy partners were waiting. As the Firebird sped past, two shots were fired toward the rear wheel, one puncturing the rear tire and halting the vehicle. All together, more than eight police cars participated in the chase or arrived immediately afterward, including a Troy patrol sergeant. Watervliet police arrested the driver and another young man who was a passenger. Unknown to the officers until the chase was over, a frightened young woman had been lying in the back seat, her head inches from where the bullets hit the car. She was placed in another police vehicle. One of the deputy sheriffs took custody of the Firebird, called for his investigator, and ordered a tow truck. Soon all officers save the deputies departed. Then two Troy officers pulled up, took a crow bar from their trunk and probed the bullet hole in the rear of the Firebird. When they had finished, the hole was a jagged gash some four inches long. In departing, one commented, "We weren't here, right?" A while later the tow truck arrived, followed by the sheriff's department investigator, who ordered the car impounded: that is, to be seen by no one without his orders.

The details of this event and its aftermath received full newspaper publicity and are unfolded during the course of this chapter. Here it provides an example of a crime of office: specifically, tampering with evidence. For both the homicide recounted above and this case of tampering, the appropriate questions for investigation are "Has a crime occurred?" and "Who committed the crime?"

Abuse of Discretion

The key investigative questions in situations involving the use of discretion are more difficult. A correct answer is needed to "What happened?" and a fair answer is needed to "Was the officer justified under the circumstances?" The departmental review of the use and abuse of discretion is an exercise in Monday morning quarterbacking by people who did not watch the game. Situations in which an officer makes an arrest for, say, disorderly conduct are sufficiently complex that not even the most careful investigation and weighing of contradictory stories afterward can establish the full truth of whether the officer made the arrest to be vindictive, whether the officer deliberately fastened the handcuffs too tightly, whether the citizen's bruises resulted from excessive or restrained use of force, and whether the officer belittled the citizen. The wide latitude of discretion that officers possess naturally provides a similarly wide range of opportunities for abuse of discretion. Malpractice of this sort is often labeled with vague and emotionally charged terms such as "police brutality" and "police harassment." Even the standard police term "use of excessive force" includes a huge variety of acts.

I have grouped abuse of discretion into six types, distinguished on the basis of the officer's actions:

1. shooting when lesser means would have brought the situation under control;
2. making arrests when lesser means would have resolved the situation;
3. using force to effect an arrest when the individual could have been persuaded to submit peaceably, or using more force than necessary to subdue an individual resisting arrest;
4. making entries, conducting searches, or interrogating in ways that infringe on an individual's constitutional rights;
5. giving special attention to individuals in ways that annoy or disturb them, practices usually termed harassment;
6. speaking or acting in ways that citizens consider discourteous.

Typically, an officer's choice of action is made in seconds, but if it is questioned, the deliberations take days before a decision is made. Officers correctly point to the world of difference between choosing a course of action in the heat of the moment and making a decision in the absence of a deadline. Another crucial difference is that the officer's actions are recorded only in the fading memories of the individuals present, whereas a judge's decision and the whole proceedings on which he or she bases a judgment are recorded verbatim. Thus, members of the legal profession have solid grounds for reviewing the quality of the judge's decision. By contrast, when a police supervisor makes an after-the-fact judgment of whether or not an officer abused discretion, the basic task of reconstructing exactly what happened is far from easy. The supervisor must also consider what the officer could reasonably have been expected to hold in mind when making the decision and what the likely outcomes might have been if the officer had chosen different courses of action. A supervisor who concludes that the officer made a faulty decision must consider what corrective actions are appropriate.

To flesh out the list of six types of incidents in which discretion may have been abused, let us look at some events in Troy. In the first, a young officer, Fred Schmidt, shot a youth.

□   One evening Officer Schmidt and several others responded to a call of an upstairs neighbor that a burglary was in progress. When officers had covered all entrances to the residence, Schmidt entered the back door and found himself on dark, cramped steps. In the darkness he saw two burglars. Both turned on him, and one threatened him with what appeared to be a long knife. Schmidt shot, wounding in the thigh a young man who turned out to be wielding a screwdriver. A departmental review determined that Schmidt had acted properly, and the young man's lawyer did not challenge that decision.

The better-managed police departments have long placed restrictions on the display and use of firearms. The emerging standard is that an officer is justified in shooting only in immediate defense of life. State statutes and departmental regulations are both moving away from the English common law tradition permitting officers to shoot fleeing felons. The Police Executive Research Forum has issued model departmental regulations specifying defense of life as the only grounds for shooting. The standards of the Commission on Accreditation for Law Enforcement Agencies permit shooting only in defense of life or if a person is in immediate danger of serious physical harm. Further, departments must require officers to submit written reports every time they discharge a firearm, other than in training or recreation.

Reflecting broadly on the need to shoot, Commissioner O'Connor commented that an officer draws his gun because he plans to use it. The simple choice he makes is to shoot or not. It is of utmost importance that departmental rules not force an officer to make a complex choice in a situation where his life is threatened. The variety of circumstances in which officers might be in mortal danger and the variety of positions of the attacker would make a very complicated set of rules for an officer to follow about where to hit somebody on what occasion. A person shot in the legs can still return fire. Developing the marksmanship of officers so that they can hit the weapon threatening them is not a practical alternative. O'Connor would not take such chances with the lives of officers.

Making only necessary arrests is the next type of action where discretion is required. An unnecessary arrest may be said to have occurred when an officer is within the letter of the law in making the arrest but professional judgment considers less punitive means appropriate. Since the law does not mandate arrests but only authorizes them, the officer must decide whether there are reasonable grounds. In judging the necessity of an arrest, it is useful to return to the distinction made in Chapter 5 between arrests for the purpose of (1) bringing the offender to court and (2) immediately restoring order. If an officer makes an arrest for an offense for which it is departmental practice to use a summons, the question may be rightly raised whether characteristics of the situation made the arrest appropriate or whether the officer was using the arrest as personal punishment.

Even more problematic are the annoying or dangerous events that require interruption. In these, prosecution is not the foremost aim of the arresting officer. For instance, individuals who are congregating in a way that disturbs others are subject to arrest for disorderly conduct, but social tranquillity may be better served if they are persuaded to quiet down and go to a park. Officers could halt a fist fight between acquaintances by arresting one or both, but a quiet cooling-off period would probably serve the individuals better than a day in court. Arrest for disorderly conduct can be used to take debilitated alcoholics off the streets, but taking them to a shelter connects them with a system more suited to their needs. This is not to imply that arrests in these circumstances are never necessary. The necessity for arrest is a matter of judgment, based on the details of the situation as they can be known by the officer on the spot and confirmed by later expert review.

Here is an example of an arrest that was called into question:

□ Accounts agree that one spring night police officers were summoned by a barmaid who was unable to persuade Hubert Brown, a disorderly patron, to leave. Brown then complied with the police request to leave. The account from David Stone, another patron, is that he protested Brown's ejection; an officer then ordered him to leave, and when he asked the sergeant for his name, he was arrested. The next day Stone filed a formal complaint that his arrest was unwarranted and that he had received bruises on the arms even though he had not resisted. To back his complaint, Stone gave the names of a barmaid and four patrons as witnesses to the incident.

More difficult than establishing whether or not an arrest is justified is determining whether or not the use of force was excessive. The most skillful of police officers must on some occasions use force to restrain otherwise uncontrollable individuals. Two examples will illustrate the complexity of determining whether the force was excessive. The first is the arrest of a thirty-one-year-old white man with a seventh-grade education, as seen both by the arresting officers and by the arrested man.

Four officers, two experienced partners and two with only a year on the job, responded one August night to a call for assistance from a teenage babysitter in an apartment of a public housing project. Later accounts by the four officers agreed that the babysitter had asked them to remove a man who was harassing her. She explained that the mother had instructed her not to allow the children's father into the apartment, because he would be dangerous to her and the children. The deposition of arrest on the charge of obstructing governmental administration reads:

At about 5:15 am . . . while your deponent was making an investigation at the above stated location after a complaint was called in to Central Station about a baby sitter being harassed, the above named defendant began yelling and screaming at your deponent, and stood up and attempted to punch your deponent at which time a scuffle ensued.

The deposition on the charge of resisting arrest states that while attempting to place the above named defendant under arrest he began to punch and kick at your deponent attempting to prevent your deponent from making a lawful arrest.

Two days after his arrest the man was interviewed in jail by the jail doctor, who found him alert, cooperative, without any neurotic disturbance, and admitting to having a bad temper. Here is the doctor's written summary of the man's account:

[He] admits that his married life has been stormy and that he and his wife have had many arguments. Approximately six weeks ago he had moved out of their apartment following an argument but had moved back in one week ago. He claims that following another argument with his wife he left the house to "cool off," returned through an open window and fell asleep on the couch. He claims he "gave the baby sitter no trouble," but when the police arrived at her request, he was told to shut up and was struck twice on the side of the head giving him a black left eye and a split left ear. He claims that he grabbed the policeman, whom he has known for many years, by the waist to prevent him from hitting him again and was then attacked by the other officers which resulted in many bruises on his chest and legs and a questionable broken nose.

Separate accounts were also given informally the next day by the two young officers who participated in the arrest. One admitted surprise that he drew blood when he used leaded gloves to punch the prisoner in the face. The young officers each described the two senior officers beating this handcuffed prisoner at the police station, one using a nightstick. The beating of handcuffed prisoners is not within the discretionary judgment of officers; it is a crime. The reasons to think about such attacks as instances of abused discretion are that the facts are unclear and that the dynamics of prisoner beating are similar to the dynamics of rough handling while subduing individuals being placed under arrest. Such situations are moments of high tension and strong conflict. Both officer and prisoner may be raw bundles of nerves responding to stimuli. The more people become emotionally involved, whether in fear or in anger, the less able they are to use their reasoning capacity. Officers behave as other people do when their emotions are aroused. Thus, if the arresting officer gets a drumming of kicks or has to haul his aging bones down streets and alleys to catch the suspect, his lashing out in retaliation is considered by police colleagues to be "normal"—although not acceptable. As time elapses after the arrest and the officer's emotions subside, vengeful blows are considered unreasonable by fellow officers.

The second example involves the use of excessive force at the end of the high-speed chase that was halted by shooting the tires. At this tense moment, officers and arrestees each had a partisan audience for whom they wished to appear as strong and as manly as possible. Further details of the incident are provided in separate sworn statements by the two deputies of the sheriff's department.

All officers were yelling to the occupants of the car to exit with their hands in sight, at which time there was no response from the occupants. Other officers including myself yelled several more times to the occupants to exit the vehicle, but got no response. Two officers unknown to me then smashed the driver's window with a flashlight and nightstick. By this time several other units had arrived on the scene including units from Troy and Watervliet. When the window was smashed two unknown officers took the driver out through the window area and placed him under arrest. There was a female passenger in the rear of the defendant's vehicle yelling and screaming, "Don't shoot." And she continued to yell and scream in a hysterical state. The male on the passenger's side was pulled from the defendant's vehicle and placed in handcuffs and escorted to a Watervliet patrol unit. . . . The female passenger exited the vehicle on her own.

The second deputy gave a more detailed account of the same events.

A Colonie policeman started banging on the driver's window with a Kel-light and couldn't break the window. A Watervliet policeman smashed the window with a nightstick. I observed a white female lying on the back seat with her hands raised yelling, "Don't shoot." The driver was taken out of the driver's window by Colonie, Watervliet and Troy police. He was struck several times by police and put on the hood of 4211 and cuffed. The male passenger in the front seat was taken out by Colonie and Watervliet P.O. passenger door and was cuffed on left by Watervliet policemen [that is, a handcuff was placed on the prisoner's left hand]. I was holding the right arm and he was cuffed on the hood of a Colonie P.D. unit. Officers [gives two names from Troy] arrived at the scene. I said to officer [name given] "How's it going, quick draw?" He stated, "That's how to end a pursuit. Can't fuck around with them all night." Officer [another name given] attempted to kick the subject who was cuffed in front of the Colonie unit in the groin area. The driver and the other male subject was put in the Watervliet unit and the female was put in another unit and driven away from the scene. I saw Sergeant [gives name] of the Troy P.D. pull his patrol car (unmarked) up Easy Street, get out, walk east about 20–30 feet, go back to the car and leave the scene. Approximately five minutes all police cars left scene.

As every police officer knows, each eyewitness account of an event will differ from the next. In this case the sheriff's deputies had at first given cursory reports; they wrote these sworn statements only after substantial discussion with their department's investigator, who was in charge of the case. These accounts may be inaccurate in some details and yet are useful for the purpose of understanding the use and abuse of force in making arrests. The scene as described by the deputies may be considered as authentic; that is, the events are true to life in the sense that similar situations arise elsewhere and develop in similar ways.

The fundamental fact about the working group that made the arrests is that it was composed of at least twelve officers from four police agencies. Because they converged only for this one event, they had had no experience in working together and thus no patterns of collaboration or common expectations of who would assume leadership. The absence of a supervisor at the time of the arrests deprived the group of an individual whose rank would immediately identify him as a leader. The intense emotions generated by the real dangers of a high-speed chase—fear, excitement, anger—do not subside immediately after the cars halt. When the occupants of the car failed to obey the order to exit, some officers may have misjudged the danger of the situation. Were the car occupants armed? Were they criminals? Almost none of the officers knew that they were confronting a teenage driver whose failure to stop after a traffic violation had prompted the chase. No one took leadership to reassess the danger to make a judgment that the danger had passed, and to impose this judgment on all the officers.

Relevant here are Friedrich's (1977) findings from the President's Commission patrol study, mentioned in Chapter 4, that officers in pairs are more aggressive toward citizens than officers working alone. In a subsequent analysis Friedrich (1980) found that the single strongest influence on whether or not officers used force was the number of officers present. In this case, some officers broke the car window and dragged the driver through it. The most thorough of subsequent inquiries could not have established whether the particular failure of each individual officer to reach through the broken window to open the door was hasty thoughtlessness in subduing an uncontrollable driver, or whether it was intended as punishment. A good deal of violence is inflicted upon police officers, but whatever kicking the passenger did to officers as they forced handcuffs on him, no one had authority to kick back. The presence of the girl in the back seat may have influenced the boys not to surrender, to show themselves strong in contrast to her hysterical screaming. For the officers, the discovery that a girl had been lying in the back seat brought the shocking realization that the bullets fired to stop the car had come close to killing her.

The question of infringing on constitutional rights involves making yet another sort of judgment call. In the present era of active judicial interpretation, the boundaries between permissible and impermissible police action are continually shifting. In recent years questionable police actions in Troy have usually been in gray areas where the precise extent of the consitutional protection was not clear. From 1974 comes a clear-cut example of disregard of rights, in which the captain of the professional standards unit reported that an officer had failed to notify the parents of a boy in custody and had interrogated him without their presence or knowledge. The commissioner issued a written reprimand to the officer, and when the man's platoon captain leaped to his defense, the commissioner sent a strong memo to the platoon captain: "I suggest you read the New York State Family Court Act with some care. I do not care that the past practices of the Department were to violate the rights of juveniles. I intend to take the necessary steps to assure that such practice does not continue."

Harassment, the fifth category of malpractice, includes all actions deliberately taken by officers to single out individuals to annoy or punish them. Obvious methods of harassment are to stop individuals without good reason, to issue tickets for minor violations when the usual practice is to ignore them, to arrest individuals for ordinance violations when the usual practice is to give a warning. The intentions of the officer determine whether an action is harassment. Officers need to be aware of the extent to which citizens view as harassment many actions that officers consider harmless or even proper. The boredom of driving around on routine patrol may nudge some officers into disturbing couples parked in lovers' lane. Sometimes what a citizen views as harassment may be a form of flirting. A young woman of eighteen briefly explained in the 1978 residential survey why she and others like her had reason to fear the Troy police:

> Because I am young and sometimes I have to walk home from work. They slow down and follow you. I just don't know what they would do. I know some of them drink because I have seen this.

Citizens may feel harassed because their perception of what is appropriate behavior differs from that of the officer. In the winter of 1977 two officers spotted the operator of a city salt spreader stopping at each red light and then proceeding through it. The officers ticketed the operator because he was not driving an emergency vehicle. The public works employee was outraged that he was stopped in the course of traveling efficiently from one work location to the next. The officers had not wanted the bystanders to think that city employees can get away with breaking the law under the noses of the police. The situation was resolved when the commissioner approved the officers' actions and the head of the public works department spoke to the operator.

A typical situation that may produce harassment is a long-standing dispute between neighbors in which one party happens to be a police officer.

□ Bad feelings had long existed between the woman running a group home next door to a commercial garage and Officer Steven Wood, who owned the garage. Sporadically, kids threw raw eggs at the garage and cars. Hostility came to a head one January when the adult son of the group home's manager was clearing snow from in front of the apartment and blew it on the officer's truck. Steven Wood and the young man exchanged heated words. It is unclear whether or not the officer landed the only blows. Wood arrested the young man for harassment, resisting arrest, and a handful of other charges, which the police department disallowed. The young man was treated in a hospital emergency room immediately after the arrest and later spent a week in the hospital under observation for internal injuries. The young man and his attorney brought the case to the department's professional standards unit and also filed criminal charges against Officer Wood.

A sixth category of abuse of discretion is discourtesy, usually a failure to speak or act with appropriate restraint. Deliberate discourtesy has no place in professional policing, whatever level of discourtesy citizens display. Occasionally an officer may have a legitimate reason to do something that offends a citizen. An officer who has just received an emergency call might curtly refuse to be drawn into conversation or brush past a bystander.

Since discourtesy between strangers is not rare in late twentieth-century America, why should police discourtesy be regarded as a serious shortcoming? An immediate answer is that when an unequal relationship exists in which one individual is far more powerful than the other, a rude remark from the powerful person must be swallowed lest a retort bring on more serious reprisal. Thus, a cutting comment from an officer is not one of several blows exchanged in verbal fisticuffs where both parties may consider themselves winners but a source of rankling displeasure. A broader answer is that government by the consent of the governed requires that all government officials treat all citizens with consideration. The ideal of equal protection under the law is closer to being realized when police officers enforce the law courteously, without malice or ill will.

Citizen complaints that an officer on patrol treated them discourteously are exceptionally difficult to investigate because the parties tenaciously hold to contradictory versions of what was said. By contrast, when a citizen charges discourtesy by a police telephone operator, almost all departments can verify what happened by playing the tapes that continuously record all calls and radio messages. An example from Troy occurred at 5:30 A.M. one summer night when an older officer working as telephone operator growled at a caller who complained of noisy people in the backyard, "Are you the same s.o.b. who called before?" Just after the citizen hung up, the dispatcher closed with, "Fuck you." The department taping system preserved the whole unpleasant exchange.

Shirking and Negligence

The origins and control of serious police wrongdoing are better understood as part of a full picture that includes less serious and more common varieties of malpractice. Shirking is avoiding work; negligence is careless work. The first abuse listed below makes explicit that police officers bear the responsibilities of office on a continual basis from the day they are sworn in. The second involves failure to comply with departmental controls. The rest of the items are failings common to many occupations:

1. failing to take appropriate police action at all times, even when not on duty;
2. failing to obey lawful orders (there is no requirement to obey unlawful orders);
3. taking unjustified sick leave;
4. coming to work late, leaving early;
5. sleeping on the job;
6. prolonged idling or working excessively slowly;
7. conducting personal business during working hours;
8. drinking on the job;
9. coming to work intoxicated;
10. carelessly using or damaging equipment;
11. improper attire and neglect of personal equipment;
12. performing tasks carelessly.

As this list indicates, most shirking and negligence are not directed against specific citizens but result from general laziness. An important exception is that some officers are selectively careless, varying the quality of their work according to the social station of the citizens served. Negligence and shirking are easy to get away with in police work. Officers on patrol have neither production targets nor close supervision. The uneven timing of calls for service requires intense effort at times, followed by slack periods that only highly motivated and creative officers can fill productively. Criminal investigations in many departments are still not managed in ways that hold detectives accountable for how they spend their time or for their production of arrests. Since shirking and negligence are relatively clear cut, relatively uncontroversial, and usually not directed at particular citizens, these acts usually come to departmental attention through the chain of command, as this incident illustrates:

☐   One August evening a patrol sergeant was unable to locate a pair of senior officers who were supposed to be running a speed trap. When he brought his suspicions to the command level, the captain in charge of the professional standards unit and the chief arranged to catch the officers in the act of shirking. At 9:10 P.M. a few evenings later they surprised the officers as they sat in their patrol car hidden from street view, drinking beer and eating ham sandwiches.

Proscribed Off-Duty Behavior

This category should be understood as a catchall of actions which many departments have specifically forbidden to police officers but which, unlike the acceptance of gratuities, are not crimes of office. The categories of regulations are listed here in rough order from rules police managers generally consider essential, to controversial restrictions, to regulations they judge to be unnecessary interference with the private lives of officers:

1. limitations on off-duty employment;
2. restrictions on solicitations and commercial testimonials;
3. prohibition of the use of the influence of office to support or oppose political candidates or parties;
4. regulation of beard and hair styles;
5. restrictions on residency;
6. prohibition of public criticism of the department.

A national study (IACP 1976) has identified off-duty employment, hair styles, criticism of the department, and residential limitations as the four out of sixteen areas of regulation where officers considered their departments' rules least fair. Restrictions forbidding off-duty employment connected with the liquor trade are generally regarded as worthwhile, in order to reduce the many opportunities for corruption in this highly regulated industry, but whether or not other employment restrictions are necessary continues to be debated. For the Troy department, off-duty employment is regulated by state law. Solicitation and endorsement should be regulated for the same reasons that acceptance of gratuities should be proscribed, to prevent officers from becoming indebted to particular interests lest they bias their enforcement of the law. The merits and drawbacks of statutes that forbid police officers to engage in political activity are considered in the next chapter. In Troy, an ill-conceived ordinance restricts residency, but speech and hair styles are left to the discretion of the individual.

Summary

As this rundown of police abuses has shown, acts of malpractice are highly diverse, given the range of police responsibilities and the variety of potential ways to abuse or neglect each one of them. The schema used here to give order to this diversity is an improvement over those underlying most departmental regulations because it groups acts of malpractice that have similar origins and that respond to similar corrective measures. Dividing all malpractice into only four categories—crimes, abuse of discretion, shirking and negligence, proscribed off-duty behavior—gives structure to a complex array of problems.

Three separate decisions must be made in sequence to fit a particular act into the larger picture of malpractice. Is the act a crime? If so it fits into the first category. For all other acts, was it committed in the officer's private capacity as a citizen? If so, it is off-duty breaking of regulations and fits into the last category. The removal of the most and least serious ends of the range leaves the core actions taken in the performance of police responsibilities. Was the act a judgment call? If experts agree that it was, the deed is an abuse of discretion. If experts agree that the act contravened standard practice, it is an instance of either negligence or shirking. The personal sources of malpractice are as richly varied as human nature: ignorance, laziness, boredom, greed, prejudice, poor judgment, lack of emotional control. It is not reasonable to expect that any single solution will reduce all types of police abuse. It is reasonable to expect that appropriate approaches, consistently applied, will keep the level of abuse within tolerable bounds.

Shortcomings of Disciplinary Systems

In coping with an overwhelming array of potential and actual malpractice, police administrators and police managers have relied on the departmental disciplinary system. When the public becomes concerned, typically it is because an outrageous incident has drawn their attention. Citizens, even more than police executives, focus on specific instances, not patterns, of abuse. Looking at how the Troy disciplinary system handled each of the incidents of malpractice described above helps to describe and explain the ways in which police discipline is obstructed by police solidarity and how the traditional locker room subculture of street officers prevents the truth from emerging. It is worth noting that most of these incidents of malpractice come from the first years of O'Connor's work in Troy, when some department members resisted assuming professional responsibility. The cover-up of events in the high-speed chase, the most serious thwarting of the disciplinary system, comes from the middle years.

How Police Discipline is Supposed to Work

Police discipline, like military discipline, has typically been viewed as bearing both a negative aspect, in which superiors become aware of and punish instances of subordinates' misconduct, and a positive aspect, in which subordinates conform to departmental procedures, policies, and rules. The text by Wilson and McLaren (1972) is still the classic statement. Both positive and negative aspects of discipline are supposed to assure uniformity of behavior. In the development of disciplinary systems, police administrators have concentrated on the negative aspect in efforts to make the sanctioning process as fair and thorough as possible.

The IACP issued a major study in 1976 that assessed problems in the disciplinary process and recommended for all departments a nine-step system that had long been standard practice in well-managed departments:

1. the department issues clear, written policies;
2. regular supervision, appropriate inspection, and a simple system to receive citizen complaints aid the detection of misconduct;
3. complaints are reviewed by a simple process;
4. the investigation is initiated by the supervisor and reviewed by the command level;
5. if warranted, the officer is temporarily suspended;
6. internal affairs oversees the supervisor's investigation or itself conducts the investigation;
7. if warranted by the findings of the investigation, the accused officer's unit commander files formal charges and recommends sanctions;
8. the accused officer may appeal to a formal trial board or to an informal conduct review board;
9. the chief decides the outcome on the basis of the board's recommendation.

The most fundamental observation is that this system is strictly an internal review. In 1960 and in 1964 the IACP had gone on record favoring a strong internal disciplinary process and against dividing disciplinary powers with an external review board.

The flow of cases through the internal system has two fundamental similarities to the flow through the courts: (1) it uses an adversarial procedure; (2) it handles a dwindling number of more serious cases at each successive stage. As the cases reach more formal stages, officers have more due process rights, such as the right to be questioned only for reasonable duration, to know the nature of the charges, and (if criminal charges are contemplated) to remain silent and have legal counsel. Such a procedurally fair system is a huge advance over the ad hoc methods that still persist in some agencies. However, the IACP system, like the military system on which it is modeled, rests on three assumptions: that the important actions of subordinates are covered by clear rules; that disobedience can be objectively identified; and that fear of punishment will deter disobedience. These assumptions, not fully in accord with the facts of American policing, are least realistic when applied to abuse of discretion.

The assumption that clear rules define appropriate action is only partially correct. Most crimes are clearly defined; some forms of negligence are also well defined, such as coming to work late and drinking on the job; and off-duty actions that have the least connection with job performance are the most clearly defined, such as wearing beards and living outside town. Abuses of discretion, however, are exceptionally difficult to define in advance. What is the proper amount of force to use in making arrests? Under what circumstances does surveillance constitute harassment? Applicable here is the argument developed in Chapter 3 that police officers work in complicated and ambiguous circumstances. Laws and departmental rules can and should define the broad outer limits of acceptable practice, but the complexity of situations renders impossible the drafting of rules to cover all contingencies.

The second assumption, that disobedience can be objectively identified, is also only partially correct. Obviously, the vaguer the rule, the harder it is to determine whether a particular action violates it. Consider these sections from the Troy departmental regulations:

> In making arrests members shall strictly observe the laws of arrest and the following provisions: only necessary restraint to assure safe custody and safety of the officer shall be employed. The arresting officer is responsible for the safety and protection of the arrested person while in his custody.

In making a particular arrest, was use of the nightstick necessary or excessive? Suppose an officer claims he gave the prisoner one blow with his nightstick to protect himself when the prisoner began pummeling him, but the prisoner claims he was clubbed several times while offering no resistance. How does someone who was not a witness determine what happened and judge whether the clubbing was necessary to the officer's safety?

The third assumption, that fear of punishment will deter wrongdoing, is based on a rational model of human behavior in which individuals make calculated choices. Yet the urgency of a situation often gives an officer no time to weigh the likelihood that his action will come to departmental attention, will be considered an abuse, will draw some punishment, or might draw severe punishment. Shirking, an entirely different problem, can be corrected early by good supervision, but the repeated shirking that comes to the attention of a professional standards unit may be an element of a self-destructive life-style such as alcoholism, again, a pattern not easily corrected by fear of punishment.

The usual fear generated by police disciplinary systems is horror and awe toward the personnel file, or "jacket." The central personnel record for each officer typically contains all evaluations by immediate supervisors and all written reprimands, however trivial the subject. For most departments the fears are exaggerated but understandable within the tradition that an officer does not know when critical comments are placed in his personnel jacket and cannot easily examine his own record. Because regular written evaluations are unusual and notes of commendation are rare, one or two negative items can stand out. Officers legitimately fear that adverse comments made long ago will haunt them when they apply for a new assignment or promotion. O'Connor once observed that reliance upon written reprimand rather than on immediately discussing the problem with the officer is like a foreman watching a carpenter at work and jotting down for the files, "Missed nail, hit thumb."

Ironically, a major way in which American police agencies depart from military structures undermines the impartiality of the system of punitive discipline. In armies, modern and traditional, the officer corps and the line soldiers have been separately recruited and socialized to the organization. The separate career systems, the many privileges of rank, the rotation of command personnel all create between officers and men a social and psychological distance that facilitates both the imposition and the acceptance of punishment. Conversely, in police work every line supervisor and every command-level officer knows from personal experience the onerous nature of departmental rules. In all probability, as a patrol officer each one deliberately broke rules, either to get the job done or for personal convenience. Contemporaries who have remained patrol officers recollect any flagrant violations of the rules and consider basically unfair any attempts to enforce a standard to which he had not adhered. Should a supervisor make a point of their present transgressions, they have the ability to embarrass him with his past. It takes unusual personal courage to say, "Never mind what I did in the past; from here on we are all going to do the right thing." Thus, an informal and unspoken constraint can operate at every level in every police department, affecting all but those rare police managers who move among departments at the top.

In work organizations as well as in their private lives, people tend to do what can easily be done. This does not always coincide with what most needs to be done. Thus, a military-style supervisory system backed by a military-style disciplinary system uses roll call to ensure that officers are properly attired, that their shoes literally shine. After roll call, however, whether officers kick anyone with their shiny shoes is not amenable to detection and correction by a military system. It is no coincidence that the very forms of police wrongdoing that have aroused the greatest public outcry are the forms most difficult to control through military-style discipline. Gary Sykes (1985) has argued that a reason the public does not press for substantial reforms in the control of police behavior is that military trappings give the illusion of officers already under firm control.

A Disciplinary System at Work

Commissioner O'Connor's working assumptions in Troy were that the preponderance of officers wanted to do their jobs, that malpractice was commonly the result of mistakes rather than deliberate intent, and that most officers would willingly accept guidance in correcting their mistakes. He further recognized that not all officers would voluntarily live up to the new standards and that a system of sanctions was therefore required. The tales of the workings of the disciplinary system include both cases thoroughly investigated and cases in which the locker room view prevailed that officers must back each other, right or wrong. Although nationally there remains widespread reluctance of officers to come forward against a fellow officer, it appears that in a growing number of agencies, officers tell the truth if directly questioned.

During his first year with the Troy department, O'Connor established a disciplinary system essentially the same as the IACP model, with full procedural safeguards. Although most departments call their disciplinary units "internal affairs," he named it "professional standards" in order to emphasize officers' responsibilities. The extract below comes from his message to the department accompanying the new manual of rules and regulations (O'Connor 1974).

I share our deep concern for the development and maintenance of sound working relationships among members. Discipline too often is seen as a negative or punitive action. As others have said, the best disciplined force is the least disciplined force. Voluntary compliance to agreed upon standards of conduct is the healthy condition of a sound force. Such compliance must spring not from fear of punishment but rather from the free adherence to a code of conduct which is reasonably established, appropriate to the times, and widely agreed upon by most members.

The commissioner had taken a first step toward peer accountability by giving the responsibility for drafting new regulations to one of the five working groups on departmental policy created in July 1973. The volunteers who formed the group were four police officers, a detective, a captain, and the chief. Rather than modify the existing regulations, which had been little used since an outside consultant had drafted them in 1964, the working group began with the Oakland, California, rule manual, which the commissioner had provided. After several months of weekly meetings the committee's product, with few changes, became the departmental rules. The only glaring omissions from the committee's list of proscribed behavior were reporting for work intoxicated, drinking on duty, and sleeping on duty. O'Connor added those three items, plus the Law Enforcement Code of Ethics and a requirement that officers speak truthfully at all times, while loosening the restriction on political activities.

To observe the system in action, recall the simple case recounted above of a departmental operator calling a citizen an s.o.b. Clear rules are the first requirement of the IACP procedure presented above. The applicable section of the departmental rules says, "Members and employees shall be courteous and orderly in their dealings with the public. They shall perform their duties quietly, avoiding harsh, violent, profane or insolent language and always remain calm regardless of the provocation to do otherwise." Point 2 is detection of misconduct, accomplished in this case through a citizen complaint. Point 3 stipulates a simple process for reviewing complaints; here the captain in charge of the professional standards unit listened to the tape of the call. The commissioner looked for circumstances beyond the immediate event which might account for the outburst and learned of the death five days earlier of a young man who had been as close as a son to the officer. Surmising that the officer's personal tragedy had interfered with his ability to keep his temper, O'Connor closed the incident with the officer's apology to the citizen.

The later stages of a fair disciplinary process are illustrated by the case of the two officers drinking on duty, both of whom had long-term alcohol problems. In accordance with points 6 and 7 of the IACP procedure, the professional standards unit conducted the investigation, and the commissioner filed three formal charges: using intoxicants while on duty; concealing themselves so as to be unavailable when on duty; and leaving their duty assignment. As standard procedure, complete copies of all investigative documents went to the accused officers. Pursuant to points 8 and 9, the officers chose to have a formal hearing by the commissioner, who determined their guilt and set their punishment at ten days' suspension without pay. He also firmly admonished them to cease accepting gratuities, a reference to the fact, which came out in the hearing, that when they bought the beer, the shopkeeper gave them the ham sandwiches. However, this decision did not close the case. In New York, as in most states, officers have the option of appealing adverse decisions to outside authorities, either to a civil service commission or to a public employment relations board. At a formal hearing held by the Troy Civil Service Commission, where the officers were represented by legal counsel and supported by their union president, the chairman of the commission found them not guilty on one of the counts and halved the punishment. The whole process took two months. As with all closed cases, the original file was sealed and kept confidential in the commissioner's office. The record in the professional standards unit was limited to details of person, place, time, and disciplinary action. "This procedure," wrote O'Connor (1974), "assures that a pattern of behavior can be detected while at the same time a minor situation does not hang over a man throughout his career."

Alcohol problems are not normally amenable to correction through punishment. In this case, the two officers split up as partners; one overcame his drinking problem, but the other stumbled through several more years of work, used his year of sick leave, and then was forced to retire. Drinking on duty or reporting to work intoxicated are often episodes in long-term problems of alcohol dependence as a response to stress. O'Connor likened his approach to "sick doctor legislation," by which some states permit doctors charged with malpractice to take sick leave for the purpose of pulling themselves together. The commissioner's efforts on behalf of more than six men with drinking problems prodded several into a residential treatment program and restored most to productive lives.

For an individual who refused to face his condition and who rejected all opportunities for rehabilitation, O'Connor sought no punishment. He simply aimed to separate the officer from the department by early retirement or, if necessary, by formal charges leading to dismissal. The department's most severe alcohol abuser, who picked fights off duty and sometimes reported to work intoxicated, was protected by the two power centers that most frequently hamper management: the union and civil service. A clause in the union's first contract prohibited the department from testing officers for alcohol levels; it was dropped in 1977 only after the New York Public Employment Relations Board ruled on a case from another city that management could not give away that power. The Troy Civil Service Commission repeatedly overruled departmental discipline. The first time O'Connor suspended the officer, for three months without pay as punishment for assaulting a man, civil service awarded him full back pay. After six years of effort, the department finally terminated him.

In acts of malpractice that are serious crimes, a well-managed department typically restricts its role to investigation of the felony in cooperation with the prosecutor. If the court acquits the officer or otherwise comes to a judgment that police leadership considers too lenient, then the department files departmental charges. In 1982 when John Logan came out of a bar, picked a fight, and killed a man, the department immediately suspended Logan but did not arrest him. A particular reason O'Connor gave for moving to indictment without an arrest is that a police officer is very unlikely to flee the jurisdiction. The department's thorough investigation in close cooperation with the prosecutor resulted in a conviction on the initial charge of first degree manslaughter. The department dismissed Logan immediately upon obtaining a copy of the conviction order. The judge imposed the maximum sentence, a marked departure from his usual leniency. Members of the department were stunned by his severity, because the judge had served as the PBA's attorney until his appointment to the bench. His sentence carried the message that police officers would be held to a higher standard of conduct than other citizens.

Consider the department's handling of three confrontations described earlier. The arrest of David Stone outside the bar gave rise to conflicting versions of the events. The four officers present stated that Stone had in no way been mistreated during his arrest and in fact had struck an officer. The platoon captain, asked to investigate by the captain in charge of the professional standards unit, took testimony supporting Stone's story from two young patrons and the barmaid. The captain explained that the department was not out to get Stone but concerned with clearing the reputation of the officer accused of brutality. Then, under intense probing, each patron admitted that he had lied, that Stone had hit the officer in the back, that Stone had offered one $50 and had promised to take care of them in exchange for false testimony. As a result, the professional standards unit exonerated the officer, and O'Connor closed the case with a letter informing Stone that the department had information that he had bribed two witnesses but had decided not to file criminal charges because he had pled guilty to the initial charge of public intoxication.

The conflict that came to blows between Officer Steven Wood and the neighbor who lived next to his garage was resolved by compromise after each side had started court action. Both brought their lawyers to a meeting with Chief Givney and Commissioner O'Connor. Both agreed to drop their charges, to avoid each other, and to call the police if they had any further trouble. In addition, Officer Wood agreed to sell his garage.

The arrest of the man in the apartment with the babysitter came to the commissioner's attention through a third party who had heard separate accounts the next day from the two young officers who had participated in the arrest. One had lost sleep over the beating of the arrestee but did not bring the incident to the professional standards unit because he felt that doing so would betray the brotherhood among officers. He likened the restraints he felt to *Omerta*, the Mafia conspiracy of silence. O'Connor turned the case over to Captain Allen Wright, head of the professional standards unit, without comment on the source of the complaint. Captain Wright spoke first with the platoon captain, who replied that he did not think he was on duty that night. The statements given Wright by the four officers and their sergeant agreed that it had been necessary to subdue the prisoner at the apartment and again at the station because of his vigorous lashing out and kicking. A week after receiving these sworn statements, Captain Wright was visited by the local reporter who covered police news. He corroborated the testimony of the officers, explaining that he had been standing in the doorway talking with the platoon captain when the struggle took place. The news that the platoon captain had been on duty shocked Captain Wright, since he had not immediately said so. Wright never sought out the arrested man for a statement or a photograph of the bruises, and the man never came forward—not surprising for a poor, ill-educated, unemployed man who can anticipate future dealings with the police. "Unsubstantiated" was the finding of the professional standards unit, indicating that the evidence was insufficient either to prove or disprove that the prisoner had been beaten.

The 1981 high-speed pursuit illustrates the cover-up of mistakes. The Troy officers involved did not give prompt and full reports on the chase. The sergeant on the scene, who was also the commanding officer that night, did not walk over to where the fleeing car had stopped and did not know at the time that shots had been fired. Departmental rules since 1974 specifically require a report on the circumstances of every decision to shoot. Only the next morning did Chief Givney learn from the sheriff that Troy officers had fired shots, that the shots had narrowly missed the young woman lying in the back seat, and that two officers had defaced the bullet hole in the car. Later, when an officer went to the assistant chief to discuss the incident, Chief Givney immediately advised him of his constitutional rights against self-incrimination. In O'Connor's judgment, the chief's action had a chilling effect on a man who was volunteering to explain what had happened. To give an officer his rights immediately casts him in the role of prisoner. Afterward, all officers declined to talk of the incident.

The department placed no disciplinary charges until the grand jury had concluded its deliberations, in order to assure that a departmental finding would not prejudice the jurors. The grand jury handed down no indictments, but its two-page report recommended administrative action to adopt policies concerning high-speed pursuit and to conduct annual training on pursuits and on the preservation of evidence. Later, the department established a policy on high-speed pursuit that (1) reiterated the departmental rule against shooting at moving vehicles, (2) permitted the pursuing officer to call off the chase if he judged that his safety or public safety was at risk, (3) required a supervisor's approval to exceed the speed limit or leave town, (4) required a supervisor to direct additional officers to assist the pursuit, and (5) forbade speeds exceeding the posted limit plus 20 MPH unless the person pursued was suspected of a violent felony.

After receiving the grand jury's report, the commissioner called the officers involved to his office, told them he expected to hear something significantly different from what was in the original reports, suspended six without pay, placed formal charges against them himself, and designated a city attorney as hearing officer in order to separate adjudication from the laying of charges. While awaiting the hearing, O'Connor informed each accused officer of what he considered to be a fair penalty for that officer's misconduct as it was then known, and he made the commitment that if they would tell the truth, he would cut the penalties. The sergeant admitted that his failure to take charge of the scene had permitted officers to evade responsibility; he accepted eight days' suspension without pay. The officer who admitted firing at the car accepted eight days' suspension and five days of work without pay as the penalty for failure to file a report on the shooting. No one gave further information on the pursuit. Since there was no way to prove exactly what happened during the shooting and the arrests, the commissioner dismissed the charges against two other officers involved.

Fourteen weeks after the chase, the hearing began for the two officers most seriously accused.

You tampered with and caused the destruction and contamination of physical evidence while it was in the custody of another law enforcement agency.

You left the City of Troy without authorization.

You submitted a report knowing information contained therein to be false . . . that Rensselaer County Sheriff's Deputies told . . . [you] a 1975 Pontiac bearing New York registration 117 PVP was not being impounded. [N.Y.S.C. 1981]

The hearing consumed two full days, pitting a city attorney against an attorney from the firm that represents the PBA. The City relied upon the testimony of the two sheriff's deputies to establish that the officers had enlarged and disguised a round bullet hole in the Pontiac while it was in the custody of the sheriff's department, and that they had lied when they claimed a deputy told them the car was not being impounded. Testimony of the chief and assistant chief attempted to establish that officers were thoroughly trained in the handling of evidence and knew they were engaging in misconduct when they tampered with the bullet hole. The accused officers had brought a cross-complaint against the commissioner for failing to provide adequate training and for harassing officers with disciplinary charges as a cover-up for inadequate training, but the hearing officer immediately ruled that civil service law does not permit members to bring charges against a department head. The double theme of the defense was that the department was deficient in training and procedures and that officers use their own judgment (to pry into what arouses their curiosity, to leave the city without authorization in an emergency) as standard practice. Here are excerpts from a typical exchange between the defense lawyer and one of the defendants (N.Y.S.C. 1981, 182, 188–192).

Q: And its your testimony that police officers are to use their best judgment in a situation such as you describe?

A: Yes. That's all we have to go by.

Q: Are there times when best judgment isn't always used?

A: I would say yes, there would have to be. But it's still the only thing you have to go by, your own judgment.

Q: Is it the practice of this department to put members on charges of misconduct when they don't use best judgment?

A: Not to my knowledge.

[The same defendant six pages later.]

A: It [City's exhibit 3] appears to be the inside cover sheet of the manual for police presented by New York State. . . . [It is] approximately 2 to 2½ inches thick.

Q: Were you ever ordered to read that book?

A: No, I was not.

Q: I show you what has been marked as City's exhibit 4 and 5 and ask you what they are.

A: *Training Keys*, volumes one and two.

Q: . . . Have you received any oral or written order to read those?

A: No, I have not.

Q: I show you what has been marked as City's exhibit 6 and ask you what it is.

A: It's the basic training course for police officers presented by the Troy Police Department and the Bureau for Municipal Police.

Q: . . . Are you aware of whether or not the City has adopted City's 3, 4, 5 or 6 as procedural manuals for you to follow?

A: To the best of my knowledge . . . the City has not adopted any of these for policy or procedure.

The second defendant and seven other officers called by the defense all testified to the same themes. A full two months later the civil service hearing officer found the police officers guilty of obliterating evidence, an act of misconduct of a "very serious nature when committed by a professional, trained police officer," but not guilty of leaving the city without authorization or of submitting a false report. He recommended six weeks' suspension without pay. The commissioner accepted the finding but increased the penalty to eight weeks. The officers appealed the decision to the state courts, which supported the commissioner.

This saga highlights several common problems. First, high-speed pursuits are the most exciting and dangerous events in the ordinary round of policing. Pursuits are dangerous to the occupants of the fleeing vehicle, the pursuing officers, other motorists, and any pedestrians nearby. A chase typically begins over a minor violation, but the driver's flight to escape arrest quickly becomes the reason for pursuit. The one who flees is often a teenager, lacking the judgment to quit. In concentrating on the chase, officers seldom reflect on whether this apprehension is worth the risks and rarely choose an alternative course of action: to break off a chase, use the computerized vehicle registration to locate the address of the owner, investigate who is driving the car, and then apprehend the driver when he or she returns home with the car. Personal courage and pride keep officers engaged in a high-speed pursuit, and a successful conclusion produces an immense sense of group achievement.

Second, unfortunate events catch newspaper headlines. Considering that the chase ended without loss of life, the public might have quickly forgotten the event if officers had quickly accepted responsibility for their actions. By coincidence, less than two months after the chase, Officer John Logan picked a fight and killed a man. This pair of events shaped a negative public image of the department for a year or more.

Third, many officers who otherwise conduct themselves professionally will lie to protect each other from punishment for breaking the rules. Four years earlier an officer had been disciplined for firing warning shots at a vehicle. Here, the two officers disguised the bullet hole apparently to prevent any questioning of their colleague's decision to shoot. In O'Connor's judgment the shooting was a less serious act of malpractice than the tampering with evidence, since the decision to shoot was made during a life-threatening crisis. Afterward, officers refused to give reports on the incident until a consistent story had been fabricated; they then lied to the extent necessary to support the story. This kind of officer solidarity has not been rare in American policing.

Fourth, when sergeants do not supervise, problematic situations get worse. If the supervisor had immediately required the officers to face up to the facts of the chase and to submit accurate reports, all would have recognized the stupidity of tampering with evidence.

Fifth, a proper balance needs to be achieved between the weight given to protecting individual police officers against arbitrary discipline and the weight given to timely correction of officers' acts of malpractice. An appeals process helps to prevent arbitrary punishment, but its protracted duration defeats the departmental need to resolve uncertainties and permit work routines to return to normal. In this case, six months elapsed between the evidence tampering and the decision of the hearing examiner—not an unusual delay.

Sixth, the whole string of events, from the chase through the last stages of the legal challenge to disciplinary sanctions, shows the difficulty of moving a police department from a military model to a professional model. At the hearing, officers testified to a man that departmental practice encouraged officers to exercise their own judgment across broad areas. They spoke easily of making difficult judgments, of sometimes making mistaken judgments, and of not being punished for mistakes. Officers used their latitude for exercising judgment to prove to the satisfaction of the hearing officer that they were not contravening narrow orders. Simultaneously, and in contradiction to their professional claims, the officers testified that they had no responsibility for the contents of any of the training materials because they had received neither direct orders to read them nor direct orders to follow them. This episode can be understood as an example of how a crisis prompted young officers who had experienced only reasonable management, and who in other capacities had acted quite professionally, to lie and to disclaim responsibility as Troy officers had done in bygone days in order to defend themselves from harsh and capricious commanders.

A Summary of the Problems of Internal Review

Sketches of unpleasant events and attempts at correction illustrate why police malpractice poses a thorny set of problems.
1. The continual necessity for officers to make independent decisions has the consequence that some of those decisions will needlessly harm citizens as the result of an officer's cynical outlook, faulty judgment, neglect, or other failing.
2. Almost all decisions by officers have low visibility; they may be hidden by incident reports, tolerated by peers, ignored by supervisors.
3. The disciplinary system handles few cases because its operation is triggered only by a complaint.
4. To protect themselves or their friends, some officers lie during official inquiries.
5. When officers lie in unison, justice is thwarted.

The cases of malpractice examined here may be set in context by looking at the work load of the professional standards unit during the first four years of upgrading in Troy. Statistical reports from a professional standards unit are like navigation charts that indicate only the parts of the shoals protruding above water. Acts of malpractice escape the count if citizens fail to complain. Cases in which supervisors themselves take steps to correct malpractice are almost always handled outside the standards unit. The first column of Table 8-1 shows that most of the complaints came from citizens and were directed against patrol officers. Eighty percent concerned abuse of discretion: specifically, insults were the source of one-third of the complaints, excessive force of one-fourth, and harassment of one-sixth. There were two citizen accusations of crimes: obstructing justice, and theft of a reporter's car as harassment. The inside complaints were also directed primarily against men of police officer rank in patrol, but over 60 percent of the charges originating within the department concerned negligence and shirking. The three crimes identified by the department, all sustained, were two cases of larceny by nonsworn members and one case of an officer's giving false information to a rape victim in order to frame another officer.

Organizational dynamics dictate that a professional standards unit will

Table 8-1 Origin and Topic of Complaints against Department Members Made to Professional Standards Unit, 1973–76

Complaint	Citizen Originated			Department Originated			Total
	Partol	Other Sworn	Nonsworn	Patrol	Other Sworn	Nonsworn	
Crime	1	0	1	0	1	2	5
Abuse of Discretion							
False arrest	5	0	0	1	1	0	7
Excessive force	24	5	0	4	0	0	33
Harassment	15	2	1	0	0	0	18
Insults	20	11	7	3	0	1	42
Private dispute	4	2	0	0	0	0	6
Other	0	0	1	2	0	0	3
Shirking and Negligence							
Failure to act	14	5	0	5	0	1	25
Shirking	0	0	0	16	1	0	17
Other	2	1	0	3	1	0	7
Total	85	26	10	34	4	4	163[a]

[a]During the four years examined, the professional standards unit received 184 complaints, but data are missing on five cases initiated by citizens and sixteen initiated by the department.

receive only serious cases from inside the department. Some sergeants so crave to be liked by their squads that they ignore or condone a great deal of shirking and considerable abuse of discretion; others view the disciplinary system as reserved for only the most serious offenses. The pervasive failure of patrol sergeants to exercise any but the most cursory supervision results both in confirmed patterns of malpractice and in the bringing of few cases to professional standards. Any lieutenant or captain in charge of a platoon or precinct who actively seeks to correct abuses of discretion through sending cases to the professional standards unit may worry that *his* supervisor will criticize him for the apparently low discipline within his command.

External Reviews As Supplements to Internal Review

Long-standing institutions in every city have the authority to investigate police malpractice, but they seldom take such action unless public protest forces them to do so. Public prosecutors can initiate criminal charges against police officers, but the fact that police bring prosecutors most of their business is a strong constraint, summed up in the proverb "Don't bite the hand that feeds you." Nor do prosecutors look for politically unpopular battles, because they either hold office as appointees of an elected executive or, as in New York state, have won election themselves.

During the upgrading in Troy there was no need for initiative from the prosecutor.

News media in Troy as elsewhere will report an incident, but once public interest flags, they turn to other news rather than probe the system. Civilian review boards, a newer effort to curb police malpractice, have received a balanced assessment by Wayne Kerstetter (1985). None was ever seriously considered for Troy.

Lawsuits for violations of civil rights increased greatly after the Supreme Court held in *Monell v. Department of Social Services*, 436 U.S. 658 (1978), that municipal governments are liable for the malpractice of their employees. Nationally, the growth of lawsuits is estimated to have been rapid until about 1984, as lawyers newly undertook these cases, and slower since then as federal judges tired of them (McCoy 1987). In 1986–87, cities served by departments with at least 135 officers averaged about one civil suit per 10,000 population (Reaves 1990). In Troy, of the eleven identified lawsuits brought against the department between 1978 and 1985, four concerned excessive use of force during arrest, and four concerned unlawful arrest. The outcomes of the eleven cases divided about evenly for the City in the number won, lost, and settled out of court.

One case shows that miscarriage of justice can occur in such lawsuits. Right after taking testimony from a woman who was in the hospital as an assault victim, an officer arrested the accused, who was quickly arraigned and charged with a felony. The commissioner's understanding is that the accused, the son of a police officer, then persuaded a friend who was guilty of a long list of felonies to plead guilty to this one as well. He did and received no additional penalties. After that, the accused brought and won a lawsuit for false arrest against the department.

Estimating Levels of Malpractice

We have a better chance of understanding the extent of malpractice in a city if we separate specific types. Standard departmental records can provide numbers of police shootings, rough estimates of the rate of unnecessary arrests, and rough estimates of the use of excessive force. Citizen surveys can provide estimates of the more numerous and less serious failings. Possible police abuse of arrest powers can be checked from the perspective of lawyers who, either as assistant prosecutors or as public defenders, have regular dealings with arrestees. For Troy, all sources agree that levels of malpractice were low.

Insights from Standard Departmental Records

The basic limitation of using departmental summaries is that they do not tell whether or not any particular action was appropriate, questionable, or wrong. If trends in the use of force are much higher than elsewhere or going up, then penetrating questions should be asked to identify particular conditions in the city that might require higher levels of the use of force.

As a whole, officers skilled in handling dangerous situations shoot less often than unskilled officers, because they do not dash into harm's way. When they are confronted, their larger repertoire of responses includes persuasion and wrestling as well as shooting. James Fyfe (1988), a leading authority on police shootings, suggests that both the level of danger in a situation and departmental philosophy, policy, and practice influence rates of shooting. Figures presented by Lawrence Sherman (1986) for the fifty largest cities show a strong recent decline in the number of citizens killed by police, dropping during a decade from 300 a year to 190. Figures from an Urban League study show that the ratio of black to white citizens killed has also fallen dramatically, from 7 to 1 in 1971 to 2.8 to 1 in 1979 (Mendez 1983). The record of a given city can be compared with published figures on the number of times citizens have been struck by police bullets and on the number of citizens killed. The number of shots fired is much less likely to be recorded accurately.

Table 8-2 shows that Troy's figures for the average rate of police bullets striking citizens are low, compared to the only other figures available: averages for cities above and below 125,000 and individual data for large cities, which are more dangerous. In Chicago, for instance, 20 percent of the police shootings took place during robberies (Geller and Karales 1981); and in cities of over a million, the rate of reported robbery with guns is five times that of cities between 50,000 and 100,000. How much of the low rate of shooting in Troy is due to the relative tranquillity of the city and how much to departmental philosophy, policy, and practice could be estimated if careful records were kept over a span of many years tracking the change in relevant variables.

Routine police tallies shed some light on unnecessary arrests. Recall that at the end of Chapter 5, in examining arrests where the purpose was to interrupt a disturbing situation, I pointed out that officers skilled in working with people find ways to halt most street disorders without making arrests. An officer who wishes to harass citizens has ready weapons in the disorderly behavior charges. Only an expert in possession of the facts can make a valid judgment on whether or not a particular arrest was necessary. The fact that the national volume of such arrests fell so precipitously, even while the Baby Boom generation was at a disorderly age, suggests that American police once made many unnecessary arrests. For a single city, a sharp increase in the volume of arrests for disorderly behavior immediately raises the question of whether new circumstances have arisen, such as a spate of brutal strikes. If police officers decrease their use of the disorderly charge while citizens continue to use the streets as before, probably officers have cut out some unnecessary arrests. It is possible, but not likely, that a decline in disorderly arrests indicates a

Table 8-2 Annual Rates of Citizens Killed or Wounded by Police Bullets (per 100,000 population)

City	Killed	Wounded	Population in 1980 (in 1,000s)
Troy[a]	.13	.26	56
30 Small cities[b]	.49	1.5	46-124
30 Mid-sized cities[b]	.61	2.0	125-200
Individual cities[c]			
St. Paul, Minn.	.07		270
Sacramento, Calif.	.11		276
Portland, Ore.	.13	.8	366
Akron, Ohio	.17		237
Rochester, N.Y.	.48		242
Wichita, Kan.	.51		279
Indianapolis, Ind.	.56	2.3	701
Tulsa, Okla.	.56		361
Louisville, Ky.	.6		298
Kansas City, Mo.	.7	2.0	448
Chicago, Ill.	.72	2.4	3,005
Washington, D.C.	.9	3.3	638
Oakland, Calif.	.94	1.9	339
Detroit, Mich.	1.19	4.6	1,387
Birmingham, Ala.	1.29	5.1	284

[a]Annual rates are computed from fourteen years of data. Between 1973 and 1986 one citizen was killed by an off-duty officer, who was found guilty of manslaughter. Two were wounded: a burglar in the dark, and an armed man who was threatening himself and the officers.

[b]Averages computed by the author from PERF and Police Foundation 1981. Included are all cities under 200,000 that provided data on both injury and death. Small cities: Alexandria, Va.; Allentown, Pa.; Ann Arbor, Mich.; Arlington County, Va.; Aurora, Colo.; Berkeley, Calif.; Charleston, S.C.; Chesapeake, Va.; Evanston, Ill.; Garden Grove, Calif.; Garland, Tex.; Hayward, Calif.; Hialeah, Fla.; Hollywood, Fla.; Lakewood, Colo.; Macon, Ga.; New Rochelle, N.Y.; Orlando, Fla.; Portsmouth, Va.; Racine, Wis.; Roanoke, Va.; Salem, Ore.; Santa Monica, Calif.; Stockton, Calif.; Sunnyvale, Calif.; Topeka, Kan.; Waterbury, Conn.; and White Plains, N.Y. Mid-sized cities: Anchorage, Alaska; Chattanooga, Tenn.; Colorado Springs, Colo.; Des Moines, Iowa; Flint, Mich.; Ft. Lauderdale, Fla.; Fresno, Calif.; Grand Rapids, Mich.; Greensboro, N.C.; Hampton, Va.; Hartford, Conn.; Huntington Beach, Calif.; Kansas City, Kan.; Lansing, Mich.; Las Vegas, Nev.; Lexington, Ky.; Lubbock, Tex.; Madison, Wis.; Montgomery, Ala.; New Haven, Conn.; Newport News, Va.; Paterson, N.J.; Peoria, Ill.; Raleigh, N.C.; Rockford, Ill.; Santa Ana, Calif.; Spokane, Wash.; Tacoma, Wash.; Torrance, Calif.; and Yonkers, N.Y.

[c]The source of the individual city figures on citizens killed is Sherman and Cohn 1986, 12. The cities selected are those under 300,000 population and those for which there are 1973-74 data on citizens wounded in Milton et al. 1977, tables 1 and 5. Chicago data are from Geller and Karales 1981, 86, 90-91.

drop in police exertion, with more officers riding by situations where they should take action.

Figure 5-6 showed that disorderly arrests in Troy plummeted from near the national average at 1,300 arrests per 100,000 population during

1970–72 to a low of 300 in 1976, rose again into the 500–600 range during the late 1970s, and then fell to 250 in the mid-1980s. During those years, public behavior in Troy underwent no dramatic change. Examination of the department's arrest blotter shows that mass arrests had ceased, such as those on 11 and 28 May 1972, when police officers broke up noisy college students by arresting 58 on the first night and 17 on the later night. The sharp drop in 1976 was due to New York state's removal of public intoxication from the criminal code.

Troy's rise in disorderly arrests in the late 1970s may have been due to an increase in unnecessary arrests, since no known changes were taking place in the level of public rowdiness. Support for this interpretation comes from an examination of 1978 arrests on the specific charge of disorderly conduct. Separately, on both the evening and midnight shifts, officers with less than five years' experience made on average three times as many of these arrests as their more experienced colleagues: on the evening tour the young officers averaged about eight per year, while their senior colleagues made three; on midnights the young officers made about three, while the seniors averaged one. Officers working days made few arrests of any kind. In 1978, 65 percent of the officers working evenings had less than five years' experience. By 1983, the proportion of young officers on that shift had dropped dramatically to 30 percent, following a decline in recruiting and an increase in senior officers' selection of evening work. This halving of the proportion of young officers on the evening shift probably helps to account for the drop in the rate of arrests for disorderly behavior from 600 per 100,000 to around 300 during 1983–86. As a percentage of all arrests in Troy, those for disorderly behavior dropped from 43 percent in 1970–72 to 8 percent in 1984–86. From this superficial inquiry, we may conclude that harassment through unnecessary arrests has not been a widespread problem since upgrading began.

Excessive force can be covered up by an arrest for interfering with an officer. The New York penal code specifies three such charges: assaulting an officer (a felony), obstructing governmental administration, and resisting arrest (both misdemeanors). Since these crime categories are not separately reported to the UCR, the counts must be obtained directly from departmental records. For convenience, I use the term "interference" to cover all three charges. Officers have made arrests for interference in circumstances ranging from the quiet subduing of a psychotic woman wielding a knife to the quick punishment of teenagers who talk back. If an officer strikes a man, the officer is likely to arrest his victim, because it is harder for an officer to hide from management the fact that he used force than to lie about the circumstances. Recall that in the incident of the prisoner beaten in the police station, the only charges against him were obstructing administration and resisting arrest. If an officer lies brazenly about a prisoner's attack on him, then when the prisoner says, "See this mouse under my eye. Let me tell you where I got it," a police supervisor can easily respond, "That's your story. We already have a report describing how you attacked the officer."

In using arrest statistics, we cannot sort the justified from the unjustified placing of interference charges. We can begin with the assumption that each year there is a roughly constant number of incidents in which officers exercising great restraint would justifiably make an arrest for interference. Oakland provides an example of a department that reduced the rate of arrests for interference by establishing a violence reduction program in which the officers most prone to use force joined a peer review panel. As documented by Grant, Grant, and Toch (1982), the Oakland department made interference arrests at the rate of 225 per 100,000 before the program and cut the rate to 143 after three years.

Table 8-3 shows the rise and drop in Troy's rate of arrests for interference. From around 100 per 100,000 population in the early 1970s, arrests for interference peaked sharply in 1979 at about 340 and then fell as sharply during the early 1980s, reaching 90 in 1983. This parallels the change in disorderly conduct arrests and likewise can be explained in part by the surge and decline in inexperienced officers on patrol in the evenings. Lack of patrol experience was found to be the most powerful predictor of the use of force, as reported on departmental forms in Rochester and Syracuse in a study conducted in 1986 (New York State Commission on Criminal Justice and the Use of Force 1987). Another explanation for the decline in Troy is that a competent police court judge took office in January 1978 who disapproved of frequent interference charges. Examination of the court records shows that he began his first year on the bench by making convictions for interference charges twice as often as he dismissed them but that by the end of the year he was dismissing all such charges. Still, it remains unexplained why the drop did not occur until two years after he took office.

Patterns Identified by Citizen Surveys

Careful surveys of a cross section of citizens can shed some light on issues of malpractice and discipline by revealing what malpractice citizens know about and under what circumstances they report it. Nothing blameworthy was recalled by 86 percent of the sample of 950 Troy residents, aged fourteen to ninety. Table 8-4 classifies the incidents mentioned by the 14 percent. Note that half are abuses of discretion, and half are shirking and negligence. Only one man mentioned a possible crime: a friend had told him that an officer had offered to fix a traffic ticket. Only one of the twelve complaints of excessive force was mentioned by a victim. Men and women had similar patterns of complaints, except that women more frequently criticized officers for double parking. A survey,

Table 8-3 Rise and Fall in Arrests for Interference

	1971	1972	1973	1974	1975	1976	1977	1978	1979	1980	1981	1982	1983	1984
Approx. arrests per 100,000 pop.	110	65		110	150	100	140	230	340	250	125	125	90	50
Percent of all arrests	4	3		4	5	4	5	7	8	7	3	4	5	3

Note: Departmental records on some 4,000 arrests were examined. The number of arrests for assaulting an officer, resisting arrest, and interference with governmental administration were tallied for four months of each year—February, May, August, November—and then multiplied by three for the approximate number of interference arrests. Exception: the figures for 1983 are a complete count. No data were collected for the year of leadership transition, 1973.

Table 8-4   Number of Persons Who Recalled Witnessing Police Malpractice during the Previous Year

Type of Malpractice	Witnesses	
	Men	Women
Crimes		
Attempted ticket fixing	1	0
Abuse of discretion		
Unjust arrest	1	1
Roughing up	4	4
Brutality, unspecified	2	1
Being gun happy	1	0
Unconstitutional stop and search	1	0
Unfair ticketing	0	3
False accusation	2	0
Closely watching or following citizens	0	5
Other harassment	3	0
Discourtesy	12	7
Other failure to handle a situation as the citizen wished	11	4
Subtotal	37	25
Shirking and negligence		
Sleeping on duty	4	1
Drinking on duty	3	4
Failing to enforce law or take report	1	3
Failing to come quickly	1	0
Improper driving practices	7	4
Other neglect	0	3
Excessive socializing	7	4
Sitting in a patrol car	7	3
Parking violations (3 took place off-duty)	2	11
Patrol car sitting empty	3	0
Subtotal	35	33
Total	73	58
Citizens recalling no blameworthy acts	349 (83%)	457 (88%)

Note: The 946 survey respondents were aged fourteen and above. Case weighting reduced the total to 937.

Survey question: In the last year . . . did you see a police officer do anything you thought should have been *complained* about? . . . What happened? What did the officer do?

no matter how carefully designed and conducted, cannot establish the truth of what happened in any incident, but it can show with some accuracy what bothers people about police behavior and to what extent they make formal complaints about serious malpractice. Unfortunately, for every type of incident, very few people complained to the department. Furthermore, the survey found that many citizens did not believe that the department was investigating complaints thoroughly and fairly.

Systematic Promotion of Professional Practice

In seeking to understand police service in Troy, we are left with two parts of a picture that do not fit together. On the negative side, we see a departmental disciplinary system that is unable to substantiate some serious abuses of discretion because officers lie to protect each other and because the majority of citizens with serious complaints of police malpractice keep silent. On the positive side, we see that minor incidents far outnumber serious ones, as shown in both the formal complaints to the department and the citizen survey, and that the volume of shootings and of arrests for disorderly behavior are low compared to that of other cities and has been dropping. Further, 95 percent of the citizens surveyed are unafraid of the police, and those groups that usually have most reason to fear—young men, black people, residents of public housing, poor people—have the same low level of fear as the average citizen. In sum, when malpractice occurs, it is almost never brought to management's attention through complaints, yet malpractice is not common. The missing piece of the puzzle is the rewards and incentives for individual officers to serve with self-restraint and courtesy.

Just as Commissioner O'Connor strove to reduce fear of crime among citizens through steps to build a positive sense of safety, so he worked to diminish malpractice by building systems, procedures, and expectations that would promote professional practice. The opening lines of the Troy department's regulations emphasize individual responsibility:

> The rules and regulations of a police agency represent a self-determined code of conduct by which members agree to behave. . . . The very fact that a police agency finds it essential to formulate and adopt a code of behavior in addition to that which applies to all citizens is an indication of the special character of the police profession. Endowed with a public trust, the police officer is given special authority and responsibility beyond that of every other citizen.

This explicit characterization of an onerous set of rules as stemming directly from special professional responsibility may contribute to an officer's sense of mission. The eloquence of a leader in defining the high purposes of an organization tends to be undervalued in the United States.

A number of books on Japanese management emphasize the motivation that employees gain from working toward goals greater than personal benefit (Pascale and Athos 1981). A leader who unabashedly extols the unique contributions of the organization to society gives members more reason to take pride in their work. The broad improvements in the Troy department's service probably also contributed to reducing malpractice. When officers have a sense of collective pride in the accomplishments of the department, they seek to keep the reputation unsullied. When incidents of malpractice became public knowledge, the commissioner told the culprits that the disgrace reflected upon the whole department.

The familiar phrase "corruption hazards" describes assignments in which illegal acts are easy and the risk of being caught is small. One can use the list of corruption hazards on page 165 to consider the many spots where prevention is necessary. O'Connor's approach to the corruption hazards surrounding the enforcement of gambling laws was to withdraw the department from enforcing those laws. He was aware that illegal gambling never became large in Troy, given low customer demand and the occasional raids conducted by the state police. He reasoned that with so much legal gambling sponsored by church and state, enforcement may help protect their share but does not end a socially undesirable practice. Without enforcement, gamblers will not pay needless protection.

Good preventive systems make illegal acts difficult to hide and increase the efficiency of work. Three examples will suffice. In 1973 the Troy department adopted a standard policy designating which garages would handle police-ordered tows in which section of town, thus making kickbacks difficult. In 1974, after the discovery that $916 had disappeared from the property room, the department established a sound system of inventory control. In 1979 it instituted computerized tickets for parking violations, primarily for efficiency but with the benefit of preventing alterations.

The most fundamental changes that reduced serious police malpractice were the positive steps described earlier to develop professional motivation. By the mid-1970s the organizational climate of the Troy department had so changed as to make unthinkable a burglary ring, despite one having been exposed on the midnight shift in 1968 (*Times Record*, 18 Nov., 18 and 30 Dec. 1968). Gratuities had been a way of life as recently as 1972, rationalized by officers as compensation for their low salaries: "The wife gets the paycheck, and I get the groceries." Commissioner O'Connor saw the 40 percent pay increase during his first three years as necessary for upgrading and for alleviating the mind set that leads officers to accept gratuities. Slowly, gratuities dried up. Whenever a source came to the commissioner's attention, he told the restaurant or shop owner to end the practice. As recently as 1983 the commissioner learned that the established practice for cashing vouchers for the $225 uniform allowance was for the clothing shop to bill the department immediately for the full amount in uniforms and then to charge against the officer's credit any items of his choosing—sneakers for the kids, a jacket for his wife. O'Connor moved to stop the abuse by requiring all clothing purchased through the vouchers to be delivered to the department for issue to the officers. The PBA immediately tried to block the change through an unsuccessful grievance.

Prevention is recognized as the primary means of reducing malpractice in a model policy statement by the Police Executive Research Forum (PERF 1981). Furthermore, departments that now work to prevent corruption through reducing corruption hazards can apply these concepts in order to safeguard against "excessive force hazards." To decrease the likelihood that officers will employ excessive force, a department should adopt regulations on the use of firearms and pursuit driving in conformance with the standards of the Commission on Accreditation for Law Enforcement Agencies.

The enhancement of officer safety, an important goal in its own right, is also likely to reduce the frequency of officers' reacting with excessive force to protect themselves. Probably an important element in an officer's sense of safety is a belief that the community is not hostile. Many abuses of discretion spring from an officer's sense of mutual hostility with citizens, specifically with poor people, members of minority groups, and those who have committed crimes. For example, Rocky Davis, who thrashed the boys he caught smashing cars, described himself as vindictive. Over the years he had generated many complaints that were reviewed by the professional standards unit. The discussion of how to prevent officers from developing the outlook of a Rocky Davis is continued in Chapters 11 and 12.

An idea considered in Chapter 3, that police departments will be more effective in controlling crime if they do not ignore helpful services in order to concentrate on suppressing crimes, has a parallel for individual officers. Officers who serve in positions that specialize in deception or force should be rotated out after brief service to positions where they can relearn that the city is full of people like themselves. Officers who are denied the opportunity to help people and given only tasks of controlling people through the use of force are likely to meet resistance from citizens and to become ever more reliant upon force. In a vicious world, attack is justified as the best defense.

For example, officers in tactical units such as robbery decoy squads are believed by police experts to treat arrestees more harshly than officers in patrol, although no systematic studies have attempted to document this generalization. Members of SWAT (Special Weapons Attack Team) units, the heavily armed teams for overpowering barricaded suspects and other dangerous people, need total reorientation to the advantages of careful negotiation. O'Connor chose to create an emergency response team for the Troy PD as an extra assignment. Team officers practice assiduously one day every two weeks and on the other days are available for an emergency while performing their regular work. The team members have quickly mobilized when called, swiftly cleared citizens from a dangerous area, and then taken their time to persuade the barricaded person to give up. Ready with rifles as necessary, in their first three years they handled situations so skillfully that the necessity to shoot did not arise.

Although long-run trends appear to be turning police work away from domineering and toward serving, for the present and the near future the serious problems of abuse of power have no fully satisfactory solutions. George O'Connor reflected in 1975 on a failure to determine the truth of the matter in a case of prisoner beating with this broad commentary.

Policing represents a major form of clustering, using and abusing power. As I think about it, it seems more apparent than it used to that power cannot be wielded by men without abuse. So long as the institution of policing is conceived as a major type of control mechanism, it will attract and protect those who seek to exercise power. Conceiving of this industry as therapeutic and/or human service oriented represents the course 180 degrees different from the present.

You have to be a cop to understand a cop.

Folk wisdom

Union Power

Police unions emerged dramatically in the late 1960s as part of the surge of public employees to form and join unions. The new militancy of police officers contrasted sharply with their long, quiet acceptance of low salaries and harsh working conditions. Citizens and police administrators were shocked, angered, or frightened by picket lines, "blue flu" and strikes. Although strikers captured headlines, very few departments ever went out on strike, and only a small proportion ever engaged in work slowdowns.

The stage had been set as one state after another followed the 1962 lead of the federal government in permitting its employees to engage in collective bargaining. The number of states allowing collective bargaining for police employees is estimated to have risen from thirteen in 1970, to twenty-five in 1980, and to thirty-four in 1983. Adding states that permit collective bargaining through local law, case decision, or attorney general's opinion brought the 1990 total to about forty-two (Dowling 1989, 1990). A Justice Department survey in 1987 found that somewhat more than half of the nation's 355,000 police officers were covered by collective bargaining agreements, and two-thirds of those in departments with at least 135 officers (Bureau of Justice Statistics 1989). The numbers continue to rise as more southern states change their laws and as smaller departments follow the lead of larger ones.

Although officers naturally welcome the benefits and protections that collective bargaining provides, some are not fully comfortable with union membership. Many officers avoid the term "union," preferring the older word "association." Police associations have long had diverse roles, which may be grouped into two broad categories: looking out for the welfare of the members; and taking active part in community affairs by sponsoring police athletic leagues, hosting charity fund raisers, and the like. In departments where the police subculture holds that only a cop can understand a cop, the association has a special attraction to its members as the only organization that is purely for cops. Officers holding an intense form of this cynical perspective believe that those who have risen above sergeant are no longer cops. A sense of brotherhood is an enduring source of strength for the association leadership. To underscore the importance of the recent collective bargaining powers, I use the new term "union" rather than the old term "association" that emphasizes the long history of the organization.

In broad perspective, unions are but one of many types of organizations created by people engaged in various lines of work to promote their common interests. Guilds, benevolent associations, fraternal organizations, professional associations, and unions have all represented their members in dealing with the powerful institutions of their day. Unions stand out by virtue of two specific formal powers: to represent the employees in the collective bargaining with management that creates the contract under which employees work, and to bring grievances when employees believe that management has violated the contract. These two powers shape an adversarial role for unions as a countervailing power to management. The general influences of unions are to compel management to articulate policies, abide by those policies, and attend to the expressed interests of the workers. When conflicts arise between efforts to improve the quality of service and efforts to improve the quality of work life, unions defend work life.

Nationally, the generally antagonistic state of union-management relations in policing has been directly attributable to management's long refusal to accept the existence of police unions as legitimate. The Boston police strike of 1919, called to protest the firing of union leaders, resulted in the firing of all the strikers—most of the department. The legacy of this episode contributed substantially to the halting of the police union movement for forty years.

This chapter considers union power from the same perspective as that from which we have been viewing management power, inquiring into how the union affects the quality of service and the quality of work life. First comes an examination of the nature of union power in its competition with management. Next are the bread-and-butter issues that dominate contract negotiations. Then we consider in some detail techniques for protecting union members from management. The following section discusses union leaders' pursuit of their goals through arbitration, court cases, city council directives, and legislation at all levels of government. The final sections of the chapter summarize contractual impediments and supports for the enhancement of professional service. The list of questions in the appendix asks only two about structure and two about performance.

Union Perspectives

The origin of police unions as local benevolent associations has shaped their structure and functions. Most began as fraternal organizations that bore the cost of members' funerals. Their concerns beyond the borders of the department tended to extend in one direction only: toward retired members. They quite naturally included all ranks within their membership and permitted retirees to retain full voting rights. The Troy Police Benevolent and Protective Association, in existence since 1903, included all ranks through the chief until 1980 and as of 1987 continued to give full votes to retirees. Such a membership structure, however, conflicts with the interests of line personnel vis-à-vis management. Everywhere, retirees have an interest in increasing pension benefits at the expense of increasing current salaries. Retirees will tend to elect to union office members they know, members close to their own age. In departments developing toward the hospital model, younger officers are more likely than older ones to seek contractual arrangements supportive of further professional development, such as educational incentives and assignments based on demonstrated ability. The presence of a retiree vote tends to perpetuate older leaders who gird to refight the old battles.

The fragmented national scene is another consequence of the local origin of police unions (Hoover and Dowling 1984). A tally of police associations in the nation's hundred largest cities found that ninety-eight have unions, and seventy- seven of the unions have concluded collective bargaining agreements (*Police Labor Monthly* 1985). Forty-five are unions without affiliation beyond the state level; thirty-six are local lodges of the Fraternal Order of Police (FOP), a confederation that forbids affiliation with any labor union; twelve belong to the International Union of Police Associations, a loose association affiliated with the AFL-CIO; four are locals of the International Brotherhood of Police Officers, a component of the National Association of Government Employees, also an AFL-CIO affiliate; one was a Teamsters' local, which has since switched its affiliation.

For the nation as a whole the pattern is similarly fragmented, as shown in Table 9-1. As of 1984 about one-third of all officers belonged to an association with a national affiliation; one-third belonged to FOP lodges, less than 10 percent were affiliated with the AFL-CIO through three different government employee unions, about 5 percent were in four industrial unions, and less than 5 percent were in an affiliated police union. During the late 1980s the National Association of Police Organizations grew rapidly because it serves independent local associations and does not attempt to amalgamate them. A major consequence of this fragmentation is that police associations are not very effective in lobbying on a national level, somewhat more influential at the state level, and most influential at the municipal level.

The magnitude of rank-and-file discontent in a few cities has been expressed in selecting the Teamsters as bargaining agent. Presenting their effectiveness in obtaining a large salary package, Teamster leaders gained a number of locals in the late 1970s and early 1980s. This development was particularly dangerous, given the Teamsters' history of corrupt leadership and intimidation of nonunion workers. Teamster affiliation dropped markedly in the mid-1980s. Because police officers have a responsibility to maintain order in industrial disputes, the question has been raised as to their impartiality if their union is part of a general industrial union.

Long before collective bargaining was permitted, police associations sought to protect their members through a wide variety of means, including political influence. Political power is considered by Robert B. Kleismet (1984), president of the International Union of Police Associa-

Table 9-1   Estimated Police Membership in Nationally Affiliated Associations

Name of Union or Association	Estimated Membership in 1,000s	
	1984	1990
Fraternal Order of Police	160	170
National Association of Police Organizations	20	105
American Federation of Government Employees	12	
AFL-CIO affiliates		
International Brotherhood of Police Officers (National Association of Government Employees affiliate)	20	30
International Union of Police Associations (Service Employees International Union affiliate)	20	
American Fedaration of State, County and Municipal Employees	12	
Teamsters	8	
Longshoremen	6	
Food and Commercial Workers	5	
Paperworkers	0.8	
Communications Workers of America	0.1	
No national affiliation[a]	200	

Sources: 1984 estimates from Kleismet (1984); 1990 estimates from Dowling (1990).
[a]Includes those who were members of state-level organizations such as the PBA in New York and PORAC in California, of local associations such as Spokane's Police Guild, or of none.

tions, to be the most valuable of all union powers. Police associations have acted politically in a manner broadly similar to that of professional associations, which protect their status and prerogatives through favorable legislation. But the differences can be clearly seen through a glance at the American Medical Association. It lobbies effectively at state and federal levels for legislation giving the members occupational monopolies and special privileges. Police associations lobby predominantly at the local level where salary and conditions of work are controlled.

A tradition of community involvement by police associations includes both service and fund raising. Through their police athletic leagues, the most common service, police officers have organized and coached basketball, boxing, and other sports for boys from poor neighborhoods. The Troy PBA sponsors outings to baseball games in New York City and an annual Christmas party for inner-city children, gives to local charities, and for a time provided a collection point for donated clothing for the needy. This same police tradition includes soliciting the public for contributions that go into the association's treasury. "Bag dragging" is the term O'Connor uses. In his first year in Troy he rebuffed the representative of the state PBA, who wanted departmental sponsorship for soliciting ads from local merchants. The Troy PBA did this very type of soliciting in 1984, selling ads in a PBA yearbook and buyer's guide that department members understood to have been created specifically as the vehicle for the ads. The fundamental problem of police solicitation, no matter how honorable the motives or worthy the cause, is that a citizen can fear that future police protection depends on a contribution.

The Troy PBA, like most police associations, exercised political influence. Unable to obtain salary raises directly from the city council, the PBA got them in 1956 by placing a proposition on the ballot and then campaigning door to door. Such success in increasing the taxpayers' burden is a measure of the strength of public support. The technique of going directly to the taxpayer to provide what elected officials refuse has been documented in other cities as well, including Oakland in the late 1950s and Newark in 1969. The Troy PBA's other political actions, which continue to the present, are election endorsements and annual awards banquets honoring selected community and political leaders. The most continuity in influence comes from close ties with key elected officials. These may be blood ties, as when the Troy PBA president was the brother of the man who served as mayor from 1970 to 1976. Or the ties may be cultivated with elected officials such as Steven Dworsky, an active member of the city council public safety committee from 1976 who subsequently became mayor and, in 1986, city manager. The value of political influence to police associations has not diminished with their acquisition of collective bargaining rights. The full range of the PBA's political actions are examined in the next chapter.

Union-management bargaining in the public sector is political bargaining, substantially different from the economic bargaining of the private sector. The essentially political nature of police bargaining results from the necessity of government to decide on the allocation of resources among various city services and to set policy for those services. In bargaining with each separate municipal union, the city's position is weakened but not destroyed by four factors: the public demand for municipal services cannot easily be slackened; the city cannot bring on any disruption of services posing a real hazard to health or safety; citizens are uninformed and unrepresented in the bargaining; and voters are in a position to punish only one party to the dispute, the elected political leadership. Cities face the demands of multiple unions, many with a parity clause and each with an eye to the concessions that others obtain. At the dawn of public-sector bargaining, cities generally came to the bargaining table less prepared than the unions and consequently bargained away management rights that they later regretted losing. In the tight times that cities have faced since the mid-1970s, some yielded management rights rather than offer satisfactory salary packages.

The City of Troy and the Troy Police Benevolent Association fought for twenty-one months before concluding their first contract in 1969. The police and fire fighters' unions joined forces for bargaining purposes and followed a common practice of hiring the same law firm. The unions forced the City to the bargaining table only through the assistance of the Public Employment Relations Board (PERB), a standard state agency that oversees public-sector collective bargaining. Eventually, the fire fighters staged a six-hour strike to force the signing of both contracts. A new city manager declared them illegal on the grounds that they were signed by the outgoing city manager, but PERB decided that they were binding. This first police contract recognized the PBA as sole bargaining agent for all sworn personnel, prohibited members from withdrawing during the life of the contract, required that union dues be deducted from paychecks, and established many conditions of work.

In 1972 John Buckley, the new acting city manager, signed a contract conceding more managerial powers over working conditions. The PBA president who had led the fight for the contract retired from office in 1972 and was succeeded by two one-term presidents who screened out frivolous grievances. In 1973 an officer highly regarded for his hard work and common sense ran for vice-president in the annual election and pulled the highest number of votes from within the department, but he lost because of the retiree vote. The winner of the vice-presidential race, a spokesman for a small circle of detectives who were suspicious of change, rose to president in the summer of 1974 on the resignation of the incumbent and was reelected annually until 1983. For this circle, the avowed purpose of the PBA was to defend every word of the contract. The consequences of their energetic defense of contractual rights was to protect benefits that accrued primarily to members with the most seniority and to thwart many management initiatives. When the president eventually retired from office in 1983, an original member of the circle won a contested election over a young member, again thanks to the retiree vote.

In 1985 an officer of the younger generation won a contested election in which he criticized the incumbents for spending so much on lawyers. Two negotiating meetings with attorneys had already taken place but accomplished nothing, because the PBA was waiting for its election results. At the new president's initiative, he and two officers put their demands directly to the commissioner and the city manager: a 12 percent annual increase and a huge fringe package. Buckley told them this was far out of line and asked them to come back with something realistic. A few days later they asked for a three-year contract with raises of 8 percent, 8 percent, and 6 percent, the Martin Luther King holiday, shift differential, and increased fringe benefits. O'Connor costed out the proposal and came back with a two-year contract specifying raises of 6 percent each year and the fringe items phased in. The city and the PBA each saved $20,000 to

30,000 in legal fees. Officers ratified the new contract 65 to 9. Since then, the PBA has not opposed management for the sake of opposition.

Union Solidarity

Police associations have a special claim on the allegiance of members. As should be abundantly clear from earlier chapters, a strong sense of occupational identity and esprit de corps among police officers is essential for quality service. Among organizations at large, the peer group is a source of security and strength. Because police officers never know how soon they will be in unexpected and dangerous situations, they need the assurance of knowing that fellow officers will back them up. Further, their day in, day out work with troubled and troublesome people persuades many officers that only other cops understand them. The immediate need to identify with fellow officers takes place within the working group, within the division, and within a police department as a whole. Across departments, however, there are far fewer organizational links, either formal or informal, than in the established professions. It is the union that permits officers from various departments to meet personally and provides the symbols of occupational identity. Union leaders in their contests with management are able to draw upon this reservoir of identification with the entire police field.

Excluding command personnel from a department's only union is hard on the individual commanders, who could lose substantial pension benefits and feel a drop in occupational identification and fellowship, although proper handling of the transition can limit their losses. Unions have compelling reasons to exclude members of management lest the traditions of chain of command operate within union governance as well, leaving leadership to lieutenants and captains, as occurs in some Fraternal Order of Police lodges. Management has an even stronger reason to separate members of the command staff, to increase their identification with service goals rather than only with the goals of a comfortable work life. The anomaly of the chief's being a member of the Troy union was the basis on which PBA leaders told Chief Givney in 1976 that he had to remain silent when he sat on the management side in contract negotiations. In 1980 the captains, assistant chiefs, and chief broke away, unopposed by the PBA, to form their own union, the Command Officers Association of Troy (COAT). They make their bargains with the city after the PBA settlements and by 1987 had brought only one grievance, an individual matter concerning vacation days.

Across the country, most officers participate little in union affairs, according to the impressions of national union organizers. In this situation it is easy for a clique to exert itself in directing the union and to pursue policies quite at variance with the wishes of the majority of members.

The Troy PBA leaders during 1975–85 consulted little with the membership outside their circle of friends. Take as an example the most important decision for a police department: who shall direct it? In the October 1977 monthly meeting, attended by about 29 of 118 members, the PBA leaders obtained a vote to support a city referendum that would have removed the public safety commissioner and made the chief's job a political appointment. Sixty-five members signed a petition opposing the referendum, but their request for a revote was refused. Yet only three months earlier a strong majority of PBA members had reported in an organizational questionnaire sponsored by management that they considered their union leaders to be representing their interests to a great extent. An explanation of PBA members' reluctance to oppose their leaders is that they do not want to undermine the union as their bulwark against management.

Low morale is a phrase often heard from union leaders. Usually this accompanies a demand for more manpower or higher pay, with the implication that such expenditures will raise morale. A claim of low morale should be treated cautiously. First, union leaders may be out of touch with the majority of their members and represent the intense discontent of only a segment of the department. Second, compared with other work organizations, police departments appear to have a higher than average proportion of perpetually discontented members, as a result of the stresses of the street, demeaning treatment by management, and a pension system that prevents individuals from resigning without a huge financial loss. When a claim of low morale is made, one can search for all substantive issues behind the claim and generally examine the degree to which administrators treat officers as though they matter. A broader view of morale was voiced by a British police leader, Geoffrey Dear (1978), when he was assistant chief constable of Nottinghamshire. He commented that the morale of British police generally fluctuates between average and high because officers are supported by a public consensus. He attributed the high status and respect that police enjoy to a consensus about the purposes and practices of policing. If public support were to diminish, then morale would necessarily fall.

Bread-and-Butter Issues

Salaries

Departments with police unions tend to pay higher salaries. A 1980 national study of departments with at least 100 officers (Pugh, Hoover, and Sapp 1981) concluded that starting salaries are 20 percent higher and maximum salaries for patrol officers 16 percent higher in union than in non-union departments. Although the region in which a city is located has the most influence on salary levels, in eight of the nine census divisions of the country, departments with unions have higher salaries. City manager governments also tend to pay higher salaries than strong mayor governments and commission governments.

The Troy department traditionally had low base pay and low increments for promotion. Comparison in 1970 with the thirty-two other New York and New Jersey cities of over 50,000 showed that Troy had the lowest base salary. Indeed, this IACP and Police Foundation study found that Troy needed an increase of 50 percent to bring salaries up to average. As Table 9-2 indicates, only with the beginning of city manager government in 1964 did salaries rise annually. O'Connor immediately saw the need for higher pay to attract and retain talented people and to lessen their need for secondary employment. In the first contract he negotiated, in 1975, police officer salaries finally equaled the average factory wage for the metropolitan area. Since 1985 they have been 10 percent higher.

Union leaders, juggling the diverse interests of a broad range of personnel, find a common denominator in higher salaries. Nationally, both police management and union leadership agree that the old tradition of pay parity with fire fighters should be broken. In the last twenty years the development of greater professional competence has justified higher police salaries, while the cut in the fire fighters' work week to two twenty-four-hour days has increased their opportunities for income from second jobs. The Philadelphia PD's 1980 salary comparison of the twenty-nine largest American cities found fire fighter salaries higher in five, parity in fourteen, and police salaries higher in ten (Kleismet n.d., 1). The police manager's interest in breaking parity is not identical to the city executive's, who must balance salary demands from all city agencies with tax resources. Troy's parity was broken not by the city manager but by a statewide PERB ruling of the late 1970s that pay parity, in effect, prevented one bargaining unit from bargaining.

Fringe Benefits

How the pay dollar should be allocated between salary and fringe benefits is usually disputed. The police associations' original concern with life after retirement has directed efforts into building generous pension plans, while police managers prefer direct salary increases and incentive pay. In Troy the 1972 consultants' report contrasted the penurious management philosophy with "the exceptionally broad and complete range of fringe benefits, most of which are provided on a non-contributory basis" (Cresap, McCormick, and Paget 1972, 1:III-21). The first contract included pensions at half pay after twenty-five years' service. In the 1972 amendment to the 1972–74 contract, the city agreed to a twenty-year noncontributory plan. Under the provisions of the New York state pen-

Table 9-2 Comparison of Troy Police Salaries with Average Factory Wage in the Metropolitan Area

Year	Top Annual Salary, Police Officer[a]	Average Annual Wages, Factory Workers	Police Salary as % of Factory Wages
1952	$3,050	$3,656	83%
1953	3,050	3,866	78
1954	3,050	3,825	80
1955	3,050	4,128	74
1956	3,050	4,391	69
1957	3,400	4,580	74
1958	3,700	4,648	88
1959	3,800	4,888	78
1960	3,900	4,990	78
1961	3,900	5,292	74
1962	4,500	5,533	81
1963	4,500	5,657	79
1964	4,500	5,848	77
1965	4,875	6,076	80
1966	5,225	6,360	82
1967	5,925	6,360	82
1968	6,100	6,777	90
1969	6,900	7,167	98
1970	7,550	7,727	98
1971	8,250	8,340	99
1972	8,600	9,171	94
1973	8,918	9,249	96
1974	9,453	9,862	96
1975	10,323	10,368	100
1976	11,673	11,761	99
1977	12,123	12,404	99
1978	13,523	14,023	96
1979	15,058	14,487	100
1980	16,112	15,725	102
1981	17,642	17,100	103
1982	18,669	17,767	105
1983	19,903	19,180	104
1984	21,520	19,727	109
1985	22,811	20,143	113
1986	24,180	21,598	112
1987	25,630	21,627	118

Sources: Police salaries for 1952–71 from New York State Public Employment Relations Board, "Recommendations of the Fact Finder in the Dispute between the City of Troy and the Troy Police Benevolent and Protective Association" (M70-536), 19 Nov. 1970, pp. 3, 12. The 1972–87 figures are from the contracts. Average annual factory wages are computed from the average hourly earnings in July of each year as recorded in New York State Department of Labor, "Area Summary: Albany-Schenectady-Troy."

[a]Base pay for the police officer rank at the highest step. In 1950–74 an officer reached top salary at the end of two years; after 1975, three and one-half years. Excluded from the salary calculations are holiday, longevity, and overtime pay.

sion system, officers who resign before eight years of service receive no pension benefits, and prior to twenty years the benefits are greatly reduced. The excessive size of Troy's fringe package persisted because the PBA was unwilling to relinquish any existing benefit. The cost of employing one sergeant in 1982, as calculated by O'Connor, is itemized in Table 9-3. The weight of a pension burden at 44 percent of base pay makes raising current salaries difficult, but retirement after twenty years provides income to the officer for almost as many years after retirement as on the job. The older an administrative system becomes, the more likely occasional tinkering will have made it complicated. Witness the scattered devices that added almost 10 percent to the sergeant's paycheck.

Table 9-3   The Cost of a Police Sergeant in Troy, 1982

Compensation Item	Dollar Cost	% of Base Pay
Base salary	$18,759	100%
Retirement	8,200	44
Medical insurance	1,629	9
FICA	1,363	7
Holiday pay	824	4
Longevity	766	4
Clothing allowance	225	1
Shift differential	100	0.5
Total	$31,866	170%

Protecting Members from Management

Harsh administration has forged police union solidarity. Conditions in the Troy department in 1972 illustrate the worst of what unions have been fighting. The incident of the yellow Mustang that opens this book, when an officer was punished for attempting to halt a reckless driver, exemplifies the extreme situation in which prolonged punishment is inflicted without explanation. Troy officers who were not favorites of the powerful felt continually vulnerable. Benefits due officers, such as vacations, had to be begged from the personnel sergeant, a confidant of the public safety commissioner. The consultants' report of 1972 remarked upon the high degree of suspicion and hostility that permeated the department. Patrol officers were not even permitted upstairs, where the detectives held sway. A squalid police station and dilapidated patrol cars were outward signs of a management that cared nothing for the quality of work life.

Against incompetent and harsh management, unions protect their members through a two-step process: contract language to define proper working conditions, and then a grievance procedure to force management to abide by the contract. The only limitations on contractual agreements are that the provisions must not contravene existing state and national laws. The employee protections in contracts may be grouped into two categories: decision mechanisms, and specific actions forbidden to or required of management. Decision mechanisms spelled out in police contracts always include the grievance process, and they sometimes include the disciplinary process. Consultation and oversight are less commonly specified.

The Grievance Process

Sound management requires establishing ways for a dissatisfied employee or group of employees to seek redress. For those departments where management treats officers as people, the overwhelming proportion of employee discontents are resolved at the level where they occur, without going to a formal grievance process. Even for the best-managed departments, however, a grievance process is an alternative channel by which members can force management to abide by the letter of the contract. In general it appears that the harsher management is, the more grievances safeguard basic employee rights, and that the more responsive management is, the more grievances give small benefits to individuals. Everywhere, grievances prevent unwanted change.

The grievance process in Troy works in typical fashion: a member gains the support of the union for redress of his personal plight, called an individual grievance; or the union judges that a situation adversely affects many officers, called a policy grievance. To illustrate, we will look at a policy grievance filed on 21 October 1985, involving a police officer who had wanted his single day off to be counted as a vacation day rather than as a personal day. The chief, the commissioner, and then the city manager had denied the grievance by 1 November on the grounds that the officer had personal days coming, which were appropriate to use for a single day off, because general order 3 of 1981, stipulated: "Vacation leave of less than one week may be allowed when an officer's Personal Leave has been expended and, in that case, only when good cause exists." The union took the case to arbitration; both sides appeared with attorneys; and the arbitrator decided one year later, on 24 November 1986, that the union was right, that management had no authority to make officers use up their personal leave. He based his decision on wording that had remained unchanged since the first contract in 1969: "All members of the Bureau shall be granted a maximum of three days per year personal leave without giving a reason therefor, which leave shall not be cumulative. Personal leave may not be consecutive working days."

Binding arbitration to decide grievances not resolved within city government is used by 80 percent of large police departments, according to

the most recent PERF study of police contracts (Rynecki and Morse 1981).
Arbitration of a simple issue typically requires a day for the hearing and a
day for writing the decision at a fee which in New York state in 1980 ran
between $300 and $400 per day. Use of lawyers in presentation before
arbitrators distinguishes police arbitration from most industrial arbitration, which typically uses direct dialogue between management and labor. The power of the grievance process depends on the strength of the
contractual clauses that limit management rights. This topic is so important that it should be examined separately.

A good working relationship between management and union prevents the extremes of management caprice or union obstinacy from mar-
ring the quality of work life. The rise and fall in the annual number of
grievances that the Troy PBA filed between 1973 and 1986 indicates the
union's shifting cooperation with management. In 1973 the PBA filed
only three grievances and went to arbitration once. After 1974, when the
new PBA leadership took charge, the average number of grievances per
year rose to twelve. During the combative years 1977–78, when O'Connor had just returned to the department and had begun team policing,
the union went eleven times to arbitration and three times to court in the
course of thirty grievances. During 1979, a year of recuperation from the
struggle over team policing, there were only four grievances; 1980 and
1981 were combative with an average of eleven; 1982 through 1986 were
tranquil, averaging two grievances per year. In a well-managed department, grievances usually concern only trivial matters. Specifically, of the
seven Troy grievances filed between 1983 and 1986, all except the one
listed first below concerned only vacation time or a few more dollars in
someone's pocket.

1. When an officer was sued for violating a citizen's civil rights, the city
   provided the city attorney but did not pay for a separate attorney for
   the officer. Union won.
2. A clothing allowance was cut pro rata for three officers who were
   suspended. Management won.
3. An officer could not carry to the next year more than twenty-two vacation days. Management compromise accepted.
4. When most sergeants were absent to take a promotion examination, a
   captain was recalled to work overtime instead of a sergeant. Union
   withdrew.
5. The department did not replace the worn-out belt of an officer. Management won.
6. A captain was recalled to work overtime instead of a sergeant. Union
   won.
7. As previously recounted, an officer was prohibited from using a vacation day and required to use a personal day to cover a single day off.
   Union won.

Contractual Limits on Departmental Discipline

Unions have made important gains in contractual guarantees of due process to reduce the likelihood of capricious actions by management. The Troy contract is typical in specifying that the officer against whom charges are brought has a right to be represented by a union member and by an attorney. Unions typically pay the attorney's fee. Procedural safeguards in Troy are illustrated by two cases discussed in Chapter 8: officers caught drinking beer on duty, and officers who tampered with evidence after a high-speed chase. But even the Troy PBA, which was energetic in defending every officer, sometimes drew the line. Eventually, for example, PBA leaders told the department's worst alcoholic that if he were brought up again on charges of coming to work intoxicated, they would not provide an attorney.

Mandatory Consultation

Some contracts require management to confer with union representatives before making basic changes in working conditions. To confer is not the same as to reach agreement. Management that treats police officers as professionals will naturally confer with those affected before implementing changes. Such contractual clauses force police administrators of dictatorial inclinations to become acquainted with the union perspective. The table of organization is the only subject on which the Troy contract requires consultation. At each change Commissioner O'Connor first discussed his proposed table of organization with the command staff and then with union representatives. These meetings served largely as a means for informing the department of the reasons behind the upcoming changes and never hampered management initiative.

Officer Safety Committee

An unusual feature of the first Troy contracts was the provision that if an officer considered a piece of equipment unsafe, he could call upon the union safety committee for a judgment. If the committee concurred, the officer had the right to refuse to use the equipment until the defect was repaired. A management headache in every police department is maintaining patrol cars in good operating condition. The sad state of Troy's patrol fleet during the 1960s had prompted the union to obtain this provision. Officers who served on the safety committee quickly informed management of every breakdown.

In the 1977–78 contract O'Connor expanded the professional authority of the union committee and all officers individually. The safety committee gained the authority to inspect on a routine basis any equipment belonging to the department and to advise the chief if it found anything faulty. All officers gained the authority to refuse to work with any piece of equipment they believe unsafe unless so directed in writing by the superior officer in charge, who must certify that the equipment is safe. This unusual explicit sharing of authority stands in contrast to more common ways of handling the problem of defective patrol cars. Robert B. Kleismet (1984), president of the International Union of Police Associations, commented that for every problem there is always an informal solution. If an officer is ordered to use a car he judges to be dangerously defective, he can always drive it a couple of blocks and park it.

Informal Protections

In Troy a pattern of weak and capricious management prior to 1973 encouraged the PBA to protect members from the criticism of their supervisors. In 1972 the consultants noted, "The only uniformly enforced system for governing day-to-day Bureau operations consists of the terms of the PBA contract with the City." An incident in 1976 illustrates Chief Givney's method of reclaiming authority by bringing disciplinary charges against two young officers who had been on the job about a year. Because they had worked after 11:30 P.M. one evening, the question arose of their eligiblity for the minimum of two hours' overtime pay. The officers admitted that the platoon captain told them they would have to stay on duty until 12:30 A.M. to be paid overtime but that they left at 12:10 because the PBA representative said they did not have to stay. They were found guilty of disobeying a direct order and were given written reprimands.

Another example comes from the late 1970s, when a pair of young officers complained to their PBA representative that their sergeant was punishing them by demanding a written explanation of why they had not been patrolling their zone. The representative immediately informed the sergeant that if the PBA executive committee found that his action had broken PBA bylaws, then they would fine him $50 and could expel him from the union for a repeated offense.

A third example comes from 1987; as Sergeant Sam Griffith recalls the problem, he persistently prodded an officer who continually avoided work. When Griffith finally warned the officer that he would write him up, the officer went to the PBA president, who questioned Griffith about the amount of time he permitted for lunch. The two agreed that the officer was shirking, and the PBA president offered to talk to him on Griffith's behalf. Griffith replied, "No, that's my job." The officer avoided Griffith for a week, but for the first time he began to work. Griffith found him, praised him, and advised him to continue now that he knew how little effort it took to do a job he could be proud of.

To the best of my knowledge, no one has traced informal union influences on supervision for any department. The backbone of the supervisors and the pride of new union leaders in quality police service account for the differences in these incidents. Apparently, interference by the Troy PBA in supervision disappeared in the 1980s.

Police Associations in Various Arenas

Union leaders can go to whatever forum they believe will give them the best hearing. Where contract language is clear, arbitration is best. Where state law is favorable, the court is best. The city executive may be a mercurial ally of the union or a consistent supporter of the police executive. Support comes to the union more often from the city council than from the city executive. Congressmen and senators, not the president, initiated the first piece of national legislation that police associations have obtained, a $50,000 death benefit for officers killed in the line of duty (LEAA 1976). This guarantee goes back to the roots of police unions as benevolent associations.

Lobbying for state legislation is a much older tradition. For example, in 1911 the PBAs of New York state obtained legislation requiring three equal shifts for patrol work, which still remained in effect throughout the 1980s. In Milwaukee, where a long-term chief had a national reputation for opposition to improving the quality of work life, union president Robert Kleismet became an advocate for reforms that could be imposed by state legislation on recalcitrant chiefs: college education for entrance, state-level certification of officers, lateral entry of personnel above the police officer rank, and compulsory management training for administrators. In one Milwaukee union-management conflict, as recounted by Kleismet (1984), the union had established an employee counseling program by covering its cost in the Blue Shield health insurance plan. The chief than used the Blue Shield billing to identify officers in counseling in order to target them for special investigation for possible misconduct. The union thwarted the chief by obtaining state legislation that forbade Blue Shield to identify psychiatric services on any insurance statements issued in Wisconsin.

Across the country in the 1970s the most important legislation sought by police associations was a set of procedural safeguards they had not entirely obtained through contracts, generally known as a "Bill of Rights." The first provision of New York's law specifies that officers cannot be prohibited from engaging in political activity, thus safeguarding their opportunity to obtain more favorable legislation. Most provisions of the law apply due process protections to any interrogation by a commanding officer, even one that results in no more than a written reprimand. An officer's right to have an attorney present makes formal and adversarial a process that should be informal and educational. Additional provisions make it difficult to obtain evidence against any corrupt officer by totally forbidding use of a polygraph and prohibiting, except in particular circumstances, financial disclosure or search of an officer's locker.

The Troy PBA's entrance into a variety of arenas illustrates how many options a police union has for reversing management decisions. Here are six decisions by outside bodies which have had a long-term effect on the department.

1. The union compelled the filling of the police chief's position after unsuccessfully going to the state court by obtaining a clause in the current revision of the city charter (see Chapter 2).
2. The union obtained ten additional police positions through the city council (Chapter 7).
3. The union impeded implementation of team policing through the city council (Chapter 10).
4. The union won an arbitrator's decision to forbid job rotation of recruits, but management won back the authority two years later through another arbitrator's decision.
5. The union won an arbitrator's decision that seniority would determine eligibility for training, but management reversed this with a new clause in the contract, which another arbitrator upheld.
6. The union, through an arbitrator's decision, ended management's authority to change the hours for patrol shifts but could not, through another arbitrator's decision, end management's right to require flexible hours for officers working in special investigative units.

Whether or not police unions should engage in political activity is a controversial question, given the special responsibilities of the police for impartiality in maintaining social order. The California experience of 1959 is an example of police associations lobbying the state legislature to build an engine of progress, the Peace Officers' Standards and Training Commission (POST). The state levies a surcharge on criminal fines that goes into the Peace Officers' Training Fund. The $38,900,000 in revenue for the fiscal year 1988–89 supported a wide variety of training across the state and reimbursed departments for 40 percent of the salary of officers in training. POST has served as a major force in making the quality of police service in California among the best in the country. Advocacy of increased political participation by officers individually and collectively as an antidote to the cynical perspective is voiced by William Muir (1983), on the basis of his familiarity with police in California.

Police are capable of employing a wide variety of improper methods to influence politicians and political discourse. Two episodes come from the early years of upgrading in Troy, when the union leaders were in the forefront of defending the department from what they perceived as political interference. A police officer who held a PBA office stopped for a traffic violation a member of the city council who had been active in attempting to obtain the records of the professional standards unit. The officer spread- eagled the councilman on his car, according to a story that went around the department. While this sort of precaution is completely appropriate when the suspect might be armed, for a cooperative citizen such treatment is harassment. The councilman was further harassed at 3:00 A.M. one night when his car was ticketed and towed for being parked facing the wrong way, a common violation in Troy that officers universally ignored at that time.

The second episode began at a December 1977 public lecture on the criminal justice system, presented by the commissioner and the newly elected municipal judge, whose opponent the PBA had supported. In the question session a respected black citizen criticized the PBA for going to the city council to oppose the commissioner. A PBA representative who had attended the meeting spoke with the union president, who telephoned the citizen to say that the union did not like his remarks. The citizen complained to the commissioner about this intimidation, and the commissioner sent a memo to the union president (8 December 1977) to inform him of the citizen's complaint of harassment.

> You can be assured that I fully understand every citizen's right to attend and/or speak at open public meetings. That right exists as much for police officers as for others, and I would not take any steps to try to curtail in any way the rights of either group.
>
> This matter, at this point, is not a formal complaint requiring an investigation or the recording of the matter. However, I thought you ought to know that at least one citizen perceived your follow-up as something more than an attempt at seeking clarification of the problem. If I can make a suggestion, it would be that you try to converse with . . . [him] in a joint effort to determine your differences.

The union leader who had been present with me at the public meeting told me that the PBA was incensed over the commissioner's reprimand.

On reflection, it appears that the breadth of police powers provides officers many legal and illegal opportunities to punish their enemies. Under what circumstances will citizens hear police officers expressing an opposing view without perceiving a veiled threat? The greatest danger of police participation in politics is that some officers will use their power and privileged information in covert ways to gain their political ends. There are no easy solutions. The pluralist approach is to permit full political participation by police unions and to encourage groups with different perspectives to contend with them in political debate, in the hope that no opposing voices will be stilled by intimidation. An alternative approach recognizes the three levels of government in the American system and weighs heavily the seriousness of misuse of police powers at the local level. Lobbying and officeholding could be forbidden to individual officers and to the union at the level of government responsible for the department. Full political participation would be permitted only at other levels, where the likelihood of intimidation would be far less.

Contractual Impediments to Enhancement of Service

Some specific do's and don'ts in police contracts hamper management's ability to set policies. Management regards flexibility as essential to meeting changing public needs with changing resources and sees limitations on flexibility as "infringements on management rights." By contrast, unions view flexibility as opening the door to capricious exploitation and punishment and see contractual limitations on flexibility as "conditions of work." A thorough review of the impact of contract language on management powers has been written to advise management how to retain maximum power. Rynecki and Morse (1981) made a detailed analysis of 140 collective bargaining agreements from more than 100 cities in a study prepared for the Police Executive Research Forum and the National League of Cities. Two contractual provisions that they single out as hampering the delivery of quality service were found in Troy: seniority rights and mandatory staffing.

The seniority clauses in the Troy contract are among the strongest in the nation. Seniority gives officers absolute priority in vacations, specialist training, and even in job positions. Picking vacation periods by seniority poses no real problem to management, affords choice to all but the most junior officers, and fits a general notion of-fairness that considers senior members to have earned a privilege that all will eventually attain. For this purpose, seniority is clean and aboveboard, giving management no opportunity for favoritism or punishment.

When job assignments are dependent upon choice by seniority, however, major damage results. When a key support position is selected by an officer without expertise or inclination to learn, street operations suffer. The uneven development of the evidence technician program, for example, was a consequence of job assignments determined by seniority. Initially, a knowledgeable and energetic identification officer held the position responsible for coordinating the work and analyzing the evidence. Then a 1975 grievance brought by a few detectives, juvenile aid detectives, and this identification officer, who all wanted to leave their positions, resulted in an arbitration decision that all these ranks were equivalent to sergeant. Nine different individuals chose the identification position between 1976 and 1980, most moving on without developing expertise. When an individual performed particularly poorly in the position, the commissioner changed the rank of the position in the table of organization prepared for the next semiannual bid, thus evicting the incumbent. Turnover slowed after 1980: one sergeant held the job for a year and a half and the next for two years; between 1983 and 1987 the same sergeant steadily held the position.

Fully half the grievances filed between 1973 and 1986 concerned seniority. When arbitrators weigh a clear criterion (seniority) against a criterion not fully specified in the contract (appropriate qualifications), clarity wins. Even though many officers expressed frustration when an unqualified senior officer chose a key position and when senior officers predominated in attending out-of-town training, they adamantly supported the seniority system. Their attitude is explained by an observation of Derek Griffiths (1983), concerning the Leicestershire Constabulary, that the ghost of the old organization haunts the new one. By 1985 half the Troy officers were too new to have experienced the bruising of the bad old days, yet they generally believed that the seniority clause in the contract was essential to prevent the return of harsh administration. Although they deemed Commissioner O'Connor free of malice, they feared an unknown future leader. They did not see that management had become too professional to use work as punishment, nor did they see that the professional development of officers had made them too valuable to waste on midnight walking posts.

Staffing requirements are infrequently mandated in large city contracts, specifically in 11 percent of the contracts covered by the PERF study (Rynecki and Morse 1981). In 1972 the Troy contract had specified the minimum number of two-officer cars per shift. A couple of years' experience with voluntary decisions to work alone, as described in Chapter 4, eliminated the belief that two-officer cars were essential for officer safety. In the 1977–78 contract the PBA agreed with O'Connor to drop the minimum staffing clauses. Subsequently, O'Connor maintained a patrol strength that permitted the department to field about twice as many cars as required by the old minimums.

Contractual Support for Professional Service

Since a contract is a device to constrain and direct management actions, provisions can be written to promote the movement of the department toward the hospital model. In four functions of personnel administration, the Troy contract promotes the development of professional police officers: restriction on who may exercise police powers, exclusion of managerial personnel from the bargaining unit, a requirement that management provide training, and incentives for individuals to pursue higher education.

In the 1975 contract O'Connor gained agreement for a clause forbidding the use of provisional employees except in an emergency. There are two reasons why departments make provisional appointments: political considerations and manpower shortage. To become a police officer in

Troy before the change to city manager government, a candidate benefited from connections to politically powerful individuals. Favored young men received temporary appointments, drew full salary, and continued as provisionals until they eventually passed the civil service examination. Of the thirty-four men at police officer rank who had been hired before 1964 and were still with the department in 1977, 70 percent had entered as provisionals, as had 36 percent of the sergeants and 58 percent of the captains and chiefs from that period. Most had gained regular appointment within a year, but the 10 percent who took longest to pass the examination had served as provisionals for more than three years. O'Connor did not need contractual restrictions to prompt him to exclude the partially qualified, but he reasoned that one of his successors might. The 1975–76 contract also extended the probationary period for new recruits from six months to one year, the maximum allowable under New York state law.

The union contract is a good vehicle for promoting training. As of 1972, 61 of the 123 officers had not passed basic training, because they had started as provisionals and state law did not require basic training until 1959. In-service training to update knowledge is still superficial in most departments. O'Connor planned to launch the first week-long in-service school in 1974 by requiring attendance. When faced with a grievance by officers whose personal lives and second jobs interfered with switching to the day shift for the week of training, O'Connor changed to voluntary participation. He then gained a clause in the 1975–76 contract making an annual week of training mandatory, even though scheduling a solid week of training for every member of the department without using overtime is a major managerial task. To O'Connor's surprise and disappointment, the union did not hold management to the observation of this contract provision. In 1978, however, when the PBA obtained a city council hearing as a forum for voicing complaints, department members repeatedly complained about the lack of the in-service school. Thereafter, management ran the school annually. Lacking the authority to select an individual to head the training division, the commissioner and chief shouldered major responsibility for its operation.

Higher education, which is central to improvement of police service, can be promoted through a contract in five ways: qualification for appointment, qualification for promotion, incentive pay, tuition reimbursement, and educational leave. Chapter 4 discussed in some detail O'Connor's early but unsuccessful attempts to obtain educational qualifications for appointment and incentive pay. He had no interest in requiring higher education for promotion, because such a change would imply that higher education was unnecessary for the police officer rank. Since 1972 all contracts have provided tuition reimbursement for courses of the officer's choosing that contribute to his professional development. Education leave is supported in principle by broad contract language that permits leave for any legitimate purpose; it occurred in practice when management granted a semester's leave for an officer to enter law school.

The brevity of this section on contractual stimulation for professional development contrasts with the length of the discussion of contractual impediments. As should be clear by now, police upgrading requires flexibility, but employee contracts are by nature fixed for their duration and hard to change at the bargaining table.

The Structural Basis of Union-Management Power Struggles

Several reasons converge to explain why union leaders fought the commissioner as he introduced changes that members generally liked and why members supported their union leaders.

The first and broadest reason for union opposition is that union power is essentially a veto power. Since unions are formed to look out for the interests of their members, some differences of opinion with management are to be expected. Moreover, the traditionally low status of the police officer rank, the length of the promotion ladder, and the scarcity of positions above the rank of sergeant emphasize differences between labor and management. The union's powers are designed not to develop leadership but to limit management power. Unions do not direct the implementation of policy; that is, they do not exercise direct power over operations or conditions of work. Rather, they narrow management's options by requiring adherence to contractually negotiated conditions of work. Questions of the extent to which individuals who enjoy combat tend to be drawn to union leadership, or the extent to which the office shapes the man, cannot be answered here. It is clear, however, that union leaders lack the right to collaborate—to participate in staff meetings, for example—but always have the right to object through the grievance process.

A second reason for union opposistion derives from the fact that few officers aspire to union leadership. Generally, members of the professions and skilled craftworkers commit little of their time or energy to union affairs. The straight-through career ladder of police departments may have a strong effect on the self-selection of union leaders. Where the bargaining unit is restricted to the police officer rank, a decision to become a union leader is tantamount to renouncing an aspiration to climb the departmental rank ladder. Can such an officer be expected to see issues from management's perspective?

The first reason why members supported the union leadership rather than the commissioner lies in their career commitment to a specific department and their awareness that the police association will endure as commissioners and chiefs come and go. Second, the retention of thoroughly disgruntled individuals who are indentured to their pension heightens antagonism in a department. They form a reservoir of support for any union leaders who pursue antimanagement policies for the sake of opposition. Serving to dilute such antagonism is the tradition of police solidarity, the sense that all police officers of whatever rank started on patrol, where they shared danger and authority. A police executive who began his career elsewhere is not felt to share fully in police solidarity, which is a department-based solidarity. Third, specifically in Troy, there is a general and widespread distrust of powerful people and a strong suspicion of outsiders. The opposition mentality of the Troy PBA leadership was buttressed by the members' beliefs that the dramatic improvements in working conditions were due to a strong and well-defended union contract rather than to enlightened management.

Police policy is public policy. There are virtually no matters of a policy nature which do not impinge upon the public. The involvement of the client in policy formation is an important goal.

George W. O'Connor, 1976

Political Accountability versus Political Interference

George O'Connor's call for public policy is now voiced by increasing numbers of police managers and stands in contrast to the advocacy of freedom from political direction that marked the previous sixty years. From the turn of the century, progressive police administrators fought hardest to remove decisions on hiring, assignment, and promotion from the influence of powerful individuals outside the department and to end corrupt ties to political bosses. They were correct in their assessment that internal accountability was not possible in the face of pervasive political interference. In striving to insulate police departments from interference, however, they rebuffed all policy direction. Exaggerated autonomy succeeded subservience to political machines. Their protective wall was the fiction that policies are unnecessary because police departments simply and automatically apply the law to lawbreakers. Police chiefs steeped in the traditions of secrecy still suggest that criticism aids the lawbreakers. One might suppose that the prevailing low levels of political accountability are exclusively the fault of police leadership. Not so. Events in Troy display impediments to political accountability even when the police manager provides full explanations of all policies and openly accepts suggestions, complaints, and criticisms.

This chapter briefly examines political interference in personnel decisions and then discusses four criteria for distinguishing between political accountability and interference: directives from officials are acts of accountability if they require actions that are legal, efficient, effective, and fair. These criteria are applied in the process of examining the nature of four mechanisms for controlling municipal police: selection of the police manager, budgetmaking, election of city officials, and city council directives. The chapter concludes with tentative generalizations about why political direction of municipal police often includes acts of interference.

Interference in Personnel Matters

At their best, personnel decisions bring qualified individuals into an agency and organize them in productive working relations to achieve quality service and high levels of work satisfaction. Personnel policies appropriately tailored to the work of an agency increase the skill and motivation of agency members. To the extent that personnel decisions are made inside an agency, the agency head can reward good work and match skills to tasks.

To protect public employees against mismanagement, a number of institutions have been created during the last century: state civil service codes, independent civil service commissions, public employee unions together with state labor relations boards, and federal legislation to prevent exploitation and discrimination. As a result, fragmentation of personnel powers is typical throughout municipal and county government. The only national study of the impact of civil service systems on municipal police management notes that over two-thirds of American cities work with independent civil service commissions (Greisinger, Slovak, and Molkup 1979, 41). In their intensive study of forty-two cities, the researchers concluded that the many varieties of dividing authority over personnel decisions are illogical and "defeat efforts to determine or fix accountability for the personnel program."

As long ago as 1970 the National Civil Service League, which had helped draft the federal Civil Service Act of 1883, recommended abolishing independent civil service commissions in order to increase the authority of executives. On the terrain of personnel decisions, an independent civil service commission commands strategic mountain passes while other officials also prevent police managers from using personnel decisions to hold department members accountable for their work. Table 10-1 groups such decisions into eight major categories of authority. The first defines the jobs, the next five determine who gets the jobs, and the last two decide how much employees are paid.

The argument advanced here is that preventing police executives from exercising a broad range of personnel powers constitutes interference. For example, in creating ten new police officer positions, Troy's city council interfered with Commissioner O'Connor's strategy to cope with fear of crime (see Chapter 7). The Troy Civil Service Commission interfered with the department's hiring of women as officers by maintaining a height standard and other actions (described in Chapter 4). Civil service procedures also prevented O'Connor from selecting for a regular position as police planner the man he had appointed to a temporary position (see Chapter 2).

Initially, City Manager John Buckley had not passed along to O'Connor

Table 10-1 Authority over Personnel Matters

Question: Who Has Authority to	Answer in Troy
Create positions?	Troy Civil Service Commission (CSC) defines each rank and job category; city council authorizes funding; police manager creates table of organization
Set position qualifications?	State and city CSC for officers; city CSC for nonsworn personnel
Select new members?	Police manager, from top three of list issued by city CSC
Assign members to positions?	No one, because of seniority clause in union contract
Promote members?	Police manager, from top three of list issued by city CSC
Terminate members?	Police manager, with concurrence of city CSC
Set pay scales?	Collective bargaining by unions and city manager, with advice from police manager
Tie pay level to performance?	No one

pressures for promotions that he received. O'Connor's appointment of John Givney as chief in 1973 came as a surprise to the city manager, who told me he had expected O'Connor to appoint the Democrat among the three eligible candidates because Democrats were then in control of the city council. Later, Buckley directly interfered in a promotion to sergeant. According to the commissioner, in the summer of 1983 he told the city manager that he wanted to promote two competent young officers from the old sergeants' list that was about to expire. Buckley's response was a flat no; he explained that he was taking a principled stand against political interference because he had been getting phone calls on behalf of one of the officers from every city council member. O'Connor pointed out that at the top of the *new* sergeants' list was a PBA leader who had used an inordinate amount of sick leave and, in O'Connor's judgment, had not invested himself in serving the public. The man had reached the top of the promotion list by using all his veteran's points and seniority points. Once the old list had expired, the city manager began telling the commissioner that he was getting pressure from the Democratic party county chairman for the promotion of the PBA official. In March 1984 O'Connor made the promotion after calling the PBA leader to his office and explaining frankly the nature of his reluctance.

The strong seniority clause of the union contract eliminated management choice in assigning department members to positions (Chapter 9). The civil service commission stalled for six years the firing of an aggressive, alcoholic officer (Chapter 8). Contract negotiation set the pay scales, in which the commissioner participated as the key member of the management team. The last item of authority in personnel matters, tying pay level to performance, was not possible in Troy and is difficult within the rank structure of police departments (Guyot 1979).

A conclusion that can be drawn from the fragmentation of personnel powers is that if police management is denied authority over who will perform the work, internal accountability is undermined. The more management is prevented from directing the work of department members, the less likely is the organization to perform well.

Distinctions between Political Accountability and Interference

Whenever police policies are framed and implemented, power is exercised over the actions of police department members. In any particular instance, this power can be exercised solely from within the department or by governmental agencies outside the department. The term "power" is used here as precisely defined by Robert Dahl (1957) and in standard use by political scientists: the ability to get someone to do something that otherwise he or she would not have done. As in daily speech, a use of power judged to be irresponsible is called "interference," while a use judged appropriate and responsible is termed "accountability." A decision can be an act of accountability and yet foolish in the view of participants and observers: for example, a legislative decision to cut services rather than raise taxes. The aim here is to develop criteria appropriate to late twentieth-century America to distinguish between interfering in police affairs and holding police accountable for their performance.

Political accountability takes place through formal agencies of government. Direct accountability to citizens (discussed in the next chapter) occurs, for example, when a citizen asks the police chief for and obtains traffic enforcement against speeders on his block or phones a sergeant to obtain an apology from an officer for a rude remark. When a citizen channels the same demands through a city councilman, that is political accountability. In contrast to both these forms is internal accountability, by which supervisors and managers coordinate the work of the department (see Chapters 2–4 and 8).

The setting of priorities among goals is an act of political accountability. In regard to specific policies, I base the distinction between accountability and interference on a framework for performance measurement developed by the Indiana University Workshop in Political Theory and Policy Analysis (Whitaker et al. 1982). Following the line of reasoning advanced by the workshop, I identify four different classes of criteria against which police policies may be measured: legality, efficiency, effectiveness, and fairness. All four should be applied so as to give the benefit of the doubt to the external agency that is directing the police. A policy that is accountable on all criteria may still be subject to debate on its wisdom. However, if a particular directive fails to meet any of the four, it is an act of political interference.

1. *Legality* is the requirement that all members of a police department obey the law. Any directive by a local government executive for police officers to take illegal actions or to protect illegal activities is political interference.

2. *Efficiency* is a measurement that compares two or more programs by assessing the value of the inputs into the programs against the benefits of their outputs. The term "efficiency" conveys precision, but in policing that precision is largely illusory because the measurement of both inputs and outputs is difficult. Unfortunately, the concept of efficiency has been blindly applied to response time, reported crime rates, traffic accident rates, arrest rates, and crime clearances. Efficiency has been properly applied to vehicle maintenance, record-keeping, and supply purchasing, areas where the straightforward nature of inputs and outputs makes them measurable.

3. *Effectiveness* is frequently used to assess policies and performance. A line between accountability and interference may be drawn between directives that define the problem and those that require some specific

steps as solution. Agreement that a particular organization is at least partially responsible for a problem is an acknowledgment that there are some goals for the organization's performance, however vague, and that the organization has not met those goals. Often goals are muddled. Measurement of effectiveness requires that the goals be clear enough so that an observer can discern whether or not they have been met. This distinction between general goals and specific solutions is blurred in practice because the very way in which a goal is formulated implies solutions. In general, demands for accountability are phrased "Do something!" Interference is usually phrased "Do this!" Although a local government executive may have the expertise in policing to choose effective measures, it is more likely that specific orders from outside the department will fit so poorly with what the department is already doing as to be ineffective.

Every organization may be regarded as having goals in many different areas. Since an organization can be more or less effective in achieving each one, there is no single question of effectiveness but as many questions of effectiveness as there are goals. Moreover, the goals are defined by a variety of constituencies: clients, agency staff, local government executives, legislatures, other organizations from which the agency receives inputs and to which it gives outputs. When an organization is not effective in meeting a goal, four different factors may be operating singly or together.

a. The goal is unrealistic; no techniques are known for achieving it.
b. The organization is applying an inappropriate technique; that is, no matter how well the agency performs a procedure, it will not achieve the desired results, because that procedure does not produce those results.
c. The organization has selected appropriate techniques but implemented them improperly.
d. The organization is appropriately implementing techniques, but the scale is too small to achieve the goal.

If the last reason alone is preventing successful resolution of the problem, policymakers outside the police department can simply mandate "more of the same" and provide funds to expand current activities. If any of the other three factors are operating, however, then selection of an effective set of solutions requires expertise. City executives and city councils rarely have the expertise to assess the effectiveness of alternative solutions. In the absence of staff with such skills, they should focus their efforts on clarifying the nature of the problems and their priorities among them. If city decisionmakers adopt specific policies that are attempts to do the impossible, then the selection of these policies may appropriately be considered political interference.

Political accountability is exercised when decisionmakers demand that specific problems be addressed. In two cities having the same reported burglary rates, one mayor can demand extraordinary effort in burglary reduction and the other require only routine efforts, yet both departments are being held politically accountable. The substance of political decisionmaking is to identify the importance of problems.

4. *Fairness*, the last criterion discussed here, has fundamental importance for policing. Everyone can agree that fairness has been achieved when similar situations are treated similarly. However, the world is full of situations where people have honest disagreements about the similarity. Moreover, people frequently disagree on what are fair ways of treating different situations. Whitaker and his colleagues have stated three definitions, any of which could be employed to judge the fairness of service distribution:

a. a single, universal standard: everyone should receive the same service;

b. a demand criterion: all who ask shall receive;

c. a need criterion: those who have more need should receive more.

Neighborhoods and interest groups tend to promote their own pet projects without attention to any standard of fairness. The city executive is likely to employ some notion of fairness, based on a concern for the welfare of the city as a whole. Promoting fairness and the perception of fairness is one of the most important responsibilities of a police manager.

In sum, various combinations of these criteria may be applied to a specific policy. Standards for judging whether a particular policy advances accountability or constitutes interference may be summarized as follows: a policy directive to a police department is an exercise of political accountability to the extent that it is legal, is not grossly inefficient, addresses attention to the problem without imposing an ineffective solution, and is fair by some standard. The less a policy directive meets these four criteria, the stronger the political interference.

The Political Context of Directing a Police Department

In order to apply these criteria intelligently, we should consider the political context. The discussion in earlier chapters examined one issue at a time, but in every city many issues coexist, their proponents vying for attention. The likelihood of conflict is high because the steps to achieve some goals make others harder to achieve. Further, citizens and elected leaders often fail to agree on what they want the police to do. A minimum expectation of elected city officials is that police managers will prevent police malpractice from becoming a hot issue. If public outrage blazes over some police action, elected officials expect the department to take the heat. Police issues, like other issues under democratic government, are not settled "once and for all," because the losers in any round have many opportunities to renew the fight.

Troy's government was the mayor and council form between 1900 and

1956. Then domination by the county Republican party was interrupted by a Democratic victory, but the Democrats' mismanagement spurred various good government groups to ally with the Republicans to pass a referendum in 1960 on a new city charter establishing a city manager form of government to take effect in 1964. The formal arrangements in the charter are standard. The city manager exercises all executive powers, including authority to appoint and dismiss, but serves at the pleasure of the city council. The council's authority to set basic policy and pass legislation brings it into conflict with the city manager about where to draw the line between policy and implementation. After each municipal election the council members elect one among them to be mayor, who thus has the spotlight for challenging the city manager. An unusual feature of Troy's election system gave the voters opportunity to unseat a majority of incumbents every two years. The volatility of Troy's elections from 1969 to 1977 was promoted by the large proportion of voters registered without party affiliation: 42 percent in 1975, compared with 33 percent Republicans and 22 percent Democrats. Increased Democratic registration of the city in the late 1970s, however, gave the council solid Democratic majorities.

Parties in Troy evoke strong loyalty among those who are politically active. County chairmen exercise direct control over city council members through their power to award or deny party endorsement. Every effort to run for city council outside the Republican or Democratic ticket has resulted in stunning defeats for a whole slate and for individual candidates. The county chairman of the party holding a council majority calls the important shots: the firing of city managers, the appointment and promotion of favored individuals. In terms of Oliver Williams's typology of what is important to politically influential people, Troy has an arbitrator style of government. Municipal problems immediately become partisan issues, and defeating opponents is more important than the content of the issues.

The first city manager, a professional from out of state, refused in 1967 to obey the order of the county Republican party to promote a particular police sergeant to captain; he arranged to resign quietly once he found another job. The second city manager made the promotion, arranged kickbacks to the county Republicans from contractors doing business with the city, and held office for seventeen months until forced out by a state criminal investigation. After an interim city manager, the fourth dominated a city council that was split four to three in the Republican's favor until the Democrats attained control of all seats through their 1971 election victory. He attributed his stormy firing in early 1972 to his refusal to obey the Democratic county chairman's direct demand to place Democrats in appointive city positions then held by Republicans. Then John Buckley stepped over from head of the water department to acting city manager. Confirmed after some months, Buckley served the fractious city council for five years, until a Republican majority fired him in mid-1977. The Democrats, who had fought with Buckley as much as the Republicans, then adopted "Bring Back Buckley" as their campaign slogan, won all contested seats, and subsequently continued their substantial majority on the council. After Buckley retired, Steven G. Dworsky became city manager in 1986. A professor of political science at the local community college, he had spent his formative years in city politics as a member of the council's public safety committee when it was most active in attempting to direct the police department; he had then spent several years as mayor, working to bring back strong mayor government.

Appointment of a Police Manager as a Tool for Accountability

A choice of managers provides the best opportunity to set new policy directions, whether in the world of business or in government. The city executive's power to hire and fire a police manager creates an overall political accountability through selection of an individual to be responsible for policies that are legal, efficient, effective, and fair. In Troy the commissioner of public safety exercised authority over the police chief and the fire chief, both tenured civil service positions. As long as the position was filled, the commissioner managed the police department. During the intervals when the commissioner's position was vacant, the police chief managed the department. The events in the appointment, reappointment, and forced retirement of George O'Connor as commissioner illustrate total lack of public participation and provide examples of decisions that were entangled in other conflicts. Chapter 2 described the fears of department members engendered by the unanticipated appointment of a commissioner in 1973. Later that year the PBA forced the appointment of a chief by persuading the charter commission to insert a clause in the overall city charter revision. On neither occasion did any public debate take place on policy goals.

The next opportunity for public discussion about overall leadership of the department occurred after O'Connor informed Buckley in July 1975 that he would be resigning to take a position in Washington. The city manager delayed making the resignation public until after O'Connor had left in September. Buckley had no intention of filling the commissioner's position; he planned to let the chief run the department. His hand was forced, however, when the 1975 election placed Dworsky and two Republican newcomers on the council's public safety committee. In January 1976 the committee began an active interest in many aspects of department management. In March, after the murder of a seventy-five-year-old woman brought one hundred citizens to a meeting of the public safety committee, it formally requested Buckley to appoint a commissioner

within six days. The top candidate was a former official of the state correction commission, who had campaigned for the Republican council
candidates the previous fall. Buckley promised to meet the deadline, but
when the favorite declined, he managed to avoid making any appointment. In November 1976 voters had a referendum opportunity to keep
the current city charter or choose between two new governmental
forms—one involving a strong mayor and the other a weakened city
manager—either of which would abolish the commissioner's position.
The voters' choice to retain the current system rekindled the council's
ambition to fill the commissioner's position. When the council by a vote
of four to three inserted it in the 1977 budget, Buckley quietly offered
George O'Connor the commissionership. O'Connor accepted, as his
work in Washington had ended and he was engaged in private consulting. He and his family had not relocated from the house purchased three
years earlier. At the regular January 1977 council meeting, the city manager replied to a councilman's question that he was working on filling
the commissioner's position. Two days later he notified council members
by letter that he intended to reappoint O'Connor. Enraged at this failure
to consult them, the council voted at its February meeting by a six-to-one
majority to put a referendum on the November ballot to abolish the position and to change the police and fire chiefs into department heads who
would serve at the pleasure of the city manager. The March council meeting included among other business the public hearing on the referendum, but only one citizen spoke, testifying that a commissioner was necessary.

The referendum on police leadership was pushed to a back burner in
July, when the Republican majority of the council fired the city manager,
and remained there through September, when O'Connor wrote the
League of Women Voters offering to assist any inquiry or discussion on
the governance of the public safety function. The league belatedly opposed the referendum, but only on its wording. The issue surfaced in late
October when a newspaper story reported that the police union's vote at
its monthly meeting had run about twenty to ten for abolishing the commissioner's position. A captain then collected signatures on a petition
from sixty-five members opposing the union vote and specifically endorsing the retention of civil service tenure for the police chief. Note that the
PBA leadership phrased its stand as an attack on the commissioner,
whereas the membership petition was phrased as protection for the
chief. When the union leaders refused the captain's request to hold a
second membership vote on the issue, he made public the stand of the
majority of officers against a "political head of the police department."
The lone councilman who spoke for preserving the commissioner's post
was not up for election. He observed that the referendum had been
transformed from a selection of governance structures into a vote on

whether George O'Connor was doing a good job. His interpretation was supported by the few letters to the editor from citizens, which urged abolishing the post in order to remove O'Connor.

The petition signed by the majority of police officers supporting the retention of the post next made headlines. The Friday before the election the late television news covered the issue by interviewing Commissioner O'Connor. That same day, the city's newspaper urgently opposed the referendum on the grounds that a commissioner was essential to prevent political interference in the police and fire departments and to protect elected officials from the power of the unions. Most people were uninformed on the issue: 44 percent of Troy's adults voted for council candidates, but only 26 percent voted on the referendum. They defeated it two to one.

In 1983, with the unexpected death of Chief Givney, the issue of selecting a department head again arose. His vigor at age forty-five had given most command officers a reason not to bother taking the civil service examination for chief; only the newest captain, William P. Miller, had passed it. Since he was one of the most capable members of the department, the selection of the new chief was a simple matter of promoting the only person on the list.

In 1987 Steven Dworsky, the new city manager, gave no public accounting in requesting O'Connor's resignation and in leaving the commissioner's post vacant. As the institutional arrangements now stand, a police chief is mandatory, must be selected from within the department according to civil service procedures, and has tenure. The city manager retains the discretion to appoint and dismiss a commissioner or to leave the position vacant.

Troy's history with the most powerful instrument of political accountability illustrates some problems in its use. First, if the city executive withholds information from the city council and the public, then the accountability of the police department stops with the executive and does not carry over to those who may represent the diverse voices of the people. During the two decisions to select a commissioner, the city manager consulted no representatives of the public. Second, changes in institutional arrangements may be made for reasons completely irrelevant to accountability issues. In 1973 the police union forced the appointment of a chief in order to obtain a promotional position. In 1977 the city council, locked in a power struggle with the city manager, attempted to cut a police leadership position as a slap at the city manager, quite apart from the merits of the issue. Third, direction of the department can change hands without any debate or effort to create debate on priorities and performance standards. Fourth, when the head of the police department must be selected from the inside, the small size of the talent pool makes luck a large factor.

Limited Accountability through the Budget Process

Police budgets are not strong instruments of accountability for three basic reasons. First, more than 90 percent of the typical police budget is for personnel (Bureau of Justice Statistics 1989; Reaves 1990). Hence, during a fiscal contraction only retrenchment of personnel provides large savings, but civil service rules and union contracts specify that layoffs will affect only the most junior personnel, regardless of the positions they fill. Nor can a budget expansion support the hiring of specialists unless they are nonsworn personnel, because police departments typically permit sworn personnel to enter only at the bottom.

Second, although two-thirds of larger cities now make some use of program budgeting for some departments (ICMA 1989), city councils cannot use it to decide on the allocation of police services because it is fundamentally inappropriate, given the way police services are structured and delivered. Police work is not divided into separate, self-contained programs provided by separate units. The diverse responsibilities reviewed in Chapter 3 belong to the patrol division. If a specialist unit is created, patrol units share the particular responsibility; and if it is abolished, the whole responsibility returns to the patrol units (see Guyot and Martensen 1991). The budget cannot re-allocate effort between immediate assistance to crime victims and the quieting of noisy parties, because patrol officers do both. Internal managerial decisions, not external budget allocations, are required to change most priorities in policing. An ironic twist is that program budgeting is most widely used in grant applications to federal and state agencies. Thus, the explicit approval of the city executive and city council is required only for programs that spend other governments' funds.

Third, budgets are annual, not long-range, and are often prepared under tight deadlines. Opportunity for reflection on long-range priorities seldom occurs in the typical three-round tussle between the city executive and department heads, between the city executive and the city council, and between the executive and representatives from special-interest groups who attend the budget hearings. The failure of many cities to reserve sufficient contingency funds often forces midyear expenditure reductions below budgeted levels. Troy, like most cities, uses a detailed line-item budget that requires legislative approval for moving funds between categories. This type of budget stifles responsiveness to changing service needs.

Commissioner O'Connor prepared lean budgets and sought no supporters to lobby for them. When forced to cut, he found creative means to avoid layoffs. He held that because the city was not growing, any growth in the slice of the pie available to police would come at the expense of some other essential service. Any expansion in the number of officers he viewed as detrimental to obtaining higher police salaries.

Three examples of budgeting in years of scarcity illustrate more interference than accountability. A lame-duck session with a Republican majority had responsibility for preparing the 1978 budget, after losing badly to the Democrats. Rather than levy higher taxes to pay for costs incurred through inflation and previously negotiated contracts, the council made a quiet decision to cut 5 percent from every departmental budget. The council was exercising accountability in deciding against higher taxes, whatever the merits of the decision. Because the Troy police department allocated 94 percent of the budget to personnel, 3 percent to supplies, 2 percent to contractual services, and 1 percent to equipment, the obvious source of saving was personnel. The commissioner chose to give up the nine vacant police officer positions, thus reducing the department's authorized sworn strength to the level of 1975, before the furor over crime. However, the council refused to accept his decision and interfered by making their own cuts without consulting him. After abolishing only five police officer positions, it then reduced maintenance positions for the central station from two to one. O'Connor's memo to the city manager noted, "It is inconceivable that the busiest public building in the city can be properly cleaned and maintained by one employee." The council's most obvious inefficiency was to cut six new vehicles while simultaneously reducing the repair service account and halving the vehicle parts account from $30,000 to $15,000. The old council's sloppiness in cutting the five police positions had inadvertently spared kindred accounts: retirement, medical insurance, holiday pay, uniform allowance, and shift differential. As requested by O'Connor through the city manager, the new city council transferred these funds to save the maintenance position and bolster the repair account.

The bleakest fiscal year occurred during 1981. The 8.6 percent budget cut that the city manager asked of the commissioner in March would have required the layoff of sixteen officers. O'Connor proposed work sharing as an alternative, with all members of the department reduced from 40-hours a week to 36½, and pay cut proportionately. When such drastic measures proved unnecessary by May, O'Connor developed a plan to save 25 percent annually on the cost of police and fire communication systems by merging them into a single operational unit. The unit was staffed by a mix of police and nonsworn personnel who in the second year of operations undertook cross-training to perform both sets of communications and dispatching responsibilities. This is accountability: the city manager demanded a dollar amount in budget cuts but permitted department heads to make the hard choices.

A quick attempt at interference occurred in early 1983 when the sole

Republican councilman sought to keep open a local branch library by transferring out of the public safety budget $10,000 apparently available as a result of vacancies. O'Connor shot back a memo itemizing five police personnel expenditures that would draw upon those funds, thus ending the matter.

A different sort of interference, which never occurred in Troy, is a budget cut made in order to punish the police executive. Although no research is available to indicate the frequency of such punishment, it is most likely to be inflicted on police chiefs with civil service tenure and elected county sheriffs. In those jurisdictions the power of the purse is one control that outside bodies retain over law enforcement.

Elections: Confusion without Accountability

Public concern over crime and police protection are issues tailor-made for politicians aspiring to office and ill suited to incumbents, who obviously have not "solved" the crime problem (see Finckenauer 1978; Buffum and Sagi 1983; McPherson 1983; and Guyot 1983). Stuart Scheingold (1984) has persuasively argued that fear of crime gives salience to the punitive strand of American culture, which yearns for the simple "cops and robbers" solutions seen on television. The fifteen years of election campaigns in Troy closely fit this pattern of the outs clubbing the incumbents with the crime issue.

As the 1973 city council election campaign began to heat up, Commissioner O'Connor drafted a press release explaining that there are no simple solutions to crime problems, but then he filed it away because candidates did not develop crime into an issue that year. The 1975 campaign issue of an imaginary crime wave propelled the city council to vote by five Democrats to two Republicans to hire ten more officers, against the advice of the commissioner and the city manager. The voters, also displeased over the gaping holes in the city landscape where urban renewal had stalled, defeated the three incumbent Democrats and elected all newcomers, one Democrat and three Republicans. In 1977 the Democrats won all four contested seats after they refocused their campaign in mid-October from developing the central business district to reinstating the city manager. The 1979 campaign had almost no issues, both parties vying for credit for the city's development. One incumbent from each party ran and won, and the addition of two Democratic newcomers continued the 6-1 Democratic majority. In 1981 the Republicans seized upon foot patrol and keeping the department fully staffed as two major issues. The *Times Record* ran a seven-part series on police manpower, painting a picture of an understaffed department. The Democratic council majority moved quickly to deprive the Republicans of the police issue by asking the state to conduct a study on the feasibility of foot patrol. Mayor

Dworsky also proposed an advisory committee to explore the possibility of establishing a neighborhood watch program. Again, the Democrats won all four seats. In 1982 the Republicans backed a charter referendum that won by a huge margin. The revised charter overhauled the composition of the council to provide only three at-large seats and six new district seats. In the 1983 campaign, candidates for the six district seats were grasping for issues and found crime. One Republican hopeful took this stand in his election flyer.

> In the beginning I was concerned about crime. Then I became frightened. The more homes I visit, the more crimes I find have been committed. I am no longer frightened. I am angry—"mad as hell" is more appropriate. I cannot fault our police officers, who are under-staffed and who have one hand tied behind their backs. They share your frustration, CITY HALL does not.
>
> The Commissioner of Public Safety stated at a public meeting in the YMCA on September 8, "It is the City's policy to reduce crime to a tolerable level." You have my pledge that policy will change, and change fast! . . . Let's all get angry together, THERE IS NO *TOLERABLE LEVEL* OF CRIME.

The PBA, which had endorsed city council and police court candidates in previous years, decided to forgo endorsement but to hold a public forum inviting all candidates to address the issues of crime and adequacy of police staffing. Before an orderly audience of two hundred, the twelve candidates agreed that the city needed more police officers, but when specifically asked where they would find the funds, none bit the bullet of higher tax rates. On the Sunday before the election the union ran an ad proclaiming no confidence in Commissioner O'Connor. The voters, however, elected five of the six Democrats, thus supporting the city manager, who supported the commissioner. The Republican who had attacked the commissioner for tolerating crime lost by a larger margin than any other candidate, Republican or Democrat.

This sequence of seven council elections interspersed with two referenda provides no example of informed debate on police issues. The 1983 candidate took his stand, that no crime level is tolerable, after a decade of public education efforts by O'Connor. Since any level of any crime can be taken as proof of the ineffectiveness of the incumbents' policies, the opposition can often win with promises to get tough. Although campaigning on fear of crime appears to have been a strong element in the 1975 success of the challengers, in 1981 and 1983, when fear had apparently ebbed, the Republican stress on crime helped win only two of the ten seats contested. The overall election history demonstrates that a police leader can keep the restraints on police power despite citizen demands for aggressive policing. When policies that had been adopted in other cities sprouted in Troy—shotguns mounted in all patrol cars, attack dogs for street patrol, a SWAT team, a curfew, a loitering law, and other repressive measures—they wilted quickly under the commissioner's disparagement.

Interference and Accountability Exercised by the City Council

Every elected official, at whatever level of government, receives a substantial number of citizen requests for assistance in dealing with bureaucracies. Most constituency service performed by elected officials is not a matter of pulling strings to obtain special treatment; it is needed assistance for citizens who have only vague ideas of which agencies have what programs and how to apply. Legislators generally consider constituency service a more powerful means of vote getting than their legislative record. Many enjoy showing their constituents that they have the power to galvanize bureaucracy into action. Consequently, legislators spend much of their time and effort meeting constituency requests.

When citizens are quite certain about what service they want and which agency they hold responsible, they are clearly capable of making demands directly to the agency. Why do they bother to go through a council member for routine problems like noisy neighbors or an absent school crossing guard? Probably because citizens expect officials to "amplify" their requests by speaking on their behalf. Commissioner O'Connor was annoyed at the implication that the police department would not be attentive without this amplification. An examination of requests channeled through city hall to the commissioner's office during the years 1979–82 shows a scattering of ongoing neighborhood problems, the most common being kids annoying adults. These requests were not interference and needed no amplification to be heard.

Police departments do receive requests for preferential treatment. An example from a councilman, who should have known better, was to offer that three downtown bar owners would pay the department $60 a month in order to have an officer posted on foot patrol. The commissioner flatly recommended that they employ private security.

More significant than constituency service was policymaking by elected representatives during three intensely active years, 1976–78. The 1975 council decision to hire ten more officers to cope with an imaginary crime wave ushered in this period. The account of that decision given in Chapter 7 explains why this addition of manpower was an ineffective policy. Here we simply take note of it as fitting the characterization of ineffective polices: orders to do something specific.

A fundamental reason for the council's particular activity in police affairs during 1976–78 was that the executive was weak. Everyone believed that Commissioner O'Connor had left for good in September 1975. Chief

Givney attempted to handle problems quietly inside the department while denying information to the media; consequently, he received a bad press. Within the department he referred to council members as the enemy. The council found ways to harass him, such as taking away his city car when he moved to a house out of town. O'Connor's return in January 1977 gave strength to the department, but by then City Manager Buckley was suffering severe attacks from the four-to-three Republican majority, spearheaded by the chief's nemesis, the councilwoman chairing the public safety committee. Of the seven Democrats who had appointed Buckley four years earlier, only two survived on the council. Both Republicans and Democrats had become restive at Buckley's practice of keeping them in ignorance. The current mayor, an old man, accused his fellow Republicans of plotting to fire Buckley, and in February he took the unprecedented step of switching his support to the three Democrats in order to prevent the firing. Democratic control of the council lasted only four months, because the mayor suffered a fatal heart attack in April, and the city court judge, a Republican, appointed a man of his own party to the empty seat. The Republicans fired the city manager in August. The new acting city manager could not gain cooperation from key city hall employees and was out of his element in dealing with the city unions. When Buckley returned to office in January 1978, a major struggle was under way between Commissioner O'Connor and the PBA leadership.

Council policies on the police matters listed in Table 10-2 show the application of the criteria distinguishing political accountability from interference. Recall that to judge a policy an act of accountability is to confirm that the council acted properly in making a decision, whether or not the decision is a wise one.

The public safety committee of the council was the source of council policy. The councilwoman elected in November 1975 who was soon to chair the committee was eager to do her best for the people of Troy. At her suggestion the *Times Record* published a brief questionnaire, for citizens to clip and return, that asked about the adequacy of police and fire protection, the need for foot patrol, and public willingness to pay for more protection. The 30 December 1975 news story covering fifty survey replies began, "By a four-to-one margin, residents are not happy with their police department." One citizen's comment, that 70 percent of the officers were drinkers, particularly riled the union leaders. After the editor refused to print a retraction, the PBA filed a $10 million libel suit against the paper.

In the city council the newcomers tended to cooperate, the one new Democrat, Steven Dworsky, giving support to the slim Republican majority. The public safety committee worked as a team to probe the performance of the police department. On 1 January 1976 a six-column newspaper story describing two arrests in which officers had employed force

Table 10-2   City Council Policies as Acts of Accountability or Interference

Year	Issue	Judgment[a]	Grounds for Judgment
1975	ten more officers	I	ineffective, not a question of scale
1975	Lansingburgh station	I	ineffective, X does not cause Y; equity, council did not address
1976	directing department attention to apparent use of excessive force	A	set priority, to check on legality of officers' actions
1976	council to read files from professional standards unit	I	would cut internal accountability
1976	foot patrol	I	ineffective, X does not cause Y
1976	shotguns in patrol cars	I	ignored effect on other priorities
1976	attempt to create police-community relations board	A	set priority, to open communication
1977	downtown safety and four other problems	A	set priorities
1977	five solutions to problems	I	ineffective
1977	ten operational directives	I	ineffective, no service goals
1977	attempt to restore youth services unit	I	ineffective and inefficient
1977	neighborhood safety centers	I	ineffective and inefficient
1977	cut budget 5%	A	global priority between services and taxes
1978	hearing on team policing	I	ineffective, confused service goals
1977–83	more foot patrol	I	ineffective, not a problem of scale

[a]A = act of political accountability; I = act of political interference

prompted the council committee to inquire whether or not officers had used excessive force. By mid-January, Dworsky had persuaded the Republicans to expand the inquiry by meeting with union members to hear their views on department management in general. The committee then pressed to obtain records from the professional standards unit, a move widely interpreted as a fishing expedition. Buckley refused on the grounds that the records were exempt from the sunshine law. When the public safety committee persisted, the PBA obtained a court injunction. In assessing these actions, we see that by directing departmental attention to excessive force complaints, the council was setting priorities, clearly an exercise of accountability. However, the attempt to read the records of the professional standards unit was prying into personnel matters, which would have been most damaging to internal accountability. A reasonable protection for employees is that the details of disciplinary measures not embarrass them before fellow employees or the public. Department members who fear exposure of their statements in disciplinary cases are likely to reduce their frankness.

The need for foot patrol was a frequent message during this period, voiced by individual citizens, citizen groups, and council members. Chief Givney was adamant that foot patrol was an anachronism and refused to make any assignments beyond the usual posting of a foot officer downtown during the Christmas shopping season. Since the chair of the public safety committee was the owner of a downtown coffee shop, she was particularly aware of the downtown merchants' desire for walking officers.

Residents of Lansingburgh had been expressing a desire for a precinct station since 1975. Because neighboring Albany had been operating a storefront as the headquarters for its single neighborhood police team, the request for a local building had become entwined with a request for team policing in Lansingburgh. The city manager and police chief eased the pressure on three fronts by proposing that expert advice be sought from the state's police training commission on appropriate departmental discipline, team policing, and the vacant commissioner's position. In September 1976 the state agency provided three reports answering the questions the way the police chief desired. The reports went on the shelf because requesting them had already served the purpose of cooling the council.

Union leaders initiated a formal request to the city council in late 1976, the first in four years. In September the PBA safety committee had initiated a grievance that the cars were unsafe because they were not equipped with shotguns. When the chief denied the grievance, three PBA officials met with the public safety committee and obtained an order to the chief to place shotguns in the station wagon used by patrol sergeants. As a side issue the PBA leaders also obtained the commitment that all new patrol cars would be air-conditioned. According to a PBA officer present at the budget hearing, the chief said that was unnecessary; the PBA officer quickly contradicted him; and the councilwoman responded, "Nothing is too good for our officers."

O'Connor returned to the commissionership before the shotgun order was implemented and ordered that the weapons be placed in the sergeants' wagon only after officers had received shotgun training. Among the officers there was initial excitement about the "war wagon," and all officers received shotgun training. In the commissioner's recollection, officers had shotguns at the ready on a few occasions but never fired them. The council's command "Do X!" was interference. Had the council directed the city manager to develop means to enable officers to feel safer, even at the risk of increased shooting of bystanders, that would have been exercise of accountability, because it asked the expert to consider the trade-offs among goals.

At its November 1976 meeting the city council considered establishing a police community relations board, which the chief had opposed on the grounds that it could become a civilian review board. In a straight party vote, the four Republicans tabled the motion. This attempted initiative was an exercise of accountability as an effort to open a new channel of communication.

When O'Connor resumed the commissionership in January 1977, the public safety committee presented him with a list of twenty-seven items, twenty-one pertaining to police and the rest to fire fighting. One item asked for legislative and budgetary recommendations. Five items called attention to service problems: traffic safety and community relations throughout the city; crime reduction, snow removal, and parking in the central business district. Five were suggested solutions to service problems—such as having meter maids issue tickets for littering, and establishing a team policing grant for Lansingburgh—each of which would have been interference if it had become a council directive. Ten items concerned management: revival of the narcotics division and the scuba team, a new system of vehicle maintenance, posting detectives to the midnight shift (discussed in Chapter 4) and the like. If these items had become council commands, they would have been interference, orders to "Do X!" without any consideration of service priorities. After O'Connor met for two hours with the committee and two additional councilmen, going over his decisions for each item, the council accepted all his decisions. As part of his plan for downtown safety, he created a regular walking post, a clear case of accountability because the council had set the priorities and the commissioner developed the specific means. In March, when O'Connor announced his plan to abolish the youth services division, the council committee again attempted to interfere (see Chapter 6). For the next few months, pressures on the police department eased as the council intensified its internal conflicts and its battle with the city manager.

As the 1977 election season warmed, the issue of a police storefront for Lansingburgh reemerged. The woman who had organized a citizens group in the Burgh at the height of the fear-of-crime episode decided to run for city council. When she approached Buckley with a plan for a storefront police station staffed by nonsworn personnel, he and O'Connor agreed. The Democrats unveiled their plan at a press conference. The Republican councilwoman who as chair of the council's public safety committee had been pressing for a storefront for fifteen months learned of the Democrats' triumph in the newspaper. The *Times Record* (28 July 1977), ordinarily highly supportive of the city manager, agreed editorially with the councilwoman's accusation that Mr. Buckley's motives "were totally political." Buckley had slapped down a strong-willed councilwoman at the same time that Republicans were receiving results from a privately commissioned opinion poll that he was not popular. This was the last straw. The Republicans fired him.

In September, O'Connor presented a different plan to the acting city manager who had replaced Buckley, for three public safety service centers to be located in fire stations and kept open during afternoons and early evenings. The staff member at each center, paid through federal training funds, would offer information on crime prevention, fire prevention, dog licensing, and social services; would register dogs, bicycles, and valuables; and would receive citizen complaints. The centers would serve as locations for meetings with police officers and would remind people of the presence of safety forces in their neighborhood. Both the councilwoman and the citizens' group from Lansingburgh liked the plan so well that they incorporated it into their storefront proposal in addition to their original ideas for assigning there two juvenile officers and two additional police cars. In early October, O'Connor told the acting city manager that he was taking on the councilwoman to prevent inequitable allocation of police personnel to Lansingburgh and to prevent the assignment of police officers to man the center. The city manager should either stay out of the fight or fire him. The acting city manager did neither. The plan as implemented staffed the three center with interns and placed the captain who was in charge of the crime prevention unit at the Burgh center three days a week. O'Connor's explanation, appearing in the *Times Record*, was that the captain's assignment was not a concession to the union and the citizens group but a move to satisfy the citizens' desire for a larger uniformed police presence. The captain would be of sufficient rank to make the police patrols respond to a problem brought to him at the center. O'Connor also changed two detective assignments from generalist to juvenile, thus salving a sore point with police officers and some citizens who were unhappy over his having abolished the juvenile unit six months earlier. As O'Connor had predicted, the Lansingburgh center was a lonely place, averaging two visitors a day. Election day came and went, the Democrats sweeping all seats on the promise to restore Buckley as city manager.

The proposal for team policing polarized the department and became a major political struggle for six months. Commissioner O'Connor introduced this new way of organizing the department in order to make broad advances toward the hospital model. Team policing divides the city into neighborhoods and assigns officers to teams, each having twenty-four hour responsibility for a neighborhood. This reallocation of responsibility increases the knowledge and commitment of officers to the neighborhood they serve and facilitates internal cooperation across shifts and specialties. O'Connor's specific goals were to increase individual officer productivity, departmental investigative effectiveness, citizen involvement, and citizen sense of safety. A form of participatory management, team policing involves officers at all levels in planning and directing service. During the summer of 1977 O'Connor had persuaded Buckley that his long-considered plan for implementing team policing was right for Troy. The telling argument was that team policing would place more officers on the street. In order to plan and implement neighborhood team policing throughout the city, O'Connor submitted an application in July for a $74,000, eighteen-month extension of the current Law Enforcement Assistance Administration crime prevention grant. The largest budget item, $36,000, was to pay police overtime for the planning task forces and the team meetings.

Team policing came to Troy as a "change machine." This term, coined by Herman Goldstein and Egon Bittner to describe the $5,000,000 Police Foundation project with the Dallas PD, means a highly publicized process of change promoted by outside experts and outside funds. It was the development of a large evaluation that gave credence to the union's depiction of team policing as an alien intrusion. Initially, I had designed a simple evaluation costing $700, but the availability of LEAA funds set aside for intensive evaluation provided an attractive opportunity to perform broad empirical research. The final design was a two-year evaluation employing extensive survey research at a total cost of $500,000 in LEAA funds.

Commissioner O'Connor had distributed a copy of his team policing proposal to every member of the department when the action grant was submitted, but few had commented. Chief Givney's opposition was based on his view that citizens had no understanding of police work and no right to delve into police affairs. He had taken sardonic satisfaction in the shock of fellow chiefs when he explained the strong seniority clause of Troy's PBA contract, and they, to a man, said that team policing would be impossible under such a contract. The chief found covert ways to undermine the plans for team policing. Officers had an underlying source of discontent because their 1975–76 contract had run out, and negotiations for the 1977–78 contract had stalled. Binding arbitration produced no new contract until 12 May 1978. When the PBA held its 1977 fall election of officers, the leaders polled the membership with a sign-up sheet headed "Team policing, yes or no." The sheet produced ninety nos and not one yes. O'Connor proceeded with the planning by offering all members opportunities to participate in task forces with overtime compensation for the time invested. Initially, only eighteen officers signed up. PBA leaders then decided that only a watchdog committee should attend, without accepting overtime pay and without participating. One young, highly respected officer who had not understood the message went to a meeting and gained the reputation of hurting the men, a canard that took him several months to live down.

"Outsider" is a very powerful epithet in Troy. The three researchers on the evaluation staff and I were outsiders, as were the three nonsworn personnel whom Commissioner O'Connor had hired on federal training funds to provide support services to the teams: two as staff for the new victim assistance unit and one as departmental information officer. The commissioner himself was regarded as an outsider because he had lived in Troy only four years. All the outsiders became targets of hostility as resistance to team policing developed.

The previous union success with the city council over shotguns and air-conditioned cars had given PBA leaders confidence that they could find allies on the council without returning to the kinds of political interference they opposed, such as the demand for files from the professional standards unit. Union opposition to O'Connor's plans gained a city council legislative hearing. The drama unfolded on two consecutive evenings in early April (Troy 1978). As the first witness, the PBA president asserted in response to questioning that the department needed a new commissioner. Fifteen officers presented eloquent testimony that team policing would ruin a good department. The council deliberated a week and decided, five Democrats to two Republicans, that the commissioner should proceed with team policing on a trial basis and decide jointly with the union whether to permit the evaluation. In response to this adverse decision, some fifty off-duty police officers took turns picketing the city hall and distributed leaflets criticizing the city council for playing partisan politics in disregard of the security needs of the community.

The PBA's specific criticisms of team policing were that it equaled the elimination of a narcotics unit, the stripping of the detective bureau, the elimination of the traffic department, and the stripping of the juvenile bureau. The union directly accused the council and the city manager of not listening to the people. The PBA gained verbal support from several other unions, including the city clerical workers. Within the department the union leaders and the chief pressured officers and command staff, with considerable success, to ostracize the commissioner. Meanwhile, the complexity of the evaluation grant had slowed LEAA's preparation of the grant contracts, which finally arrived in early July. The city manager refused to sign them, thus ending the evaluation.

Commissioner O'Connor went ahead with team policing, without the evaluation. The program operated all summer, while some members of the department felt rancor, and others despaired that the struggle had not yet ended between the commissioner and the union. O'Connor kept close watch on all indicators of performance, noting that easily measurable indicators such as response time and arrests had remained good. At the end of the summer, however, the commissioner developed a replacement for team policing, worked out with the city manager, the chief, and the captains. In September, after O'Connor announced the termination of team policing, he said flatly in a television interview that there had been political interference and that he had been disappointed by the failure of community groups to be more active in support of the program. All parties to the conflict cooled down and eventually resumed good working relationships. Stung and angered by the union criticism, city council members put some distance between themselves and union concerns. The city manager exercised more power vis-à-vis the council because the Democratic majority continued to be elected on their pledge to support him. Neither the scope nor the hectic pace of council policymaking for police had recurred in Troy through 1989. After 1981 the chairman of the council's public safety committee explicitly left operational questions to the department.

What explains the predominance of political interference over political accountability in eleven of the fifteen issues listed in Table 10-2? The two major motivators for council members to interfere appear to have been an election-year need to be seen in the forefront of the fight against crime and a desire to please the union. The police union supported none of the four acts of accountability. Conversely, of the eleven acts of interference, the union instigated or actively supported five and opposed only one. The small size of the public attentive to police affairs and the episodic nature of attention from the broader public left the stage to police management and the police union, who in public policy debates usually staked out two sides of the issues. Team policing was by far the most fiercely contested issue, yet if the union had not opposed it, opposition would not have emerged.

One reason the union has such strength is that political leaders strongly desire to avoid a bad police image. They fear that adverse publicity concerning the police will lessen the city's attractiveness as a place to live, work, and play. The credible threat that police may strike, picket, conduct a public campaign decrying a shortage of officers, or go on a parking ticket binge is enough to make council members tremble for the reputation of the city and for their reelection prospects.

Summary of Accountability on Service

This close look at four means of political direction is a story of opportunities missed. Appointment of the department head, annual budgeting, biennial municipal elections, and city council deliberations did not come near their potential as forums for informed debates on priorities.

We have not looked systematically at the most common type of accountability, when the police manager answers directly to the city's chief executive, nor are there any detailed studies from other cities of working relations between a city executive and a police executive. Although city executives routinely give direction to the heads of agencies such as public works and sanitation, some are extremely reticent to give orders to the head of the police department for fear of being branded as committing political interference. At the other extreme a city executive may use a police department to protect racketeers. An examination of political direction of the police agencies serving three metropolitan areas (Mastrofski 1988) found political interference most pronounced in the smallest towns and departmental insulation from outside direction more common than political accountability.

Differences between the demand for accountability and the imposition of interference may be illustrated by possible alternative directives from a hypothetical city executive in response to two problems. They show that accountability is a complex task requiring accurate information to assess the problems and expert knowledge to design and implement the solutions. Interference is often a snappy command.

A. Problem: burglary
Accountability: "Identify the nature of the city's present burglary problems and explain current and anticipated steps to reduce the incidence of various types of burglary."
Interference: "Assign more detectives to burglary investigation."

B. Problem: fear of crime
Accountability: "Identify what kinds of people in what neighborhoods fear what kinds of criminal attacks and develop plans to assist people to enhance their actual safety and sense of safety."
Interference: "Assign more officers to foot patrol."

In addition to the overall modes of accountability, police departments operate under specialized review processes concerned with specific subject areas (many of these are discussed in Chapter 8, on police malpractice). Prosecutors and courts routinely review the legality of arrests. The better-managed state governments automatically initiate an investigation when a suicide occurs in a police lockup. An audit to review the gathering of political intelligence has been established in Seattle (Walker 1985). When other means are not available, citizens can bring lawsuits in federal or state courts to hold individual officers and department heads accountable for specific acts of malpractice (see Chapter 8). Civilian review boards operate in more than forty cities, according to the International Association of Civilian Oversight for Law Enforcement. The reason to mention all these special agencies is that they, too, are capable of interfering or of assisting to hold a police department to reasonable performance standards.

Summary on Police Power

The chapters on malpractice and unions, together with this one on policy, examine the problems of police power in three different contexts. Police officers' discretion underlies the rich variety of malpractice that occurs in American police departments. In Troy, malpractice was viewed solely as an individual abuse of power, since the city was free of systematic departmental abuses of police powers. To the extent that malpractice persists, such acts weaken the movement toward the hospital model. The solutions examined for reducing malpractice are techniques within a managerial philosophy that accepts the hospital model. As a contrast, Chapter 9 concerns a counterweight to managerial powers, the police union. The purpose of unions is to safeguard the interests of the members against abuses of power by management. The chapter concluded that the contract the PBA defended had far more impediments than supports for professional service. The comprehensive view of the police union was a necessary prelude to understanding political conflicts over the direction of the department. The union and management are the two power centers with lasting interest in police issues as they emerge and fade in municipal politics. Further, this chapter on political power over the police department has found that the fragmentation of personnel powers systematically impedes growth toward the hospital model.

IV

Excellence in Police Service

Americans are a spirited people.

Officer Carl Peterson

11 Building Bridges between Police and Public

Carl Peterson, discussing how he handles a wide variety of disputes and annoyances, explained that he does not give orders, because people would resist them. Rather, he plants ideas and then works to encourage the people to take them as their own. The lasting gratitude that Officer Peterson cultivated and the burst of anger that were the reaction when Officer O'Reilly pulled his wad of hundreds, plus every other exchange between officers and citizens in Troy, may be regarded as the sum of that city's police-community relations.

A common and serious confusion is to suppose that police-community relations consist primarily of public relations campaigns. The underlying misconception views the police department and the public each as a mass. A mass problem can be solved by a mass solution, such as mass media. Many police-community relations programs degenerate into public relations selling jobs. As advertising, they are amateurish, unpersuasive to tastes developed by Madison Avenue; as solutions, they do not address real problems. Police work is not performed by a phalanx of officers encountering a massed citizenry.

Public safety and public order are produced through the cooperation of police and citizens. The growing police efforts to promote cooperation have been described by Herman Goldstein (1987). Police departments rely upon citizens to alert them to the occurrence of more than 90 percent of the crimes known to them. Patrol officers and detectives rely upon information from citizens to solve crimes and arrest the offenders. Only if someone calls them and only if the people in trouble listen to their advice can officers assist people in danger and resolve conflicts. Police officers facilitate traffic flow only because drivers obey their directions. The nearly total dependence of effective police work upon citizens can be imagined by picturing an America where all municipal employees speak only French: public works could still make street repairs, and sanitation could collect garbage, but police could do little more than drive on preventive patrol.

This chapter introduces the issues of police-community relations by looking at the exposed tip of the iceberg, demonstrations and crowds; then it turns to the daily personal relations that build common bonds between citizens and the officers who protect them. Next, a consideration of ways to promote harmonious relations begins with criticism of three frequent and superficial policies: community relations specialists, foot patrol, and residency requirements. The major portion of the chapter returns to the theme introduced in the chapter on the hospital model: how police leadership fosters the development of good relations between individual officers and the individual citizens they serve. One powerful cement is the kind of confidence in the police department that prevents the rise of vigilantes. Another is the department's provision of multiple services. Crucially important are the openness of the department to public scrutiny and the willingness of citizens to provide commentary on police service. The last section looks at desires of police officers and citizens to belong to the same community and observes that communities are home to diverse people with conflicting life-styles.

Peaceful Use of the Streets by Everyone

Police in a democratic society are essential for assuring that views of all persuasions may be put before the public. Protecting First Amendment rights requires the active participation of police departments as policy-makers to set guidelines for peaceable demonstrations, plus active commitment by individual officers to help the events run smoothly. City governments need procedures for obtaining advance knowledge of planned demonstrations in order to protect the demonstrators from traffic and to separate demonstrators and any counterdemonstrators. A police department committed to protecting freedom of speech is an appropriate agency for granting street use permits, because police officers need to be on hand during demonstrations to assure that they proceed peacefully, to direct traffic, and to render any immediate medical assistance needed by individuals. No matter what agency is authorized to issue parade permits, the procedure must be simple, the route must be an appropriate one to facilitate public impact and minimize public inconvenience, and the police department must know of the plans in advance.

A sketch of two different situations quickly gives a picture of how a police department can facilitate free speech. Back in 1973 a garment workers' union leader sat down with Commissioner O'Connor to discuss his plans to picket a factory that was employing nonunion labor to produce a line of slacks. In Miami a year earlier O'Connor had brought together police officials and protest leaders to plan orderly demonstrations at the national political conventions and thus prevent repetition of the police riots that occurred at the 1968 Democratic convention in Chicago. O'Connor's conversation in Troy ran like this.

"Do you want anyone arrested?" he asked.

"What do you mean?"

"Well, I assume if you're demonstrating, you want some publicity to draw attention to your cause. If you want, we can work it out so that we arrest as many of your people as you want arrested. But if we are going to get into that kind of situation, I want to plan ahead and not have it happen on the street when nobody's prepared for it."

"No, no. Nothing like that," said the union leader. "We're just going to picket."

On 1 October 1983 the Upper Hudson Nuclear Weapons Freeze Campaign held a well-planned march for six miles along Troy's main and secondary streets and rallied at the riverfront park. O'Connor checked on the march at two points to make sure that all was going well. Officer Albert Vincente in his patrol car escorted the ninety marchers and directed traffic at major intersections. Unfortunately, at the park the public address system would not function. Officer Vincente and Sergeant Joseph Ricco immediately began tinkering with the system, discovered that there was no electricity, and radioed police headquarters to call the city engineer at home to get the electricity flowing. Within fifteen minutes the system was working. These two officers, with twenty and thirty years of experience in policing, had no special interest in the movement. Rather, their job was to assist every group of citizens to hold their rallies, whatever their cause.

Use of the streets for informal socializing, group enjoyment, and just hanging around often creates tougher problems for police than do planned demonstrations. Some conflicts between segments of the community are irreconcilable in the terms in which they are posed, as between a few debilitated alcoholics who want to relax all day on benches in front of stores and a few merchants who believe the loungers drive away customers. An example of harmonious reconciliation occurred in the early 1980s when a group of white police officers peaceably dispersed a crowd of black people. A new sergeant, Doug Martin, tells this story:

About 2:00 A.M. one summer night we received a complaint from a black neighborhood of loud rock music making sleep impossible. Because there was a large crowd, the dispatcher sent several cars. I stopped about half a block away to get a sense of the crowd. Two hundred young people were dancing in the street. I came up to the disc jockey, who had a phonograph powered through an extension cord running out of the apartment on the far side of the street. I took a close look to figure out if I knew him. Yes, I had arrested him once. Too bad I didn't know him in some other way. I went up to him and began, "You probably know why we are here."

"Yeah, you white cops are picking on us black folks when we're having a good time."

"That's not it at all. As far as we're concerned, you can have your good time. We're here because your neighbors can't sleep. This is your neighborhood, and your people are complaining."

"Those no good old people are spoiling the fun of us young people."

"We talked several minutes, and I offered him the chance to continue the dancing with the volume turned down. We would go away and not come back unless we got another call. He didn't go for that. I was trying to find some way of cutting the noise without making him lose face in front of the partying crowd. Finally, I said, "I'm going to have to be the bad guy in this. I'm going to pull the plug on the record player, and we're all going to leave." The disc jockey didn't like that, but he didn't want to try running the party with the music low, so we talked some more. Finally, I called out, "Okay men, it's time to leave." I leaned down and pulled out the plug. "You're on your own," I told him. As we were leaving he shouted out, "All right, everybody, that's it for tonight."

Several elements of good police work are evident in Sergeant Martin's recollection of the evening. First, he took time to sense the mood of the crowd and then took charge of the scene, so different from the sergeant who drove out to check on the high-speed chase and then did not bother to walk over to the halted Firebird. Second, Sergeant Martin began conversing with the leader of the crowd, knowing that the crowd would obey him. The fundamental principle of crowd control is to direct groups through their leaders, and the corollary is to avoid creating a leaderless crowd. Third, Martin immediately redefined the situation away from the disc jockey's view that the problem was created by the police to a new definition as a neighborhood problem. Fourth, through explanation and persuasion Martin sought a way to satisfy the sleepless neighbors and yet save the pride of the disc jockey in front of his dancers. Fifth, having failed, Martin did not give any orders to the disc jockey or threaten him. The presence of about six officers at the fringe of the crowd and the sergeant's decisive manner conveyed the message that anyone who wanted trouble could have it. Sixth, Martin explained the solution he planned to impose before he took action. Seventh, he ended the impasse first with a shout to his men to leave and then by pulling the plug. This lowest possible level of interference gave the decision to the disc jockey of whether or not to accept the sergeant's solution. The whole exchange might have gone very differently, because the sergeant and the disc jockey were each in a position to make things unpleasant for the other. Instead, they talked man to man.

Sometimes crowd situations begin in such a way that they quickly turn hostile. Then officers must exercise great courage and forbearance to prevent a scuffle from becoming a brawl. A street conflict near midnight on a warm evening in April 1985 had the potential to become a mass fight between officers and the residents of a housing project. The account is from the incident report filed by Mike Mullin, a straightforward and thoughtful officer who had put his college education to work during his five years with the department. Although relying here solely on the incident report for the details of the event, we should be aware that no official police report describing discretionary judgment should be read as though it tells the whole story. O'Connor commented that, in his twenty-five years of reviewing police incident reports, he had never seen one in which an officer gave an inkling that he might have made a mistake. Every official report extracts selectively from all the elements of an event those aspects most important to the report writer, aspects that more or less deliberately show the writer in the best light. This police report gives an authentic account in the sense that the details are believable and can be treated as accurate for the purposes of understanding how difficult crowd control can be.

The site of the conflict was the courtyard in front of one of two high-rise housing projects at the southern edge of the central business district. Officers Mike Mullin and Jack Rice had each worked four years in the poorest residential neighborhood, north of the business district, and had joined as partners a year before. Here is Officer Mullin's report on the scuffle, with only the names of participants changed.

While on patrol we received a call for a domestic disturbance at Ahern 2 7C. Upon our arrival a Sandra King advised us she wanted a Leroy Friend out of her apartment. While we were sorting out this complaint, an altercation ensued between two other females in the apartment. While breaking up the fight between these two, the original complainant collapsed. We called for backup and an ambulance. Mr. Friend carried Ms. King downstairs, outside by the front door to expedite her treatment. At that point the situation appeared to be diffused. The paramedics and the ambulance arrived, and our backups left. While the paramedics looked at Ms. King, a large crowd gathered quickly. At one point a man we now know to be William Butts started fighting with Leroy Friend. We separated the two and wanted Butts to leave. Shortly after that Butts started fighting again. We broke the two up again and advised Butts to leave again. Within one minute Butts started fighting with Friend again. I grabbed Butts and pulled him off of Friend and advised him he was under arrest. As I started to walk Butts to my patrol car, several people gathered around me. As I got to my car, someone struck me in the back of the head a couple of times. When I turned around, I found myself and my partner in the middle of a crowd of about fifty people. At one point, while trying to handcuff my prisoner, someone was trying to pull my gun out of my holster while other people were hitting me and pulling my hair. I had difficulty defending myself as I had one hand on my gun and the other on my prisoner. As our backup units arrived I was struck in the side of the head with a cane and punched repeatedly. At this point Mr. Butts started helping my partner pull people off me. As more police arrived, more arrests were made. Eight people are arrested [six black men and two black women between the ages of twenty and thirty]. As the crowd dispersed, Mohawk Ambulance got Sandra King into the ambulance and transported her to Samaritan Hospital. Once the crowd had completely dispersed, all units cleared.

Given this book's claim that police-community relations in Troy are generally good, why did this fight occur? A general answer is that in late twentieth-century America, the living conditions in high-rise public housing projects and in inner-city neighborhoods tend to crowd together people who have more than an average number of problems and few socially acceptable outlets for their frustrations. Some young men growing up in these circumstances resent authority and on occasion give physical expression to their resentment. Police officers tend not to become as well acquainted with housing project residents as with other apartment dwellers on the excuse that the layout of the projects makes it difficult to find one's way.

Specifically, in this incident the partners who responded to the call had not yet become well acquainted with people of the neighborhood, including residents of the project, because they had been working in this zone for less than four months (see Goldstein 1990, 159–61). The triggering event was a domestic dispute, a situation where the absence of a "bad guy" gives bystanders no immediate recognition that officers there are engaged in serving the community. Note also the absence of the constraints that Sergeant Martin brought into play with the street dancers. The crowd at the housing project had no purpose other than to view the excitement. Leaderless, it was uncontrolled. Lacking the foresight to anticipate trouble, the zone officers sent the others cars away. At the point when individuals in the crowd began tussling for Officer Mullin's gun, he and his partner were the only officers present. Thus, when six other officers and a sergeant arrived, the time had passed when words and mere police presence could have prevented a melee. At the street disco party, police gave no orders and made no threats but gave full explanations. Police here threatened and made arrests; members of the housing project crowd defined the situation as a direct conflict with the officers. It is remarkable that William Butts, whose arrest gave him the most immediate reason to be hostile, joined Officer Mullin in fighting off the attackers. Officers then arrived in sufficient numbers to break up the crowd by making a total of seven additional arrests. All individuals arrested were booked and immediately released.

Officer Mullin exercised great self-restraint while some of the crowd took cracks at him, because he considered holding his prisoner and keeping his gun securely in its holster more important than protecting himself. What manner of man does not immediately lash back? Officer Mullin is the same man who joked with Sarah Brown and her tough friends from Schenectady to prevent a feud from turning into a racial fight. Day in and day out he had stayed concerned and exerted a calming influence when others were beset, and now that he was attacked, he remained level-headed.

Officers and Citizens Being Human Together

Personal exchanges between one or two officers and one or two citizens are the bedrock of a city's police-community relations. The daily contacts of individual officers with individual citizens and the memory of those contacts year in and year out add up to the police-community relations of a city. To put the focus on personal exchanges, here are the words of a woman in her early thirties who called the police in the spring of 1978; she is describing the work of Officer Chuck Holt.

I came home from work, and my babysitter told me my daughter was beat up by five kids. So I called the police right away, and an officer came right away. I was upset. He talked to my daughter and myself and took down everything she said. He told me someone from Juvenile would contact me later, but I haven't heard from anyone else. He was sincere and very concerned about the incident. He was like a father trying to calm a typical mother down. He tried to calm me down by talking to my five-year-old and keeping him occupied while my daughter answered his questions. I felt very calm when he left.

The department's failure to follow up on the incident is common in Troy and in most cities. Specialist units often fail to keep appropriate commitments made by patrol officers. Coordination failures are due not only to around-the-clock operations but also to the structure of police departments, which confers high status on members of the specialist units. Individual patrol officers are not in a position to require youth officers, detectives, or other specialists to adhere to departmental policy on behalf of their clients. If a police department were run like a hospital, the patrol officer, in the role of attending physician, would direct the attention of the specialist to his client's problem. Still, Officer Holt's quick arrival and concern at least gave reassurance to this worried mother. His ease in talking to both children at once made him like a father to her children, and his helping her recover her composure was an important police service. The sum of such services builds good relations.

When participants and bystanders tell their families and friends about their experiences, the impact of an event spreads over several small circles. When the newspapers pick up the event, it lightly touches many in the large circle of readership. Unfortunately, instances of police malpractice are made known by the mass media far more frequently than instances of good police work. A general explanation is that bad news is less routine and hence more interesting than good news. Citizens with little direct police contact who rely on the mass media for their impressions of police service will have a more jaundiced view than most of those who have had personal experience. All retellings of events go into the recollections that form the tapestry of police-community relations. The time when police have the most control over the substance of these relations is when incidents occur.

The basic concerns in community relations are to increase the number of incidents that all participants agree were well handled and to reduce the number of damaging incidents. A secondary concern is to amplify knowledge of well-handled events through encouraging word of mouth and through coverage in the mass media. Police management and city leaders need to devise organizational structures that encourage, support, and foster good individual relations.

Common Misguided Attempts to Build Bridges

Since a city's quality of life and reputation can suffer greatly from adverse police-community relations, city officials often act on partial understanding to advocate superficial policies. Neighborhood storefronts have already been criticized (in Chapter 7) as wasteful. Here are three other widespread but misguided proposals: a police-community relations unit, foot patrol, and a requirement that officers live within city limits.

Police-Community Relations Units

In the 1960s the standard police response to newly critical police-community problems was to create specialized units charged with improving relations. In fact, however, the creation of such units probably undermined community relations. The explanation of this paradox lies in the nature of large organizations. As we have seen, officers in the patrol division have the most opportunity to enhance or damage police-community relations because they are the most numerous and have the most varied responsibilities. Whenever a specialist unit is created, be it meter attendants or a vice squad, the generalists in patrol slack off on their activity in that unit's sphere because they see the problems as having become someone else's headache. Evaluations of programs with officers specializing in community relations show that there is typically a gulf between those officers and the rest of patrol. When a specialist unit is abolished, as was Troy's youth services unit in 1977, patrol officers who think the activity is important pick up the work. Commissioner O'Connor holds that community relations are so central to the police mission that officers should be given no excuse to slough off the responsibility of creating friendly, supportive relations whenever possible in the course of their work.

Foot Patrol

The immense popularity of foot patrol appears to stem from nostalgia coupled with the general public desire for more police protection. When public opinion polls offer the choice of more or fewer officers on foot patrol, people naturally opt for more because the choice is stated as though increased police service comes without the cost of increased taxes. Two major experiments with foot patrol, in Newark, New Jersey, in 1978–79, and Flint, Michigan, in 1978–86, added officers on foot to the existing complement of officers in patrol cars. Evaluations by the Police Foundation (1981) and Trojanowicz et al. (1982; 1986a) both reported modest positive results.

The arguments in favor of foot patrol are that an officer on foot appears to be more accessible and in closer contact with the neighborhood than when he or she is sealed off from the public by the glass and steel walls of a patrol car. The anecdotes of officers who started their careers on foot provide rich evidence of how individuals can develop friendships with people of the neighborhood. Here are some of Carl Peterson's recollections.

> I walked for my first three years on the job. The Eye-talians—I always call them Eye-talians—used to kid me and call me a sardine packer. Then they would offer me wine and insist that I come inside. I always said, "No, I can't. Now I'm on the job. Can't do it." I would return after work and have wine and cheese. Afterwards, when I was walking on cold nights, there would always be someone who would invite me in to have a bowl of soup.

A walking post probably assisted Peterson to develop his breadth of understanding of what is common in human nature. Whether or not his perspective would be narrower if he had begun patrol work in a car is impossible to know. Earlier discussion suggests that many other factors may be more crucial in an officer's development of a tragic perspective: initial motivation to become an officer, skill and enjoyment in talk, guidance from sergeants and senior colleagues, choice of role models within the patrol division, and the mission of the department as expressed by its leaders. Walking posts can have a negative influence if officers view them as punishment. Recall Officer Turner, who was thwarted in his pursuit of the yellow Mustang, was yanked from the car and ordered to walk. During those nine months he neither sought nor found friendly people behind the doorways he passed.

A variant on foot patrol is a mandatory park-and-walk program in which officers are ordered to spend a fixed span of hours on walking patrol. This is a mechanistic attempt to get officers out of their vehicles.

The park-and-walk program merely requires officers to step out from behind the wall; it does not otherwise assist them in developing the outlook and skills to build good relations with the people they serve.

Now that cars are so essential to the American life-style, at the density of more than one motor vehicle for every two people, will officers feel other than punished if they are ordered to walk instead of ride? Will they have to walk on rainy days? One should not naively assume that the mere assignment of officers to foot patrol will naturally result in greater rapport between police and citizens. Thoughtful supervisors, recognizing that motivation is the key to an officer's expanding his contacts with the people of a neighborhood, will assign only volunteers to foot patrol.

Police managers' fundamental criticism of foot patrol is that an officer in a car can provide much more service than one on foot. Managers note that the demographic trends of the last forty years, with movement out of the central city to less densely populated suburbs, require officers to travel farther to serve the same number of people. To citizens streaming by in their cars, an officer on the empty sidewalk is inaccessible. Foot patrol is appropriate only in the areas where and during the hours when many pedestrians are about. In most cities only the central business district and the entertainment district during business hours have sufficient pedestrian density. The complex peacekeeping carried out by a seasoned officer on Skid Row in a west coast city is described by Muir (1977) as an example of foot patrol at its best. The officer prided himself on knowing at least five thousand people by their first names and was trusted for his evenhandedness in doing small, legal favors for those in need.

The tiny share of the law enforcement work load that is accomplished by officers on foot is seen in the statistics from the Police Foundation (1981) study in Newark. During a year, the most energetic of the eight officers recorded in his research log that he wrote 131 reports and made 115 arrests; another logged 67 crime reports and 53 arrests; the remaining six officers logged an average of 10 crime reports and 5 arrests each during a full year. Logs should be used cautiously by researchers, since officers often refer to them as lie sheets, but these Newark statistics do show that on average officers on foot make little claim to handling crime incidents or to making arrests. The disparity between one officer's energy and six others' avoidance of reports and arrests raises the suspicion that the six may have been lazy in other respects. An officer on foot can find a friendly store in which to while away the evenings. Thirty years ago, when police salary packages were low compared to the price of patrol cars and officers worked overtime without compensation, departments were profligate in assigning officers to foot patrol. Now that the cost picture has changed, well-managed departments make foot patrol assignments very selectively.

Residency Requirements

The Supreme Court has held that cities have authority to require local residency as a condition of municipal employment. As of 1987, one-third of cities with populations over 250,000 required new police officers to live within the jurisdiction (Reaves 1990). This a large drop from the finding of the administrative study of the Police Executive Research Forum and Police Foundation (1981) that 57 of 122 cities required residency *prior* to employment, and an overlapping 54 cities required residency *during* employment. Troy still requires preemployment residency, but state law permits residence in nearby counties during employment. Considering the prevalence of regulations requiring officers to live in town, there is surprisingly little research on compulsory residence or even on the quite different matter of voluntary residence within a jurisdiction. Few small jurisdictions imposed these restrictions as of 1987: 8 percent of the departments serving cities of 50,000–100,000 and less than 1 percent of the smaller departments.

How effectively residency legislation is enforced is another matter. Officers can flout the spirit of the law with impunity because there is widespread consensus that such laws are unfair. For example, when Newark attempted strict enforcement of the residency ordinance, officers formed groups to rent one-room apartments in town as their official residences. The Newark PBA won the battle in 1969 by collaborating with the two other most powerful public employee unions—teachers' and fire fighters'—to obtain state legislation exempting all of them throughout the state from municipal regulation of residence. Such are the lengths to which people go in order to live where they choose.

Over the decades, residency requirements for city employees have been thought to serve several purposes. First, when city leaders gave out jobs as patronage, they expected job holders to be available to repay the party at the polls. Second, when cities were in fiscal straits during the Great Depression and again in the 1970s, they wanted employees to spend the bulk of their paychecks within the city limits to help stimulate the city's economy. Third, residency requirements have been seen as assisting officers to diminish their alienation from the people of the city. Fourth, the neighborhoods where officers live may benefit from their off-duty presence because of their twenty-four-hour commitment to uphold the law.

The most powerful argument against residency as a *prerequisite* for appointment is that it reduces the talent pool (see Chapter 4). The most powerful argument against residency *during* employment is the civil liberties case that only a compelling public interest justifies regulating the private lives of government employees. Police officers must feel that their families will be safe in the community before they will make their homes and raise their children there. Fire fighters and coal miners leave the dangers of the job when they clock out, but a police officer can feel threatened even at home. Police officers who believe that the community is full of people who hate them, either personally or because they hate all cops, may not feel safe in the community after work. Ways of increasing officer safety and the perception of safety were described in the discussion of the hospital model (Chapter 4). High levels of both are probably essential prerequisites to officers' willingness to live in the community they serve.

Officers, like everyone else, use many different criteria in choosing a good place to live. Any policy that limits an officer's freedom of choice should be based on careful research to demonstrate the value of the policy. As individuals grow old in a service profession, even the most dedicated may feel from time to time that they want to get far away from their work during their leisure hours. Carl Peterson described his feelings when he had been about ten years on the job:

> There's a big change in me. Now I just do the job and leave it. People are crybabies, complaining all the time. They are calling me at all hours for some kind of help. The other night at 11 P.M. when I was asleep, someone called about a cat that had kittens. I don't want to be Mr. Policeman to Lansingburgh. I want to be Mr. Peterson to my wife.

Peterson continued to live in the same house, but he put some distance between himself and the people of Lansingburgh by choosing to work at the other end of town. The pestering during his private time abated, and he so appreciated the thanks he received from his new clients that his enjoyment in his work returned to its previous high level. In Commissioner O'Connor's view, it is entirely up to the individual officer whether he lives in the neighborhood where he works, elsewhere in town, or out of town. Those leading an organization, he observed, do need to live in town as a symbol of commitment.

The grain of value in residency requirements, community relations units, foot patrol, park-and-walk, and neighborhood storefronts is that the structures of the police job set the conditions under which officers are allowed to relate to citizens. The hospital model encourages officers to view citizens as their clients and to make a professional commitment to those clients' well-being. If a military model is at the core of a department, community relations will be a veneer.

Four Fundamental Ways to Build Bridges

The Prevention of Vigilantes

Where citizens generally feel safe, they will not welcome any private group of volunteers who claim a special role in providing public protection. Both professional police administrators and police managers are firmly opposed to vigilantes, citizens who organize to take action outside the law. Fear of crime coupled with racial tension is a breeding ground for vigilantes.

In Troy members of a local motorcycle club called the Breed Gang, who later renamed themselves the Hell's Angels, moved into a rundown house in a neighborhood in racial transition. They apparently saw themselves as protectors of the white people of the neighborhood from black teenagers and young men. The years 1975 to 1978 appear to be the period when residents of Troy most feared crime. The spring of 1977 was marred by three incidents in three weeks that built toward serious interracial conflict. In Prospect Park a black driver accidentally ran over a dog belonging to a white man. The driver apologized and promised to make amends, but a group of white men jumped on the hood of his car. Then a carload of white men with shotguns arrived and began shooting at the black men. Immediate police response caused the white men to flee. Next, gangs of black and white youth in the transitional neighborhood had a brawl. In another night's clash, Breed Gang members fired rifle shots at a Volkswagen carrying two black men past their house. In every instance, police officers were on the scene very quickly to quell any further disturbance, but the climate seemed ripe for the Breed Gang to step forward as a vigilante group. Commissioner O'Connor approached members and met with them quietly in their house to discuss his concerns for the safety of all residents of the city. For whatever reasons, the spring's incidents were followed by a quiet summer, and no vigilantes emerged.

The Provision of Multiple Services

The most fundamental decisions for any organization are what goods and/or services it will produce. For members of a work organization, the strongest and most persistent incentives come from the nature of the work. To the extent that the leaders of service agencies can determine what services are delivered and to what clients, they can have strong influence on the satisfactions that come from performing the work. The deliberate policy of the Troy PD since the beginning of upgrading in 1973 has been to provide a wide range of human services, many of which are unrelated to crime prevention and crime control. The department welcomes the fact that the twenty-four-hour presence of officers throughout the community gives them particular advantage as first responders to a broad range of social and individual problems. This policy holds that real police work includes assisting the injured, rescuing victims of fires, calming landlord-tenant disputes, doing something about the noisy kids hanging out on the corner, and helping in numerous other situations where people are endangered or merely inconvenienced. In sum, patrol officers are seen as the professionals who guard the safety, health, and welfare of the social body.

A clear policy to respond to a wide variety of community needs can easily be distinguished from a lack of policy that leads to automatically providing police officers at every request. Happenstance, rather than rational decision, has involved police in many aspects of social life and in the provision of many private services to individuals. When O'Connor took charge of the Troy PD, he immediately terminated a number of ceremonial services and protective services for the well-to-do. He ended the election-day posting of eighteen officers to polling places on the grounds that the officers were merely ornamental. The popular motorcycle escorts for funeral processions were discontinued because they were largely ceremonial and generally served only the prosperous. The department also stopped escorting local merchants making their daily bank deposits, on the grounds that they could afford to employ private security services. A count of 1972 radio transmissions showed that about 7 percent of all dispatches had been for escort services. New departmental policy further excluded investigations to help businesses locate customers who had failed to pay their bills. In declining to provide such special services for businesses and individuals, the department reduced the work load of patrol officers and gave them more time to provide assistance of their own choosing.

These selective cutbacks in services to special clients are not the same as the differential police response that has been widely adopted in larger departments since the late 1970s (Farmer 1981). Both changes seek to make better use of patrol time by removing some of the work load. O'Connor eliminated only one type of dispatch that can be clearly distinguished, bank escorts, plus assorted tasks that did not originate as calls. Separately he set up priorities in urgency among calls, but he expected all calls other than requests for information and referrals to be answered by the arrival of an officer. Differential police response sets priorities for the rapidity of dispatching a patrol car and also sets criteria for police operators to handle a substantial portion of the calls without dispatching a car. Departmental policy usually stipulates substituting telephone reports, but other options are walk-in or mail reports, or referral to other agencies. Theft, vandalism, and burglary were the types of calls most commonly handled by telephone reports in three cities where the program was carefully evaluated, although some assaults, disturbances, and suspicious circumstances were also handled at a distance. Differential response is harsh on any victim who has been upset by the crime and quietly complies when the operator asks if a telephone report is acceptable. Moreover, information from differential response units tends to flow poorly to the zone officers, resulting in their being out of touch with some of their neighborhood's problems.

The patrol division must have adequate staffing to encourage officers to commit themselves to quality service in noncriminal matters. If the number of dispatches overwhelm the available officers so that they hurry without a break from one job to the next, they are likely to protect themselves from an unreasonable work load by giving cursory attention to some calls and then delay in notifying the dispatcher that they are available for the next call until they have taken their own break. Under a patrol overload, officers probably cut their initiation of assistance and give short shrift to the so-called "low priority" calls, the noncriminal ones that do not require a report. Mastrofski's (1981) analysis of the Indiana University data on twenty-four police departments shows that individual officers varied tremendously—from none to thirteen—in the number of times per shift they stopped to offer assistance. This variation was not explained by steady assignment to a small neighborhood, compared to assignment over a huge geographic area. It may be that an officer's curiosity and tragic perspective provide the most powerful motivation for volunteering assistance. The conditions of patrol work and the expectations of supervisors may also encourage officers to look upon the multiple problems of people in their neighborhood as opportunities to be of service.

When officers are attuned to the needs of people in their assigned neighborhood, they take the initiative to inquire whether they can be of help. A woman in her mid-seventies told of this recent event:

I was going away with a friend, and my son took me to pick her up, and she didn't answer the door. My son said, "Let's try calling in case she can't get to the door. Maybe she could answer the phone." But there wasn't any answer. Two policemen saw us standing by the phone booth. They stopped and asked if we needed any help. We told them the whole story, and they followed us back to my friend's house. I was terribly upset. They roused the man downstairs and asked if he had keys for upstairs, which he did, because he was going to take care of things while she was gone. My son, the officers, and the man went upstairs. One of the officers came down to me and put his arm around me and told me she was dead in her bed. He was so gentle and nice. They called the coroner's office and stayed there with us all the while. I was very upset to begin with. I liked that they were so gentle and nice to us, not at all matter-of-fact or gruff. I've had officers talk down to me in the past, but these two young officers made me feel good about the police. They were concerned and seemed to know how I felt. They really calmed me.

This elderly woman probably feared the worst as she tried to reach her friend. Of the four men who mounted the stairs to her friend's apartment, it was an officer, not her son, who descended to break the sad news. The law places responsibility on police officers to safeguard a dead body until a medical examination determines whether or not the death was due to natural causes. While these officers waited for the coroner, they consoled the grief-stricken woman. Officers with a narrow interpretation of their responsibilities could have isolated themselves in the patrol car. The elderly woman praised the officers' gentleness and perceived that they had lingered out of concern for her.

No studies have been conducted so far to test the effect on the development of human understanding in young officers of a department's embracing multiple services, but groundwork has been laid by the thinking of William Muir and in the practices of a growing number of police managers. What appears to happen is that when officers repeatedly assist diverse individuals and receive heartfelt thanks, they come to see beyond the jumbled fragments of others' lives to recognize the common humanity they share with people who ask their help and even with many of the people they arrest. In learning to care for the people they serve, officers develop a tragic perspective on life that makes them less susceptible to cynical views. They become strengthened in their personal commitment to helping people. By contrast, if officers narrow their responsibility to dealing with crime—to attacks that people make on each other and their property—and focus on the lawbreakers, then they have fewer opportunities to feel kinship with their clients.

By no means do all officers learn the same things from the diversity of human problems they confront. Repeated contacts with the public appear to have an amplifying effect on the early orientation of officers. Those who initially experience basic sympathy for the plight of others may tend to be trusted and to find that their own trust is not disappointed. Through finding satisfaction in their work, they may develop more skills in helping people. On the contrary, officers who early develop a dislike for many of the people they encounter may tend to stimulate distrust and hostility, and they may react to the hostility by becoming vindictive. The events officers encounter are so varied that officers can make their own meanings for the whole of police work by recalling selectively the times when someone said "Bless you" or the times when someone muttered "Damn you."

Provision of multiple services also includes lighthearted events that provide relief for officers and citizens alike. The appearance of animals where they do not belong is "something-that-ought-not-to-be-happening-and-about-which-somebody-ought-to-do-something-now." By chance, three such events occurred within a few hours on 9 August 1979. In the afternoon, officers were called because a swarm of bees had appeared in front of a residence; that evening, a woman called about a bat in her house; at about the same time, the Jack-in-the-Box restaurant reported a chicken running around the floor. When a level-headed and resourceful officer takes charge at such events, everyone has a good time. A carnival atmosphere prevailed also on a day in the late spring of 1985 when a bear rambled down from the woods and appeared on the grounds of the girls' boarding school. Frightened, he climbed a sixty-foot tree. During the three hours it took for veterinarians to arrive, shoot tranquilizers into him, and extract him from the tree, the large crowd had a fine time watching, secure in the knowledge that police officers would protect them if the bear turned savage.

The provision of multiple services also appears to have positive effects on citizens' own abilities to cope with crime. Recall that for women and the elderly, knowing officers personally reduced their fear of being attacked as they went about alone at night. When officers render assistance to citizens in all manner of situations, citizens apparently increase their acquaintance with individual officers, feel more comfortable contacting the police, and increase the likelihood that they will report minor crimes.

In Troy, the effect of knowing police officers personally has been measured as it influences the degree of citizen cooperation. The 1978 residential survey asked people whether they had recently seen any of six different situations and what they did about them. Table 11-1 shows both the percentage of citizens who recalled each type of incident and the proportion who took some action, on their own or with other citizens or with the police. Over one-third of the citizens recalled witnessing some act of juvenile delinquency; fewer recalled seeing a crime or a suspicious event; only 46 percent of the respondents recalled seeing one or more of these three acts within the last year. "Mind your own business," as a view probably held by many citizens, helps explain the difference between only about half initiating action but almost everyone cooperating fully with a direct police request. An explanation of why a somewhat smaller proportion took action in response to crimes than to kids doing damage and suspicious events may be found by looking more closely at the nature of the crimes witnessed. Most were minor: vandalism, speeding, running a stop sign, and smoking pot accounted for 60 percent of the crimes witnessed but not reported.

As might be supposed, younger people saw more lawbreaking than their elders, men more than women. Boys aged fourteen to seventeen had the most opportunity of all to take action to stop incidents. Fully 85 percent of them had seen at least one instance of destructive acts by other teenagers, a crime occurring, or a suspicious event. What was the single most influential factor prompting the boys to seek police assistance in stopping the crime or delinquent act? Their personal acquaintance with at least two officers who worked in their neighborhood. Table 11-2 shows that of the twenty-one boys who knew at least two officers, twelve said they called the police, and every one took some action. Of the fifteen boys who knew no officers, three said that they called the police, and five did nothing.

Table 11-1 Citizen Cooperation in Crime Control

Question	Percentage Saying "Yes"	Proportion of Those Saying "Yes" Who Took Positive Action
In the last year have you seen any children or teenagers damaging property, such as throwing rocks at cars, defacing signs, or breaking windows?	37%	65%
In the last year . . . did you see anything happen that you thought was against the law, a crime or probably a crime? [Added questions if necessary] Did you see somebody hurt somebody deliberately? Did you see somebody's property being taken or damaged?	13	48
In the last year did you see anything suspicious that made you think someone might be going to commit a crime?	13	67
In the last year . . . did a police officer ask you about some trouble that had just happened?	15	97
In the last year did anyone in your neighborhood have an argument or fight that disturbed the peace?	22	52
In the last year have you been away from home for a few days?	62	75
$n = 946$		

Note: This is the wording and order of the questions used in the survey. After individuals identified all opportunities for action, they were asked whether they did anything.

Table 11-2 Effect of Knowing Officers Personally on the Frequency of Teenage Males Taking Cooperative Action

	Number of Officers He Knows		
Action Taken by Teenager[a]	None	One	Two or More
Did nothing	5	0	0
Acted on his own or with friends	7	2	9
Called the police	2	0	1
Did both	1	0	11
Totals ($n = 38$)	15	2	21

Note: Kendall's tau is .48, significant at less than .001.

[a]The three questions about actions: (1) In the last year have you seen any children or teenagers damaging property, such as throwing rocks at cars, defacing signs or breaking windows? Did you happen to do anything about it or talk to anybody about it? (2) In the last year, since March 1977, did you see anything happen that you thought was against the law, a crime or probably a crime? Did you see somebody hurt somebody deliberately? Did you see somebody's property being taken or damaged? Did you tell the police about it, did someone else report it to the police, or did no one report it? (3) In the last year did you see anything suspicious that made you think that someone might be going to commit a crime? Did you happen to do anything about it?

The question about knowing officers: Do you know any police officers who patrol your neighborhood well enough to speak to them? About how many?

A summary of the arguments in this section can be stated as an agenda for future research, since research has not yet demonstrated the effects of police departments' provision of multiple services. Demographically similar cities should be studied to compare departments that are competent in providing multiple services with those competent in crime control alone. There are several interesting hypotheses to test. In cities where the department embraces multiple services,

(1) a higher proportion of officers will have a tragic perspective;
(2) the least advantaged citizens will have satisfaction levels that are higher than in comparison cities;
(3) the rate of citizens' crime prevention calls will be higher;
(4) the most vulnerable people, such as elderly women, will feel safer going out alone at night.

Informing the Public

Popular interest in police work is evident in the large audience for television police dramas and the lasting readership for detective stories, yet departments often evince little interest in informing the public. The principle that police business is the public's business places the burden on every department to justify any holding back of information. In the 1978 Troy survey, half the respondents agreed with the statement "The police don't tell us enough about how we can help them." Sixty-eight percent agreed in London in 1972 (Belson 1975).

Police have many opportunities to inform citizens in the course of daily work. A citizen information card that patrol officers leave at the conclusion of handling a call for service is a simple tool for communicating the next step the department will take and what action a citizen should take. The 8- by 4-inch card that O'Connor designed for the Troy department also contained phone numbers for twenty-six offices to which police frequently refer citizens. Explanations of what they are doing can be offered by all department members who meet the public: patrol officers, dispatchers, crossing guards, meter attendants, detectives, and youth officers. Most members are sufficiently informed about departmental affairs to answer many questions beyond those concerning the immediate situation. Unfortunately, many departments have regulations explicitly forbidding employees to comment on department policies, and thus they stifle opportunities to inform citizens. If department leaders make efforts to keep officers fully informed of the reasons behind policy changes and maintain an organizational openness, city residents will become better informed regarding police matters.

Police departments have many opportunities for direct contacts with neighborhood, civic, and religious organizations. Waxing and waning is typical of association and neighborhood needs for police information and assistance. It is an art to be receptive to the fresh enthusiasm of a group that newly wrestles with enduring problems and not to be overly disappointed some months later when the group melts away. Among the many kinds of outreach the Troy department has undertaken during the last dozen years, the simplest have been to meet requests for officers to give talks on safety and crime reduction. The department has presented demonstrations in the public schools and made the station house a destination for class trips. The department sponsored an Explorer Scout post in the mid-1970s, but interest declined after a few years. Whenever requested, a department member has addressed, become adviser to, or otherwise worked with citizen groups, including churches, boys' clubs, a rape crisis program, a dispute mediation center, and neighborhood associations. The department set up a simple ride-along system whereby any officer could choose to host an adult rider who signed a release absolving the City from liability. Begun for college students majoring in criminal justice, the program initially had few riders, stopped entirely between 1978 and the early 1980s because of active PBA disapproval, and later was little used.

In some cities, police departments have become deeply involved in organizing citizen groups around issues of neighborhood safety. The most widespread are block-watcher programs, systems in which citizens receive some training in identifying suspicious events and take responsibility for calling the police. Police managers have facilitated the creation of block associations and neighborhood groups. An example of long-term community building comes from the work of Chief Ray Davis in Santa Ana, California (Skolnick and Bayley 1986). At their best, such associations facilitate information flow and development of neighborhood priorities.

In all the types of communication discussed so far, police officers and commanders make direct contact with citizens to spread the message that together police and citizens can build toward safety and security for all. Now we turn to the mass media. Newspapers, radio, and television amplify the information about a local department and are joined by magazines, broadcasting networks, books, and films in carrying national messages about policing. Chapter 7 looked at the 1985 policy conflict between the *Times Record* and the Troy PD over the new departmental policy of withholding incident reports on felonies under investigation, in order to prevent the newspaper from using such stories as filler in ways that could heighten public fear of crime. The conclusion drawn was that for both mass media and police departments the safeguards against public damage from the flow of information and also from self-serving withholding of information lie largely within each organization.

The flip side concerns benefits to the public from dissemination of human interest stories and reasoned presentation of police issues. On a daily basis, police officers encounter people whose problems could be the material for human interest stories if the stories were told with sensitivity and compassion. All the issues presented in the discussion of politics (Chapter 10) provide material for ongoing adult education in public affairs. An example of education to improve the quality of newspaper reporting has been provided by Herman Goldstein (1980). Reporters who have taken his law school course in police issues find that the questions they ask have changed. Regarding a department's decision to purchase dogs, they no longer ask, "What are their names?" or "Where will they be housed?" Instead, they ask, "What are the specific tasks for which the dogs will be used?" and "What is the basis for determining whether the dogs add to the department's effectiveness?" Because the rookie journalist's first assignment is usually as police reporter, city editors are pivotal in defining what is important on the police beat. Vanderbilt University's law school houses an institute in collaboration with a southern association of news editors for education in the complex issues of law and policing. As already noted, however, a trend working against newspaper responsibility for civic education is the absorption of family newspapers by chains, which tend to build circulation through sensational stories. In cities where newspapers assist opinion leaders and the public at large to develop better understanding of police issues, confused political conflicts like Troy's should become rare.

Listening to Citizens

Complaints about services delivered and not delivered are the bedrock of citizen feedback. Citizens know whether or not officers' actions met their expectations. Criticism can stem either from poor police performance or from poor citizen understanding of what police can reasonably be expected to do. As policing becomes less secretive, public understanding will improve, and expectations will become more realistic. Unfortunately, complaints represent opportunities to improve service only if they are voiced to those responsible for the service. The absence of complaints to a department does not mean absence of dissatisfaction. Recall that Officer Holt promised follow-up by a youth services officer to the woman whose daughter was beaten by a gang of kids. In city after city, people almost never call the department to complain about the failure of a specialist officer to appear. In general, citizens tend to treat the police with kid gloves as a means of keeping good relations. Fear of police is a minuscule part of the problem. The root may be the monopoly that the local department has as the public supplier of patrol and general investigative services. Dissatisfied people cannot switch without moving out of the community; hence, they accept a low quality of service. Since police handle matters both minor and major, citizens may be reluctant to take them to task over failures in minor matters lest antagonism jeopardize their service on a future important matter. In London in 1972, Belson

(1975) reported, 57 percent of citizens agreed with the statement "Police get fed up with people who come to them over trivial things." In Troy in 1978, 62 percent agreed.

Few police departments have anything resembling the active customer service departments so common in business. The only topics of complaint handled systematically are malpractice charges. Departments do not have the means of attracting and channeling daily run-of-the-mill complaints. The usual response to complaints is an attempt to limit the damage rather than to use the information to understand patterns of problems. The survey finding in Troy is probably true of most cities: people tend to share their complaints with their friends and take only the most serious ones to the department. Conscientious police managers, well aware of this reluctance, patiently listen to the outpouring of pent-up complaints whenever they talk to citizens groups—often lists of problems that need police attention. Illustrations of the police manager as the channel for complaints are both the fearful Germania Hall meeting described in Chapter 7 and a low-keyed meeting with elementary school parents, described by this excerpt from O'Connor's subsequent memo to the chief.

> The agenda was concerned with the school crossing problem. However, as is usually the case, a number of persons pointed out other problems. . . . [The following comments refer to the] Hells' Angels loud mufflers on cycles
> using dealer plates on several cars—switching plates from car to car
> out-of-state plates (Rhode Island) on a car there for a long time
> they are peddling bumper stickers—do they have a permit to solicit from door to door?

Likewise, citizens lack a regular way to applaud the good police work they witness. The residential survey in Troy shows that citizens pass praise among themselves much more often than they give it directly to officers. About 45 percent of the citizens who witnessed praiseworthy actions took the step of expressing their appreciation directly to the officers involved, but citizens' estimates of how many friends they told averaged ten. Thus, even if a department is gaining an excellent reputation among citizens, the officers may continually underestimate public appreciation because they most frequently deal with people in unpleasant situations. Studies of traditional departments have shown that officers consistently underestimated the esteem in which the public held them (Bayley and Mendelsohn 1969; Reiss 1971). If a department would make energetic efforts to pass words of appreciation along to the officers involved, officers would be encouraged to increase their concern for the people they serve.

A large variety of actions are considered praiseworthy by citizens who

Table 11-3   Police Services Praised by Citizens

Action		Number of Citizens Praising that Action
Assistance		35
Resolving conflicts	13	
Helping people who cannot care for themselves: children, aged, intoxicated	11	
Following medical and fire emergencies	5	
Other	6	
Facilitating Traffic		31
Assisting individual drivers and pedestrians	22	
Maintaining general flow	7	
Stopping dangerous drivers	2	
Saving Lives		22
In medical emergency	10	
By fire rescue	9	
From other physical danger	3	
Crime Control		17
Investigation	12	
Victim assistance	3	
Crime prevention	2	
Generally Good Work		9
Total ($n = 948$)		114

witness them. Table 11-3 shows that assistance of all types most commonly evoked admiration, whereas excellence in criminal investigation netted praise much less often. Recall that about 30 percent of the calls for service handled by the Troy department concerned crimes. If praise came in proportion to work load, we would expect about 30 percent of the praise to concern crime control—yet the table shows that only 17 of the 114 specific instances of praise concerned officers' handling of crimes. This finding is consistent with the results of the Indiana University study (Mastrofski 1983) that citizens across twenty-four towns rated about 70 percent of crime calls and 80 percent of noncrime calls as satisfactorily handled. The department policy that officers respond immediately to medical and fire emergencies is a reason for the frequency of praise in these relatively rare events.

A serious shortcoming in police-community relations is that citizens seldom know how to request an alteration in the delivery of police services. The 1978 Troy residential survey posed this hypothetical situation:

"Suppose that you wanted to change the way police do their work in your neighborhood. Is there any person or organization you would contact about this?" A substantial 49 percent knew no one to contact, and 24 percent were unsure; only about 15 percent would go directly to the police department, and the remaining 12 percent would divide among city councilmen, the city manager, and individuals active in community affairs. A smaller proportion of Troy citizens could identify some advocacy channel than could the 45 percent of respondents in the St. Louis, Rochester, and Tampa–St. Petersburg metropolitan areas (Sharp 1980, 367).

If a department receives citizen feedback, it can use the information to set departmental priorities. Troy residents responding to the 1978 survey mentioned vandalism as by far the most common problem needing police attention. When William Trigg, a graduate student at the State University of New York, Albany, requested to work with the Troy department in applying a systematic method of problem solving, O'Connor suggested that he work on vandalism. Through small-group discussion with all police officers and sergeants in the in-service school and by creating a task force, Trigg (1984) developed his understanding of officers' current approaches and assisted them to view the problem systematically. The department also sought out citizen complaints and praise on service via letters to burglary victims (Chapter 5).

Police Officers and Citizens as Part of the Same Community

Informal, casual contact between police and public occurs at very different rates in different communities. At social gatherings, some people distance themselves from officers on the assumption that they are on the lookout for law enforcement opportunities, much as some people distance themselves from psychiatrists on the assumption that they want to perform an instant psychoanalysis. American studies show high social isolation of police officers in comparison with people in other occupations. Maureen Cain (1973) has written a classic study of police-community relations, in England in the 1960s, examining the friendship patterns and attitudes of both officers and their wives. In comparing constables serving in rural and urban areas, she found that rural officers had more social contacts and considered their recognition from the community to be more satisfactory. American officers as individuals can become involved in community, church, scouting, and other neighborhood affairs. Through their benevolent associations, officers have traditionally sponsored police athletic leagues. Charity drives, such as a cerebral palsy telethon, provide occasions for officers as a group to become involved.

If citizens are looking at their own police department without the benefit of a survey or other intensive study, several outward signs can show the degree to which officers as a group and individually feel they belong to the community they serve. One sign that patrol officers feel comfortable being recognized as officers is that they choose to report to work in uniform. When the station house has good locker rooms and showers, officers have the option of commuting without revealing their occupation. In Troy, since the installation of good facilities in 1977, officers have consistently continued to wear their uniforms on the way to work. Another outward sign is whether officers choose to eat at local spots rather than returning to police companionship at the station or sitting isolated in their patrol cars.

Young children have a special place among the many clients of police officers. Their innocence is refreshing after numerous encounters with hostile or jaded adults. When parents teach their children to trust and rely upon police officers, they are building bridges for the next generation. The 1978 Troy survey asked what parents should tell children about the police and whether there is anything to tell children to be aware of about police. "Tell children that police officers are their friends" was the advice from 20 percent of the residents. Over 90 percent gave positive or neutral advice.

Children's words of praise are especially appreciated by officers because they are likely to be sincere. Sam Griffith, an officer with a thoroughly professional outlook, discussed his work in these terms.

> Many times I had been to the home of this common-law couple. She was white and he was black. I remember a particularly bad dispute when their six-year-old kid was taking in every move they made. It took me a long time, but eventually they came to a peaceable understanding with each other. Some months afterwards I was feeling blue as I went for lunch in the local fast food place. When I walked in the door, there was the kid. He was dirty with summer sweat on his face, a runny nose, shining eyes, and a big grin. He was so cute he was adorable. He sang out to his friends, "There's Sam. There's Sam." "How's it going?" I replied. He came right up to me. "Know what, Sam? When I grow up I want to be just like you."

The more responsive to community desires police officers become, the more they find conflicting desires. This chapter opened with the opposition of the sleepy neighbors to the street disco dancers. It closes with this point made at a community meeting where Commissioner O'Connor received complaints and requests from the people of a middle-class neighborhood. Young people drinking and making noise on a hillside behind the synagogue had become a particularly sore point with many of the citizens. One of the most outspoken was the woman who ran the little corner store. Then a well-dressed young man stood up and said as politely as you please, "Mrs. Johnson, you know where we buy our beer."

"To keep different moral worlds from colliding" is the phrase of Police Chief David Couper of Madison, Wisconsin (Couper 1979). The larger the city, the more likely it is to be the home of people with diverse life-styles, some of whom will take offense at the life-styles of their neighbors. For the most part, Americans accommodate each other's diverse ways, but when tolerance wears thin, police have a crucial role in building bridges between citizens.

Today, each of you [graduates of basic training] enters into a new phase of your life and of your career, and from this point forward you must demonstrate a kind of courage which too few possess. Everyone perceives the police officer as a strong and fearless person—and while each of you will live up to that expectation sooner or later, I would speak to you today of a different form of bravery. . . .

What I call upon you to find within yourselves and make the hallmark of your career is the courage

... to cling forever to those ideals which have brought you to this moment; the courage

... to reject the gifts of coin, of coffee or of flesh which others would offer in order to place you in their debt; the courage

... to forgive the ignorant and the confused; the courage

... to calm the angry and the hostile; the courage

... to bear the disappointment of other people's narrow judgments of your work; the courage

... to be intolerant of those around you who would seek to be taller, to be better or to be smarter by belittling others because they have different skins or beliefs or background; the courage

... to care so deeply for the people you serve that you will feel their sorrow, their pain and their joy.

George O'Connor, 1984

12 Fairness

A challenge like the one above could have been given by any police manager in America to young men and women entering police service. George O'Connor chose to take the opportunity of Troy's March 1984 police graduation ceremony to impress these aspirations upon new officers. Personal courage probably more strongly influences an officer's action than does supervision, since officers rarely work in view of a sergeant and rarely are called upon to explain their action and inaction. Day in and day out patrol work thrusts officers into conflict after conflict where they have the opportunity to decide what is the fair thing to do. To follow the advice of the commencement address is to bypass the stage of excessive aggressiveness characteristic of young officers. When police officers bring courage to the troubles of the people they serve, they will not find easy answers, but they will have a coherent outlook, a tragic perspective, to guide their efforts to be fair.

Fairness is a particularly appropriate standard by which the powerless judge the powerful, the governed judge the government, the citizens judge the police. Judgments of fairness are appropriate for every action that individual officers direct toward citizens and for every departmental policy. Fairness is so central to law enforcement and police services that it is hard to conceive of a city with a broadly admired police department where the majority of citizens consider officers unfair. In putting forward the citizen as judge of police fairness, we recognize that citizens are partisan and that situations are complex; consequently, citizens are likely to disagree in many instances over the fairness of an officer's actions. The fundamental reasons to stay with the citizen's perspective are that democratic systems place authority in the citizenry, and that the sense of having been treated fairly is an end in itself. If citizens are informed of police department policies, they can judge the fairness of those policies. Citizens as participants, bystanders, and disinterested third parties do make judgments of fairness in the handling of incidents. There are two separate questions—is the action fair? and do the citizens involved see the action as fair?—but we will consider only the second.

Citizen perceptions of the fairness of all police action, behavior, operations, practices, and policies may be viewed in terms of two dimensions or aspects. One dimension is the difference between enforcement and service. This rough division may be made for each incident according to whether a citizen is being subjected to some enforcement action he or she would rather avoid or receiving some service he or she wants. An officer's action in a conflict among citizens may be viewed quite differently by the parties involved. For example, when a bartender asks police to eject an unruly patron, the police response is service to the bartender but enforcement to the customer. The bartender is more likely to agree that the service was performed in a fair manner than the patron is to agree that the enforcement against him was fair.

The other dimension is who makes the decision. Actions of street officers arise from a variety of sources and combinations of sources: state law, local ordinance, explicit departmental policy, traditional departmental practice, precinct or shift commander's directive, supervisor's directive, and the individual officer's own values.

These two dimensions are the basis for the presentation in Table 12-1 of some of the more common types of action and policies that citizens judge as fair or unfair. One may scan each column as an introduction first to the discussion of law enforcement and then to the discussion of service. Individual officers are listed first because they directly carry out almost all the decisions, regardless of who made them.

The most obvious instances of unfairness in enforcement have already been discussed in the analysis of police malpractice: illegal arrest, excessive force, failure to observe constitutional rights, harassment, and discourtesy. Recall that abuses of discretion are far more prevalent than outright crimes. Illegal actions are excluded from consideration here in order to focus on more problematic situations in which officers have taken actions that are legal yet widely considered unfair.

Recall that Chapter 10 introduced three alternatives for determining

Table 12-1   Policies and Actions Subject to Judgments of Fairness

	Types of Decisions	
Decisionmaker	Enforcement	Service
Individual officers	stopping on street ticketing arresting physically restraining detaining overnight killing	investigating crimes maintaining order providing other service allocating time committing effort
Dispatchers	sending a car sending backup notifying other agencies	sending a car sending backup notifying other agencies
Supervisors and commanders	setting priorities and standards for actions by individual officers	setting priorities and standards allocating patrol cutting time on calls screening cases
Department	setting priorities and standards for actions by individual officers	setting priorities and standards adding specific services cutting specific services
City	passing and repealing municipal ordinances	siting precinct stations
State	passing and repealing provisions of criminal code and criminal procedure code	passing and repealing crime victim compensation laws

fairness in the distribution of service. First, a policy can be judged fair if it applies a single universal standard to all. Second, a policy can be considered fair if those who ask for a service receive it. Third, a policy can be considered fair if it meets needs proportionately: that is, if those in greater need receive greater services. These three definitions compare fairness across incidents. If all members of a department adhered to any of these measures of equity, that new condition would be fairer than the previous haphazard state. To distinguish among many fair and unfair actions, we do not need to undertake a rigorous inquiry into which of these principles ought to be applied, for reasons that may be explained through an example of service.

The idea of "fairness" goes beyond equity to include the notion of what is appropriate and right for the situation. In the search for fairness we ask the practical question "Is today's investigation into the burglary of Joe Brown's apartment as well performed as the investigation yesterday at the mansion of Alice Vanderbilt?" If Mr. Brown, Ms. Vanderbilt, and every other citizen whose home was burglarized receive only insults and spilled dusting powder, they are treated equally—but this is not fairness in the common understanding of the term. The element of appropriateness is clearly part of the notion of fairness, however taxing it may be to define for every single situation.

Clear thinking about fairness does not require a long list of detailed definitions of what is appropriate for each situation. In practice, no department's service is unvaryingly shabby. When the homes of people who are rich and powerful are burglarized, the police investigations are typically the most courteous and careful that officers know how to give. Raising the standard of service for underprivileged people to the level provided to the rich and powerful—that is, merely applying the first of the three standards of equity—will greatly increase a department's fairness in delivering service.

Fairness in Law Enforcement

On the one hand, fair law enforcement is the first step in a fair judicial process; on the other hand, unfair law enforcement can have disastrous consequences for the citizen. The specific provisions of the laws and every step in enforcing them can affect the fairness of the outcome. When police attempt to enforce laws that are widely considered unfair, such as Prohibition's ban on alcoholic beverages, they are in great ethical and practical quandaries. Here we focus on laws supported by a public consensus, in the recognition of how difficult is fair enforcement even of laws generally regarded as fair.

Police managers today hold that when individual officers are well educated and well motivated, their individual interpretations of standards of fairness will produce fairer outcomes than will blanket directives. They consider 100 percent enforcement of the laws impossible and not an appropriate goal. Officers should be encouraged to develop and use their discretion in the application of municipal ordinances, traffic laws, and even state criminal codes. Fairness includes lenience in enforcing the law through taking into account the social purpose of the particular law and the situation of the individual against whom it could be enforced. This is what William Muir in *Police: Street Corner Politicians* (1977) has called an officer's situational judgment, which is based on his or her perception of the moral character of the participants and on an estimate of the likely effect of enforcement actions.

The first distinction that police officers make is to recognize the great range in the seriousness of lawbreaking. Laws forbid both murder and jaywalking. Police managers join with police administrators in insistence that laws at the serious end of the spectrum be enforced as fully and vigorously as resources permit; both condemn the old, informal bargains still made by some officers to let the thief go if he returns the stolen property. In Troy in the mid-1970s, such bargains by older officers occasionally came to Commissioner O'Connor's attention. Police managers likewise work to prevent certain quiet bargains by detectives, such as ignoring an informer's continuing burglaries in exchange for receiving information to incriminate others in narcotics deals. Administrators and managers agree that adults who inflict injury on others should be brought into the criminal justice system. The national rise in arrests for drunken driving is a current example of how a changing view of seriousness has pushed up arrests, from about 556,000 in 1970 to about 1,778,000 in 1982. Since public education campaigns have given ample warning of the new strictness, yesteryear's fairness of letting drivers sleep it off is different from today's fairness of arrest and sentence.

Police managers see lenience as an appropriate police response to illegal actions that are neither dangerous nor damaging. Three brief examples illustrate criteria for department-level decisions not to issue parking tickets. First, permitting delivery trucks to double-park is a common practice in many cities, even by those departments that generally set a goal of full enforcement. Police administrators who hold to a standard of fairness through uniformity see the exemption of a specific class of vehicles as a refinement in what remains a single standard. Police managers tend to look at the social needs of a neighborhood and to balance the need to facilitate the flow of traffic with the need to make deliveries. Their general principle is to resolve conflicts in such a way that many different, non-harmful activities are accommodated in public places.

A second example of fairness concerns consistency over time. Drivers in Troy had long been accustomed to parking illegally on the left side of the street, facing the wrong way. But one day in 1978, when an illegally parked driver pulled out and almost smashed into a patrol car, the officer—a loner in the department—resolved to enforce the parking ordinance. That very day he issued over one hundred tickets. Commissioner O'Connor asked the judge to invalidate these tickets so that citizens could receive a fair warning in advance of such a change in enforcement policy. After that demonstration and the accompanying publicity, O'Connor announced that future tickets would not be dismissed. The presence on the statute books of far more ordinances than are regularly observed, or even remembered, provides weapons for unfair enforcement if an individual officer or a department chooses to harass particular citizens. Given the general enthusiasm of city councils and county and state legislatures for solving problems through passing laws and their disinclination to go through the codes to purge unused legislation, police will always have plenty of obscure statutes and ordinances that can be arbitrarily enforced. Thus, prevention of harassment cannot be achieved through limiting the weapons but appears to rest first on each officer's commitment to fairness and second on thorough and fair review processes.

A third example of fairness is taking into account the special hardship that enforcement inflicts on particular individuals. In November 1982 a woman who lived at the edge of the central business district was so ill that she required around-the-clock nursing. The nurses who attended her at night were receiving parking tickets for violating the ban on all-night parking in the central business district. The purposes of the ban were to facilitate street cleaning and to prevent the accumulation of derelict vehicles. When O'Connor learned of the problem through the sick woman's sister, he advised the nurses to park in the nearby bank parking lot and only as a fallback to park on the street. Then he issued a memo to all officers working midnights, explaining the sick woman's problem and outlining his solution: that any nurses who did park on the street were to call the radio room so that officers on patrol could identify their cars and avoid ticketing them. This departmental decision for lenience to meet the special needs of individuals employs the same sort of reasoning as do officers with a professional outlook when they decide whether or not to make an arrest.

Fairness as experienced by citizens rests largely in the hands of individual members of the police department. As Table 12-1 shows, officers on the street make by far the most frequent decisions on the application of the laws, application to situations as diverse as street discos, dangerous driving, and barricaded suspects. Officers at the scene have more direct knowledge of the situation than do supervisors and managers who are distant from the street. How wisely officers will apply these laws depends on how far they have developed a tragic perspective and how well they have molded their personal courage.

An example of active police participation in the evolving societal definition of fairness is the changing response to public intoxication (Aaronson, Dienes, and Musheno 1984). Viewed superficially, laws against public intoxication, disorderly conduct, loitering, and vagrancy set universal standards. In practice, however, enforcement falls heavily upon poor people, because any of their actions that could cause annoyance to others take place disproportionately within police view. Nationally, arrests for all types of disorderly behavior declined from 1,900 per 100,000 in 1970 to 850 in 1988, thanks to the combined actions by the Supreme Court in ruling unconstitutional specific statutes that forbid intoxication, loitering, and vagrancy; by state governments in repealing their statutes; by local governments in setting up new services such as detoxification centers; and by police officers in declining to make arrests. Typical disorderly conduct statutes are so broadly drawn that officers can easily construe them to cover the behavior of individuals who previously could have been arrested specifically for drunkenness, vagrancy, or loitering, a point discussed in Chapters 5 and 8 in connection with patterns of arrest. Officers with the kind of courage that O'Connor praised are slow to make disorderly conduct arrests, because they recognize that the criminal justice system is not designed to help individuals who exhibit these problem behaviors.

Akin to handling a disorderly situation without arrest is releasing an arrested individual before court appearance. Requiring an arrestee to post bail might appear to set a universal standard, but in fact it harshly discriminates against the poor. Release on one's own recognizance (ROR), a court-authorized program to address this problem, has substantially reduced the numbers of people who are locked up overnight. Before the Troy department made extensive use of ROR, Officer Bill Keller, who had been with the department eight years, made this observation:

I feel sorry for the poor white man we lock up who doesn't have connections. The white people with connections get out on bail and then get their charges dropped. Last Fourth of July we arrested two black men and a white man. The black guys called up the NAACP and got to the judge, who let them go ROR. They turned up in court on Monday because the NAACP said to them, "Don't disgrace us blacks by not appearing." But the white guy had to stay in the lockup all weekend.

The views of citizens subjected to enforcement powers are important in their own right, whether or not an objective observer would agree with their judgments on the fairness of their treatment. The most common type of enforcement, being stopped while driving or walking, was experienced in 1977–78 by about 10 percent of Troy residents. Of the men and women who had been stopped, 81 percent believed the officers were justified, only 3 percent were unsure, and 16 percent believed that the stop was unjustified. We also asked people about a hypothetical situation: "Suppose a Troy police officer pulled you over as you were driving and told you that you had been speeding. Suppose you told the officer that you had not been speeding." Of the residents surveyed, 65 percent considered it *very likely* that an officer would treat them courteously, 22 percent said *somewhat likely*, 6 percent said *not likely*, and 7 percent did not know. The officer who aims to educate drivers is invariably courteous, helps drivers to see the seriousness of their careless driving, and leaves them feeling fairly treated.

Ten percent of the Troy residents interviewed anticipated getting another ticket for arguing, 5 percent thought they would be ticketed even if innocent, and 4 percent thought they would be insulted. An important finding is that people who were socially disadvantaged expected unfair treatment at the same low rate as people who had social advantages. Specifically, the few who anticipated an additional ticket, an unfair ticket, or discourtesy were found among the rich as often as among the poor, among college graduates as often as among high school dropouts, among white people as often as among minority group members. Citizens were most divided over whether or not an officer would be lenient by giving a only a warning if they claimed to have been obeying the speed limit: 27 percent said very likely, 30 percent said likely, 26 percent said not likely, and 17 percent had no guess. People expecting lenient treatment were also found equally among the various levels of income, education, and racial grouping, though women did show consistently higher expectations of leniency than men. Surprisingly, people who knew no officers personally expected leniency as often as people who had officers among their relatives and close friends. These survey findings show that citizens at large shared a view of police fairness of a fundamental sort.

Let us look at an actual case of enforcement against a powerful man. In 1975 a sergeant arrested the Democratic party county chairman for failing to stop at a stop sign and driving on the wrong side of the street. A Breathalyzer test proved that he was intoxicated. Two days later a captain told the patrol captain that the sergeant had been put up to making a politically motivated arrest, had been waiting at the restaurant for the political leader to leave, and had called for a tow truck in advance. A police officer echoed these accusations and added that simultaneously the sergeant had neglected his duty to go to the scene of a nearby accident. Investigation by the professional standards unit supported the sergeant, but the attacks on his judgment suggest that in the old days he would have been punished.

O'Connor's sense of fairness in enforcement requires as little intervention as possible into people's private lives. Across the nation a popular form of intrusive policing has been to catch drunken drivers by setting up road blocks on weekend nights to stop all drivers. Here power is applied to the public at large in order to curb a few dangerous individuals. O'Connor is clear that his department does not do business that way. An enforcement mode that does not interfere with the law-abiding driver is to create a temporary traffic detail composed of volunteers who seek out and ticket reckless drivers, among whom are many under the influence of alcohol. Other modes of addressing the problem include driver education, media campaigns, municipal ordinances to require that bars serve food, enforcement of existing laws against serving intoxicated patrons, installing mechanical devices to test sobriety in the cars of repeat offenders. For a problem as deeply rooted in American habits as driving after drinking, a sound approach engages the police as but one of several governmental and voluntary agencies that can cooperate to reduce the accident toll. An attempt to solve a complex problem solely by reliance upon police power has a strong probability of encouraging oppressive and unfair use of power as the problem fails to yield to moderate amounts.

Being fair is relatively easy in traffic stops when the citizen's behavior is obvious, laws are clear, and laws are supported by a consensus. In other situations where people annoy or endanger each other, in conflicts, disturbances, and harassments, officers have difficulty in creating outcomes that all participants consider fair. In fact, some street situations produce unfair outcomes in the eyes of the participants, regardless of how hard the officers may try to act fairly. For example, when Officers Mullin and Rice summoned assistance to disperse the crowd at the housing project, each of the six men and two women who were arrested could easily have considered their treatment unfair because they were singled out for arrest among the others whose behavior was similar.

Inconsistency is a source of unfairness for which police departments have no easy answer. Listen to Mike Mullin describe a problem recurring every spring:

> Kids get beer and drink on the hill. Jack and I did it when we were young, and so of course we expect kids do it now. Kids have been drinking since Christ was a cowboy. As long as the kids are back in the woods and not disturbing anyone, that's fine. However, there is another officer, Jones, who also patrols this zone, who thinks that kids should be prevented from drinking. When Jack and I come to the area, we have to talk to the kids over the car's PA system: "Don't run. We're not Officer Jones."

Inconsistencies of this sort abound. People engaged in antisocial and illegal actions are calmed down by one officer, courteously arrested by another, arrested with insults by yet another. Sam Griffith quickly talked the friend of the barricaded man into going home when the younger officers were ready to arrest him. Rocky Davis beat the kids wrecking the cars in the garage, but another officer would have taken them to family court. Sergeant Martin maneuvered the street disc jockey into ending the party, but a less skillful officer could have provoked a confrontation ending in a melee and a dozen arrests. A few lazy officers in Troy ignore dangerous drivers weaving down the street; a few conscientious ones spot every vehicle with an expired registration and pull the driver over for a warning. Troy has no zealots who ticket every driver who fails to signal turns. Troy officers seeing young men angrily trading punches or trespassing across a back yard do not arrest all of them.

A fundamental method for controlling decisions not to arrest would be to adopt state statutes that explicitly define and permit police discretion in the enforcement of the law. A number of police managers, including Commissioner O'Connor, believe that the time is ripe for this step, but states have not as yet adopted such legislation. On the contrary, New Jersey officers work under an attorney general's ruling that officers *must* arrest whenever they have sufficient evidence. A far-reaching definition of discretion not to arrest was made in 1978–80 by the prosecutor of Jefferson County, Colorado, a suburban area adjacent to Denver (Leahy 1980). There, the prosecutor worked with effective officers from the local police departments to develop a list of twenty-six criteria for deciding upon follow-up investigation and arrest. The arrest standards set five outcomes: permanent resolution by the officer without a charge; no charge but open to review; charges pending further investigation; charge and release; charge and incarceration. Permanent resolution without a charge could occur if (1) the victim suffered a minor loss and sought only to recover for the loss or damage; (2) the victim and any witnesses were unwilling to prosecute and unwilling to testify; (3) the violations were conditional. The standards gave each police agency scope to set written guidelines to increase consistency in arrest practices within its jurisdiction. Unfortunately, the whole system quickly fell into disuse under the subsequent prosecutor.

Fairness in the Provision of Service

According to a modern folk saying, "You can never have too much money or too much police protection." The most frequently voiced suggestion from citizens for better police service is to put more officers on patrol. In Troy, over 50 percent of the citizens wished for more patrol when asked in the 1978 survey, "What steps should police take to improve service in your neighborhood and improve relations with people?" If all neighborhoods received patrol protection to the levels requested, cities would have to increase the number of officers far in excess of the present level of 2.1 per 1,000 population. Neighborhood problems requiring police attention are always waxing and waning. Whenever vandalism, purse snatching, burglary, or teenage rowdiness increases, people tend to demand more cops. Whenever these ills abate, no one speaks up to say that a neighborhood has excessive patrol coverage. Basic questions of fairness at the departmental level concern the allocation of patrol coverage to different neighborhoods. Better-managed police departments have long used work-load studies to assist decisions on assignment of patrol personnel. Common to all methods of work-load analysis is an estimation of current calls for service by geographic area and time of day. This is a form of fairness based on need.

Too much political debate about police revolves around issues of quantity. Are there enough cops? Enough foot cops? Scant attention is paid to issues of quality. Are officers providing consistently good service to everyone?

Learning the Courage of Commitment

Subtle and profound changes take place in individuals who become police officers. Many grow in moral courage as they learn the job. Police responsibilities, in their complexity and variety, all require the exercise of discretion. When an officer seriously addresses the question of how he or she will achieve fairness, one of the possible outcomes is a commitment such as Officer Frank Baldwin made after one year on the job.

> When I had been an evidence technician for about three months, I began to get very discouraged by all the burglaries I was going to day in and day out. I found myself cutting corners, not bothering with that messy dusting powder if nothing really valuable was taken. Then I stopped myself with the realization that these people were counting on me. Even if only a small black and white TV was taken, that might be all some families had. It occurred to me that if they didn't have any money to buy a new one, they could feel worse about it than I would feel if burglars cleaned out the whole house. I decided that I should make a rule for myself. You know, I don't rush into making personal rules, because when I make them, I stick to them. I made a rule that I would do as careful a job for the poor person who had nothing worth stealing as for the richest person in town.

Department leadership can set expectations that every officer will treat every citizen fairly. For example, during his first weeks in Troy, Commissioner O'Connor heard complaints from residents of public housing projects and summarized his understanding of the problems in a departmental memo to all personnel.

> At the present time approximately 10 percent of the population of the City lives in projects under the jurisdiction of the Troy Housing author-

ity. . . . At a recent meeting with representatives of the various resident councils of the housing projects, a considerable number of concerns were presented by them regarding the manner in which we respond to their calls for service.

The purpose of this memorandum is to remind all personnel of the Department that the quality and quantity of police service rendered to them by this department shall in no way be less than that rendered to any other person within the City.

Police leaders, having started their careers as officers on patrol, know the personal courage they are calling upon officers to exhibit in giving equal service to the people with intractable problems who live crowded together in public housing. This account by a divorced mother, aged thirty-two, gives a glimpse of her ongoing problems. Although shaking with fear, she had not initially thought to call the police.

I was having trouble with a neighbor who was mentally unbalanced. I've gone to Troy Housing about it. I'm divorced. There had been incidents with my kids. A man came to my door with a pizza which I had not ordered. . . . I thought it was her kids playing a possible joke. Then there was another knock. That's when I found a letter, like a blackmail letter. It had a riddle written in magic marker. "When is a rich person a poor person? . . . You are going to be robbed. Ha, ha, ha." It really scared me. I called the security police. He came up to my apartment. . . . The security guard asked me if I wanted to make a report, and I said "Yes." So he called the police. I called my ex-husband and he came out.

One officer took the report from my "ex," and the other was out in the kitchen trying to calm me down. They said it was like someone is reading a Batman book or watching Batman. They knew we were having trouble with next door, so they took the letter over to show her. I don't know what they said to her. They were reassuring and said to call right away if anything happened. My security guard tracked down where the pizza came from. A kid had called. They didn't know who. The kids' father is down in Poughkeepsie and the mother is really weird. They don't let up on me. She eggs them on, makes them do things.

I particularly liked that the officers made you feel as if you just weren't sick, as if you were somebody. They didn't just ask questions. They reassured me, and I wouldn't feel funny about asking again. They really were concerned. They said, "Calm down. Can I get you anything?" I was shaking. They went out of their way by going over to the apartment next door. They told my "ex" not to go over to their apartment. Just to stay calm and call again right away if you need to. They promised to keep a report on it in case something happened. They said to try to get a good night's sleep, asked if I wanted water.

Let me tell you, I fell right asleep. Like a weight was taken off my shoulders.

Here Officers Chuck Holt and Al DeCarlo used their insight, concern, and understanding to help a woman weather the immediate crisis in a long-standing problem. Given the woman's overwrought state, Officer Holt turned to her former husband for factual background on the problem. Officer DeCarlo began allaying her fear by pointing out that the childishness of the threatening note made it similar to notes in Batman comic books. To address the root of the problem, the officers showed the threatening note to the neighbor she suspected of writing it. To minimize the likelihood of a blowup, they advised both the woman and her ex-husband to stay clear of the neighbor and to call the police immediately if they needed help. Relieved by this concern for her well-being, the woman decided that she could rely on the police another time. Her summary of her reassuring treatment suggests that in previous encounters, though not necessarily with police, she had felt treated like a nobody. "They made you feel as if . . . you were somebody."

All the evidence we have examined about the nature of police work shows that people want personal service. Precisely equal, businesslike treatment is not satisfying to people in distress. Consider the findings · discussed in Chapter 3, that people get more satisfaction from reassurance than from officers' task accomplishment. The national trends of reduced political interference and increased professional commitment by officers help prepare them to make sound judgments. Today's police managers aim to motivate officers to tailor their responses to the particular needs and concerns of the citizens served and to support them when they do.

Structures to Increase Fairness

As we have seen throughout this book, when citizens turn to the police, they want attention to their particular concerns, not mere routine treatment. In their absorption with their personal distress, they are unlikely to consider whether the services they desire are unfair favors not provided to all. Officers have the dual responsibility to tailor their actions to the particular circumstances and yet to maintain evenhandedness overall. When officers have developed the personal courage O'Connor described, they are striving toward the goal of fairness.

A future is possible in which supervision appropriate to professionals and review by peers will enable officers to fine-tune their judgment to consistency with departmental standards and the practice of their colleagues. Years will be required to complete the transition from a crude standard of fairness based on adherence to procedures to a refined standard based on the thoughtful judgment of officers with a professional perspective. Essential to this transition are structures that permit and encourage officers to relate directly to the citizens of the neighborhood and to one another. This final section of the book points to structures at the department level and at the state level that can support the professional development of officers on the street, the development of officers who grow skilled in making instant decisions fairly. Here we conclude the discussion opened in Chapter 1 with the timetable of the two transitions in American policing and amplified in Chapter 4 through the discussion of the hospital model.

Department-level practices and structures supporting fairness can begin with a leadership that articulates a sense of mission. Police leaders with a sense of where the department should be going communicate it to members. Officers who are suffering from dealing with irreconcilable conflicts that frustrate fairness or who are depressed by viciousness they have just faced can draw some strength from the confidence that their department leaders understand the importance and difficulty of their work.

Fairness toward citizens is increased when departments upgrade their management practices to meet the standards of the Commission on Accreditation for Law Enforcement Agencies. Departments must set down in writing explicit policies in areas where old habits and individual preferences previously held sway. The lack of material incentives or sanctions in the accreditation process is a major reason why police accreditation had been achieved by only 143 agencies from 1983 through March 1990. By contrast, hospital accreditation established early in this century immediately permitted only accredited hospitals to enjoy the services of interns and residents. Since the establishment of Medicare and Medicaid in 1965, only accredited hospitals receive these payments.

Police supervisors may come to regard themselves as moral educators. When I asked Sam Griffith what important things he teaches his officers, this was his reply:

> I talk to officers about how to be manly. They need to learn to control their emotions, so I explain it this way. I say that it is manly as an officer to take an insult that you wouldn't stand for before you became an officer. A man who backed down from insults before he became an officer is probably not decisive enough to be a good officer. A man who fought rather than take an insult before, now needs to learn a new way to be manly.

Other skills and attitudes to be learned by young officers are curiosity, judgment of danger, a tragic perspective, and decisiveness. A next step is for supervisors and managers to puzzle out how to teach them. The argument of Donald Schon in *Educating the Reflective Practitioner* (1986) is that teaching professional judgment and artistry are similar across professions as different as architecture, music, and psychiatry. In the future, police supervisors may apply themselves to teaching young men and women how to see situations with the eyes of a professional officer.

Collegial consultation is critically important to facilitating officers' development of common understandings of fairness, and yet it is extremely limited in practice. A visit to a department's roll call will show whether officers are seated around a conference table to discuss the current situation on the street or whether they stand at attention so that the sergeant can inspect the shine of their shoes. It is unusual for a department to set aside any time other than the few minutes of roll call for patrol officers to confer. Hence, consultation across the three shifts of patrol is particularly spotty. Consultation across unit boundaries is also rare. For example, hardly ever do police officers, investigators, and youth service officers confer when they are all concerned with the crimes committed by a pair of young purse snatchers. In some departments a young officer may not easily find an experienced officer or a sergeant with whom to discuss ethical quandaries. Formal peer review is not practiced. At present, much informal collegial consultation takes place quietly, out of earshot of bosses who would punish and of locker room critics who would sneer.

Listening to the many voices of the community is essential for police officers and police managers in their striving for fairness. Police departments need structures that can encourage officers to be more attentive to the diversity of views in a neighborhood. This geographic level for coordination and accountability is below the department level. Experiments with modes of listening to citizens, such as team policing, community boards, "cop of the block," and community organizing, are not well developed.

Problem-oriented policing is the most promising current method for increasing fairness in both enforcement and service. When conflicting interests are clearly articulated in the analysis of a problem, a more balanced view can emerge of what is fair to all concerned. When new policies are discussed, debated, and analyzed before adoption, those who are affected by the policy will have opportunity to learn what the policy is— no mean achievement in the police field, where unwritten, informal practices are the effective policy. When the problem-oriented approach leads to the implementation of new policies, officers will see the limits on their use of discretion. When problem-oriented policing is working well, the huge divergence in officers' individual approaches will be reduced; individual approaches in conflict with department policy will eventually be eliminated; the values underlying policy decisions will be clarified (Goldstein 1990, 40–41, 152–54). At neighborhood and city levels, challenging agendas lie ahead.

The most crucial state-level actions to promote fairness in policing are to set appropriate criteria for admission to practice. The timetable of

Chapter 1 noted that mandatory training began in Cincinnati in 1888, within forty-three years of the establishment of the first American police department, in New York City. However, the first states to make training mandatory, New York and California, did so only in 1959. The state mandate did change practices in Troy, but in the vast majority of departments, officers were already receiving some preservice training.

Organizations staffed by professionals generally do not bear the cost of the professional training but place that burden upon the individual and, in the case of medicine, government subsidy. The recognized professions, from accounting to veterinary medicine, require the aspiring individual to invest years in professional training at universities. However, police departments are so accustomed to training their own that they tend to ignore whether new officers come with only a high school education or with a college degree by putting them all through the same preservice training and then assigning them to the same work situations.

Although Berkeley introduced college education to policing in the 1910s, a bachelor's degree as a prerequisite was first set by Multnomah County, Oregon, in 1964. Large departments following suit include Nassau and Suffolk counties in New York and Lakewood, Colorado. That these four departments are suburban does not mean that a better-trained mind is required to penetrate suburban problems—far from it. Rather, suburbs can more likely afford the salaries that attract college graduates. The practical ways for a department to reallocate its budget to accommodate higher salaries are, first, to replace officers in support positions with nonsworn personnel; and second, to cut the number of officers providing direct service, because a few motivated officers will outperform many lethargic ones.

Psychological assessments of new officers were mandated by the Commission on Accreditation more than sixty years after they were tried in Berkeley. National data from an IACP and Police Foundation study (Eisenberg, Kent, and Wall 1973) showed that only 167 of the 375 municipal departments employing at least fifty officers used an assessment by a psychologist or a psychiatrist. The time is ripe for states to require these assessments.

States generally have removed the inappropriate barriers that prevented those of short stature, those with less than 20-20 vision, and women from becoming officers. The new view of the police job recognizes that physical size, keenest vision, and upper body strength are useful but not of paramount importance. Acceptance of women as street officers is proceeding more slowly than acceptance of black men as officers. One explanation is that as white Americans reduce their general prejudice against blacks, black men are coming to be viewed as capable officers. The present degree of acceptance results more from the changing views of black people than from changed notions of police work.

Women, on the contrary, will be more fully accepted as capable officers when Americans go beyond their understanding that police officers need decisiveness and emotional self-control—characteristics traditionally considered masculine—to see that they also need skill in judging character, persuasiveness, tact, and compassion, characteristics traditionally considered feminine. A theme of the hospital model for policing is that essential skills and attributes include an ability to think clearly; a tolerance and understanding of differences between cultures; personal values supporting the controls on police practice; a moral calm in making difficult decisions, including the decision to use coercion; and firm control of one's own emotions. Each new officer should already possess or have a high potential for developing these qualities.

Dismissal of unfit individuals has long been made difficult by state laws, state and city civil service commissions, and unions authorized by states as bargaining agents for officers. Even during the early months, when dismissal power lies entirely within the department, academy trainees rarely flunk out, and rookie officers whose actions are grossly unfair are seldom advised to find another career. This legacy of the era when police jobs were patronage appointments is understandably slow to change. One of the reasons for reluctance to terminate marginal performers is the sizable financial investment a city has in each individual by the end of the probation period, conservatively estimated at an average of $30,000. Nevertheless, some states have established review procedures to bar from practice, in any department, officers who have shown themselves clearly unfit. The standards range from the Texas requirement of a felony conviction for decertification to the Florida requirement of a demonstration of gross incompetence or the practice of willful harm.

Taken as a whole, police decisions in America appear to be fairer today than they ever were. Increased fairness contributes in no small part to the overall quality of police service. However, departments still exist in which much work is needed to bring up the level of fairness. The importance of the Troy experience is that a police manager who has clear ideas about where policing ought to be going undertook a dozen years of work with a department that was far behind the times. That department has grown into an organization that supports the professional commitment of officers. These changes occurred in a city not conducive to change and in a department where managerial choice was limited by tight city budgets, constricting clauses in the police union contract, and a rigid civil service commission. The evolution toward a hospital model in this one city reveals the fundamental issues of police upgrading that will be with us well into the twenty-first century.

Appendix,
Bibliography,
and Indexes

Appendix:
Some Worthwhile
Questions

Anyone who wonders "How good is this police department?" can learn a great deal by asking specific questions based on the commonsense understanding that police departments exist to serve the public. The list below presents questions to highlight each chapter's inquiry into the redesign of the police organization to improve the quality of service. In a sense, the questions are a summary of the main points of the book because they are meant to carry the argument beyond the case study to every corner of the American police scene. They inquire both about performance and about management practices to support excellence in performance.

Many of the questions are easier to ask than to answer. In general, asking the people who are directly affected is a sound approach. The wide variety of citizens who interact with police officers as well as officers themselves can provide insights into the quality of police services. The inquirer should attempt to verify the information received by using more than one source. A practical difficulty for any outsider in understanding a poorly managed department lies in finding thoughtful officers who are willing to risk being frank. Police department policies may be so unrealistic that officers contravene them in order to do their work, yet they risk reprimands if they acknowledge such practices.

This list contains only a fraction of the tough questions worth asking. Nevertheless, if "Yes," "To a great extent," and "Many" are the answers to most of these questions, then the department under scrutiny is meeting high standards. If the answer to a particular question is negative, exploring the full circumstances may help determine in what ways, if any, the current condition is unsatisfactory.

Chapter 1. Two Transformations in Police Upgrading

The Transformation to Professional Administration
1. Do police officers obey the law?
   A. Do officers safeguard the rights of people they arrest?
   B. Does the department have the reputation of being free of graft?
2. To what extent do police officers act impartially and courteously?
   A. What proportion of citizens stopped by police officers understand why they were stopped and consider the officers justified?
   B. What proportion of citizens who receive police service praise the courtesy of officers?
3. To what extent do performance statistics show high productivity?
   A. Is the department making arrests for certain serious crimes at rates as high as should be expected?
   B. Does the department use traffic enforcement to reduce accidents?

The Transformation to Professional Officers

4. To what extent do police officers use discretion to help people solve their problems?

    A. Do officers tailor their solutions to the nature of the problems?

    B. Do officers use explanations with citizens much more often than they use commands and threats?

5. To what extent is the department managed to support wise use of discretion?

    A. Does the department encourage officers to take as long as necessary to handle incidents well?

    B. Do police supervisors and commanders use explanation with police officers much more often than they use commands and threats?

6. To what extent does the department inform the public?

    A. Do members throughout the department take initiative in educating the public on what they are doing and why?

    B. Do department members provide helpful answers to citizens' questions?

Chapter 2. Overcoming Inertia

1. Does the city executive either work with the head of the police department or remove him, but not attempt to work around him?

2. To what extent does the department head have authority over hiring, transfers, promotions, and dismissals?

3. Is the head of the police department held accountable through a fixed-term, renewable contract?

4. If the decision is to look outside the department for a head, does the city hold an open, national competition?

Chapter 3. Patrol Officers: General Practitioners Who Make House Calls

Skills That May Enhance Wise Use of Discretion

1. Do officers generally develop a keen curiosity about individuals and patterns of behavior?

2. Do officers generally develop correct judgments of danger?

3. Do officers generally develop a compassionate understanding of the people they serve, a tragic perspective on life?

4. Do officers generally develop decisiveness and come to terms with the necessity to use coercion?

5. Do officers generally have firm control over their emotions?

Outcomes as Viewed by Citizens

6. To what extent do people who seek police assistance feel that officers are concerned about their problems?

7. To what extent do citizens feel calmed after receiving police service?

Outcomes Measured by Departmental Statistics

8. Has overall response time been discarded as a measurement of patrol performance?

9. Are the department's trends in the annual volume of calls for service and dispatches appropriate to the city's societal conditions?

Chapter 4. The Hospital Model

1. To what extent does the department employ a diverse group of talented individuals?
2. To what extent is the work of the department structured to encourage each officer to hold himself or herself accountable for the quality of service to the citizens?
3. To what extent are the support systems well managed? For example, are the patrol cars maintained in good operating condition?
4. Do supervisors treat poor decisions as correctable mistakes?
5. To what extent does the department promote the professional growth of the members?
6. To what extent does the department inform and involve the public in police activities?
7. To what extent does the department employ problem-oriented policing?

Chapter 5. Arrests

1. Is the department vigilant to prevent illegal arrests?
2. Do officers assure the physical safety of everyone they arrest?
3. Is the department making arrests for each type of serious crime at rates per 100,000 population that are as high as should be expected?
   A. Has the rate risen to the national average for cities of this size?
   B. Does consideration of criminological factors suggest that deviation from the national average is appropriate in this city?
4. To what extent are arrests for serious crimes, such as robbery and burglary, resulting in convictions?
5. Is the rate of arresting citizens for all types of disorderly behavior below the national average for cities of that size? Has the rate been declining as fast as the national rate?

Chapter 6. Solving Crime Problems

Working with Potential and Actual Youth Offenders

1. To what extent do patrol officers know the kids making trouble in their zone and know who has a steadying influence on them?
2. To what extent do officers throughout the patrol division and the youth unit make individually tailored efforts to guide youths away from criminal behavior?

Working to Reduce the Access of Potential Offenders

3. To what extent do officers conduct field interviews and use the information?
4. To what extent does the department respond creatively and energetically to crime problems as they emerge?

Working with Potential Victims

    5. Does the department advise every burglary victim of techniques to decrease the likelihood of a recurrence?

    6. To what extent does the department promote protective neighboring through programs such as neighborhood associations, cop of the block, and neighborhood watch and through the efforts of individual officers?

    7. Does the department have an increasing or a high level of calls which could prevent crimes: e.g., concerning suspicious circumstances?

Working with Individual Victims

    8. Does the department leadership promote a victim assistance program, and to what extent do officers cooperate with it?

    9. To what extent do victims of crimes feel comforted by officers?

Chapter 7. From Fear of Crime to Sense of Safety

    1. To what extent does the department distinguish between crime problems and fear of crime?

    2. To what extent does the department use a problem-solving approach to assess the causes of citizens' fears?

    3. To what extent do officers in their daily encounters avoid promoting fear and a fortress mentality but instead focus on building a realistic sense of safety?

    4. To what extent does the department support or sponsor community programs that promote protective neighboring?

Chapter 8. Police Malpractice

Officers' High Standards

    1. To what extent do officers express distaste or lack of interest when fellow officers brag about their successes in assaulting, harassing, or belittling citizens?

    2. When an officer is baiting a citizen, to what extent do fellow officers step in to end such treatment?

    3. How seriously do supervisors treat the tendency of an officer to be quick to resort to force?

    4. When officers are formally questioned about the conduct of fellow officers, do they refuse to lie?

Discovery and Correction of Malpractice

    5. Is there an easy system enabling citizens to make a complaint and know the outcome?

    6. Is there a professional standards unit, and does it conduct thorough and fair investigations?

    7. When a department dismisses an officer for malpractice, do the courts and the civil service agency confirm the dismissal?

Rates of Police Actions that Have High Potential for Abuse of Power
8. Is the rate at which citizens are killed by officers or struck by police bullets low compared to the rates for other cities?
9. Is the rate of arrest for interfering with an officer declining or low?

Policies to Reduce the Likelihood of Abuse of Power
10. Does the department have policies meeting the Accreditation Commission standards for situations involving serious "excessive force hazards," such as firearms, injury, high-speed pursuit?
11. Does the department organize the work so that individuals and units rarely specialize in the application of physical force?

Chapter 9. Union Power
1. Are retirees excluded from voting?
2. Are command personnel excluded from the union that represents the police officer rank?
3. To what extent do union members judge that union leaders represent their interests?
4. To what extent do union and management representatives confer to solve problems at the levels where they arise?

Chapter 10. Political Accountability versus Political Interference

Avenues of Accountability
1. Does the police executive have both responsibility for the quality of service and authority over personnel decisions?
2. To what extent does discussion of priorities for the police department inform the selection of the police executive?
3. Does the police executive manage the department budget, effecting savings in some areas and spending more in others?
4. To what extent do candidates for office refrain from promising quick solutions to long-term problems and instead engage in informed discussion of police issues?

Distinguishing Accountability from Interference
5. Do orders from the city leadership not compel acts that are illegal?
6. Do orders from the city leadership specify the problems and set priorities rather than select the solutions?

Chapter 11. Building Bridges between Police and Public

Peaceful Use of the Streets
1. Does the city government have a simple system that allows citizens to get permits to use the streets for special political, social, and cultural events?
2. Do officers protect people in crowds and (when necessary) disperse crowds peacefully?

Provision of Multiple Services

3. To what extent does the department wholeheartedly provide a broad range of services?
4. To what extent does the department treat problems as serious on the basis of the harm they cause, rather than in terms of whether or not they are crimes?

Community-Based Policing

5. Does the department reject thoughtless application of community relations techniques such as storefronts staffed by officers, foot posts in residential areas, and mandatory park-and-walk programs?
6. To what extent do people know officers who serve their neighborhood?
7. To what extent does the department keep officers informed on policy matters and place no obstacles in the way of individuals who want to speak out?
8. To what extent do individual officers and the departmental leaders engage citizens in discussion of how to solve community problems?
9. To what extent does the department involve local citizens in the solution of problems?

Chapter 12. Fairness

Enforcement

1. To what extent does the department have a reputation for fairness in stopping drivers and pedestrians? in making arrests? in using force?
2. Are traffic laws and ordinances enforced against prominent people and the sons of police officers in the same way as against other citizens?
3. Does the department work with standards for releasing arrestees on their own recognizance, which results in the release of most prisoners?
   If the court has not authorized such a program, does the department work to obtain one?
4. To what extent do officers working in a neighborhood apply consistent standards of enforcement from one day to the next in dealing with kids hanging out on the corner, speeding and dangerous driving, noise complaints, and the like?

Service

5. Does the department allocate more resources to services especially needed by socially disadvantaged people and fewer resources to services especially used by people who can afford to purchase private services?
   E.g., robbery: It investigates every purse snatching but does not provide merchants with escort service to the bank.
   E.g., fraud: It vigorously investigates flimflam operations, such as tricking elderly people out of their life savings, but does not trace customers who have not paid their bills.
   E.g., household burglary: It does not base the decision for follow-up investigation solely on the dollar value of the possessions taken.
6. Do people who live in poor neighborhoods or in public housing consider

that the service to their neighborhood is as good as that given to other neighborhoods?

7. Do people who belong to socially disadvantaged groups consider that the crimes against them are investigated with the same vigor as the crimes against everyone else?

8. Do people who belong to socially disadvantaged groups consider themselves treated with as much courtesy and concern as everyone else?

Bibliography

Chapter 1. Two Transformations in Police Upgrading

A T and T (American Telephone and Telegraph). 1983. *Events in Telecommunications History*. New York: A T and T.

Bittner, Egon. 1970. *The Function of Police in Modern Society: A Review of Background Factors, Current Practices, and Possible Role Models*. U.S. DHEW Publication 73-9072. Chevy Chase, Md.: National Institute of Mental Health.

Block, Peter, and David Specht. 1973. *Neighborhood Team Policing*. Washington, D.C.: Law Enforcement Assistance Administration.

Blum, Richard H., ed. 1964. *Police Selection*. Springfield, Ill.: Charles C. Thomas.

Brewer, Jesse A. (Assistant Chief, Los Angeles). 1988. Letter to the author, 31 Aug.

CALEA (Commission on Accreditation for Law Enforcement Agencies). 1985. *Law Enforcement Agency Accreditation to 1985*. Fairfax, Va: Commision on Accreditation for Law Enforcement Agencies.

Carte, Gene E. and Elaine H. Carte. 1975. *Police Reform in the United States: The Case of August Vollmer*. Berkeley: University of California Press.

Clark, Donald E., and Samuel G. Chapman, 1966. *A Step Forward: Educational Backgrounds For Policemen*. Springfield, Ill.: Charles C. Thomas.

Deakin, Thomas J. 1988. *Police Professionalism: The Renaissance of American Law Enforcement*. Springfield, Ill.: Charles C. Thomas.

FBI. *See* U.S. Department of Justice.

Fosdick, Raymond B. 1920. *American Police Systems*. New York: Century.

Goldstein, Herman. 1977. *Policing a Free Society*. Cambridge, Mass.: Ballinger.

———. 1979. "Improving Policing: A Problem-Oriented Approach." *Crime and Delinquency* 25:236–58.

———. 1990. *Problem-Oriented Policing*. Philadelphia: Temple University Press.

Greenberg, Bernard. 1972–73. *Enhancement of the Investigative Function*. Vols. 1–2. Menlo Park, Calif.: Stanford Research Institute.

Lawrence, Neil, Paul McIver, John Henderson, and Norm Croker. 1989. *Tribute: A Day on the Beat with America's Finest*. Washington, D.C.: Police Executive Research Forum and Tribute Book.

Milton, Catherine. 1972. *Women in Policing*. Washington, D.C.: Police Foundation.

Monkkonen, Eric H. 1981. *Police in Urban America: 1860–1920*. Cambridge, University Press.

Muir, William Ker, Jr. 1977. *Police: Streetcorner Politicians*. Chicago: University of Chicago Press.

O'Connor, George W. 1957. "Vollmer Memorial Scholarship Fund." *California Peace Officer* 7, no. 3: 33–34.

———. 1962. "Survey of Selection Methods." *Police Chief*, Oct.–Dec.

Ostrom, Elinor, Roger B. Parks, and Gordon P. Whitaker. 1978. *Patterns of Metropolitan Policing*. Cambridge, Mass.: Ballinger.

Owen, Sharon (Management Analyst, Sheriff's Office, Multnomah, Ore.). 1988. Letter to the author, 10 Aug.

Parker, Alfred E. 1972. *The Berkeley Police Story*. Springfield, Ill.: Charles C. Thomas.

Reppetto, Thomas A. 1978. *The Blue Parade*. New York: Free Press.

U.S. Department of Justice, Federal Bureau of Investigation, and IACP (International Association of Chiefs of Police). 1930. *Uniform Crime Reports*, vol. 1, no. 1.

U.S. President's Commission on Law Enforcement and Administration of Justice. 1967a. *The Challenge of Crime in a Free Society*. Washington, D.C.: Government Printing Office.

————. 1967b. *Task Force Report: The Police*. Washington, D.C.: Government Printing Office.

Vollmer, August. 1971. *The Police and Modern Society*. (1936; rpt.) Montclair, N.J.: Patterson Smith.

Vollmer, August, and Albert Schneider. 1917. "The School for Police as Planned at Berkeley." *Journal of the American Institute of Criminal Law and Criminology* 7:877–96.

Walker, Samuel. 1977. *A Critical History of Police Reform: The Emergence of Professionalism*. Lexington, Mass.: D. C. Heath, Lexington Books.

Wilson, James Q. 1968. *Varieties of Police Behavior: The Management of Law and Order in Eight Communities*. Cambridge, Mass.: Harvard University Press.

Wilson, O. W. 1942. *Police Records*. Chicago: Public Administration Service.

Wilson, O. W., and Roy C. McLaren. 1972. *Police Administration*. 3d ed. New York: McGraw-Hill.

Chapter 2. Overcoming Inertia

Baker, Mark. 1985. *Cops: Their Lives in Their Own Words*. New York: Simon & Schuster.

Black, Donald. 1980. *The Manners and Customs of the Police*. New York: Academic Press.

Bouza, Anthony V. 1990. *The Police Mystique: An Insider's Look at Cops, Crime, and the Criminal Justice System*. New York: Plenum.

Cresap, McCormick, and Paget, Inc. 1972. *City of Troy, New York: A Management Study of the Bureau of Police*. Vols 1 and 2. Washington, D.C.: Cresap, McCormick, and Paget.

Eisenberg, Terry, Deborah Ann Kent, and Charles R. Wall. 1973. *Police Personnel Practices in State and Local Governments*. Washington, D.C.: International Association of Chiefs of Police and Police Foundation.

Goldstein, Herman. 1977. *Policing a Free Society*. Cambridge, Mass.: Ballinger.

Greisinger, George W., Jeffrey S. Slovak, and Joseph J. Molkup. 1979. *Civil Service Systems: Their Impact on Police Administration*. 1979-331-379/1685 Washington, D.C.: Government Printing Office.

Guyot, Dorothy, and Kai Martensen. 1991. "The Governmental Setting." In *Local Government Police Management*, ed. William Geller. Washington, D.C.: International City Management Association.

IACP (International Association of Chiefs of Police). 1976. *The Police Chief Executive Report*. Washington, D.C.: Government Printing Office.

Kelly, Michael J. 1975. *Police Chief Selection: A Handbook for Local Government*. Washington, D.C.: Police Foundation and International City Management Association.

Manning, Peter K. 1977. *Police Work: The Social Organization of Policing*. Cambridge, Mass.: MIT Press.

Manning, Peter K., and John Van Maanen, eds. 1978. *Policing: A View from the Street*. Santa Monica, Calif.: Goodyear.

National Civil Service League. 1970. *A Model Public Personnel Administration Law*. Chevy Chase, Md.: National Civil Service League.

O'Connor, George W. 1977. "Providing a Professional Police Service." *Law Enforcement News* 3 (6 December): 10–11.

Ostrom, Elinor, Roger B. Parks, and Gordon P. Whitaker. 1978. *Patterns of Metropolitan Policing*. Cambridge, Mass.: Ballinger.

PERF (Police Executive Research Forum). 1980. "Elements of an Employment Agreement for Police Chief Executives." Washington, D.C.: Police Executive Research Forum.

Punch, Maurice. 1983. "Officers and Men: Occupational Culture, Inter-Rank Antagonism, and the Investigation of Corruption." In *Control in the Police Organization*, ed. Maurice Punch, 227–50. Cambridge, Mass.: MIT Press.

Reuss-Ianni, Elizabeth. 1983. *Two Cultures of Policing: Street Cops and Management Cops*. New Brunswick, N.J.: Transaction Books.

Rubinstein, Jonathan. 1973. *City Police*. New York: Farrar Straus, & Giroux.

Van Maanen, John. 1974. "Working the Street: A Developmental View of Police Bahavior." In *The Potential for Reform of Criminal Justice*, ed. Herbert Jacob, 83–100. Beverly Hills, Calif.: Sage.

Vaughn, Jerry. 1989. *How to Rate Your Police Chief*. Washington, D.C.: Police Executive Research Forum.

Williams, Oliver. 1961. "A Typology for Comparative Local Government." *Midwest Journal of Politics* 5:150–64.

Witham, Donald C. 1984. *The American Law Enforcement Chief Executive: A Management Profile*. Washington, D.C.: Police Executive Research Forum.

Chapter 3. Patrol Officers: General Practitioners Who Make House Calls

ABA (American Bar Association). 1973. *Standards Relating to the Urban Police Function*. Chicago: American Bar Association.

Andrews, Allen H., Jr. 1985. "Structuring the Political Independence of the Police Chief." In *Police Leadership in America: Crisis and Opportunity*, ed. William Geller. New York: Praeger.

Antunes, George, and Eric J. Scott. 1981. "Calling the Cops: Police Telephone Operators and Citizens Calling for Service." *Journal of Criminal Justice* 9:165–79.

Bayley, David H. 1985. *Patterns of Policing: A Comparative International Analysis*. New Brunswick, N.J.: Rutgers University Press.

Bayley, David H., and James Garofalo. 1989. "The Management of Violence by Police Patrol Officers." *Criminology* 27:1–25.

Bennett, Richard R., ed. 1983. *Police at Work: Policy Issues and Analysis*. Perspectives in Criminal Justice 5. Beverly Hills, Calif.: Sage.

Bieck, William, William Spelman, and Thomas J. Sweeney. 1990. "The Patrol Function." In *Local Government Police Management*, ed. William Geller. Washington, D.C.: International City Management Association.

Bittner, Egon. 1974. "Florence Nightingale in Pursuit of Willie Sutton: A Theory of Police." In *The Potential for Reform of Criminal Justice*, ed. Herbert Jacob, 17–44. Sage Criminal Justice Annuals, vol. 3. Beverly Hills, Calif.: Sage.

Brown, Michael K. 1981. *Working the Street: Police Discretion and the Dilemmas of Reform*. New York: Russell Sage Foundation.

Cunniff, Mark A. 1983. *Beyond Crime: Law Enforcement Operational and Cost Data*. Statistical Series Project Report 1. Washington, D.C.: Bureau of Justice Statistics.

Farmer, Michael T., ed. 1981. *Differential Police Response Strategies*. Washington, D.C.: Police Executive Research Forum.

Force, Robert. 1972. "Decriminalization of Breach of the Peace Statutes: A Nonpenal Approach to Order Maintenance." *Tulane Law Review* 46:367–493.

Fyfe, James J., ed. 1981. *Contemporary Issues in Law Enforcement*. Sage Research Progress Series in Criminology, vol. 20. Beverly Hills, Calif.: Sage.

Goldstein, Herman. 1979. "Improving Policing: A Problem-Oriented Approach." *Crime and Delinquency* 25:236–58.

Griffiths, Derek. P. 1983. "The Police Sergeant—Gatekeeper Extraordinary." Paper presented to the American Society of Criminology, Denver, 10 Nov.

Kansas City Police Department. 1977. *Response Time Analysis*. Vols. 1 and 2. Kansas City, Mo.: Police Department.

Klockars, Carl B. 1985. *The Idea of Police*. Law and Criminal Justice Series, vol. 3. Beverly Hills, Calif.: Sage.

McEwen, J. Thomas, Edward F. Connors III, and Marcia I. Cohen. 1984. *Evaluation of the Differential Police Response Field Test*. Alexandria, Va.: Research Management Associates.

Martin, Susan Ehrlich. 1980. *Breaking and Entering: Police Women on Patrol*. Berkeley: University of California Press.

Mastrofski, Stephen. 1983. "The Police and Non-Crime Services." In *Measuring Performance of Criminal Justice Agencies*, ed. Gordon P. Whitaker and Charles David Phillips. Sage Criminal Justice Annals 18. Beverly Hills, Calif.: Sage.

Mastrofski, Stephen, and Roger B. Parks. 1990. "Improving Explanatory Studies of Police Behavior." *Criminology* 28:475–96.

Mastrofski, Stephen D., R. Richard Ritti, and Debra Hoffmaster. 1987. "Organizational Determinants of Police Discretion: The Case of Drinking-Driving." *Journal of Criminal Justice* 15, no. 5: 387–402.

Muir, William Ker. 1977. *Police: Streetcorner Politicians*. Chicago: University of Chicago Press.

Parks, Roger B. 1982. "Citizen Surveys for Police Performance Assessment: Some Issues in Their Use." *Urban Interest* 4:17–26.

Percy, Stephen L., and Eric J. Scott. 1985. *Demand Processing and Performance in Public Service Agencies*. Tuscaloosa: University of Alabama Press.

Reiss, Albert J., Jr. 1971. *The Police and the Public*. New Haven, Conn.: Yale University Press.

Sherman, Lawrence W. 1987. *Repeat Calls to the Police in Minneapolis*. Washington, D.C.: Crime Control Institute.

Skolnick, Jerome H. 1966. *Justice without Trial: Law Enforcement in a Democratic Society*. New York: Wiley.

Spelman, William, and Dale K. Brown. 1984. *Calling the Police: Citizen Reporting of Serious Crime*. Washington, D.C.: Government Printing Office.

Sykes, Richard E., and Edward E. Brent. 1983. *Policing: A Social Behaviorist Perspective*. New Brunswick, N.J.: Rutgers University Press.

U.S. President's Commission on Law Enforcement and the Administration of Justice. 1967. *The Challenge of Crime in a Free Society*. Washington, D.C.: Government Printing Office.

Whitaker, Gordon P., ed. 1984. *Understanding Police Agency Performance*. Washington, D.C.: National Institute of Justice.

Whitaker, Gordon P., Stephen Mastrofski, Elinor Ostrom, Roger B. Parks, and Stephen L. Percy. 1982. *Basic Issues in Police Performance*. Washington, D.C.: National Institute of Justice.

Wycoff, Mary Ann. 1982. "Improving Police Performance Measurement: One More Voice." *Urban Interest*, 4:8–16.

Chapter 4. The Hospital Model

Aaronson, David E., C. Thomas Dienes, and Michael C. Musheno. 1984. *Public Policy and Police Discretion*. New York: Clark Boardman.

ABA (American Bar Association). 1973. *Standards Relating to the Urban Police Function*. Chicago: American Bar Association.

AMA (American Medical Association). 1988. *Physician Characteristics and Distribution in the United States*. 1987 ed. Chicago: American Medical Association.

Angell, John E. 1971. "Toward an Alternative to the Classic Police Organizational Arrangements: A Democratic Model." Pts. 1 and 2. *Criminology* 9 (Aug., Nov.):185–206.

Baer, William J. 1976. *Police Personnel Exchange Programs: The Bay Area Experience*. Washington, D.C.: Police Foundation.

Bayley, David H. 1985. *Patterns of Policing: Comparative International Analysis*. New Brunswick, N.J.: Rutgers University Press.

Bittner, Egon. 1983. "Legality and Workmanship: Introduction to Control in the Police Organization." In *Control in the Police Organization*, ed. Maurice Punch, 1–11. Cambridge, Mass.: MIT Press.

Boydstun, John E., Michael E. Sherry, and Nicholas P. Moelter. 1977. *Patrol Staffing in San Diego: One or Two Officer Units*. Washington, D.C.: Police Foundation.

Bureau of Justice Statistics. *See* U.S. Department of Justice.

CALEA (Commission on Accreditation for Law Enforcement Agencies). 1983. *Standards for Law Enforcement Agencies*. Fairfax, Va.: Commission on Accreditation for Law Enforcement Agencies.

———. 1990. *Commission Update* 43 (March): 1.

Carter, David L., Allen D. Sapp, and Darrel W. Stephens. 1989. *The State of Police Education: Policy Directions for the 21st Century*. Washington, D.C.: Police Executive Research Forum.

Cresap, McCormick, and Paget, Inc. 1972. *City of Troy, New York: A Management Study of the Bureau of Police*. Vols. 1 and 2. Washington, D.C.: Cresap, McCormick, and Paget.

Eck, John E., and William Spelman. 1987. "Who Ya Gonna Call? The Police as Problem Busters." *Crime and Delinquency* 33:31–52.

Eck, John E., William Spelman, Diane Hill, Darrel W. Stephens, John R. Stedman, and Gerard R. Murphy. 1987. *Problem-Solving: Problem Oriented Policing in Newport News*. Washington, D.C.: Police Executive Research Forum.

Fields, Kenneth, Betty Lipskin, and Marc Reich. 1975. *Assessment of Professionals in the Forensic Science Field*. Washington, D.C.: Forensic Science Foundation.

Flanagan, Timothy J., and Katherine M. Jamieson, eds. 1988. *Sourcebook of Criminal Justice Statistics—1987* Washington, D.C.: Bureau of Justice Statistics.

Friedrich, Robert. 1977. "The Impact of Organizational, Individual, and Situational Factors in the Behavior of Policemen." Ph.D. diss, University of Michigan.

Goldstein, Herman. 1979. "Improving Policing: A Problem-Oriented Approach." *Crime and Delinquency* 25:236–58.

———. *Problem-Oriented Policing*. 1990. Philadelphia: Temple University Press.

Guyot, Dorothy. 1977a. "the Organization of Police Departments: Changing the Model from the Army to the Hospital." *Criminal Justice Abstracts* 9:231–56.

———. 1977b. "Planning Begins with Problem Identification." *Journal of Police Science and Administration* 5:324–36.

———. 1985. "Building Bridges between Police and Public." *FBI Law Enforcement Bulletin* 54, no. 11: 1–8.

Habenstein, Robert W. 1970. "Occupational Uptake: Professionalizing." In *Pathways to Data*, ed. Robert W. Habenstein. Chicago: Aldine.

Hobson, David. 1989. Telephone conversation with author, Lakewood, Colo., 14 Dec.

Kanter, Rosabeth Moss. 1983. *The Change Masters: Innovation for Productivity in the American Corporation*. New York: Simon & Schuster.

Kelling, George L., and Mark H. Moore. 1987. "From Political Reform to Community: The Evolving Strategy of Police." Working Paper 87-08, John F. Kennedy School of Government, Harvard University.

Lawrence, Michael D., John R. Snortum, and Franklin E. Zimring, eds. 1988. *Social Control of the Drinking Driver*. Chicago: University of Chicago Press.

Lawrence, Paul R., and Jay W. Lorsch. 1967. *Organization and Environment*. Cambridge, Mass.: Harvard University Press.

Leonard, V.A., and Harry W. More, Jr. 1975. *Police Organization and Management*. 5th ed. Mineola, N.Y.: Foundation Press.

Marder, William D., David W. Emmons, Phillip R. Kletke, and Richard J. Willke. 1988. "Physician Employment Patterns." *Health Affairs* 7:137–45.

Mastrofski, Stephen. 1986. "Police Agency Accreditation: The Prospects of Reform." *American Journal of Police* 5:45–81.

Meier, Robert D., Richard Farmer, and David Maxwell. 1987. "Pyschological Screening of Police Candidates: Current Perspectives." *Journal of Police Science and Administration* 15:210–15.

Mitler, Merrill M., Mary A. Carskadon, Charles A. Czeisler, William C. Dement, David F. Dinges, and R. Curtis Graeber. 1988. "Catastrophes, Sleep, and Public Policy: Consensus Report." *Sleep* 11:100–109.

Monk, Timothy. 1988. "Coping with the Stress of Shift Work." *Work and Stress* 2:169–72.

———. 1989a. "Human Factors Implications of Shiftwork." *International Review of Ergonomics* 2:111–28.

————. 1989b. "Social Factors Can Outweigh Biological Ones in Determining Night Shift Safety." *Human Factors* 31:721–24.

Naitoh, Paul. 1982. "Chronobiologic Approach for Optimizing Human Performance." In *Rhythmic Aspects of Behavior*, ed. Frederick M. Brown and R. Curtis Graeber, 41–103. Hillsdale, N.J.: Lawrence Erlbaum Associates.

Nardulli, Peter F., and Jeffrey M. Stonecash. 1981. *Politics, Professionalism, and Urban Services: The Police*. Cambridge, Mass.: Oelgeschlager, Gunn & Hain.

O'Connor, George W. 1973. "Memo to the City Manager." 17 Dec.

————. 1976. "Some Not So Random Thoughts on Police Improvement." (Available from Police Development Services, Inc., 1 Warren Ave., Troy, NY 12180.)

Ottmann, W., M. J. Karvonen, K.-H. Schmidt, P. Knauth, and J. Rutenfranz. 1989. "Subjective Health Status of Day and Shift-Working Policemen." *Ergonomics* 32:847–54.

Parsons, Talcott. 1968. "Professions." In *The International Encyclopedia of the Social Sciences*, 12:536–47. New York: Macmillan and Free Press.

PERF (Police Executive Research Forum). 1988. *Problem Solving Quarterly* 1.

Reaves, Brian. 1990. Letter to the author reporting unpublished data from Bureau of Justice Statistics program on Law Enforcement Management and Administration Statistics, 6 June.

Reppetto, Thomas A. 1979. "Bachelors on the Beat: Organizational Design of the Educated Police Department." *Journal of Police Science and Administration* 7:1–11.

Rice, Dorothy P., Ellen J. MacKenzie, et al. 1989. *Cost of Injury in the United States: A Report to Congress*. San Francisco: Institute for Health & Aging, University of California, and Injury Prevention Center, Johns Hopkins University.

Sherman, Lawrence W., and National Advisory Commission on Higher Education of Police Officers. 1978. *The Quality of Police Education*. San Francisco: Jossey-Bass.

Skolnick, Jerome H. 1988. "Community Policing: Issues and Practices around the World." Washington, D.C.: National Institute of Justice.

Skolnick, Jerome H., and David H. Bayley. 1986. *The New Blue Line: Police Innovation in Six American Cities*. New York: Free Press.

Smith, R. Dean. 1975. Interview with author, Gaithersburg, Md., 9 June.

Starr, Paul. 1982. *The Social Transformation of American Medicine*. New York: Basic Books.

Taft, Philip B., Jr. *Fighting Fear: The Baltimore Cope Project*. Washington, D.C.: Police Executive Research Forum, 1986.

Taylor, James C., and David G. Bowers. 1972. *The Survey of Organizations: A Machine Scored Standardized Questionnaire Instrument*. Ann Arbor: Institute for Social Research, University of Michigan.

Thompson, James D. 1967. *Organizations in Action*. New York: McGraw-Hill.

Troy Department of Public Safety. 1984. "Memorandum to Men and Women with a Need to Help."

Tumin, Zachary. 1986. "Community Based Policing: The Houston Experience." Working paper C87-01. John F. Kennedy School of Government, Harvard University.

U.S. Department of Justice, Bureau of Justice Statistics. 1989. *Profile of State and Local Law Enforcement Agencies, 1987*. Washington, D.C.: Government Printing Office.

Van Maanen, John. 1983. "The Boss: First-Line Supervision in an American Police Agency." In *Control in the Police Organization*, ed. Maurice Punch, 275–317. Cambridge, Mass.: MIT Press.

Wilensky, Harold. 1964. "The Professionalization of Everyone?" *American Journal of Sociology* 70:142–46.

Wycoff, Mary Ann. 1982. "Evaluation Report on Training for First Line Supervisors: A Program Conducted for the City of Minneapolis by the Police Foundation." Preliminary Report. December.

Chapter 5. Arrests

Black, Donald. 1976. *The Behavior of Law*. New York: Academic Press.

Brosi, Kathleen B. 1979. *A Cross-City Comparison of Felony Case Processing*. IN-SLAW study, (GPO 027-000-00808-9). Washington, D.C.: Law Enforcement Association Administration.

Bureau of Justice Statistics. *See* U.S. Department of Justice.

Burrows, John. 1986a. *Burglary: Police Actions and Victims' Views*. Home Office Research and Planning Unit Paper. London: Her Majesty's Stationery Office.

———. 1986b. *Investigating Burglary: The Measurement of Police Performance*. Home Office Research Study. London: Her Majesty's Stationery Office.

Chaiken, Jan, and Marcia Chaiken. 1982. *Varieties of Criminal Behavior*. Santa Monica, Calif.: RAND.

Clarke, Ronald V. G., and J. Michael Hough, eds. 1980. *The Effectiveness of Policing*. Westmead, Eng.: Gower.

———. 1984. *Crime and Police Effectiveness*. Home Office Research and Planning Unit Report. London: Her Majesty's Stationery Office.

Cohen, Lawrence, and David Cantor. 1981. "Residential Burglary in the United States: Life-Style and Demographic Factors Associated with the Probability of Victimization." *Journal of Research in Crime and Delinquency* 18:113–27.

Doleschal, Eugene. 1978. "Social Forces and Crime." *Criminal Justice Abstracts* 10: 395–410.

Eck, John E. 1983. *Solving Crimes: The Investigation of Burglary and Robbery*. Washington, D.C.: Police Executive Research Forum and National Institute of Justice.

Edgar, James M. 1977. "Information Model Policing—A Design for the Systematic Use of Criminal Intelligence in a Team Policing Operation." *Journal of Police Science and Administration* 5:272–84.

FBI. *See* U.S. Department of Justice.

Forst, Brian, Frank J. Leahy, Jr., Jean Shirhall, Herbert L. Tyson, and John Bartolomeo. 1982. *Arrest Convictability as a Measure of Police Performance*. INSLAW research. Washington, D.C.: U.S. Department of Justice. National Institute of Justice.

Forst, Brian, Judith Lucianovic, and Sarah J. Cox. 1977. *What Happens after Arrest*. Washington, D.C.: INSLAW.

Friedrich, Robert J. 1980. "Police Use of Force: Individuals, Situations, and Organizations" *Annals* 452 (November): 82–97.

Gay, William G., Thomas M. Beall, and Robert A. Bowers. 1984. *A Four-Site Assessment of the Integrated Criminal Apprehension Program.* Washington, D.C.: University City Science Center.

Gay, William G., and Robert A. Bowers. 1985. *Targeting Law Enforcement Resources: The Career Criminal Focus.* Washington, D.C.: National Institute of Justice.

Goldstein, Herman. 1990. *Problem-Oriented Policing.* Philadelphia: Temple University Press.

Goldstein, Herman, and Charles E. Susmilch. 1982. "The Drinking-Driver in Madison: A Study of the Problem and the Community's Response." Project on Development of a Problem-Oriented Approach to Improving Police Service, vol. 2, University of Wisconsin Law School. Photocopy.

Greenwood, Peter, and Allan Abrahamse. 1982. *Selective Incapacitation.* Santa Monica, Calif.: RAND.

Greenwood, Peter, Joan Petersilia, Jan Chaiken. 1975. *The Criminal Investigation Process.* 3 vols. Santa Monica, Calif.: RAND.

Guyot, Dorothy. 1979. "Bending Granite: Attempts to Change the Rank Structure of American Police Departments." *Journal of Police Science and Administration* 7:253–84 (based on a consultant's report to the Police Foundation). Reprinted in *Thinking about Police: Contemporary Readings,* ed. Carl B. Klockars, 400–22. New York: McGraw-Hill, 1983.

IACP (International Association of Chiefs of Police). 1976. *The IACP-UCR Audit/Evaluation Manual.* Gaithersburg, Md.: International Association of Chiefs of Police.

Jacob, Herbert. 1984. *The Frustration of Policy: Responses to Crime by American Cities.* Boston: Little, Brown.

Leahy, Frank. 1980. "A Report on Criminal Justice System Activities in Jefferson County, CO." INSLAW internal report.

Martin, Susan E., and Lawrence W. Sherman. 1986. *Catching Career Criminals: The Washington, DC, Repeat Offender Project.* Washington, D.C.: Police Foundation.

Morris, Norval, and Gordon Hawkins. 1970. *The Honest Politician's Guide to Crime Control.* Chicago: University of Chicago Press.

Nettler, Gwynn. 1984. *Explaining Crime.* 3d ed. New York: McGraw-Hill.

New York State Commission on Criminal Justice and the Use of Force. 1987. *Report to the Governor.* Vol. 1. Albany, N.Y.: Office of the Governor.

O'Connor, George W. 1976. "Allocation and Reorganization of Investigative Resources." (Available from Police Department Services, Inc., 1 Warren Avenue, Troy, NY 12180.)

Parks, Roger B. 1982. "Citizen Surveys for Police Performance Assessment: Some Issues in Their Use." *Urban Interest* 4:17–26.

PERF (Police Executive Research Forum). 1989. *Taking a Problem-Oriented Appraoch to Drug Enforcement.* Washington, D.C.: U.S. Department of Justice, Bureau of Justice Assistance.

Petersilia, Joan, Allan Abrahamse, and James Q. Wilson. 1987. *Police Performance and Case Attrition.* Santa Monica, Calif.: RAND.

Rubinstein, Jonathan. 1973. *City Police.* New York: Farrar, Straus, & Giroux.

Schneider, Anne L. 1976. "Victimization Surveys and Criminal Justice Evaluation."

In *Sample Surveys of Victims of Crime*, ed. Wesley Skogan. Cambridge, Mass.: Ballinger.

Sherman, Lawrence W., and Barry D. Glick. 1984. "The Quality of Police Arrest Statistics." Police Foundation Reports 2.

Skogan, Wesley G. 1975. "Measurement Problems in Official and Survey Crime Rates." *Journal of Criminal Justice* 3:17–32.

Skogan, Wesley G. 1985. "Making Better Use of Victims and Witnesses." In *Police Leadership in America: Crisis and Opportunity*, ed. William Geller. New York: Praeger.

Smith, Douglas A., and Christy A. Visher. 1981. "Street Level Justice: Situational Determinants of Police Arrest Decisions." *Social Problems* 29:167–77.

Spelman, William. 1987. *Beyond Bean Counting: New Approaches for Managing Crime Data*. Washington, D.C.: Police Executive Research Forum.

Sykes, Richard E., and Edward E. Brent. 1983. *Policing: A Social Behaviorist Perspective*. New Brunswick, N.J.: Rutgers University Press.

Sykes, Richard E., James C. Fox, and John P. Clark. 1976. "A Socio-Legal Theory of Police Discretion." In *The Ambivalent Force*, 2d ed., Arthur Niederhoffer and Abraham Blumberg, 171–83. Hinsdale, Ill.: Dryden Press.

U.S. Department of Health and Human Services, Office of the Surgeon General. 1989. *Surgeon General's Workshop on Drunk Driving: Proceedings*. Washington, D.C.: Government Printing Office.

U.S. Department of Justice, Bureau of Justice Statistics. 1985a. *Criminal Victimization of District of Columbia Residents and Capitol Hill Employees*. NCJ-97982. Washington, D.C.: Government Printing Office.

———. 1985b. *Data Quality of Criminal History Records*. NCJ-98079. Washington, D.C.: Government Printing Office.

———. 1985c. *The National Survey of Crime Severity*. NCJ-9601. Washington, D.C.: Government Printing Office.

———. 1987a. *Criminal Victimization in the United States, 1985*. Washington, D.C.: Government Printing Office.

———. 1987b. *Jail Inmates, 1985*. Washington: Government Printing Office.

———. 1987c. *Prisoners in 1986*. NCJ 104864. Washington: Government Printing Office.

———. 1990. *Criminal Victimization in the United States, 1988*. Washington, D.C.: Government Printing Office.

U.S. Department of Justice, Federal Bureau of Investigation. 1986. *Uniform Crime Reports: Crime in the United States, 1985*. Washington, D.C.: Government Printing Office.

U.S. Department of Justice, National Institute of Justice. 1982. *The Effects of the Exclusionary Rule: A Study in California*. Criminal Justice Research Report Series. Washington, D.C.: Government Printing Office.

U.S. President's Task Force on Victims of Crime: 1982. *Final Report*. Washington, D.C.: Government Printing Office.

Waller, Irvin, and Norman Okihiro. 1978. *Burglary: The Victim and the Public*. Toronto: University of Toronto Press.

Wilson, James Q., and Barbara Bolland. 1979. *The Effect of the Police on Crime*. Criminal Justice Perspectives. Washington, D.C.: Law Enforcement Association Administration.

Wilson, James Q., Mark H. Moore, and George L. Kelling. 1983. "Crime in America." *Public Interest* 70:49–65.

Wolfgang, Marvin, Robert Figlio, and Thorsten Sellin. 1972 *Delinquency in a Birth Cohort.* Chicago: University of Chicago Press.

Chapter 6. Solving Crime Problems

Bard, Morton, and Dawn Sangrey. 1986. *The Crime Victim's Book.* 2d ed. New York: Brunner/Mazel.

Barnett, Arnold, Alfred Blumstein, and David P. Farrington. 1987. "Probabilistic Models of Youthful Criminal Careers." *Criminology* 25:83–107.

Bolen, David C. 1980. "Police-Victim Interactions: Observations from the Police Foundation." *Evaluation and Change,* special issue, pp. 110–15.

Boydstun, John E., Michael E. Sherry, and Nicholas P. Moelter. 1977. *Patrol Staffing in San Diego: One or Two Officer Units.* Washington, D.C.: Police Foundation, 1977.

Bureau of Justice Statistics. *See* U.S. Department of Justice.

Clark, Ronald V. S., and Derek B. Cornish. 1983. *Crime Control in Britain: A Review of Policy Research.* Albany: State University of New York Press.

Goldstein, Herman. 1990. *Problem-Oriented Policing.* Philadelphia: Temple University Press.

Guyot, Dorothy. 1976. "What Productivity? What Bargain?" *Public Administration Review* 36:340–43.

———. 1983. "Newark: Crime and Politics in a Declining City." In *Crime in City Politics,* ed. Anne Heinz, Herbert Jacob, and Robert Lineberry, 23–96. New York: Longman.

Hough, Mike. 1987. "Thinking about Effectiveness." *British Journal of Criminology* 27:70–80.

Kelling, George L., Tony Pate, Duane Dieckman, and Charles E. Brown. 1974. *The Kansas City Preventive Patrol Experiment: A Technical Report.* Washington, D.C.: Police Foundation.

Langworthy, Robert H. 1989. "Do Stings Control Crime? An Evaluation of a Police Fencing Operation." *Justice Quarterly* 6:27–46.

National Institute of Justice. *See* U.S. Department of Justice.

O'Connor, George W. 1975. "Special Report to the City Manager: Crime in Troy—1973 vs. 1975." (Available from Police Development Services, Inc., 1 Warren Ave. Troy, NY 12180).

Schneider, Anne L. 1987. "Coproduction of Public and Private Safety: An Analysis of Bystander Intervention, Protective Neighboring, and Personal Protection." *Western Political Quarterly* 40:611–30.

Skogan, Wesley G. 1985. "Making Better Use of Victims and Witnesses." In *Police Leadership in America: Crisis and Opportunity,* ed. William Geller. New York: Praeger.

Spelman, William. 1988. *Beyond Bean Counting: New Approaches for Managing Crime Data.* Washington, D.C.: Police Executive Research Forum.

Spelman, William, and John E. Eck. 1989. "Sitting Ducks, Ravenous Wolves, and Helping Hands: New Approaches to Urban Policing." In *Police Management*

Today: Issues and Case Studies, ed. James J. Fyfe. 2d ed. Washington, D.C.: International City Management Association.

U.S. Department of Justice, Bureau of Justice Statistics. 1983. *Bulletin: Victim and Witness Assistance*. Washington, D.C.: Government Printing Office.

———. 1989. *Criminal Victimization in the United States, 1987*. National Crime Survey Report, NCJ-96459. Washington, D.C.: Government Printing Office.

U.S. Department of Justice, Federal Bureau of Investigation. 1989. *Crime in the United States, 1988*. Washington, D.C.: Government Printing Office.

U.S. Department of Justice, National Institute of Justice. 1987. *NIJ Reports: Helping Crime Victims*. No. 203. Washington, D.C.: Government Printing Office.

Winchester, Stuart, and Hillary Jackson. 1982. *Residential Burglary: The Limits of Prevention*. Home Office Research Study 74. London: Her Majesty's Stationery Office.

Winkel, Frans Willem, and Leendert Koppelaar. 1988. "Police Information for Victims of Crime: A Research and Training Perspective from the Netherlands." *Police Studies* 11:72–80.

Chapter 7. From Fear of Crime to Sense of Safety

ABA (American Bar Association). 1973. *Standards Relating to the Urban Police Function*. Chicago: American Bar Association.

ABC. 1982. *ABC News Poll on Public Opinion on Crime*, No. 8100. Ann Arbor: ICPSR.

Altheide, Fritz, and David Altheide. 1987. "The Mass Media and the Social Construction of the Missing Children Problem." *Sociological Quarterly* 28:473–92.

Baumer, Terry L. 1985. "Testing a General Model of Fear of Crime: Data from a National Sample." *Journal of Research in Crime and Delinquency* 22:239–55.

Biderman, A. D., L. A. Johnson, J. McIntyre, and W. A. Wier. 1967. *Report of a Pilot Study in the District of Columbia of Victimization and Attitudes toward Law Enforcement*. Field Surveys for the President's Commission. I. Washington, D.C.: Government Printing Office.

Bureau of Justice Statistics. *See* U.S. Department of Justice.

Cordner, Gary W. 1986. "Fear of Crime and the Police: An Evaluation of a Fear-Reduction Strategy." *Journal of Police Science and Administration* 14:223–33.

Dertouzos, James N., and Kenneth E. Thorpe. 1982. *Newspaper Groups: Economies of Scale, Tax Laws, and Merger Incentives*. R-2878-SBA. Santa Monica, Calif.: RAND.

Deutschmann, P. J. 1959. *News-Page Content of Twelve Metropolitan Dailies*. Cincinnati, Ohio: Scripps-Howard Research Center.

Doob, A. N., and G. E. MacDonald. 1979. "Television Viewing and Fear of Victimization: Is the Relationship Causal?" *Journal of Personality and Social Psychology* 37:170–79.

Fishman, Michael. 1980. *Manufacturing the News*. Austin: University of Texas Press.

Furstenberg, Frank F., Jr. 1971. "Public Reaction to Crime in the Streets." *American Scholar* 40:601–10.

Garofalo, James. 1981. "Crime and the Mass Media: A Selective Review of Research." *Journal of Research in Crime and Delinquency* 18:319–50.

Garofalo, James A., and J. Laub. 1978. "Fear of Crime: Broadening Our Perspective." *Victimology* 3, nos. 3–4: 242–53.

Gerbner, G., et al. 1980. "Television Violence, Victimization, and Power." *American Behavioral Scientist* 23:705–16.

Graber, Doris. 1980. *Crime News and the Public.* New York: Praeger.

Higdon, Richard Kirk, and Phillip G. Huber. 1987. *How to Fight Fear: The Citizen Oriented Police Enforcement Program Package.* Washington, D.C.: Police Executive Research Forum.

Hindelang, Michael J., Michael Gottfredson, and James Garofalo. 1978. *The Victims of Personal Crime.* Cambridge, Mass.: Ballinger.

Jacob, Herbert, and Robert Linebarry with Anne M. Heinz, Michael Rich, and Duane Swank. 1982. *Governmental Responses to Crime: Crime and Governmental Responses in American Cities.* Washington, D.C.: National Institute of Justice.

Kelly, Patricia A. 1987. *Police and Media: Bridging Troubled Waters.* Springfield, Ill.: Charles C. Thomas.

Koppel, Herbert, C. 1987. *Lifetime Likelihood of Victimization.* Technical Report. Washington, D.C.: Bureau of Justice Statistics.

LaGrange, Randy L., and Kenneth F. Ferraro. 1989. "Assessing Age and Gender Differences in Perceived Risk and Fear of Crime." *Criminology* 27:697–719.

Lavrakas, Paul J., and Elicia J. Herz. 1982. "Citizen Participation in Neighborhood Crime Prevention." *Criminology* 20:479–98.

Lewis, Dan A., Ron Szoc, Greta Salem, and Ruth Levin. 1979. *Crime and Community: Understanding Fear of Crime in Urban America.* Reactions to Crime Project, vol. 3. Evanston, Ill.: Northwestern University.

McGahan, Peter. 1984. *Police Images of a City.* Series 11, Anthropology/Sociology, vol. 4. New York: Peter Lang.

Moore, Mark H., and Robert C. Trojanowicz. 1988. "Policing and the Fear of Crime." Working paper, John F. Kennedy School of Government, Harvard University.

O'Connor, George W. 1975a. "Citizen Participation = Crime Prevention." Grant application to the New York Division of Criminal Justice Service, no. 8158. (Available from Police Development Services, Inc., 1 Warren Ave., Troy, NY 12180.)

———. 1975b. "Special Report to the City Manager: Increasing Patrol Services." (Available from Police Development Services, Inc. 1 Warren Ave., Troy, NY 12180).

Ortega, Suzanne T., and Jessie L. Myles. 1987. "Race and Gender Effects on Fear of Crime: An Interactive Model with Age." *Criminology* 25, 1: 133–52.

Pate, Anthony, Mary Ann Wycoff, Wesley G. Skogan, and Lawrence W. Sherman. 1986. *Reducing Fear of Crime in Houston and Newark: A Summary Report.* Washington, D.C.: Police Foundation.

Skogan, Wesley. 1986. "Fear of Crime and Neighborhood Change." In *Communities and Crime,* ed. Albert J. Reiss, Jr., and Michael Tonry. Vol. 8 of *Crime and Justice: A Review of Research.* Chicago: University of Chicago Press.

Skogan, Wesley, and Michael Maxfield. 1986. *Coping with Crime: Individual and Neighborhood Reactions.* Beverly Hills, Calif.: Sage.

Slovic, Paul. 1987. "Perception of Risk." *Science* 236 (17 April): 280–85.

Smith, Tom W. 1985. "The Polls: America's Most Important Problem." *Public Opinion Quarterly* 49:264–74.

Taft, Philip B., Jr. 1986. *Fighting Fear: The Baltimore Cope Project.* Washington, D.C.: Police Executive Research Forum.

Troy City Manager's Office. 1975. "Statement." 15 July.

U.S. Department of Justice, Bureau of Justice Statistics. 1984. *Criminal Victimization in the United States, 1982.* Washington, D.C.: Government Printing Office.

Walker, Sam. 1984. "'Broken Windows' and Fractured History: The Use and Misuse of History in Recent Police Patrol Analysis." *Justice Quarterly* 1, no. 1: 75–90.

Wilson, James Q., and George Kelling. 1982. "Broken Windows: The Police and Neighborhood Safety." *Atlantic Monthly* 256 (March): 29–38.

Wilson, Richard, and E. A. C. Crouch. 1987. "Risk Assessment and Comparisons: An Introduction." *Science* 236 (17 April): 267–70.

Wycoff, Mary Ann. 1987. Interview with the author. Philadelphia.

Wycoff, Mary Ann, and Wesley G. Skogan. 1985. *Police Community Stations: The Houston Field Test, Technical Report.* Washington, D.C.: Police Foundation.

Yin, Robert. 1977. *Patroling the Public Beat.* Washington, D.C.: Government Printing Office.

Zahn, Margaret A. n.d. "Homicide in the Twentieth Century United States." Unpublished paper in NCDD Collection (R-25613), Rutgers University Law Library, Newark, N.J.

Chapter 8. Police Malpractice

Bayley, David H., and James Garofalo. 1989. "The Management of Violence by Patrol Officers." *Criminology* 27:1–25.

Brancato, Gilda, and Elliot E. Polebaum. 1981. *The Rights of Police Officers.* American Civil Liberties Union Handbook. New York: Avon Books.

Carter, David L., and Allen D. Sapp. 1989. "The Effects of Higher Education on Police Liability: The Implications for Police Personnel Policy." *American Journal of Police* 8, no. 1: 153–66.

Carter, David L., and Darrel W. Stephens. 1988. *Drug Abuse by Police Officers: An Analysis of Critical Policy Issues.* Springfield, Ill.: Charles C. Thomas.

Center for Research in Criminal Justice. 1977. *The Iron Fist and the Velvet Glove: An Analysis of the U.S. Police.* 2d ed. Berkeley, Calif.: Center for Research on Criminal Justice.

Delattre, Edwin, J. 1989. *Character and Cops: Ethics in Policing.* Washington, D.C.: American Enterprise Institute.

Friedman, Ruth. 1988. "Municipal Liability for Police Misconduct: Must Victims Now Prove Intent?" *Yale Law Journal* 97:448–65.

Friedrich, Robert J. 1977. "The Impact of Organizational, Individual, and Situational Factors in the Behavior of Policemen." Ph.D. diss, University of Michigan.

———. 1980. "Police Use of Force: Individuals, Situations, and Organizations." *Annals* 452 (November): 82–97.

Fyfe, James J. 1988. "Police Use of Deadly Force: Research and Reform." *Justice Quarterly* 5:165–205.

Geller, William A., and Kevin J. Karales. 1981. *Split Second Decisions: Shootings of and by Chicago Police*. Chicago: Chicago Law Enforcement Study Group.

Goldstein, Herman. 1977. *Policing a Free Society*. Cambridge, Mass.: Ballinger.

Grant, J. Douglas, Joan Grant, and Hans Toch. 1982. "Police-Citizen Conflict and the Decision to Arrest." In *The Criminal Justice System: A Social-Psychological Analysis*, ed. Vladimir J. Konecni and Ebbe B. Ebbesen. San Francisco: W. H. Freeman.

Guyot, Dorothy. 1976. "Preliminary Report on the Police Accountability Project, Newark." Rutgers University School of Criminal Justice. Mimeo.

IACP (International Association of Chiefs of Police). 1964. "Police Review Boards." *Police Chief* 31, no. 2: 12–13, 34–36.

———. 1965. "IACP Position Statement." *Police Chief* 32, no. 6: 8–9.

———. 1976. *Managing for Effective Police Discipline*. Gaithersburgh, Md.: International Association of Chiefs of Police.

Kerstetter, Wayne. 1985. "Who Disciplines the Police? Who Should?" In *Police Leadership in America: Crisis and Opportunity*, ed. William A. Geller. New York: Praeger.

Klockars, Carl. 1980. "The Dirty Harry Problem." *Annals* 452 (November): 33–47.

McCoy, Candace. 1987. "Survey Results—Police Legal Liability." *Police Manager* 2, no. 3: 11–12.

Marx, Gary T. 1988. *Undercover: Police Surveillance in America*. Berkeley: University of California Press.

Mendez, Gary. 1983. *The Role of Race and Ethnicity in the Incidence of Police Use of Deadly Force*. Washington, D.C.: National Urban League.

Milton, Catherine H., Jeanne W. Halleck, James Lardner, and Gary L. Albrecht. 1977. *Police Use of Deadly Force*. Washington, D.C.: Police Foundation.

New York City Police Department Civilian Complaint Review Board. 1987. *Nationwide Survey of Civilian Complaint Systems*. New York: New York City Police Department.

New York State Commission on Criminal Justice and the Use of Force. 1987. *Report to the Governor*. 3 vols. Albany, NY: Office of the Governor.

N.Y.S.C. (New York State Supreme Court) Appellate Division Reports. 99 AD 2nd 916. In the matter of Police Officer v. City of Troy, 23 February 1984.

O'Connor, George W. 1974. "Memo accompanying the Rules and Regulations for the Troy Bureau of Police." Office of the Commissioner of Public Safety, Troy, N.Y. 10 June.

Pascale, Richard T., and Anthony G. Athos. 1981. *The Art of Japanese Management*. New York: Simon & Schuster.

Perez, Douglas. 1978. "Police Accountability: A Question of Balance." Ph.D. diss. University of California.

PERF (Police Executive Research Forum). 1985. "Police Agency Handling of Citizen Complaints: A Model Policy Statement." In *Police Management Today: Issues and Case Studies*, ed. James J. Fyfe, 88–89. Washington, D.C.: International City Management Association.

PERF (Police Executive Research Forum) and Police Foundation. 1981. *Survey of Police Operations and Administrative Practices, 1981*. Washington, D.C.: Police Foundation.

Pomeroy, Wesley A. Carroll. 1985. "The Sources of Police Legitimacy and a Model for Police Misconduct Review: A Response to Wayne Kerstetter." In *Police Leadership in America: Crisis and Opportunity*, ed. William A. Geller. New York: Praeger.

Punch, Maurice, ed. 1983. *Control in the Police Organization*. Cambridge, Mass.: MIT Press.

Reaves, Brian. 1990. Letter to the author reporting unpublished data from Bureau of Justice Statistics program on Law Enforcement Management and Administrative Statistics, 6 June.

Scharf, Peter, and Arnold Binder. 1983. *The Badge and the Bullet—Police Use of Deadly Force*. New York: Praeger.

Shearing, Clifford D., ed. 1981. *Organizational Police Deviance*. Toronto: Butterworths.

Sherman, Lawrence W. 1978. *Scandal and Reform: Controlling Police Corruption*. Berkeley: University of California Press.

———. 1983. "Reducing Police Gun Use: Critical Events, Administrative Policy, and Organizational Change." In *Control in the Police Organization*, ed. Maurice Punch, 98–125. Cambridge, Mass.: MIT Press.

Sherman, Lawrence W., and Ellen C. Cohn. 1986. *Citizens Killed by Big City Police*. Washington, D.C.: Crime Control Institute.

Smith, Douglas A., and Christy A. Visher. 1981. "Street Level Justice: Situational Determinants of Police Arrest Decisions." *Social Problems* 29:167–77.

Sykes, Gary W. 1985. "The Myth of Reform: The Functional Limits of Police Accountability in a Liberal Society." *Justice Quarterly* 2:51–66.

Toch, Hans. 1977. *Police, Prisons, and the Problem of Violence*. Crime and Delinquency Monograph Series. Rockville, Md.: National Institute for Mental Health.

Toch, Hans J., Douglas Grant, and Raymond T. Galvin. 1975. *Agents of Change: A Study in Police Reform*. New York: Wiley.

U.S. Civil Rights Commission. 1981. *Who Is Guarding the Guardians? A Report on Police Practices*. Washington, D.C.: Government Printing Office.

Wilson, O. W., and Roy C. McLaren. 1972. *Police Administration*. 3d ed. New York: McGraw-Hill.

Chapter 9. Union Power

Bouza, Anthony V. 1985. "Police Unions: Paper Tigers or Roaring Lions?" In *Police Leadership in America: Crisis and Opportunity*, ed. William Geller. New York: Praeger.

Burpo, John H. 1979. "Police Unions in the Civil Service Setting." Washington, D.C.: Public Administration Service.

Cresap, McCormick, and Paget, Inc. 1972. *City of Troy New York: A Management Study of the Bureau of Police*. Vols 1 and 2. Washington, D.C.: Cresap, McCormick, and Paget.

Dear, Geoffrey James. 1978. "The Community Voice in British Policing." *Law Enforcement News*, 25 Dec.

Dowling, Jerry L. (editor of *Police Labor Monthly*), 1989. Telephone communication, 24 May.

————. 1990. Telephone interview with author, 24 April.

Dowling, Jerry L., and Larry T. Hoover 1984. *History of Police Labor Unions in the United States.* Huntsville, Tex.: Justex Systems.

Downie, Bryan M., and Richard L. Jackson, eds. 1980. *Conflict and Cooperation in Police Labour Relations.* JS 62-35/1980E. Hull: Canadian Government Publishing Centre.

Greisinger, George W., Jeffrey S. Slovak, and Joseph J. Molkup. 1979. *Civil Service Systems: Their Impact on Police Administration.* Washington, D.C.: Law Enforcement Assistance Administration.

Griffiths, Derek P. 1983. "The Police Sergeant—Gatekeeper Extraordinary." Paper presented to the American Society of Criminology, Denver, 10 Nov.

IACP (International Association of Chiefs of Police) and Police Foundation. 1971. *Police Personal Selection Survey.* Washington, D.C.: Police Foundation.

Kleismet, Robert B. n.d. *A Discussion of the Issues Involved in Pay Parity between Police Officers and Fire Fighters.* Washington, D.C.: International Union of Police Associations.

————. 1984. Interview with the author, Washington, D.C., 24 April.

————. 1985. "The Chief and the Union: May the Force Be with You." In *Police Leadership in America: Crisis and Opportunity,* ed. William Geller. New York: Praeger.

LEAA. *See* U.S. Department of Justice.

Levy, Margaret M. 1977. *Bureaucratic Insurgency: The Case of the Police Unions.* Lexington, Mass.: Heath.

Martin, Susan Ehrlich. 1982. *Breaking and Entering: Police Women on Patrol.* Berkeley: University of California Press.

Muir, William Ker, Jr. 1983. "Police and Politics." *Criminal Justice Ethics* 2, no. 2: 3–8.

Police Labor Monthly, 1985. "Patrol Officer Labor Organizations Representing Nation's Largest Cities." September.

Pugh, Michael P., Larry T. Hoover, and Allen D. Sapp. 1981. "The Effect of Unions on the Wages of Municipal Police Officers." Criminal Justice Center, Sam Houston State University, Huntsville, Tex.

Reaves, Brian. 1990. Letter to the author reporting unpublished data from Bureau of Justice Statistics Program on Law Enforcement Management and Administrative Statistics, 6 June.

Rynecki, Steven B., and Michael J. Morse. 1981. *Police Collective Bargaining Agreements: A National Management Survey.* Washington, D.C.: Police Executive Research Forum and National League of Cities.

Swanton, Bruce. 1979. *Police Institutions and Issues: American and Australian Perspectives.* Canberra: Australian Institute of Criminology.

Tannenbaum, Arnold. "Unions." 1965. In *Handbook of Organizations,* ed. James March. Chicago: Rand McNally.

Troy Police Benevolent and Protective Association. 1947. *Constitution and By-Laws.* Troy, N.Y.

U.S. Department of Justice, Bureau of Justice Statistics. 1989. *Profile of State and Local Law Enforcement Agencies, 1987.* Washington, D.C. Government Printing Office.

U.S. Department of Justice, Law Enforcement Assistance Administration. 1976. *Indexed Legislative History of the Public Safety Officers' Benefits Act of 1976*. GPO 57-139. Washington, D.C.: Government Printing Office.

Chapter 10. Political Accountability versus Political Interference

Buffum, Peter C., and Rita Sagi. 1983. "Philadelphia: The Politics of Reform and Retreat." In *Crime in City Politics*, ed. Anne Heinz, Herbert Jacob, and Robert L. Lineberry. New York: Longman.

Bureau of Justice Statistics. *See* U.S. Department of Justice.

Dahl, Robert A. 1957. "A Rejoinder." *American Political Science Review* 51:1053–61.

Finckenauer, James O. 1978. "Crime as a National Political Issue, 1964–76: From Law and Order to Domestic Tranquility." *Crime and Delinquency* 24:13–27.

Greisinger, George W., Jeffrey S. Slovak and Joseph J. Molkup. 1979. *Civil Service Systems: Their Impact on Police Administration*. Washington, D.C.: Law Enforcement Assistance Administration.

Guyot, Dorothy. 1979. "Bending Granite: Attempts to Change the Rank Structure of American Police Departments." *Journal of Police Science and Administration* 7:253–84 (based on a consultant's report to the Police Foundation). Reprinted in *Thinking about Police: Contemporary Readings*, ed. Carl Klockars, 400–422. New York: McGraw-Hill, 1983.

———. 1983. "Newark: Crime and Politics in a Declining City." In *Crime in City Politics*, ed. Anne Heinz, Herbert Jacob, and Robert Lineberry, 23–96. New York: Longman.

Guyot, Dorothy, and Kai Martensen. 1991. "The Governmental Setting." In *Local Government Police Management*, ed. William Geller. Washington, D.C.: International City Management Association.

IACP (International Association of Chiefs of Police). 1976. *The Police Chief Executive Report*. Washington, D.C.: Government Printing Office.

ICMA (International City Management Association). 1989. *Municipal Government Yearbook*. Washington, D.C.: International City Management Association.

Kelly, Michael J. 1975. *Police Chief Selection: A Handbook for Local Government*. Washington, D.C.: Police Foundation and International City Management Association.

McPherson, Marlys. 1983. "Minneapolis: Crime in a Politically Fragmented Arena." In *Crime in City Politics*, ed. Anne Heinz, Herbert Jacob, and Robert L. Lineberry, 148–92. New York: Longman.

Mastrofski, Stephen. 1988. "Varieties of Police Governance in Metropolitan America." *Politics and Policy* 8:12–31.

Reaves, Brian. 1990. Letter to the author reporting unpublished data from Bureau of Justice Statistics program on Law Enforcement Management and Administrative Statistics, 6 June.

Scheingold, Stuart A. 1984. *The Politics of Law and Order*. New York: Longman.

Simon, Herbert A. 1976. *Administrative Behavior: A Study of Decision Making Processes in Administrative Organizations*. 3d ed. New York: Free Press.

Troy City Council. 1978. "Legislative Hearing on Team Policing and Other Related Matters," 3 and 4 April. Transcript.

U.S. Department of Justice, Bureau of Justice Statistics. 1989. *Profile of State and Local Law Enforcement Agencies, 1987.* Washington, D.C.: Government Printing Office.

Walker, Samuel. 1985. "The Politics of Accountability: The Seattle Police Spying Ordinance as a Case Study." In *The Politics of Crime and Criminal Justice*, ed. Erika Fairchild and Vincent J. Webb, 144–57. Beverly Hills, Calif.: Sage.

Wasserman, Robert. 1977. "The Governmental Setting." In *Local Government Police Management*, ed. Bernard L. Garmire. Washington: International City Management Association.

Whitaker, Gordon P., Stephen Mastrofski, Elinor Ostrom, Roger B. Parks, and Stephan L. Percy. 1982. *Basic Issues in Police Performance.* Washington, D.C.: National Institute of Justice.

Williams, Oliver. 1961. "A Typology for Comparative Local Government." *Midwest Journal of Politics* 5:150–64.

Chapter 11. Building Bridges between Police and Public

Alpert, Geoffrey P., and Roger G. Dunham. 1988. *Policing Multi-ethnic Neighborhoods: The Miami Study and Findings for Law Enforcement in the United States.* Westport, Conn.: Greenwood Press.

Bayley, David H., and Harold Mendelsohn. 1969. *Minorities and the Police: Confrontation in America.* New York: Free Press.

Belson, William A. 1975. *The Police and the Public.* London: Harper & Row.

Bittner, Egon. 1974. "Florence Nightingale in Pursuit of Willie Sutton: A Theory of Police." In *The Potential for Reform of Criminal Justice*, ed. Herbert Jacob, 17–44. Sage Criminal Justice Annals 3. Beverly Hills, Calif.: Sage.

Cain, Maureen. 1973. *Society and the Policeman's Role.* London: Routledge & Kegan Paul.

Cohen, Bernard, and Jan M. Chaiken. 1972. *Police Background Characteristics and Performance.* New York: New York City RAND Institute.

Couper, David. 1979. "Police: Protectors of People's Rights." *Law Enforcement News* 5 (12 March): 8.

———. 1983. *How to Rate Your Local Police.* Washington, D.C.: Police Executive Research Forum, 1983.

Davis, Raymond C. 1985. "Organizing the Community for Improved Policing." In *Police Leadership in America: Crisis and Opportunity*, ed. William Geller, 84–95. New York: Praeger.

Farmer, Michael T., ed. 1981. *Differential Police Response Strategies.* Washington, D.C.: Police Executive Research Forum.

Goldstein, Herman. 1980. Interview with author. Madison, Wis., 13 August.

———. 1987. "Toward Community-Oriented Policing: Potential, Basic Requirements, and Threshold Questions." *Crime and Delinquency* 33:6–30.

———. 1990. *Problem-Oriented Policing.* Philadelphia: Temple University Press.

Greene, Jack R., and Stephen Mastrofski, eds. 1988. *Community Policing: Rhetoric or Reality.* New York: Praeger.

Guyot, Dorothy. 1985. "Building Bridges between Police and Public." *FBI Law Enforcement Bulletin* 54, no. 11: 1–8.

Kelling, George L. 1987. "Acquiring a Taste for Order: The Community and the Police." *Crime and Delinquency* 33:71–89.

Lindsey, William H., Ronald Cochran, Bruce Quint, and Mario Rivera. 1985. "The Oasis Technique: A Method of Controlling Crime and Improving the Quality of Life." In *Police Leadership in America: Crisis and Opportunity*, ed. William Geller, 322–31. New York: Praeger.

Mastrofski, Stephen. 1981. "Policing the Beat: The Impact of Organizational Scale on Patrol Officer Behavior in Urban Residential Neighborhoods." *Journal of Criminal Justice* 9:343–58.

———. 1983. "The Police and Non-Crime Services." In *Measuring Performance of Criminal Justice Agencies*, ed. Gordon P. Whitaker and Charles David Phillips. Sage Criminal Justice Annals 18. Beverly Hills, Calif.: Sage.

Muir, William Ker, Jr. 1977. *Police: Streetcorner Politicians*. Chicago: University of Chicago Press.

Murphy, Gerald R. 1985. *Special Care: Improving the Police Response to the Mentally Disabled*. Washington, D.C.: Police Executive Research Forum.

———. 1989. *Managing Persons with Mental Disabilities: A Curriculum Guide for Police Trainers*. Washington, D.C.: Police Executive Research Forum.

PERF (Police Executive Research Forum) and Police Foundation. 1981. *Survey of Police Operations and Administrative Practices, 1981*. Washington, D.C.: Police Foundation.

Police Foundation. 1981. *The Newark Foot Patrol Experiment*. Washington, D.C.: Police Foundation.

Reaves, Brian. 1990. Letter to the author reporting unpublished data from Bureau of Justice Statistics program on Law Enforcement Management and Administrative Statistics, 6 June.

Reiss, Albert J., Jr. 1971. *The Police and the Public*. New Haven, Conn.: Yale University Press.

———. 1985. *Policing a City's Central District: The Oakland Story*. Washington, D.C.: National Institute of Justice.

Reiss, Albert J., Jr., and Michael Tonry, eds. 1986. *Communities and Crime*. Vol. 8 of *Crime and Justice: A Review of Research*. Chicago: University of Chicago Press.

Sharp, Elaine B. 1980. "Citizen Perception of Channels for Urban Service Advocacy." *Public Opinion Quarterly* 44:362–76.

Skolnick, Jerome H., and David H. Bayley. 1986. *The New Blue Line: Police Innovation in Six American Cities*. New York: Free Press.

Trigg, William C., III. 1984. "Police and Vandalism: A Study of Task Problem Definition and Response Formulation in Police Work." Ph.D. diss. State University of New York, Albany.

Trojanowicz, Robert. 1986. *Community Policing Programs: A Twenty-Year Review*. East Lansing: Neighborhood Foot Patrol Center, Michigan State University.

Trojanowicz, Robert, Robert Baldwin, et al. 1982. *An Evaluation of the Neighborhood Foot Patrol Program in Flint, Michigan*. East Lansing: School of Criminal Justice, Michigan State University.

Trojanowicz, Robert, Marilyn Steele, and Susan Trojanowicz. 1986. *Community Policing: A Taxpayer's Perspective*. East Lansing: School of Criminal Justice, Michigan State University.

Chapter 12. Fairness

Aaronson, David E., C. Thomas Dienes, and Michael C. Musheno. 1984. *Public Policy and Police Discretion*. New York: Clark Boardman.

Delattre, Edwin J. 1989. *Character and Cops: Ethics in Policing*. Washington, D.C.: American Enterprise Institute.

Dreyfus, Hubert L., and Stuart E. Dreyfus. 1986. *Mind over Machine: The Power of Human Intuition in the Era of the Computer*. New York: Free Press.

Eisenberg, Terry, Deborah Ann Kent, and Charles R. Wall. 1973. *Police Personnel Practices in State and Local Governments*. Washington, D.C.: International Association of Chiefs of Police and Police Foundation.

Elliston, Frederick A., and Michael Feldberg. 1985. *Moral Issues in Police Work*. Totowa, N.J.: Rowman & Allenheld.

Goldstein, Herman. 1990. *Problem-Oriented Policing*. Philadelphia: Temple University Press.

Leahy, Frank J., Jr. 1980. "A Report on Criminal Justice System Activities in Jefferson County, CO." INSLAW internal report.

Muir, William Ker, Jr. 1977. *Police: Streetcorner Politicians*. Chicago: University of Chicago Press.

Ostrom, Elinor. 1983. "Equity in Police Services." In *Evaluating Performance of Criminal Justice Agencies*, ed. Gordon P. Whitaker and Charles David Phillips. Sage Criminal Justice Annals, vol. 19. Beverly Hills, Calif.: Sage.

Schon, Donald. 1986. *Educating the Reflective Practitioner*. San Francisco: Jossey-Bass.

General Index

210–11; contracts, 31, 212, 214, 222–23; functions of, 204–5; grievances in a well-managed department, 216; history, 204–5; lobbying, 219; membership participation low, 210; national scene, 204–7; opposition to one-officer cars, 77; political influence, 206–7; protecting members from management, 214–15, 220; reasons for opposition, 225–26; referendum on salaries, 208. *See also* Police Benevolent Association of Troy
Upper Hudson Nuclear Weapons Freeze Campaign, 257

Vacant home inspection, 132
Vacation days, 210, 215
Vagrancy, 289
Vandalism, 88, 136, 146–47
Vanderbilt University, 276
Vernon, Wyman, 32
Veteran's preference, 70, 82, 230. *See also* Personnel
Vice, 199
Victimization, 120; age, impact of, 128, 144–45; and fear, 146, 148; risk assessment, 144–45; surveys, 103–6
Victims, 120, 269; assistance program, 133, 249, 306; blaming the, 52; comforted, 53, 306; privacy from media coverage, 150–54; rights, 133
Vigilante groups, 268
Vollmer, August, 7
Voluntary associations, 127, 274–75, 279
Volunteers, 129–32, 140, 148–49
Voting. *See* Elections, for city council

Walk-in complaint, 269
Walking post: in appropriate places, 142, 246, 265; punishment, 4, 223. *See also* Patrol
War on crime, inappropriate concept, 93–94

Warrants for arrest, 109. *See also* Criminal investigation
Washington, D.C., 78, 95, 106, 193
Watches. *See* Shift work
Watchman-style policing, 5, 15–18, 22–24, 214–15
Wave of fear, 136–38, 150, 246. *See also* Fear of crime
Weapons. *See* Firearms, police; Guns
Well-being of citizens, 69, 119
White, Officer Tom, 40, 50, 51, 78
Wichita, Kans., 109, 193
Williams's typology on municipal government, 15
Wilson, James Q., 7
Wilson, O. W., 121
Witnesses: at the scene, 100, 272–73; testifying, 111
Women: fear of crime, 144–45, 147–49, 272; police officers, 9, 73–74, 298–99; risk of victimization, 144–45
Wood, Officer Steven, 174, 184
Working conditions, consistency in, 75–76
Working hard, lack of reasons for, 83–84
Worklife, 10, 267, 268
Work load, 42–43. *See also* Patrol work load
Wounded, citizens by police, 192–93
Wright, Captain Allen, 184–85
Wrongdoing. *See* Malpractice

YMCA courtesy memberships, 25
Youth: continued misbehavior may cause fear of crime, 136–42; misbehavior, 262, 280; officer beating, 126; police notification of parents, 173; police work with, 41–42, 78, 124–27, 305; reporting crimes to police, 272–73
Youth services unit, 125–26, 244, 246, 247, 262

Zone, 75; profiling, 88

Author Index